PRECARIOUS TIMES

signale
modern german letters, cultures, and thought

Series editor: Peter Uwe Hohendahl, Cornell University

Signale: Modern German Letters, Cultures, and Thought publishes new English-language books in literary studies, criticism, cultural studies, and intellectual history pertaining to the German-speaking world, as well as translations of important German-language works. *Signale* construes "modern" in the broadest terms: the series covers topics ranging from the early modern period to the present. *Signale* books are published under a joint imprint of Cornell University Press and Cornell University Library in electronic and print formats. Please see http://signale.cornell.edu/.

PRECARIOUS TIMES

Temporality and History in Modern German Culture

ANNE FUCHS

A Signale Book

CORNELL UNIVERSITY PRESS AND CORNELL UNIVERSITY LIBRARY
ITHACA AND LONDON

Cornell University Press and Cornell University Library gratefully acknowledge the College of Arts & Sciences, Cornell University, for support of the Signale series.

First published 2019 by Cornell University Press and Cornell University Library

Printed in the United States of America

Library of Congress Cataloging-in-Publication Data

Names: Fuchs, Anne, author.
Title: Precarious times : temporality and history in modern German culture / Anne Fuchs.
Description: Ithaca : Cornell University Press, 2019. | Series: Signale : modern German letters, cultures, and thought | Includes bibliographical references and index. | Summary: "Explores how works of German literature, film, and photography reflect on the temporal anxieties precipitated by contemporary experiences of atomization, displacement, and fragmentation that bring about a loss of history and of time itself and is peculiar to our current moment"— Provided by publisher.
Identifiers: LCCN 2019027737 (print) | LCCN 2019027738 (ebook) | ISBN 9781501735103 (paperback) | ISBN 9781501734816 (pdf) | ISBN 9781501734823 (epub)
Subjects: LCSH: German literature—20th century—History and criticism. | German literature—21st century—History and criticism. | Time in literature. | Anxiety in literature. | Time in art. | Anxiety in art. | Arts and society—Germany—History—20th century. | Arts and society— Germany—History—21st century.
Classification: LCC PT148.T57 F83 2019 (print) | LCC PT148.T57 (ebook) | DDC 830.9/33—dc23
LC record available at https://lccn.loc.gov/2019027737
LC ebook record available at https://lccn.loc.gov/2019027738

In memory of my parents, Ilse and Klaus Fuchs

Contents

Illustrations

Acknowledgments

Many colleagues, friends, and family members have directly or indirectly aided the completion of this book, which preoccupied me much longer than I had originally planned. It developed over many years and came with unexpected detours that turned out to be more fascinating than the straight and high-speed route of my original plan. Special thanks are due to the University of Warwick, which granted me generous research leave in 2014. My former colleagues in the German Department at Warwick stand out in my memory for their incredible generosity of spirit and genuine collegiality. My warm thanks go to Christine Achinger, Helmut Schmitz, James Hodkinson, and Jim Jordan. I also want to especially acknowledge Jonathan J. Long, Ines Detmers, and Aleida Assmann, with whom I co-organized two inspiring international conferences on time and temporality: "Faster than Light? Historical Experience and Memory in the Age of Acceleration" at the Warwick Institute of Advanced Study in 2013, and generously funded by the Institute of Advanced Study, the Humanities Research

Centre, and the Faculty of Arts, University of Warwick; and "The Longing for Time: *Ästhetische Eigenzeit* in Contemporary Film, Literature, and Art," which followed a year later at the Kultur-wissenschaftliches Kolleg of the University of Konstanz, Germany, funded by the Max Planck research group Memory and History and the International Office, University of Konstanz. Jonathan J. Long and I subsequently coedited *Time in German Literature and Culture, 1900–2015: Between Acceleration and Slowness* (Palgrave Macmillan, 2016), and Ines Detmers and I coedited the double issue "*Ästhetische Eigenzeit* in Contemporary Literature and Culture," *Oxford German Studies* 46/3 and 46/4 (2017). I want to thank my coeditors for their wonderful stewardship of these publications, and all contributors for their inspiring conference papers, discussions, and ensuing publications. The different perspectives and approaches have enriched my approach to the complexities of time and temporality.

Parts of this book had an earlier gestation in journal articles and book chapters. I wish to acknowledge the editors of the following journals and publishing houses who have given me kind permission to reuse and adapt these previous publications. The section on Stadler in chapter 4 in this book is based on my article "An Awareness of What Is Missing: Voyeurism and the Remediation of Transcendence in Arnold Stadler's *Sehnsucht* and *Salvatore*," which appeared in *German Life & Letters* 67/3 (2014): 435–49. The section on Genazino in chapter 4 builds on "After the Flâneur: Temporality and Connectivity in Wilhelm Genazino's *Belebung der toten Winkel* and *Das Glück in glücksfernen Zeiten*," which was published in *Modern Language Review* 109/2 (2014): 435–50. The section on Kafka's *Der Proceß* in chapter 2 in this book draws on my chapter "The Trouble with Time: Kafka's *Der Proceß*," which appeared in *Franz Kafka's The Trial*, edited by Espen Hammer (Oxford: Oxford University Press, 2018), 173–200; by permission of Oxford University Press, USA. Sections of chapter 2 use some material from "Temporal Ambivalence: Attention, Acceleration, and Lateness in Modernist Discourse," which appeared in *Time in German Literature and Culture, 1900–2015: Between Acceleration and Slowness*, edited by Anne Fuchs and J. J. Long (Houndmills:

Palgrave Macmillan, 2016), 21–38. All previously published material has been substantially revised for this book.

I wish to express my gratitude to Kehrer publishing house and the photographer Ulrich Wüst for providing digital files and generously allowing me to reproduce several photographs from his photobook *Später Sommer/Letzter Herbst*. My very special thanks are due to Michael Wesely, who corresponded with me about his photography, while also providing me with digital files of his photographs. My thanks extend to The National University of Ireland, whose generous publishing grant made possible the color reproduction of Wesely's "Blick von der Glienicker Brücke auf Schloss Babelsberg."

I am deeply indebted to Aleida Assmann, who invited me as a guest researcher to my alma mater, the University of Konstanz, in 2014: I spent three most productive and enjoyable months at the Max Planck research group Memory and History, and as a guest of the Kulturwissenschaftliche Kolleg, where I benefited from regular seminars and discussions.

I am also grateful to Andrew Webber, who gave me very productive feedback on chapter 3 of this book. My greatest thanks, however, are reserved for Elizabeth Boa, my friend, mentor, and critic, who has provided the most generous support, astute commentary, and nuanced editorial suggestions on several drafts of this book. Last but not least, I want to thank my partner, Helen, for her inspiring curiosity, intelligent comments, and unflinching encouragement to keep going when I wanted to chuck it in. This book is dedicated to the memory of my parents, Ilse and Klaus.

Berlin, 5 July 2019

ABBREVIATIONS

(in order of appearance)

VNN   Friedrich Nietzsche, *Vom Nutzen und Nachteil der Historie für das Leben* (Stuttgart: Reclam, 1999)

UaD   Friedrich Nietzsche, *On the Uses and Disadvantages of History for Life*, trans. R. J. Hollingdale (Cambridge: Cambridge University Press, 1997)

DZ   Thomas Mann, *Der Zauberberg* (Frankfurt a. Main: Fischer, 1979)

MM   Thomas Mann, *The Magic Mountain*, trans. John E. Woods (New York: Everyman's Library, 2005)

GG   Georg Simmel, "Die Großstädte und das Geistesleben," in *Gesamtausgabe*, ed. Rüdiger Kramme (Frankfurt a. Main: Suhrkamp, 1995), 7:227–42

MML   Georg Simmel, "The Metropolis and Mental Life," in *Simmel on Culture*, ed. David Frisby and Mike Featherstone (London: Sage, 1997), 174–85

DV   Franz Kafka, *Der Verschollene: Roman in der Fassung der Handschrift* (Frankfurt a. Main: Fischer, 1994)

A Franz Kafka, *Amerika (The Man Who Disappeared)*, trans. Michael Hofmann (London: Penguin, 1996)

DP Franz Kafka, *Der Proceß: Roman in der Fassung der Handschrift* (Frankfurt a. Main: Fischer, 1995)

TT Franz Kafka, *The Trial*, trans. Breon Mitchell (New York: Schocken, 1998)

SW Robert Walser, *Sämtliche Werke in Einzelausgaben*, ed. Jochen Greven, 20 vols. (Frankfurt a. Main: Suhrkamp, 1986).

AdE Robert Walser, "Auf der Elektrischen," in *Kritische Ausgabe sämtlicher Drucke und Manuskripte*, ed. Wolfram Groddeck and Barbara von Reibnitz, vol. III.1, *Drucke im Berliner Tagblatt*, ed. Hans-Joachim Heerde (Frankfurt a. Main: Stroemfeld, 2013)

DS Robert Walser, *Der Spaziergang*, in *Sämtliche Werke in Einzelausgaben*, ed. Jochen Greven (Zurich: Suhrkamp, 1986), 5:7–77

TW Robert Walser, *The Walk and Other Stories*, trans. Christopher Middleton (London: Serpent's Tail, 1992), 54–104

Awt Clemens Meyer, *Als wir träumten* (Frankfurt am Main: Fischer, 2011)

MdG Julia Schoch, *Mit der Geschwindigkeit des Sommers* (Munich: Piper, 2009)

T Karen Duve, *Taxi* (Frankfurt a. Main: Eichborn, 2008)

BtW Wilhelm Genazino, *Die Belebung der toten Winkel: Frankfurter Poetikvorlesungen* (Munich: Carl Hanser, 2006)

GigfZ Wilhelm Genazino, *Das Glück in glücksfernen Zeiten* (Munich: Hanser, 2009)

EadW Arnold Stadler, *Einmal auf der Welt. Und dann so* (Frankfurt a. Main: Fischer, 2009)

Se Arnold Stadler, *Sehnsucht: Versuch über das erste Mal* (Cologne: DuMont, 2002)

S Arnold Stadler, *Salvatore* (Frankfurt a. M: Fischer, 2008)

GGG Jenny Erpenbeck, *Gehen, ging, gegangen* (Munich: Knaus, 2015)

GWG Jenny Erpenbeck, *Go, Went, Gone*, trans. Susan Bernofsky (London: Portobello Books, 2017)

LH Juli Zeh, *Leere Herzen* (Munich: Luchterhand, 2017)

Precarious Times

INTRODUCTION

Temporal Anxieties

Time is intangible and yet omnipresent: its flow is measured and controlled, but it is also controlling; it governs every aspect of our lives from cradle to grave. It expresses itself through timetables, schedules, temporal imperatives, modes of sequencing, and processes that create "orders of time," to appropriate François Hartog's phrase.[1] As Norbert Elias so succinctly put it, time is above all a "cognitive symbol" that allows human actors to monitor their behavior with reference to three interdependent levels: the cycles of nature, the social setting, and their individual biographies.[2] As a

---

1. François Hartog, *Regimes of Historicity: Presentism and the Experiences of Time*, trans. Saskia Brown (New York: Columbia University Press, 2015), 1.

2. Norbert Elias, *Über die Zeit*, ed. Michael Schröter (Frankfurt a. Main: Suhrkamp, 1988), xvii and xxiv.

complex synthesis, relating events across different times and places, time is a regulatory mechanism that is internalized by social actors.[3]

Although Elias emphasized the social dimension of human temporality, he did not explicitly address the role of technology in our relationship with time. Since the invention of the World Wide Web in 1990, digital technologies have revolutionized the relationship between individuals, their worlds, and their temporal horizons.[4] There is a widespread perception that digital devices are causing frenetic activity as the constant stream of Twitter feeds, news alerts, WhatsApp messages, and Facebook posts drive us to stay connected. The ever-tighter enmeshing of human worlds with digital media alters the very notion of experience. The advent of Web 2.0 with its built-in capacity for interactivity in real time has led to the ubiquitous growth of social media platforms that have produced new forms of participatory online communication. The ontological difference between lived and virtual experience is diminishing as technology transmutes dispositions, habits, and perceptions. Because the information age promotes instant access, it also erodes the expectation of temporal processing. The new era of the "digital now" challenges not only established notions of delayed gratification but also the very idea of time as a multidimensional concept that integrates past, present, and future into human experience. In 2016, participation in social media networks surpassed 2 billion users globally, with an average daily social media usage of 135 minutes.[5] Teenagers in the US are reported to spend up to nine hours per day on digital devices, either chatting on social media, playing games, listening to music, or

---

3. Elias, *Über die Zeit*, xxxiii.

4. Tim Berners Lee is credited for the invention of the World Wide Web: in March 1989, Berners Lee wrote "Information Management: A Proposal," which formulated his vision of the web. By October 1990, he had written the three cornerstones that remain the foundation of today's web: HTML (HyperText Markup Language), URI (Uniform Resource Identifier), and HTTP (HyperText Transfer Protocol). At the end of 1990 the first web page was launched in CERN, and in 1991 the new web community was opened to users outside. See http://webfoundation.org/about/vision/history-of-the-web/ (accessed 27 December 2016).

5. See https://www.statista.com/statistics/433871/daily-social-media-usage-worldwide/.

watching TV.[6] Health experts and educators are worried about the detrimental effect this is having on the physical and mental well-being of these so-called digital natives. Disorders attributed to heavy social media usage include sleep deprivation, lack of physical exercise, reduced attention spans, digital addictions, increased loneliness, stress, and lack of self-esteem. Besides growing concerns about excessive social media usage, there is widespread temporal anxiety about the loss of time as duration. The vocabulary of crisis is omnipresent; it infects not only media coverage but also sociological debates on the transformation of society in the age of social acceleration. Anthony Giddens already employed the metaphor of a "runaway world" in the 1990s; Thomas Hylland Eriksen spoke of the "tyranny of the moment," Manuel Castells coined the oxymoron "timeless time," and Paul Virilio diagnosed a "dictatorship of speed," terms I will discuss in chapter 1.[7] Evidently, much of the initial optimism that the continuous technology revolution would create ever more leisure and overcome social inequality has evaporated.

At the other end of the spectrum are the technology optimists and cyber gurus who welcome new modes of citizenship and online participation. For example, Scott McQuire analyzes the "smart mob" as a self-organizing and self-directing urban phenomenon that makes use of precisely the same technologies that are usually employed by the state for surveillance purposes.[8]

---

6. Hayley Tsukayama, "Teens Spend Nearly 9 Hours Every Day Consuming Media," *Washington Post*, 3 November 2015, https://www.washingtonpost.com/news/the-switch/wp/2015/11/03/teens-spend-nearly-nine-hours-every-day-consuming-media/?utm_term=.d93d18429e9b.

7. Anthony Giddens, *Runaway World: How Globalisation Is Reshaping Our Lives*, 2nd ed. (London: Profile Books, 2002); Thomas Hylland Eriksen, *Tyranny of the Moment: Fast and Slow Time in the Information* Age (London: Pluto Press, 2001); Manuel Castells, *The Rise of the Network Society: The Information Age—Economy, Society, and Culture*, 2nd ed. (Oxford: Blackwell, 2000); Paul Virilio, *Negative Horizon: An Essay in Dromoscopy*, trans. Michael Degener (London: Bloomsbury Academic, 2008).

8. Scott McQuire, "City Times: Negotiating Public Space in the Twenty-First-Century City," in *Time, Media, and Modernity*, ed. Emily Keightley (Basingstoke: Palgrave Macmillan, 2012), 123–42.

Similarly, Carmen Leccardi celebrates resistance to neoliberal corporate governance in the antiglobalization movement through clever deployment of digital technologies as smart, flexible forms of self-organization.[9] And, according to Robert Hassan, digital technologies can give rise to new asynchronous experiences of time that overturn the rule of the clock and our regimentation by linear time.[10]

Even though the two sides in the debate are polarized, at bottom they both subscribe to various degrees of technological determinism: both cyber-optimists and resigned techno-pessimists have a tendency to regard technology as an objective historical agent beyond human control. As the sociologist Judy Wajcman observes, "Temporal demands are not inherent to technology. They are built into our devices by all-too-human schemes and desires."[11] Technological determinism whether of the optimistic or dystopian kind leads to one-dimensional accounts of modern temporality that are excessively totalizing. While it is undeniable that our lives have been transformed by rapidly advancing digital technologies, we must be mindful of the fact that time remains an embodied and embedded mode of experience that is shaped by complex biological, cultural, social, and economic factors in interaction with technology. It is often not technology as such but the prevailing social narrative that massively influences our social experience of time, as, for example, in the modern celebration of speed as progress during the Industrial Revolution. Modern art and literature then punctured the one-dimensional vision of the industrial age by way of aesthetics of slowness that aimed to recover nonutilitarian experiences, a point to which I return in chapter 2. Instead of adopting a technology-driven focus on time in network society, this

---

9. Carmen Leccardi, "New Temporal Perspectives in the High-Speed Society," in *24/7: Time and Temporality in the Network Society*, ed. Robert Hassan and Ronald E. Purser (Stanford, CA: Stanford Business Books, 2007), 25–36.

10. Robert Hassan, "Network Time," in *24/7: Time and Temporality*, 37–61.

11. Judy Wajcman, *Pressed for Time: The Acceleration of Life in Digital Capitalism* (Chicago: University of Chicago Press, 2015), 3.

study therefore investigates our temporal anxieties from a broad cultural-historical perspective that illuminates alternative temporal trajectories and experiences. Alarmist metaphors abound in the contemporary imaginary: according to many commentators, we are moored in an everlasting present without any future horizon; we are simultaneously flooded by pasts that we can no longer integrate into meaningful narratives. We are stagnating at top speed; our experience of time is flat, disembedded from context and without duration. Our sleep has been wrecked by the 24/7 imperative of uninterrupted standby. We have entered the era of the fragmented now, bereft of past and future. The anxiety that we are no longer the authors and agents of our own fate is pervasive. This is precisely the territory of my study: I ask how and to what extent cultural attachment to the past and experience of the length and depth of time are being reconfigured in our globalized era of turbocapitalism. Given the premium placed on instant delivery, liveness, and connectivity, how are the temporal conditions in the twenty-first century to be understood? Have we entered the age of a timeless connectivity that depletes the future while also eroding our relationship to the past?

My study probes this crisis narrative by analyzing how contemporary literature, film, and photography stage, perform, and bring forth other kinds of time. Instead of merely tracking the discursive exploration of time in our anxiety-ridden era, I focus on aesthetic interventions in a debate that is far too monolithic and deterministic. Literature, films, and artworks do not merely represent the times we live in but can challenge prevailing consensus and open up alternative trajectories. My analysis of contemporary aesthetic interventions in the debate on time unfolds in dialogue with the history of modernity and of modernism. The comparison of our age with the shifting conceptualizations of time through different phases of modernization will help to draw out continuities and discontinuities in the multifaceted history of lived time from the late nineteenth century to the present. Even though the very idea of modernization seems to entail the speeding up of change to reach a better future, the modern imaginary was overall much more pluritemporal than is commonly recognized.

Modern Speed Politics

One of the most cited passages from Karl Marx's *Communist Manifesto* is his dramatic summation of the sweeping transformation of nineteenth-century society by the ruling bourgeoisie:

> Die fortwährende Umwälzung der Produktion, die ununterbrochene Erschütterung aller gesellschaftlichen Zustände, die ewige Unsicherheit und Bewegung zeichnet die Bourgeoisepoche vor allen anderen aus. Alle festen eingerosteten Verhältnisse mit ihrem Gefolge von altehrwürdigen Vorstellungen und Anschauungen werden aufgelöst, alle neugebildeten veralten, ehe sie verknöchern können. Alles Ständische und Stehende verdampft, alles Heilige wird entweiht, und die Menschen sind endlich gezwungen, ihre Lebensstellung, ihre gegenseitigen Beziehungen mit nüchternen Augen anzusehen.[12]

> Constant revolutionizing of production, uninterrupted disturbance of all social conditions, everlasting uncertainty and agitation distinguish the bourgeois epoch from all earlier ones. All fixed, fast-frozen relations, with their train of ancient and venerable ideas and opinions, are swept away, all new-formed ones become antiquated before they can ossify. All that is solid melts into air, all that is holy is profaned, and man is at last compelled to face with sober senses his real conditions of life, and his relations with his kind.[13]

As Marshall Berman observes, the impassioned style and dramatic imagery of Marx's analysis of the process of modernization and of the historical struggle between the bourgeoisie and the proletariat re-enact the frenzied pace of capitalist expansion.[14] "He makes us feel," Berman comments, "that we are part of the action, drawn into the stream, hurtled along, out of control, at once dazzled and menaced by the onward rush."[15] Marx describes the bourgeoisie positively as a pivotal revolutionary force that liberated humankind from the

---

12. Karl Marx and Friedrich Engels, *Das Manifest der kommunistischen Partei*, Kommentierte Studienausgabe, ed. Theo Stammen and Alexander Classen (Munich: Fink/UTB, 2009), 23.

13. Karl Marx and Friedrich Engels, *Manifesto of the Communist Party: A Modern Edition*, with an Introduction by Tariq Ali (London: Verso, 2016), 10.

14. Marshall Berman, *All That Is Solid Melts into Air: The Experience of Modernity* (1982; London: Verso, 2010), 91–98.

15. Berman, *All That Is Solid*, 91.

shackles of tradition. As *the* agent of the capitalist economy, the bourgeois class embraces perpetual innovation, ruthless competition, and a politics of high speed to reach new markets. Of course, for Marx this explosive acceleration of historical change does not stop here: the energies unleashed by the bourgeoisie will sweep it away when the oppressed proletariat discovers its collective power and finally engages in a revolutionary struggle of world-historical proportions.

Marx's metaphoric language vividly captures the dramatic acceleration of history in the age of industrial modernity. His materialist critique of capitalism is laced with a deep fascination with the vitality and inventiveness of his age.[16] Modern man inhabits a dynamic and transitory present that reaches into a radically new future. As a result of this investment in a new and better life the relationship between past, present, and future becomes asymmetrical. The emphatic orientation toward the future forges a strong alliance between modern time and progress: in measuring the gap between what has been achieved so far and what can be achieved in the future the idea of progress propels modern time forward. As the British sociologist John Tomlinson observes, toward the end of the nineteenth century the acceleration of history increasingly also produced unruly speed and an unstable dynamic of social and economic modernization. This risk could be intermittently contained by the enforcement of social time-discipline through the promise of the good life. "The intrinsic benefits of mechanical production in delivering the fruits of material modernity, then, tends," Tomlinson comments, "to bind speed in with progress. To this extent, an increase in the pace of life, though it may not be particularly attractive in itself, may appear as a matter for pragmatic acceptance as part of the cultural bargain with modernity."[17] Even though capitalism depended on the temporally disciplined subject for its success, it ultimately favored speed over discipline to drive modernization. And this is why, as Enda Duffy argues, the modern imaginary conceives of movement and speed not merely as objective agents of

---

16. John Tomlinson, *The Culture of Speed: The Coming of Immediacy* (London: Sage, 2007), 4.

17. Tomlinson, *The Culture of Speed*, 22.

change but rather as genuinely modern desires that bind the modern self to the capitalist project of innovation.[18]

> As a desire clearly nurtured by capitalism, it [the desire for speed] may be the desire par excellence in Western culture that is fostered and tolerated in order to reconcile human actors to their lot as actors in a "dynamic" capitalist economic milieu. Speed, intimately woven into a new paradigm of the modern subject's nexus of desires, becomes the new opiate and the new (after)taste of movement as power.[19]

The Futurists' obsession with speed is an extreme but nevertheless symptomatic example of a specifically modern semantics of speed as pleasure. Filippo Marinetti's Futurist manifesto, published in 1909, declared with programmatic panache: "The world's magnificence has been enriched by a new beauty, the beauty of speed. . . . We already live in the absolute, because we have created eternal omnipresent speed."[20]

Temporalization

The modern speed fantasy, as outlined above, is part of a long-term process that already begins in the premodern period with the introduction of the clock and results in what the German historian Reinhart Koselleck called "Verzeitlichung," the temporalization of history. The introduction of the mechanical clock in the thirteenth century progressively led to a new organization of human time: the division of the day into twenty-four hours prepared the ground for a competition between commercial time and liturgical time in the early modern period.[21] The clock spread quickly from

---

18. Enda Duffy, *The Speed Handbook: Velocity, Pleasure, Modernism* (Durham, NC: Duke University Press, 2009), 23.

19. Duffy, *The Speed Handbook*, 35.

20. Filippo Tommaso Marinetti, "The Founding and Manifesto of Futurism," in *Futurist Manifestos*, ed. Umbo Apollonio (London: Thames and Hudson, 1973), 22.

21. Rather than simply replacing liturgical time, modern clock time began to overlay other time practices, creating complex local temporal zones. On the

the church tower to the town hall, and then into the living rooms of wealthy tradesmen and merchants before it made its way inside the watch pockets of the bourgeoisie. While in the sixteenth century the clock could indicate minutes, by the seventeenth century its hand showed seconds. It thus not only indicated the progressive "denaturalization of time" but actually prompted "a disciplining and rationalizing of the human world of work and its latitude for action."[22] However, it was only in the eighteenth century in the context of the Enlightenment and the French Revolution that the idea of historical time began to challenge and replace the notion of a chronological order that was preordained by God. The process of temporalization affected all areas of life. As Dirk Göttsche observes, from now on "subjectivity, history, nature, culture and even the universe all become subject to historicity and open to change."[23] Once history was subject to "criteria which could only be derived from an understanding of history itself," people could discover an open future as horizon for political, social, and economic planning.[24] The Enlightenment notion of progress thus emerges in the eighteenth century as an instrument of historical acceleration: once the difference between the past, the present, and the future was brought into view, the future became the horizon of urgent human planning and action. Acceleration, Koselleck explains, "provides evidence of a history in which time continually seems to overtake itself."[25]

---

complexity of the history of clock time, see Paul Glennie and Nigel Thrift, *Shaping the Day: A History of Timekeeping in England and Wales, 1300–1800* (Oxford: Oxford University Press, 2011).

22. Reinhart Koselleck, "Time and History," in *The Practice of Conceptual History: Timing History, Spacing Concepts*, trans. Todd Samuel Presner, foreword by Hayden White (Stanford, CA: Stanford University Press, 2002), 104. See also Gerhard Dohrn-van Rossum, *Die Geschichte der Stunde: Uhren und moderne Zeitordnungen* (Cologne: Anaconda, 2007).

23. Dirk Göttsche, "Introduction," in *Critical Time in Modern German Literature and Culture*, ed. Dirk Göttsche (Oxford: Peter Lang, 2016), 3.

24. Koselleck, "Concepts of Historical Time and Social History," in *The Practice of Conceptual History*, 120.

25. Koselleck, "Time and History," 113.

Picking up this thread, Peter Osborne explains that the temporal matrix of modernity comprises the following three facets: firstly, it valorizes the *historical* present over the past "as its negation and transcendence," thereby making it possible for an event to change its meaning according to shifting interpretive parameters. Secondly, the modern orientation toward the future "is characterized only by its prospective transcendence of the historical present, and its relegation of this present to a future past." Thirdly, it tendentially eliminates the present "as the vanishing point of a perpetual transition between a constantly changing past and an as yet indeterminate future."[26] Together these three temporal moves offer a dynamic vision of history that turns it into an always as yet unaccomplished project.

Multiple Modernities

Neither Koselleck's nor Osborne's reflections on the modern transience of the present suggest that modernity followed a singular trajectory or narrative. In Osborne's words, the modern politics of time contains "a range of possible temporalizations of history within its fundamental most abstract temporal form."[27] In order to avoid painting a monochrome picture that is blind to the plurality of temporal perspectives and experiences in modernity, it is therefore useful to distinguish between, first, *modernity* as a datable period; second, the *modern* as an experiential notion that is subject to continual and dynamic change; third, the technological, administrative, and social processes of *modernization* that steer social change; and fourth, *modernism* as a divergent and highly self-reflexive discourse about the above phenomena. Once we move away from the monolithic notion of a homogeneous modernity toward the pluralistic idea of what Lutz Koepnick terms "multiple modernities, alternate modernism, and vernacular modes of

---

26. Peter Osborne, *The Politics of Time: Modernity and Avant-Garde* (London: Verso, 1995), 14.

27. Osborne, *The Politics of Time*, 118.

modernist experience,"[28] we can also bring into view temporal pluralism and heterogeneity as defining signatures of a divergent modernity that, by valorizing the new, also produces new attachments to the past and new forms of traditionalism. What is at stake then, Koepnick comments, "is to show that the normative association of Western modernism with pleasurable speed and ceaseless movement often rested on rather lopsided definitions of the temporal as a sphere of dynamic change and of space as a dimension of static simultaneity."[29]

The approach adopted here will complement and extend Koepnick's book *On Slowness*, which analyzes the ways contemporary visual art forms complicate time:

> The wager of aesthetic slowness is not simply to find islands of respite, calm, and stillness somewhere outside the cascades of contemporary speed culture. It is to investigate what it means to experience a world of speed, acceleration, and cotemporality, experience understood—in Miriam Hansen's words—as "that which mediates individual perception with social meaning, conscious with unconscious processes, loss of self with self-reflexivity . . . ; experience as the matrix of conflicting temporalities, of memory and hope, including the historical loss of these dimensions."[30]

Aesthetic slowness today, Koepnick argues, "recalibrates how certain modernists of the early twentieth century already questioned the dominant association of modernism with speed, acceleration, shock and ceaseless movement."[31]

Following in the footsteps of Peter Osborne, Marshall Berman, and Lutz Koepnick, I attempt to map our own anxieties onto the modern temporal imaginary with its contradictory pathways. Temporal anxiety, I argue, is a feature of a multifaceted modernity, whose future-oriented optimism has always been haunted by the

---

28. Lutz Koepnick, *On Slowness: Toward an Aesthetic of the Contemporary* (New York: Columbia University Press, 2014), 18.
29. Koepnick, *On Slowness*, 18–19.
30. Koepnick, *On Slowness*, 10.
31. Koepnick, *On Slowness*, 11.

copresence of other timescapes. To be sure, the arrow of time is a central figure in the speed-as-progress narrative. However, the modern discourse on time also abounds in images of cyclicality, lateness, and distraction that puncture the very idea of human-kind's linear progression through history.

Contingency

An important by-product of modern temporalization is the notion of historical contingency. In opposition to necessity, contingency is the child of the turn from theology to history that, in the words of Richard Rorty, "has helped free us, gradually but steadily, from the-ology and metaphysics—from the temptation to look for an escape from time and chance."[32] Following the German historian Ernst Troeltsch, Hans Joas explains that the modern scientific revolu-tion created the "image of a causally determined universe, ruled by the laws of nature in the sense of a clock-work like mechanism."[33] While this shift destroyed the metaphysical certainty of a preor-dained world, only to replace it with mechanical determinism, par-adoxically, it also gave birth to contingency in the dual sense of chance and free will. "The longing for complete certainty," Joas argues, "moved from the ontological to the epistemological level—the clearest expression of this move is the Cartesian belief in the pos-sibility of a methodical procedure in human cognition as warranting complete certainty."[34] The modern turn toward reason undermined the preordained authority of the divine Creator and gave rise to liberal notions of individual autonomy and self-determination that promised to free the self from the chain of tradition. Embracing the future as a field of action emancipates the modern self from the bur-den of the past. And so the dialectical flipside of contingency is the

---

32. Richard Rorty, *Contingency, Irony, and Solidarity*, 28th ed. (Cambridge: Cambridge University Press, 2009), xiii.
33. Hans Joas, "Morality in the Age of Contingency," *Acta Sociologica* 47/4 (2004): 394.
34. Joas, "Morality," 394.

effort to control its effects: the more contingent history is, the more it requires human planning. Contingency in this sense services historical acceleration on the journey toward a brighter future that is—at least theoretically—open to all.

Precariousness

In our own era, the liberating dimension of contingency and a brighter future appear to have morphed into the anxious experience of a precarious present. The future is no longer the horizon of ideological contestation but rather the projection screen for dystopian visions of the final ecological catastrophe. Countless blockbusters imagine the apocalyptic end of humankind. In the so-called age of the Anthropocene, that is, the epoch in which human activity has a decisive impact on the earth, the planetary risks appear to be reaching the tipping point at which minor developments could precipitate major catastrophes. According to the risk theorist Ulrich Beck, we now inhabit a "world risk society" in which the negative effects of global capitalism, and the risks of global terrorism and irreversible global ecological disaster, outrun the ability of sovereign nation-states to contain and control them.[35] The notion of risk, according to Beck, addresses the possibility of future events; risks anticipate catastrophes.[36] The less calculable a risk is, Beck argues, the more it is subject to cultural interpretations and perceptions.[37] For Beck, then, the transition from the modern risk society into the world risk society is marked by the revocation of the type of insurance policy that, in the modern period, turned risk into a calculable quantity. Global risks are for Beck fundamentally deterritorialized, incalculable, and noncompensatory; they therefore fuel a pronounced sense of ontological precariousness.[38] Whereas Beck developed a global risk theory, other sociologists tend to debate precariousness in terms of the growth of global inequality and

---

35. Ulrich Beck, *Weltrisikogesellschaft: Auf der Suche nach der verlorenen Sicherheit* (Frankfurt a. M.: Suhrkamp, 2008), 61.
36. Beck, *Weltrisikogesellschaft*, 29.
37. Beck, *Weltrisikogesellschaft*, 34.
38. Beck, *Weltrisikogesellschaft*, 103.

with reference to the erosion of the social security systems in much of the Western world. Precariousness in this sense is the effect of globalization, which, instead of distributing wealth downward, has exacerbated existing inequality. As global companies ruthlessly outsourced their production to cheaper Asian countries, blue-collar workers in the US and in Europe saw their industrial jobs in steel and coal production and in other manufacturing industries disappear. The Brexit referendum and the US election in 2016 underline the failure of mainstream political parties—including those on the left—to adequately respond to the growing misery of their former constituencies in the American postindustrial "rust belt," in areas of industrial decline in northern England, or in Wales where voters began to embrace postliberal right-wing populism. Precariousness is the dark underside of modern contingency: while contingency enables the modern self to convert chance into free will, precariousness tips the experience of chance into incalculable risk.

When it comes to artworks, however, the term conveys more than the dismal prospects of our worried age. As I shall argue, contemporary art practice often explores the precariousness of living in the present through an aesthetics of the unfinished. Contemporary art and literature have lost faith in the chronological imagination that presents history in terms of an overarching master narrative. I borrow the term "chronological imagination" from Peter Fritzsche's essay of the same title, which analyzes the way in which the historian emplots history as a series of turning points that demarcate periods.[39] The literary texts, films, and works of photography under discussion here intervene in the current discourse on time. They bring into view alternate experiences that rupture the chronological imagination as well as our immersion in the new culture of immediacy. They articulate radical uncertainty about time as a

---

39. Peter Fritzsche, "1989 and the Chronological Imagination," in *Debating German Cultural Identity since 1989*, ed. Anne Fuchs, Kathleen James-Chakraborty, and Linda Shortt (Rochester, NY: Camden House, 2009), 17–29. For a discussion of Fritzsche, see chapter 2 in this study. See also Hayden White's seminal analysis of the literary tropes that shaped historical discourse in the nineteenth century. Hayden White, *Metahistory: The Historical Imagination in Nineteenth-Century Europe* (1975; Baltimore: Johns Hopkins University Press, 2014).

mode of order that can generate biographical, social, and historical meaning. They also query the positive potential of historical contingency. And so the experience of historical chance in these works oscillates between meaningful moments of ultrasubjective freedom at one end of the spectrum and a profound sense of ontological disorientation at the other.

Aesthetic precariousness, as I use the term, designates the various artistic and literary strategies through which subjective time is tentatively recovered in these works. Photography and films in particular are "slow" art in Koepnick's sense: their slow plotlines and minimalist aesthetics turn the act of reception into a mode of attentiveness that also cares for the Other. The ethical dimension of aesthetic precariousness ties in with the etymological meaning of the term: while the Latin noun *prex* means "request, petition, and prayer," the verb *precor* translates as "to beg, beseech, and entreat."[40] The term *precariousness* captures both the experience of an atomized, displaced, and fragmented reality as well as resistance to the loss of "proper time." Aesthetic precariousness also accounts for the myriad ways in which works of literature and art can engender *Eigenzeit*, that is, intimately subjective modes of temporality that dislodge the temporal imperative to be always live and connected.[41] The literary and artistic examples discussed in this study are very diverse, but they all pay attention to interiority and intimacy as essential conditions of cultural connectedness.

Eigenzeit

From around 1800 the separation of the public and private spheres evolved in step with modern civic society, which also brought forth the self-restrained bourgeois subject. According to Helga Nowotny,

---

40. According to Korte and Regard, "Precariousness forces me to acknowledge the presence of an other as an addressee." Barbara Korte and Frédéric Regard, eds., *Narrating Precariousness: Modes, Media, and Ethics* (Heidelberg: Universitätsverlag Winter, 2014), 9–10.

41. See Helga Nowotny, *Eigenzeit: Entstehung und Strukturierung eines Zeitgefühls* (Frankfurt a. Main: Suhrkamp, 1993); Helga Nowotny, *Time: The Modern and Postmodern Experience* (Cambridge: Polity Press, 1996).

Eigenzeit designates the modern subject's ability to cultivate "temporal sovereignty" over local time in the face of the commodification and acceleration of time in the public sphere. The modern era, Nowotny argues, gave rise to a specific "I-time," a time of the self, by polarizing the public time of work and the self's private time of leisure.[42] It was precisely this division of human temporality into two opposing time regimes that helped to legitimate modern subjectivity because the self's time was now part of "the objective spatio-temporal reality."[43] *Eigenzeit* emerges in Nowotny's book as a fundamentally ambivalent category: on the one hand, it is an integral part of the capitalist temporal economy that subjugates all aspects of human temporality to the rule of the mechanical clock. *Eigenzeit* is permissible only to the extent that it does not threaten the modern valorization of accelerated speed and perpetual innovation as quintessential temporal resources in the pursuit of profit. On the other hand, the very notion of the subject's own time entails the possibility of temporal resistance to modernity's regimented time regime. The potential of *Eigenzeit* to resist or disrupt the dominance of public time was then delegated to a different arena: as technological innovation, accelerated social change, and an increased tempo in everyday life were harnessed in the service of progress, modern aesthetic discourse became the domain that took care of the subject's desire for *Eigenzeit*. The dandy's ennui and mannered cultural boredom at the end of the nineteenth century, the literary exploration of *durée*, the celebration of a new intensity of life in short prose, and the cultural fascination with the condition of lateness underline the deep modernist engagement with diverse modes of temporality that challenged the capitalist time regime by way of a differentiated aesthetics.

What gives the texts and artworks discussed in my study a particular edge is the precariousness of *Eigenzeit*: as an unstable category that remains tied to temporal anxieties, *Eigenzeit* in these texts is simultaneously recuperative and abysmal. And this is so

---

42. Nowotny, *Time*, 13.
43. Nowotny, *Time*, 28.

because our era has eroded the binary division between the private and the public spheres, which are becoming enmeshed in ever more complex ways through new modes of connectivity and liveness. While the perspective of I-time or *Eigenzeit* enabled the modern self to exercise relative temporal sovereignty, this realm has now been destabilized by the culture of 24/7 connectivity, which even has the power to invade our sleep. The penetration of everyday life with streams of information produces a new economy of attention that favors interruptive action. The continual information stream binds the self into feedback loops that generate the illusion of agency and choice, while in reality undermining the conditions for *Eigenzeit*.

Chapter Outline

Times and temporalities in the plural, then, are the focus of this study, which takes its cue from the fall of the Berlin Wall and the invention of the World Wide Web, which occurred in close historical proximity. My focus is on the Western experience of time, in particular on German culture, which, as I aim to demonstrate, is a particularly fertile field of inquiry because, after the fall of the Berlin Wall, many writers, intellectuals, and artists responded to the shocking experience of a radically contingent history.

Chapter 1 analyzes the key terms in the debate on time. Acceleration, atomization, immediacy, the extended present, and time-space compression capture a pervasive sense of crisis. François Hartog has coined the term "presentism" for the experience of an omnivorous present that, in his view, has taken the place of authentic historical time.[44] One symptom of a profound crisis of time is the current memory boom that, for Hartog, reacts to the disappearance of the open future by transmuting memory into a "theological category."[45] But presentism also extends into the future itself through catastrophism—a presentist figure of thought that

---

44. Hartog, *Regimes of Historicity*, xviii.
45. Hartog, *Regimes of Historicity*, 7.

attempts to manage uncertainty through risk management, prevention, and security.[46] For Hartog, presentism is deeply pathological precisely because it extends our present into the future and into the past, thereby destroying our historical relatedness to both the past and the future as ontological categories. Burdened with its "twofold memory of the past and the future," Hartog concludes, "it is also shadowed by entropy"—presentism is therefore a "monstrous time."[47] Aleida Assmann too diagnoses a reconfiguration of our relationship to past, present, and future: she argues that the time regime of modernity ended in the late 1980s when the future finally lost its shiny gloss against the backdrop of the unparalleled violence of twentieth-century history and in the context of emerging ecological threats.[48] But Assmann evaluates the disappearance of the modern time regime in a very different light: even though the future as horizon of ideological investment has collapsed, the present remains a site where social actors manage to construct and synthesize their experiences of the past and expectations of their future.[49] For Assmann, cultural memory is the key instrument in the handling of our temporal experiences, as it provides us with indispensable cultural frames. Assmann's reading of the "culturalization" of time thus deontologizes the very category of time in favor of a constructivist perspective that takes account of the genuinely human ability to recall the past and project expectations into the future.[50]

Other terms in the debate on time also point to a new temporal ecology that engenders opportunities alongside threats: resonance, time-space, and network time promise to overcome the rule of the clock but also threaten our chronological imagination, which is wedded to the kind of historical narrative that we tell about our lives. Chapter 1 engages with the temporal anxiety that we

46. Hartog, *Regimes of Historicity*, 199.

47. Hartog, *Regimes of Historicity*, 203.

48. Aleida Assmann, *Ist die Zeit aus den Fugen? Aufstieg und Fall des Zeitregimes der Moderne* (Munich: Hanser, 2013), 18.

49. Assmann, *Ist die Zeit aus den Fugen?*, 273.

50. Assmann, *Ist die Zeit aus den Fugen?*, 277.

can no longer narrate history and our own lives as coherent stories and concludes with a more detailed discussion of the idea of precariousness.

Chapter 2 returns to the fin de siècle to show that our temporal anxieties are part and parcel of the complicated story of modernity. A wide range of examples from the domains of literature, sociology, philosophy, and psychology from the 1870s to the late 1930s showcases the rich modernist discourse on time. Neither modernity nor modernism can be adequately summed up under the heading of the speed-as-progress narrative: even though the processes of modernization invest in the future by driving technological innovation and rationalizing time, the modern imagination was also hugely fascinated by foreign and distant pasts, as the rise of disciplines such as archaeology, psychoanalysis, geology, and anthropology, whose time frames reach far back into the (pre)history of humankind, provides witness. Nietzsche, Simmel, and Freud are among those pivotal figures that provided the theoretical scaffolding for human untimeliness and asynchronicity. Thomas Mann, Franz Kafka, Robert Musil, and Robert Walser are modernist writers who explored very different temporal itineraries that disrupt modern speed politics. Chapter 2 therefore offers deliberately disparate readings that, together, complicate the story of modernity. I also track how acceleration and progress are crosscut with attention, lateness, and slowness in the modern debate on time.

The earliest text discussed is Nietzsche's *Über den Nachteil und Nutzen der Historie für das Leben* (*On the Use and Abuse of History for Life*): published two years after German unification in 1873, it is a milestone marking the modernist fascination with radically different time spans and itineraries that stretch from the shortest moment of attention and the modern experience of immediacy, as exemplified by Simmel's seminal essay *Die Großstädte und das Geistesleben* (*The Metropolis and Mental Life*, 1903) and Robert Walser's short prose pieces, to the extended present of Thomas Mann's *Der Zauberberg* (*The Magic Mountain*, 1924) or the metaphysical and transcendent other time in Kafka's *Der Proceß* (*The Trial*, 1914). Freud, whose writings reach into the prehistory of humankind, exemplifies the modern enthrallment with an ultimately inaccessible and far-flung past that haunts the present. Mapping the complex and contradictory temporal itineraries of the modern imagination from a cultural-historical perspective, chapter 2 abandons chronological narration: although it deals with texts that were written or published between 1873 and the late 1930s, it deliberately defies decisive turning points and moments of innovation. I view the period rather in terms of a rich cultural tapestry or spatiotemporal map that comes with diverse speeds and temporal directions. The metaphor of the map reminds us that the debate about time is always also a debate about space and place: the discussion of time-space compression in chapter 1 takes issue with the misleading dualism of time and space that characterizes much of the current debate on time. With geographers David Harvey and Doreen Massey, I argue throughout this study that space and time are performative categories that are tied to social, material, and cultural processes that can produce very uneven time spaces.

These theoretical and cultural-historical perspectives prepare the ground for the analysis of time in contemporary culture. Focusing on visual art, chapter 3 debates the concept of slow art in dialogue with international art practice, as exemplified in the performance art of Lee Lozano and Marina Abramović, before analyzing the representation of time in the works of two prominent German photographers: West German Michael Wesely and East German Ulrich Wüst. I show how Wesely's time photography invalidates the indexicality of the photograph through radical experiments with exposure times. Wüst's *Später Sommer/Letzter Herbst* (Late Summer/Final Autumn, 2016) plays with the representational conventions of the photobook to displace the drama of the summer of 1989—in his narrative the fall of the Berlin Wall appears as an unreadable and strangely absent event that nevertheless haunts his photographs of the GDR. Christian Petzold is an internationally renowned German filmmaker: his acclaimed film *Barbara* (2012) is another example of a slow artwork that engages with the memory of the GDR from enhanced historical distance. Petzold's strikingly slow cinematography not only foregrounds a two-speed Germany before the fall of the Berlin Wall; it also probes the protagonist's search for subjective time under the conditions of surveillance. The chapter continues with a discussion of the aesthetic of stillness in Austrian filmmaker Ulrich Seidl's feature film *Paradise: Glaube* (Paradise: Faith, 2012), the second part of a trilogy that explores the doomed quest for happiness and transcendence in the lives of three female protagonists. The analysis of disruptive performances in Maren Ade's acclaimed tragicomedy *Toni Erdmann* (2016) focuses on the quest for *Eigenzeit* and the good life in the age of turbocapitalism. The works discussed in this chapter exemplify the contemporary interest in slow art in response to the culture of immediacy and instant delivery. They envisage an aesthetics of precariousness that foregrounds the fragility of our anchorage in social time.

Chapter 4 turns to the experience of precarious times in contemporary German fiction. The first part of the chapter queries the binary distinction between modernist and postmodernist literature in the light of striking epistemological and narratological continuities that capture the uneven experience of time. The ensuing close readings then analyze diverse articulations of precariousness in contemporary literature: Julia Schoch's novel *Mit der Geschwindigkeit des Sommers* (With the Speed of the Summer, 2009), Karen Duve's *Taxi* (2008), and Clemens Meyer's *Als wir träumten* (When We Were Dreaming, 2006) deal with protagonists for whom 1989 represents a nonevent yet also, paradoxically, a disturbing rupture in their biographies. Schoch's novel is set in provincial East Germany close to the Polish border, Duve's narrative in Hamburg, and Meyer's text in Leipzig before and after the fall of the Berlin Wall. The protagonists of these texts are drifters who know their locality well but have no sense of orientation. In their existential dislocation they are akin to Wilhelm Genazino's protagonist in *Das Glück in glücksfernen Zeiten* (Happiness in Unhappy Times, 2009), who embodies the new educated precariat facing social and economic decline. In his encounter with a reality that is simultaneously drab yet demanding, Genazino's hero fine-tunes a tactics of temporal resistance to the just-in-time ideology of the neoliberal era. Similarly, the protagonist of Arnold Stadler's *Sehnsucht: Versuch über das erste Mal* (Longing: Attempting to Capture the First Time, 2002), is a first-person manic-depressive narrator who ekes out his living with consumer advice seminars, an idea that he developed after dropping out of his university degree in forestry. Embroiled in a mundane world of consumption, the protagonist regularly succumbs to sexual voyeurism as a mode of transcending the here and now. But the protagonist's carnal desires are also the underside of his religious longing for transcendence. Stadler's intriguing text *Salvatore* (2008) is the companion piece to the novel: it employs a complex circuit of exchange between diverse genres and media to recover the possibility of transcendence as a precarious experience.

The chapter concludes with an in-depth analysis of Jenny Erpenbeck's novel *Gehen, ging, gegangen* (2015; *Go, Went, Gone*, 2017), which tackles one of the most urgent political issues of our times: the refugee crisis. Besides discussing the narratological handling of time in dialogue with the prominent chronotopes in this text, I show how the narrative envisages a precarious politics that recognizes cultural difference alongside a shared humanity.

Thematically and stylistically diverse, these texts have one feature in common: they all explore highly individualistic temporal itineraries that collide with the prevailing desire for digital connectivity without, however, reinstating the historical imagination. Each of these works homes in on the experience of being out of sync with one's time through a mode of writing that displaces the culture of immediacy and liveness. They all protest against the imaginative poverty and temporal scarcity of a reality that is perceived as atomized, disembedded, and without future horizons. My epilogue attempts to connect the analysis of time and temporality with a broader perspective on the future direction of the humanities.

1

THEORETICAL PERSPECTIVES

Temporal Anxieties in the Digital Age

Timeless Time

Many contributors to the debate on time in the digital era have diagnosed a paradigm shift toward a timeless present that has swallowed up the past. Manuel Castells's trilogy on the information age provided the first sustained theory of the economic, social, and cultural effects of network society and the collapse of time. Examining how an inescapable network logic affects all domains of life, Castells arrived at this overarching conclusion:

> Networks constitute the new social morphology of our societies and the diffusion of networking logic substantially modifies the operation and outcomes in the processes of production, experience, power and culture. While the networking form of social organization has existed in other times and spaces, the new information

technology paradigm provides the basis for its pervasive expansion throughout the entire social structure.[1]

For Castells the new social morphology of network society shifted power away from established institutions such as governments, political parties, and labor movements. A new "space of flows" has emerged that escapes the conventional and comparatively slow mechanics of modern political governance by breaking down the spatial barriers that delay the instant delivery of information. Castells argued that in network society space organizes time and not vice versa, as suggested by classical social theories. The space of flows is made up of three layers: firstly, the circuit of electronic exchanges that provides the "material support of simultaneous practices";[2] secondly, the nodes and hubs that link the network up with specific places "with well-defined social, cultural, physical and functional characteristics,"[3] and, thirdly, the spatial organization of the managerial elites "that exercise the directional functions around which such space is articulated."[4] The space of flows, as Castells explained it originally in *The Rise of the Network Society*, thus refers to a new feature of network society: the possibility enabled by technology of practicing simultaneity without spatial contiguity. On the other hand, it also allows for asynchronous interaction at a distance.[5] In this way the space of flows produces a new experience of a "timeless time" that overcomes the linear predictability of clock time as well as the context-dependent nature of our temporal experiences. Castells

---

1. Manuel Castells, *The Rise of the Network Society*, 2nd ed. (Oxford: Blackwell, 2000), 469.

2. Castells, *The Rise of the Network Society*, 442.

3. Castells, *The Rise of the Network Society*, 443.

4. Castells, *The Rise of the Network Society*, 445.

5. Castells usefully differentiates between the space of flows and real places, i.e., our material, social, and cultural habitats. While the space of flows is a form of domination over such habitats, he qualified his argument in later publications to make room for resistance to domination by grassroots groups or social movements that exploit the net for countercultural or alternative political and social purposes. See Manuel Castells, "Grassrooting the Space of Flows," *Urban Geography* 20/4 (1999): 294–302.

describes this profound transformation of time in network society in terms of a

> mixing of tenses to create a forever universe, not self-expanding but self-maintaining, not cyclical but random, not recursive but incursive: timeless time, using technology to escape the contexts of its existence, and to appropriate selectively any value each context could offer to the ever-present.[6]

Network society thus displaces the sequential order of lived experience by way of a "real virtuality" that immerses us into a world of instantaneity.[7] As Jan van Dijk notes, Castells's great achievement was to provide us with a far-reaching analysis of the transformation of time and space in network society at a very early point in the history of the development of the World Wide Web. For van Dijk, however, Castells's argument is ultimately too one-dimensional, as it adopts an instrumental or overly deterministic view of technology that, in van Dijk's view, negates the possibility of a social struggle over networks. "Social actors," comments van Dijk, "take positions inside the networks, communicating at centres, nodes and terminals, and they are engaged in daily struggles over the construction and use of these networks, in the role of managers and employees, producers and consumers or governors and citizens."[8] Rapidly evolving digital technologies have certainly infiltrated nearly all aspects of our daily lives, but their impact is more complex, heterogeneous, and unpredictable than Castells suggested. Judy Wajcman rightly observes that "the relationship between technological change and temporality is dialectical, not teleological."[9] A proponent of STS (Social Technology Studies), she emphasizes that the design of technology is not simply the outcome of indisputable technical imperatives but rather

---

6. Castells, *The Rise of the Network Society*, 464.

7. As noted by Jan van Dijk, Castells's concept of a "timeless time" draws on Baudrillard's notion of simulacra. Jan van Dijk, "The One-Dimensional Network Society of Manuel Castells," *New Media & Society* 1 (1999): 127–38.

8. Van Dijk, "The One-Dimensional Network Society," 135.

9. Wajcman, *Pressed for Time*, 9.

the product of complex social processes that reflect gender biases, racial inequality, educational gaps, and class differences as well as the unevenness of geography. Society and technology are, as Wajcman puts it, "mutually constitutive": they form "sociomaterial 'assemblages.'"[10] The social significance of technology also points to myriad usages in everyday life: social actors are not simply passive recipients of technological innovations but active producers and users who come up with unforeseen ploys, tactics, and subterfuges that secure unique spaces of agency. As I will argue throughout this study, this subversive surplus of subjectivity escapes both discursive categorization as well as the disciplinary logic of Foucauldian systems.

Nevertheless, twenty years after the publication of *The Rise of the Network Society*, the anxiety about the disembedding effects of an unpredictable and ungovernable space of flows in the age of globalization and a new culture of immediacy that requires us to be always connected and live has not been put to rest. The ongoing debate on time and temporality revolves around a range of interconnected diagnostic tropes that aim to illuminate a fundamental recalibration of the conditions of temporality in the network era: acceleration, resonance, atomization, immediacy, the extended present, time-space compression, network time, and precarious times.

Acceleration

The ever-tighter enmeshing of human worlds with digital media and the new culture of liveness have unleashed fears about the loss of democracy, about the erosion of the very notion of experience, about the loss of both past and future as horizons of orientation, and about the atomization of our biographies into incoherent episodes. Because the new culture of immediacy promotes instant access, it erodes the expectation of temporal processing. This new

---

10. Wajcman, *Pressed for Time*, 31–32.

era of the "digital now" where the furthest goal is only a click of the mouse away challenges not only established notions of delayed gratification but also the very idea of time as a multidimensional concept that integrates past, present, and future into human experience. The sociologist Hartmut Rosa therefore argues in his influential book *Beschleunigung: Die Veränderung der Zeitstrukturen in der Moderne* (2005; *Social Acceleration: A New Theory of Modernity*, 2015) that the prospect of maintaining reciprocal relations between selves, others, and their human habitats has been unhinged in the twenty-first century. He contends that the acceleration of all aspects of life has now reached the critical point where social integration is no longer possible.[11] In physics, acceleration refers to the rate of change of velocity of an object with respect to time. According to Newton's Second Law, an object's acceleration is the net result of all forces acting on the object. The speed of an object is the rate of change of its position. While the scientific terms *speed* and *acceleration* are by no means identical, the modern discourse on social time interweaves them in a narrative that champions scientific, technological, and social progress. Acceleration emerges in this discourse as the central agent that can close the gap between a present that is rich in creative potential and an even brighter future as the horizon of humankind's self-realization. Rosa argues that in high modernity the technological acceleration that was achieved by more efficient modes of production, faster transportation and communication networks, and so on also facilitated the acceleration of social change and as such continual social innovation. As past experiences began to lose their relevance more quickly, individuals experienced the acceleration of their entire lives.[12] For Rosa the unstoppable tempo of modern

---

11. Hartmut Rosa, *Beschleunigung: Die Veränderung der Zeitstrukturen in der Moderne* (Frankfurt a. Main: Suhrkamp, 2005), 48. See also Peter Borscheid, *Das Tempo-Virus: Eine Kulturgeschichte der Beschleunigung* (Frankfurt a. Main: Campus, 2004). Some authors promote specific forms of resistance to the regime of acceleration. See Friedhelm Hengsbach, *Die Zeit gehört uns: Widerstand gegen das Regime der Beschleunigung* (Frankfurt a. Main: Westend, 2012).

12. Rosa, *Beschleunigung*, 190.

rationalization and differentiation has brought forth late modernity as an arena where the latent pathologies of the modern time
regime could finally erupt: late modernity has devoured the specifically modern horizon of expectation that propelled human beings
toward the future. We now inhabit a much more fragmented and
contingent temporality that turns life into a series of short-term
projects. And so, ironically, acceleration gives rise to a new detemporalization of history that collapses the epistemological difference
between past, present, and future in favor of the directionless experience of "rasender Stillstand" (stagnation at top speed).[13]

Because Rosa views acceleration as the unrestrained engine of
modern history, all alternative temporalities and modes of agency
must inevitably appear as by-products of social and technological
acceleration. For Rosa the temporal pathologies of late modernity
are embodied in the figure of the time juggler and time gambler
whose sense of self has shrunk to a tiny atomized dot that reacts to
the fast-paced change by way of a new flexibility and a "situated
identity" that is lacking in any sense of continuity.

In his book on acceleration in modernity Rosa removes culture
entirely from his analysis: rather than an essential component in the
story of modernity, he views culture merely as a capitalist by-product.
In liberal-capitalist societies, he argues, the fields of production and
consumption, and our social relationships, are being controlled by
the behavior patterns of the producer or consumer.[14] Not surprisingly then, Rosa arrives at the utterly dystopian conclusion that
expressive notions of selfhood that he associates with Romanticism
have been entirely colonized by a naturalist notion of selfhood that
ensures conformity with the systemic requirements of capitalism. In
the age of postmodernity, Rosa concludes, the romantic-expressive
paradigm loses its oppositional character and its potential to resist
the naturalist or capitalist imperatives of the system.[15]

---

13. Rosa, *Beschleunigung,* 479.
14. Hartmut Rosa, *Weltbeziehungen im Zeitalter der Beschleunigung: Umrisse
einer neuen Gesellschaftskritik* (Frankfurt a. Main: Suhrkamp, 2012), 167.
15. Rosa, *Weltbeziehungen,* 176.

While Rosa's vision of the commodified self is perhaps exaggerated, the rise of occupational stress in postindustrialized society seems to validate his diagnosis that many people are struggling to manage the pace of life at the beginning of the twenty-first century: in 2015 the Bertelsmann Foundation published a representative German survey on stress at the workplace. The study showed that 42 percent of the German workforce felt that their performance targets were constantly increasing, and 51 percent reported that they could not influence the volume of work they had to do.[16] Similar results are reported in British and US health surveys.[17] In response to these trends, the stress management industry has sprung up as a burgeoning economic sector that not only fills the shelves of bookshops with self-help books but also offers professional online training courses and corporate workshops on stress control. So-called time-saving techniques such as "trashing perfectionism," "multitasking," "power napping," or "power reading" play a prominent role alongside relaxation techniques that include physical exercise, a balanced diet, yoga, and mindfulness training. The commodification of well-being by the new time management industry corroborates Rosa's dystopian vision of the colonized self: both time-saving and relaxation techniques make us fit for life in the age of high speed and continual innovation.

Too much speed also featured prominently in the recent debate about particle physics that was ignited in 2011 when a team of Italian particle physicists called OPERA made the startling announcement that they had found particles traveling at a speed faster than light, a discovery that—if corroborated—would overturn the very

---

16. See "Studie zu Stress am Arbeitsplatz," *Spiegel Online*, 16 March 2015, http://www.spiegel.de/karriere/stress-am-arbeitsplatz-jeder-dritte-fuehlt-sich-ueberfordert-a-1023685.html (accessed 26 October 2016).

17. See "Work-Related Stress, Anxiety, and Depression Statistics in Great Britain 2015," Health and Safety Executive, http://www.hse.gov.uk/statistics/causdis/stress/stress.pdf (accessed 25 October 2016). The data shows that in 2014–15 stress accounted for 35 percent of all work-related ill health and 43 percent of all working days lost due to ill health. The main factors cited by respondents as causing work-related stress, depression, or anxiety were workload pressures, including tight deadlines, too much responsibility, and a lack of managerial support.

foundations of Einstein's theory of relativity.[18] The Italian researchers reported that neutrinos—subatomic particles—had traveled the distance of 730 kilometers from CERN, Europe's particle-physics lab near Geneva, to the Gran Sasso lab in Italy at a speed that exceeded the speed of light by a fraction of 20 parts per million. The speed of light is 299,792,458 meters per second; they believed that the neutrinos were traveling at 299,798,454 meters per second. As Subir Sarkar, head of Particle Theory at Oxford University, explained, "The constancy of the speed of light essentially underpins our understanding of space and time and causality, which is the fact that cause comes before effect."[19] Six months later the head of the Italian research team resigned when repeats of the test showed that the particles were traveling at the speed of light.[20] The science journal *Nature* reported that OPERA team members had detected two possible sources of error:

> The initial result suggested that the neutrinos were reaching the detector 60 nanoseconds faster than the speed of light would allow. Both potential errors would affect the neutrinos' arrival time, as measured by OPERA's master clock. . . . The first is a faulty connection at the point at which the light from a fiber-optic cable brings a synchronizing Global Positioning System (GPS) signal into the master clock. The fault could have delayed the GPS signal, causing the master clock to run slow and thus causing the neutrinos' travel time to appear shorter than it actually was.[21]

The second error occurred when "tests of the timing system turned up a second, opposing effect: an oscillator within the master clock that keeps time between the arrivals of synchronization signals

18. Ian Sample, "Faster Than Light Particles Found, Claim Scientists." *The Guardian*, 22 September 2011.

19. Quoted in Ian Sample, "Faster Than Light Particles Found."

20. Jason Palmer, "Neutrinos clocked at Light-Speed in New Icarus Test," *The Guardian*, 16 March 2012; Geoff Brumfiel, "Neutrinos Not Faster Than Light: ICARUS Experiment Contradicts Controversial Claim," *Nature: International Weekly Journal of Science*, 19 March 2012, http://www.nature.com/news/neutrinos-not-faster-than-light-1.10249 (accessed 12 October 2014).

21. Eugenie Samuel Reich, "Time Glitches Dog Neutrino Claim: Team Admits to Possible Errors in Faster-Than-Light Finding," *Nature: International Weekly Journal of Science*, 1 March 2012, 17.

was running fast. That would have made the neutrinos' travel time seem longer."[22] Clocks running too slow or too fast are not what we expect of particle physics. A further factor contributing to the premature publication of faulty test results may have to do with human hastiness in response to the pressure to produce revolutionary scientific findings where the investment of financial resources has been high: OPERA team members conceded that they published their results too soon without carrying out sufficient checks.

This intriguing case, involving faulty clocks and human error, accentuates not merely the scientific but also the social dimension of time. Even though Rosa's theory of unstoppable acceleration is too one-dimensional, it does convey how acceleration as an agent of change has nurtured a speed politics that impacts all aspects of life.

Resonance

Rosa's latest book *Resonanz: Eine Soziologie der Weltbeziehung* (2016; *Resonance: A Sociology of Our Relationship to the World*, 2019) attempts to correct the underlying determinism of his earlier theory of acceleration by developing a "sociology of the good life."[23] Rosa now argues that the good life in the twenty-first century hinges on the development of relations of resonance between self and world. As long as the modern state continues to obey the imperatives of acceleration, innovation, and persistent investment in economic growth, it impairs the conditions for a resonant relationship between the self and her world. Rosa understands resonance as a mode of being in the world that can redress modernity's multiple alienations, including the Cartesian split between mind and body and the disjuncture between the individual, society, and nature.[24] For Rosa, resonance is a basic

---

22. Reich, "Time Glitches Dog Neutrino Claim," 17.

23. Hartmut Rosa, *Resonanz: Eine Soziologie der Weltbeziehung* (Frankfurt a. Main: Suhrkamp, 2016), 14; Rosa, *Resonance: A Sociology of Our Relationship to the World*, trans. James C. Wagner (Cambridge: Polity, 2019).

24. Rosa, *Resonanz*, 293.

human need and innate ability that connects human beings with others. Rather than appropriating or erasing the experience of otherness, it is premised on the recognition of a fundamental difference between the self and the Other: the resonant encounter with the Other sets in train a dialogic process of "Anverwandlung," that is, partial absorption by or entry into the Other's sphere.[25] Rosa's theory of the good life in the twenty-first century is steeped in Romanticism: he draws on poets from Friedrich Schlegel to Eichendorff, Novalis, and Hölderlin to call for responsive and reciprocal world relations.[26] Rosa champions resonance as the potential cure for the ills of modernity's crippling time regime: resonant experiences, he argues, overcome acceleration by creating a temporal bridge between past and future and transcending the chronology of linear time.[27] But he also concedes that his vision of the good life would require a radical political, economic, and cultural revolution.[28]

Rosa makes no mention of book 12 of Homer's *Odyssey*, which, in the Sirens episode, tells a foundational story about the allure, power, and threat of resonance. It is worthwhile recapitulating this story in detail because Homer tells Odysseus's encounter with the Sirens three times: first, when the sorceress Circe advises the Greek hero about how to escape the danger of the Sirens' song:

> Plug your comrades' ears with softened beeswax lest they listen, and row swiftly past. And if you must hear, then let them first tie you hand and foot and stand you upright in the mast housing, and fasten the rope ends round the mast itself, so you can delight in hearing the Sirens' voices. And should you beg your crew to free you, let them only bind you more tightly.[29]

---

25. Rosa, *Resonanz*, 317.
26. Rosa, *Resonanz*, 599–614.
27. Rosa, *Resonanz*, 693.
28. Rosa, *Resonanz*, 56.
29. Homer, *The Odyssey*, trans. A. S. Kline, Poetry in Translation 2004, http://www.poetryintranslation.com/PITBR/Greek/Odyssey12.htm#anchor_Toc 90268047 (accessed 15 April 2015).

The second telling occurs immediately before the encounter with the Sirens when Odysseus—the first-person narrator of books 9 to 12—instructs his men to tie him to the mast and, should he beg them to free him, to tighten the ropes even more. The third telling immediately follows this instruction: Odysseus now recalls the unfolding events through an epic narration that includes the citation of the Sirens' complete song:

> Famous Odysseus, great glory of Achaea, draw near, and bring your ship to rest, and listen to our voices. No man rows past this isle in his dark ship without hearing the honeysweet sound from our lips. He delights in it and goes his way a wiser man. We know all the suffering the Argives and the Trojans endured, by the gods' will, on the wide plains of Troy. We know everything that comes to pass on the fertile Earth.

The three retellings of the Sirens' episode can be read as a contest over whose voice should be heard: because Circe possesses the knowledge of the future she has the authority to instruct Odysseus. However, by communicating her warning to his men Odysseus establishes the power of the Western male subject who has access to privileged information. The switching of voice from Circe to Odysseus thus transfers authority: even though it is Circe who holds knowledge of the future, she is displaced in the retelling so that Odysseus emerges as a man of intellectual guile and cunning. When Odysseus reenacts the actual encounter through epic narration, Circe's gesturing to a perilous future has already been absorbed by the epic past tense of Odysseus' intradiegetic narration. Epic narration thus contains the dangerous allure of the Sirens' irresistible song whose singing we can only hear from the safe distance of the narrative present.

According to Horkheimer and Adorno's famous interpretation in *The Dialectics of the Enlightenment*, the episode therefore symbolizes the very moment when domination was institutionalized in Western thought: Odysseus's upright posture and his delectation at the Sirens' song turn him into a precursor of the bourgeois subject. The sailors are engaged in manual labor and cannot hear the beautiful singing because their ears are stuffed; they therefore represent for Adorno and Horkheimer a version of the modern proletariat.[30] Indeed, Odysseus's upright posture asserts his phallic power: while the sailors are laboring at his feet, their master takes time out from the toil of travel to enjoy the Sirens' performance. But we should also note that Odysseus could bear to hear the Sirens' honeysweet song only when he is tied to the mast. It is precisely the sadomasochistic dialectic between control (of the present and future) and seduction (to the past) that unsettles the simple enactment of domination in this scene. However, this episode does not exhaust itself in the relationship of domination between Odysseus and his men: it is also a story about how the Sirens' honeysweet song enters Odysseus's ear. As Rebecca Comay points out, the ear is not just the organ of equilibrium and control but also an intricate labyrinth that renders "precarious the sense of balance and upright posture."[31] The content of the Sirens' song adds additional complexity to the scene, as their song is anything but sweet: it provides not only a painful cultural memory of the Trojan War and of Odysseus's banishment but also the ghastly vision of everything that comes to pass on earth. While the gods may hold such knowledge, in the hands of mortals it would be deadly. By performing an omniscient and as such total memory of past, present, and future, the Sirens' song interjects radical achronicity into Odysseus's phallic and future-oriented trajectory. The interpolation of the female voice into Odysseus's passage thus foregrounds the gendered nature of chrono-politics: the achronicity of the Sirens' song remains episodic, as Odysseus manages to circumvent their deadly allure. And so book 12 of the *Odyssey* already complicates the very idea of resonance: resonance is not a panacea for the temporal pathologies of late modernity, because it is imbricated in power and gender relations.

Kafka's *Das Schweigen der Sirenen* (*The Silence of the Sirens,* 1917) demystifies the ancient myth because in his modern parable the Sirens no longer sing at all. Their silence, Kafka asserts, is an

---

30. See Theodor Adorno and Max Horkheimer, *Dialektik der Aufklärung,* in *Gesammelte Schriften* (Frankfurt a. Main: Suhrkamp, 1981), 3:64. See Rebecca Comay, "Adorno's Siren Song," *New German Critique* 81 (2000): 21–48.

31. Comay, "Adorno's Siren Song," 27.

even deadlier weapon than their singing.[32] According to Kafka's version, Odysseus stuffs wax into his own, rather than his men's, ears, even though it is well known that such measures are childish and offer no protection against the Sirens' penetrating song. Yet Odysseus, so it appears, believes that the Sirens are singing: for a fleeting moment he sees their throats rising and falling, their breasts lifting, their eyes filled with tears, and their lips half-parted before he fixes his gaze on the distance where they literally vanish from his sight. And as the ship draws nearer, Odysseus—far from succumbing to the Sirens' song—proves to be oblivious to their charm. The impersonal narrative voice observes that had the Sirens possessed any consciousness, they would not have survived this moment of their erasure. Kafka's story thus enacts a decisive shift from sound and hearing to sight: by describing what Odysseus sees rather than hears, Kafka introduces the notion of visual mastery into the story as a decisive moment in Western history. By fixing Odysseus's gaze on the distance, he exposes the hero as master of all he surveys and as the proverbial male subject.

Kafka concludes with a further twist in a codicil: Odysseus knew all along that the Sirens were not singing and merely employed pretense as a protective shield. But whether Odysseus was oblivious to the singing or knew all along of the silence, the story disrupts a naive model of resonance: Odysseus merely pretends to listen to something that he cannot hear or that he knows does not exist. Kafka turns the Sirens' desire for resonance into an instrument of male power: phallic Odysseus outwits the female Sirens with guile and displaces Circe's voice through his own authoritative retelling.

Kafka wrote his last story, *Josefine, die Sängerin oder Das Volk der Mäuse* (*Josefine the Singer or the Mouse People*) in 1924 when

---

32. Franz Kafka, "Das Schweigen der Sirenen," in *Beim Bau der chinesischen Mauer und andere Schriften aus dem Nachlaß* (Frankfurt a. M.: Fischer, 1994), 168–70. On this parable, see Vivian Liska, "Was weiß die Literatur? Das Wissen der Sirenen: Adorno, Banchot, Sloterdijk," *KulturPoetik: Zeitschrift für kulturgeschichtliche Literaturwissenschaft* 4 (2004): 1–18; Liliane Weissberg, "Myth, History, Enlightenment: The Silence of the Sirens," *Journal of the Kafka Society of America* 9 (1985): 131–48.

advanced tuberculosis was ravaging his voice. It too explores the achronic temporality of voice and resonance: the story unfolds in terms of a male discourse on the effect of female performance on a downtrodden and disempowered community, the mouse people. Surrounded by enemies and pressured by poor economic conditions, the mouse people are engaged in a never-ending battle for survival that leaves no room for childhood, youth, and pastimes. The mouse folk live in a timeless time of an everlasting present without historical depth. Kafka skillfully contrasts the gender identity of the patronizing male mouse narrator who acts as spokesperson for his people with Josefine's identity as a female performer whose voice we never hear outside this male discourse.[33] And yet, even though the narrator goes out of his way to denigrate Josefine's art—he claims that her singing is nothing but the most ordinary mouse piping and furthermore that the mouse people are unmusical—he unwittingly acknowledges the utopian power of her concert performance to lift the mouse people out of the common drudgery of life. At the very end of the story the narrator attempts to reassert his authority by assigning her voice to oblivion:

> Bald wird die Zeit kommen, wo ihr letzter Pfiff ertönt und verstummt. Sie ist eine kleine Episode in der ewigen Geschichte unseres Volkes und das Volk wird den Verlust überwinden. Leicht wird es uns ja nicht werden; wie werden die Versammlungen in völliger Stummheit möglich sein? Freilich, waren sie nicht auch mit Josefine stumm? War ihr wirkliches Pfeifen nennenswert lauter und lebendiger, als die Erinnerung daran sein wird? War es denn noch bei ihren Lebzeiten mehr als eine bloße Erinnerung? Hat nicht vielmehr das Volk in seiner Weisheit Josefinens Gesang, eben deshalb, weil er in dieser Art unverlierbar war, so hoch gestellt?
>
> Vielleicht werden wir also gar nicht sehr viel entbehren, Josefine aber, erlöst von der irdischen Plage, die aber ihrer Meinung nach Auserwählten bereitet ist, wird fröhlich sich verlieren in der zahllosen Menge

---

33. See Elizabeth Boa, "Performance and Femininity: *Josephine the Singer or the Mouse People*," in *Kafka: Gender, Class, and Race in the Letters and Fictions* (Oxford: Clarendon, 1996), 175–80; Ruth V. Gross, "Of Mice and Women: Reflections on a Discourse in Kafka's *Josefine, die Sängerin oder Das Volk der Mäuse*," *Germanic Review* 60 (1985): 59–68; Michael Minden, "Kafka's *Josefine die Sängerin oder Das Volk der Mäuse*," *German Life & Letters* 62 (2009): 297–310.

der Helden unseres Volkes, und bald, da wir keine Geschichte treiben, in gesteigerter Erlösung vergessen sein wie alle ihre Brüder.[34]

Soon the time will come when her last whistle sounds and falls silent. She is a little episode in the never-ending story of our people, and the people will get over her loss. It won't be easy for us; how will our assemblies be possible in complete silence? Then again, were they not silent, even with Josefine there? Was her actual whistling noticeably louder and livelier than in our memory it was? Was it ever more than a memory, even while she was alive? Was it not rather the people in their wisdom valueing Josefine's song so highly, because in such a way, it was impossible for them ever to lose it?

Perhaps therefore we shall not even miss her, but Josefine, released from the earthly torment that in her opinion is the lot of the chosen ones, will happily lose herself in the numberless crowds of the heroes of our people, before long—as we don't keep any history—to be accorded the heightened relief of being, like all of her brothers, forgotten.[35]

The narrator's blatant attempt to erase Josefine from cultural memory is, however, undercut by his intense and, arguably, obsessive preoccupation with a voice that has escaped his own phallic discursive practice. And so in spite of his denunciatory intentions, his own narration unwittingly assigns her voice a place in cultural memory and as such resonance. In Kafka's last story resonance overcomes domination by traveling in an unpredictable fashion across space and time. This is perhaps Kafka's most optimistic story, as it does not so much stage the absence of Josefine's voice but her continued presence through absence. Her absence irritates and beguiles the narrator who fails to master or curb her cultural resonance through his controlling narration.

The literary examples sketched here accentuate the gendered conditions of resonance; in so doing they foreground conditions of domination and power alongside a radically alternative temporality that disrupts the linearity of time. While in Homer the Sirens' ghastly and honeysweet song contains all times ever, Josefine's singing enters a latent cultural memory that punctures the seeming

34. Franz Kafka, "Josefine, die Sängerin oder Das Volk der Mäuse," in *Ein Landarzt und andere Drucke zu Lebzeiten* (Frankfurt a. Main: Fischer, 1994), 294.

35. Franz Kafka, "Josefine, the Singer, or The Mouse People," trans. and with an introduction by Michael Hofmann (London: Penguin Books, 2007), 244.

rationality of the male mouse narrator. Separated by 2,000 years, these two examples also voice a surplus that eludes the discursive practice of phallic protagonists and male mouse narrators.

Atomization

The notion that acceleration has been the driving engine of modernity is a commonplace in much of contemporary discourse. Like Hartmut Rosa, Fredric Jameson argues that "time is today a function of speed, and evidently perceptible only in terms of its rate or velocity as such."[36] Paul Virilio, the maverick French critic, goes even further by making time the main principle of power: in his view history is an ever-accelerating competition of speed. For Virilio it is the fastest mover in history who holds political power.[37]

In sharp contrast, Byung-Chul Han holds that it is a mistake to attribute the temporal crisis of today's world to acceleration. He diagnoses instead a state of "dyschronia" for which he blames the atomization of time and the attendant dissolution of narrative integration. People in today's world, he argues, are bereft of duration and the notion of the right time because they lack the "temporal gravitation" that, in his view, is indispensable for the experience of a meaningful present that is enclosed by the past and the future.[38] Time, suggests Han, tumbles down on us like an unstoppable avalanche precisely because it is divested of anchorage and the possibility of closure.[39] Network society has relinquished the possibility of meaningful experience and the condensation of time felt as significant in favor of the timeless neutrality of the information that savagely annihilates memory.[40] Time in the information

---

36. Fredric Jameson, *The Cultural Turn: Selected Writings on the Postmodern* (London: Verso, 1983), 50.

37. Paul Virilio, *Negative Horizon: An Essay in Dromoscopy*, trans. Michael Degener (London: Continuum, 2005).

38. Byung-Chul Han, *Duft der Zeit: Ein philosophischer Essay zur Kunst des Verweilens* (Berlin: Transcript, 2009), 10.

39. Han, *Duft der Zeit*, 12

40. Han, *Duft der Zeit*, 13.

age, contends Han, consists of a series of disconnected points that "buzz" around without direction: discontinuous and unstructured, this new temporal dissipation results in a lack of orientation rather than enhanced freedom.[41] A directionless movement characterizes this new "point time," a form of continual "buzzing" that is indifferent to historical acceleration.[42] For Han, acceleration is therefore not the cause of our sense of stagnating in an unbounded present but merely a symptom of deeper processes that have to do with the lack of temporal direction. He writes, "Acceleration and deceleration have their joint origin in narrative detemporalization. They are different manifestations of the same process."[43] By offering countless arbitrary options and links, the internet intensifies for Han the atomization of time: it favors browsing and surfing and such directionless movement.[44] Net space and net time are discontinuous and as such imprisoned in a now without duration.

In his discussion of time Han employs a strikingly Heideggerian spatial metaphoric: he invokes the notion of a gravitational time-space that embeds, holds, and anchors the self through modes of communicative relatedness.[45] Conceding that Heidegger's model of ontological groundedness produces the dead end of an antimodern apotheosis of an archaic world,[46] he then attempts to resolve the dilemma by way of a second metaphoric that is extremely evocative and sensual: time should be "fragrant," he suggests, like Proust's madeleine, which, steeped in lime blossom tea, releases a sense of duration free from the contingency of life. Such metaphors feed into a sensorium of temporality that helps to translate the abstract notion of time into lived experience: while singing, piping,

---

41. Han, *Duft der Zeit*, 38.
42. Han, *Duft der Zeit*, 39.
43. Han, *Duft der Zeit*, 31.
44. Han, *Duft der Zeit*, 44.
45. Commenting on Proust, he writes: "Man braucht nur tiefer ins Sein hineinzublicken, um zu erkennen, daß alle Dinge miteinander verwoben sind, daß jedes geringste Ding mit einer Weltganzheit kommuniziert." (You only need to look deeper into Being to recognize that all things are interwoven and that even the smallest thing communicates with the totality of the world.) Han, *Duft der Zeit*, 51.
46. Han, *Duft der Zeit*, 79.

and buzzing appeal to the aural sense, the Proustian notion of fragrance adds the sense of smell to the vocabulary of duration. Han adds a further example of a sensual temporality that has the power to reanimate duration and the conditions for a *vita contemplativa*: the ancient Chinese hsiang yin clock apparently measures the passage of time by burning off incense.[47] But the poetic turn of Han's argument begs the question of whether and how such bounded experience of duration can repair the atomization of time in the age of dyschronia. Does his argument not reinstate precisely the narrativization of time, the conditions of which, as he insists, no longer really exist? In the last analysis, the idea of the "fragrance of time" is a poetic metaphor that simply bypasses the challenges of temporality in the digital era.

Han's reading of atomized time is reminiscent of philosophical impressionism around 1900: his temporal metaphors resonate with the work of Ernst Mach, who in his seminal *Die Analyse der Empfindungen* (*The Analysis of Sensations*, 1897) described the modern self in terms of a fleeting *Elementenkomplex* (complex of elements) without the Kantian unity of apperception. The disintegration of the grand historical narratives and the experience of an atomized time without an integrative horizon already characterize much of the literature of classical modernism.[48] Looked at from a historical angle, Han's argument is thus not new: it is a continuation of the modernist fascination with a temporally unstable and fragile subjectivity.

However, his philosophical eclecticism takes on a more problematic tenor in his later essay on the transformation of democracy in the age of big data.[49] Debating the dissolution of Habermas's communicative public sphere in the digital era, Han suggests that

---

47. Han, *Duft der Zeit*, 59–63.

48. See Johannes Pause, *Texturen der Zeit: Zum Wandel ästhetischer Zeitkonzepte in der deutschsprachigen Gegenwartsliteratur* (Cologne: Böhlau, 2012), 52.

49. Big data is the term used for extremely large and complex data sets that are submitted to so-called data mining, i.e., sophisticated computational analysis that captures patterns and trends by way of algorithms.

the web might bring about a new form of a "pre-communicative" and "prediscursive rationality" to replace the Habermasian discursive idealism with a new form of digital materialism.[50] Instead of dialogic participation in the public sphere, Han envisages a democracy based on the digital rationality of big data. Because big data has the capacity to map and objectify the totality of our desires, inclinations, beliefs, fears, and wishes, it makes possible a new digital biopolitics that, in his eyes, can respond to the collective unconscious in real time.[51] Euphorically celebrating the egalitarian potential of digital rationality in real time, he perversely suggests that it is precisely the absence of the requirement to actively participate in the public sphere that might create a more inclusive democracy.[52] Rather than an instrument of surveillance and behavioral manipulation, data mining is welcomed here as a democratic tool that would no longer require conscious input by active and emancipated citizens. For Han this objectified collective unconscious is beginning to evolve passively through billions of mouse clicks, thus eliminating the need for a Habermasian discursive rationality, which demands from citizens the effort of participation in argumentation and dialogue. In my view this dream of "direct" democracy unfolds a totalitarian vision of society as a messy soup of unconscious desires and inclinations that no longer need discursive expression. There is no recognition here that coding technologies and digital protocols can also "impose a hegemonic logic onto a mediated social practice,"[53] thereby designing and steering the behavior of users of the net. But does the largely asymmetrical power relation between the corporate organizations and individual users not raise the question of "what is social about social media"?[54]

---

50. Byung-Chul Han, *Digitale Rationalität und das Ende des kommunikativen Handelns* (Berlin: Matthes & Seitz, 2013), 19.

51. Han, *Digitale Rationalität*, 27.

52. Han, *Digitale Rationalität*, 33.

53. José van Dijck, *The Culture of Connectivity: A Critical History of Social Media* (Oxford: Oxford University Press, 2013), 31.

54. Van Dijck, *The Culture of Connectivity*, 27.

Immediacy

The question raised at the end of the last paragraph prepares the ground for the third diagnostic trope in the discourse on time: the idea that a new culture of immediacy has superseded the modern culture of speed. So what does the shift toward a culture of immediacy entail? For John Tomlinson it denotes first of all "a culture of instantaneity—a culture accustomed to rapid delivery, ubiquitous availability and the instant gratification of desires." Secondly, it involves a "sense of directness, of cultural proximity" that finds expression in "an increasing sense of connectedness with others, or as a prevailing sense of urgency and, perhaps, of compulsion and drivenness in our short-term preoccupations."[55] However, we need to note that Tomlinson does not propose a naive binary model that posits an authentic subject that confronts an alienating technological world. He argues rather that the inescapable embedding of human selves in a technologically mediated world has gained a new quality by, thirdly, *ostensibly* closing the gap that separates "now from later, here from elsewhere, desire from its satisfaction—the gap which . . . constituted the motivating challenge of speed-as-progress."[56] In this way the cultural imaginary of the early twenty-first century has conjured away the human effort that, as I would argue, also lent classical modernity a particular heroic tone. As long as the pursuit of progress required effort, modernity remained a deeply heroic project that accentuated the perfectibility of man. Pleasure and effort were intertwined in a modern speed politics that produced a simultaneously disciplined and temporally sovereign subjectivity. And so the figure of the (male) inventor plays such a central role in the modern imagination: the inventor demonstrates an ingenuity and resourcefulness that services the common good. By sharp contrast, the new script of effortlessness in the digital era erodes the conditions for a heroic subjectivity: if everything is—at least in theory—always just a computer click away,

---

55. Tomlinson, *The Culture of Speed*, 74.
56. Tomlinson, *The Culture of Speed*, 74.

then everything is equally banal. Accordingly, I suggest that the culture of immediacy might be termed "disenchanted accessibility" in an age that disavows the heroism of effort that was at the very heart of the age of mechanical modernization.

Because the new culture of immediacy promotes instant access to goods, services, and media, and the constant availability of social interaction (be it work- or leisure-related), it also erodes the expectation of temporal processing and of the duration of time. In the modern age of mechanical acceleration at the turn of the nineteenth century, by contrast, the dream of ever-greater speed was still bogged down by the wear and tear of machines and infrastructures. In spite of the ideological nexus between speed, power, and capitalism, the speed fantasies of what Tomlinson terms "mechanical modernity" were hampered by the relative slackness of the age of machine acceleration. In contrast, the new age of immediacy comes with the promise and the threat that temporal delays are a thing of the past: pressing the transaction button on one of our digital devices is now sufficient to move vast amounts of capital or to create global audiences for local events. Of course this does not mean that this new culture has really overcome temporal inefficiencies: these still show up in the slow delivery of goods, unplanned waiting periods, and unwanted delays in service provision and travel. Broadband congestion, long airport security queues, automated answering loops of service providers, and the permanent traffic congestion in and around urban centers are everyday experiences in the twenty-first century. They show that the gap between departure and arrival remains an integral part of the human experience. However, the cultural script of instant delivery does make immediacy a new cultural value and a prized asset that arguably delegitimizes slower forms of temporal processing, the value of memory, and the idea of duration as a prerequisite of human experience.

A striking symptom of this new culture of immediacy is the ubiquitous phrase 24/7 ("twenty-four/seven"), which, as Jonathan Crary argues, "announces a time without time, a time extracted from any material or identifiable demarcations, a time without sequence or recurrence."[57] Following Deleuze and Guattari, Crary interprets 24/7 as a "mot d'ordre," an order word, which commands human time:

> It effaces the relevance or value of any respite or variability. Its heralding of the convenience of perpetual access conceals its cancellation of the periodicity that shaped the life of most cultures for several millennia: the diurnal pulse of waking and sleeping and the long alterations between days of work and a day of worship or rest.[58]

And so 24/7 is *the* imperative of our culture of immediacy. Its time regime of uninterrupted connectivity requires the contemporary self to constantly download system updates and novelties that herald greater choice, while in reality entrapping us in a compulsory system of capitalist consumption. The promise of continual innovation at an ever-accelerating rate wrecks the conditions of familiarity with new technologies and with the rapidly changing environment: forever attempting to catch up with the latest "digital revolution" and new information, the self is always behind and ultimately estranged from the very products that augur enhanced experiences and performances.

Enabled by the World Wide Web as well as the neoliberal penetration of the economic and social spheres, the new culture of immediacy is characterized by the following features: it has eroded the clear demarcation line between work and home life or leisure, while also favoring flexibility and short-term gains at the workplace above and beyond loyalty, stability, and experience. The cult of immediacy undermines the conditions for familiarity with systems and technologies, thereby contracting the self to the project of continual self-innovation. Further to this, it erases both past and future by turning the present into a sphere of never-ending, fast-paced consumption of technological innovation. As a new delivery norm,

---

57. Jonathan Crary, *24/7: Late Capitalism and the Ends of Sleep* (London: Verso, 2013), 29. Crary demonstrates that the time regime of 24/7 even invades our sleep by undermining "distinctions between day and night, between light and dark, and between action and repose" (17).

58. Crary, *24/7*, 29–30.

immediacy comes with opportunities and challenges for established institutions, such as libraries, archives, academies, that no longer control access to learning and knowledge. It aids information rather than learning, which is a hermeneutic process across time, while also engendering the expectation of the real-time transmission of historical events on a global scale. The ubiquity of screens and digital media in our everyday environment has virtually closed the gap between the simulacrum and reality. Arguably, the expectation of immediacy has also had profound political implications: it has facilitated the shift away from the social-democratic vision of a consensus society toward the neoliberal shareholder society, which favors short-term gains and short-term transactions over long-term results and social contract. The cult of immediacy also enthralls a global youth culture for which technological gadgets and social media are indispensable modes of experience. Connected with this, immediacy fuels new social pathologies, such as cyberbullying and tech addictions. While the above list is of course not exhaustive, it makes clear how the radical transformation of social life and human experience by a culture of immediacy has created the right ecosystem for neoliberal capitalism.

The Extended Present

The map of our temporal anxieties places immediacy in close proximity to the chronotope of an extended or burgeoning present that is divorced from the future as the human horizon of orientation. Besides François Hartog, the literary critic Hans Ulrich Gumbrecht has written an apocalyptic crisis narrative about the present that is colored by a good dosage of posthistorical melancholia. Analyzing the transition from classical modernity to postmodernity, Gumbrecht suggests that postmodernity is marked by the shocking realization in the aftermath of the Second World War that the entire catalogue of Enlightenment promises proved illusory. Indeed, the idea that all life on the planet could be ended by the continued exploitation of all natural resources and the cumulative destruction of the environment no longer appears as the hysterical vision of a minority of eco-freaks but rather as the likely scenario within our lifetime. Faced with this dystopian prospect, Gumbrecht glumly observes that the Enlightenment discourse on human perfectibility has had to give way to a new discourse on the preservation of the planet, which, however, appears already belated.[59] Under the condition of a profoundly threatening future, Gumbrecht suggests, the only horizon of expectation left to humanity is that of the end of all times. From Gumbrecht's posthistorical perspective of the future perfect, then, the present comes into view as a stranded object of reflection, or, as Gumbrecht puts it, a past that is made up of the totality of missed final chances.[60] Gumbrecht's dystopian reflection on the end of all times does not, as one might expect, really prepare the ground for a sustained ecological critique; rather, he merely gestures toward eco-criticism in order to set in train a melancholy lament that is conservative in its cultural sensibility, caught up in a particular generational identity, and gendered as male.

So what, according to Gumbrecht, defines living in our postmillennium "broad present"? To understand Gumbrecht's argument, we need to briefly recapitulate the salient traits of modern historical consciousness, as he sees them: first, in this form of consciousness the subject imagines a linear pathway that aligns past, present, and future. Second, all phenomena are subject to historical change because time is the absolute agent of history. Third, modern subjects believe that they continually shed their pasts. Fourth, the future appears as an open horizon of endless possibilities that, fifth, turns the present into a short moment of transition. Finally, this temporal linearity of modernity creates a short present that is the epistemological habitat of the Cartesian subject.[61]

As discussed above, like Hartog, Gumbrecht argues that modern historical consciousness has been irretrievably replaced by the new chronotope of a broad and ultimately timeless present. On

---

59. Hans Ulrich Gumbrecht, *Präsenz*, ed. with an afterword by Jürgen Klein (Frankfurt a. Main: Suhrkamp, 2012), 42.

60. Gumbrecht, *Präsenz*, 17.

61. Hans Ulrich Gumbrecht, *Unsere breite Gegenwart* (Frankfurt a. Main: Suhrkamp, 2010), 15.

the one hand, the broad present is closed off from the future as an open horizon; on the other, it is flooded by pasts that we can no longer shed in our hypermediated world. As a point of convergence between a multitude of electronically mediated pasts and a threatening future, the present expands ever more into a time of intransitive simultaneity. Aleida Assmann observes that for Gumbrecht the present is thus no longer a moment of transition but merely the "Wartesaal der Weltgeschichte," the waiting room for the world-historical end of all time.[62] She rightly places Gumbrecht's dystopian vocabulary in the tradition of a hyperbolic rhetoric that, as she notes, risks attachment to a depressed mood.[63] For Gumbrecht it is only embodied presence that could possibly heal the Cartesian split between mind and body as well as the painful dislocations of our globalized nonexistence. Like Han, he draws on Heidegger's ontology to envisage the alternative of an embodied presence. However, his palliative prescription of temporary relief from the painful entrapment in a broad presence takes an altogether problematic turn in the apotheosis of sport (especially American football) as the realization of a true corporeal experience through performance and spectacle. Surprisingly, Gumbrecht ignores the fascist celebration of the collective experience of the body in the modern sport arena, as paradigmatically enacted in Leni Riefenstahl's film aesthetics of corporeal presence.

In contrast to Gumbrecht's linear reading of the modern historical consciousness Peter Osborne takes a different, less monochrome line. He argues that modernity does indeed "valorize the new as a product of a constantly changing self-negating temporal dialectic." But he also emphasizes that it remains open "to a variety of competing articulations."[64] Moreover, the modern obsession with the new also leads to the remorseless production of the old that, in turn, provokes "forms of traditionalism, the temporal logic of which is quite different from that of tradition

---

62. Assmann, *Ist die Zeit aus den Fugen?*, 255.
63. Assmann, *Ist die Zeit aus den Fugen?*, 256.
64. Osborne, *The Politics of Time*, xii.

as conventionally conceived."[65] Indeed, as the next chapter will demonstrate, from the 1870s onward European culture—and its German form in particular—was concerned with lateness as an "untimely" temporal trope that, to quote Nietzsche, runs "counter to our time," thereby "acting on our time and, let us hope, for the benefit of a time to come."[66] A different type of lateness also features in Freud's psychoanalysis: he showed that we can never really know ourselves because our conscious being is always punctured by a repressed past. Psychoanalysis provided a method for indirectly recovering the memory of this hidden past through retrospective acts of interpretation. In this way, psychoanalysis established itself as a modern discipline that, by foregrounding the relevance of the subject's repressed past for the present, explicitly challenged the modern attraction to and investment in a rapidly passing present. And Bergson's hugely influential antireductionist theory of memory challenged the old Cartesian split between mind and body. Only insofar as we are able to delay the automated reaction to external stimuli and remember our past, Bergson argues, do we possess consciousness. For Bergson, the "movement of memory" requires a temporal operation that involves "pure memory, memory-image, and perception, of which no one, in fact, occurs apart from the others."[67]

---

65. Osborne, *The Politics of Time*, xii.

66. Friedrich Nietzsche, *On the Uses and Disadvantages of History for Life*, trans. R. J. Hollingdale (Cambridge: Cambridge University Press, 1997), 60.

67. Henri Bergson, *Matter and Memory*, trans. Nancy Margaret Paul and W. Scott Palmer (London: George Allen and Unwin, 1911), 169. He writes: "Whenever we are trying to recover a recollection, to call up some period of our history, we become conscious of an act *sui genesis* by which we detach ourselves from the present in order to replace ourselves, first in the past in general, then in a certain region of the past—a work of adjustment, something like the focusing of a camera. But our recollection still remains virtual; we simply prepare ourselves to receive it by adopting the appropriate attitude. Little by little it comes into view like a condensing cloud; from the virtual state it passes into the actual; and as its outlines become more distinct and its surface takes on color, it tends to imitate perception. But it remains attached to the past by its deepest roots, and if, when once realized, it did not retain something of its original virtuality, if, being a present state, it were not also something which stands out distinct from the present, we should never know it for a memory" (170).

These examples illustrate that modern "politics of time" are—in the words of Peter Osborne—defined by "a competition or struggle between these different forms of temporalization."[68] Around 1900 the ideal of a future that could be attained through a rational process of modernization had already been frustrated by the experience of a contradictory and often unpredictable social dynamic that, as Lucien Hölscher has shown, escaped the control mechanisms of continual technological innovation and enhanced administrative planning. And so the very social dynamic that had been unleashed by the modernization of society created a massive clash between people's experience of history and their expectations.[69]

The ideological fixation on the future was further eroded by the peculiarly modern fascination with the past as an object of inquiry. Modernity's "self-negating temporal dialectic"[70] and the modern apprehension of history thus brought forth a variety of dynamic pasts that were filtered through the lens of a fast-paced present. Stephen Kern argues that the modern heightened sense of the value of the past centered around four key issues: "the age of the earth, the impact of the past on the present, the values of that impact, and the most effective way to recapture a past that has been forgotten."[71] Bergson, Freud, and Benjamin demonstrated the relevance of the human past for the present; scientific debates about the age of the earth then added a hitherto unimaginable timescale of millions of years to the modern imagination. "While geologists and biologists tried to work out patterns of development through those vast stretches of time," comments Kern, "the history of man came to appear increasingly as a parenthesis of infinitesimal brevity."[72]

---

68. Osborne, *The Politics of Time*, 116.

69. Lucian Hölscher, *Die Entdeckung der Zukunft* (Frankfurt a. Main: Suhrkamp, 1999), 131.

70. Osborne, *The Politics of Time*, xii.

71. Stephen Kern, *The Culture of Time and Space, 1880–1918* (Cambridge, MA: Harvard University Press, 2003), 37.

72. Kern, *The Culture of Time and Space*, 38.

From the perspective of evolutionary or geological timescales, modernity was less than a tiny dot in natural history.[73]

Time-Space Compression

The modern fascination with vastly different times and places manifested itself in the discovery of primitivism in fine art, the cubist break with linear perspective, and the embrace of an aesthetics of simultaneity, the quest in modernist literature for both the shortest moment as well as extended memory, the philosophical inquiry into both duration and the fragmented moment or the psychoanalytical investigation of the dynamic interrelationship of past and present in the subject's formation. All of these movements foreground asynchronous timescapes that infiltrate the modern narrative about speed as progress. Only if one ignores the modern enthrallment with a multiplicity of temporalities, can one claim that speed is the sole pleasure invented by modernity or that the modern subject—which in this narrative tends to be gendered as male—continually sheds his past. This misconception of a modernity that is fundamentally deprived of temporal complexity is the necessary building bloc in a disaster narrative that understands the digital era only in terms of a flat, homogeneous, and intransitive present moored in a sea of everlasting and timeless simultaneities.

This grim view of life in our posthistorical global era also rests on a misleading dualism of space and time. As Doreen Massey notes, the triumphant narrative of globalization glorifies the "free"

---

73. Darwin's theory of evolution also undermined the idea of human free will and with it the notion that human beings can determine their future. As Martin Middeke argues, even though Darwin's notion of evolution accentuates the idea of progress through evolutionary development, his large timescale undermines the importance of individual action and planning. Darwin's timescale places the individual "in eine indifferente Zeitreihe, deren Bestandteil der Mensch ist und nichts weiter" (on an indifferent timescale of which the human being is one component and nothing more). Martin Middeke, *Die Kunst der gelebten Zeit: Zur Phänomenologie literarischer Subjektivität im englischen Roman des ausgehenden 19. Jahrhunderts* (Würzburg: Königshausen & Neumann, 2004), 51.

movement of capital by subsuming space into time. In her view the victory of neoliberal globalization is

> a sleight of hand in terms of the conceptualisation of space and time. The proposition turns geography into history, space into time. And this again has social and political effects. It says that Mozambique and Nicaragua are not really different from "us". We are not to imagine them as having their own trajectories, their own particular histories, and the potential for their own, perhaps, different futures. They are not recognised as coeval others. They are merely at an earlier stage in the one and only narrative it is possible to tell.[74]

The triumph of time over space has been somewhat misleadingly associated with Marxist geographer David Harvey's work on time-space compression. In his seminal *The Condition of Postmodernity* Harvey recognized "the multiplicity of the objective qualities which space and time can express, and the role of human practices in their construction."[75] Adopting a materialist perspective, he then argued that space and time are tied to material practices and processes and hence to social life. Even though space is a seemingly commonsense category in our daily lives and as such part of our tacit knowledge,

> conflicts arise not merely out of admittedly diverse subjective appreciations, but because different objective material qualities of time and space are deemed relevant to social life in different situations. Important battles likewise occur in the realms of scientific, social, and aesthetic theory, as well as in practice. How we represent space and time in theory matters, because it affects how we and others interpret and then act with respect to the world.[76]

Ever since Adam Smith, Marx, and Weber, social theory has tended to privilege time over space because it foregrounds social change and as such processes of technological, social, and political

---

74. Doreen Massey, *For Space* (London: Sage, 2010), 5.

75. David Harvey, *The Condition of Postmodernity: An Enquiry into the Origins of Cultural Change* (Cambridge: Blackwell, 1989), 203.

76. Harvey, *The Condition of Postmodernity*, 205.

modernization. By positing that temporal processes transform pre-existing spatial orders, social theory thus turns space into a secondary category of analysis. Harvey notes that, by contrast, the aesthetic thrust of modernism is to investigate "how different forms of spatialization inhibit or facilitate processes of social change."[77] Interlacing his discussion of the dynamics of time in social theory with the representation of time and space in modernism, Harvey then analyzes the radical readjustment of time and space in the wake of 1848 and the economic depression that engulfed "the whole of what was then the capitalist world."[78] For Harvey the crisis of 1848 called into question the time-as-progress narrative, "as too many people had been caught up in the maelstrom of hopes and fears, not to appreciate the stimulus that comes with participant action in 'explosive' time."[79] These events then also gave rise to the "insecurities of a shifting relative space in which events in one place could have immediate and ramifying effects in several other places."[80] While European modernism reflected on a profound crisis of representation by exploring the heterogeneity of time and space through experimental forms, imperialism responded to the rapacious need of capitalism for ever-expanding markets through colonial conquests that simultaneously deterritorialized and reterritorialized space according to the requirements of competing colonial administrations.[81] Facilitated by new communication and transport technologies, the modern phase of time-space compression thus serviced capitalist growth.

So how has globalization affected the contemporary experience of time and space? Harvey discusses the transition from modernity to postmodernity as an intensification of time-space compression by electronic means. The post-Fordism era promotes not only flexibility, instantaneity, and innovation as social values but above all continual image production and marketing. Such unprecedented

---

77. Harvey, *The Condition of Postmodernity,* 207
78. Harvey, *The Condition of Postmodernity,* 260.
79. Harvey, *The Condition of Postmodernity,* 261.
80. Harvey, *The Condition of Postmodernity,* 261.
81. Harvey, *The Condition of Postmodernity,* 264.

mediatization also transforms the experience of space. "The image of places and spaces," comments Harvey, "becomes as open to production and ephemeral use as any other."[82] Citing Marshall McLuhan's vision of the global village in which electronic technologies "have extended our central nervous system itself in a global embrace, abolishing both space and time as far as our planet is concerned,"[83] Harvey argues that the elimination of spatial boundaries in network society does not decrease the significance of space:

> Not for the first time in capitalism's history, we find the evidence pointing to the converse thesis. Heightened competition under conditions of crisis has coerced capitalists into paying much closer attention to relative locational advantages, precisely because diminishing spatial barriers give capitalists the power to exploit minute spatial differentiations to good effect. Small differences in what the space contains in the way of labor supplies, resources, infrastructures, and the like become of increased importance.[84]

Under the conditions of a global market, the uniqueness of locality matters ever more. And so the dissolution of spatial barriers in the global era results precisely in the emphatic reaffirmation of place within the space of the global. Local food production, the revival or invention of local traditions, and the focus on local politics are prominent trends that underline "the search for secure moorings in a shifting world."[85] Harvey sees such investment in place-bound identity as an understandable reaction against globalization, which, however, runs the risk of becoming "a part of the very fragmentation which a mobile capitalism and flexible accumulation can feed upon."[86] He thus makes the case for a theory of uneven geographical development that takes account of "the different ways in which different social groups have materially embedded their modes of sociality into the web of life, understood as

---

82. Harvey, *The Condition of Postmodernity*, 293.
83. Marshall McLuhan, quoted in Harvey, *The Condition of Postmodernity*, 293.
84. Harvey, *The Condition of Postmodernity*, 106.
85. Harvey, *The Condition of Postmodernity*, 302.
86. Harvey, *The Condition of Postmodernity*, 303.

an evolving socio-ecological system."[87] The rich metaphor of the "web of life" evokes the idea of inhabited places as sites of diverse social, symbolic, and temporal practice.

Harvey's notion of the web of life resonates with the work of Yi-Fu Tuan, who describes place as a "field of care" brought about by the "affective bond between people and places."[88] Places are not only composed of material objects and defined by power relations but also made up of imprints of past attachments, present perceptions and feelings, and future orientations. Jon May and Nigel Thrift too accentuate the disparate geography of lived temporality: "The picture is less of any simple acceleration in the pace of life or experiences of spatial 'collapse' than of a far more complex restructuring in the nature and experience of time and space reaching through the nineteenth and in to the early decades of the twentieth century."[89] They argue that for most people the experience of acceleration and time-space compression is more intermittent and less dramatic than is commonly acknowledged:

> Thus, the picture that emerges is less that of a singular or uniform social time stretching over a uniform space, than of various (and uneven) networks of time stretching in different and divergent directions across an uneven social field. . . . The result is therefore a radical unevenness in the nature and quality of social time itself, with this spatial variation a constitutive part rather than an added dimension of the multiplicity and heterogeneity of social time or what, for precisely these reasons, we prefer to call "SpaceTime."[90]

Doreen Massey's book *For Space* also refutes the "discursive victory of time over space."[91] For Massey "the really serious question which is raised by speed-up, by the communications revolution,

---

87. David Harvey, *Spaces of Global Capitalism: Towards a Theory of Uneven Geographical Development* (London: Verso, 2006), 77.

88. Yi-Fu Tuan, *Topophilia: A Study of Environmental Perception, Attitudes, and Values* (New York: Columbia University Press, 1990), 4.

89. Jon May and Nigel Thrift, eds., *TimeSpace: Geographies of Temporality* (London: Routledge, 2001), 10.

90. May and Thrift, *TimeSpace*, 5.

91. Massey, *For Space*, 71.

and by cyberspace is not whether space will be annihilated but what kinds of multiplicities (patternings of uniqueness) and relations will be co-constructed with these new kinds of spatial configurations."[92] Space is "always under construction"—it is "a simultaneity of stories so far."[93] Her performative notion of multiple, contested, and open spaces not only rewrites the narrative of the information age from the perspective of the local production of the global, but it roundly rejects all deterministic interpretations of human subjectivity and agency. Like Harvey, May, Thrift, and Massey, this book too argues that subjectivity in the twenty-first century is capable of negotiating varied temporalities in multiple spaces by way of differentiated modes or tactics of social relatedness. While cyberspace and the culture of immediacy do indeed constitute genuinely new arenas of social interaction, these do not necessarily signal the end of social relations, the flattening of time, the erosion of presence, or the end of memory.

Network Time

That the World Wide Web and cyberspace have created a new, totally unparalleled reality of connectivity is a commonplace observation. Digital technologies have moved the broadcast age into the postbroadcast era, in which production and reception are fundamentally intertwined. Social media and new forms of mediatized interaction have given birth to new forms of agency and participation in the public domain.[94] But, as José van Dijck argues, whether this new culture of connectivity really delivers more citizenship is doubtful in the light of the rapid commodification of a "platformed sociality" that manipulates and quantifies social

---

92. Massey, *For Space*, 91.
93. Massey, *For Space*, 9.
94. See Andrew Hoskins, "Anachronisms of Media, Anachronisms of Memory: From Collective Memory to a New Memory Culture," in *On Media Memory: Collective Memory in a New Media Age*, ed. Motti Neiger, Oren Meyers, and Eyal Zandberg (Basingstoke: Palgrave Macmillan, 2011), 278–88.

notions, such as popularity, friendship, participation, and citizenship.[95] For example, on Facebook, the idea of friendship no longer involves social investment over a period of time but has been turned into a quantifiable commodity. Users of these platforms are often unaware that they

> produce a precious resource: connectivity. Even though the term "connectivity" originated in technology, where it denotes computer transmissions, in the context of social media it quickly assumed the connotation of users accumulating *social* capital, while in fact this term increasingly referred to owners amassing *economic* capital.[96]

The coding techniques behind these platforms are neither neutral nor innocent: they alter the very nature of our social experience in that they demand certain activities, such as "sharing" or "following."[97] As van Dijck further notes, this culture of connectivity services neoliberal principles: "Connectivity," writes van Dijck, "derives from a continuous pressure—both from peers and from technologies—to expand through competition and gain power through strategic alliances."[98]

And yet, in spite of the radical transformation of the social sphere in networked society, we need to be mindful of the social embeddedness of the experience of time. Our biological body clocks, the natural world with its rhythms of seasons, the passage of day and night, the cycle of birth and death, continue to shape our experience of time even though these spheres have been infiltrated by digital technologies.[99] In social life, notes Barbara Adam, time is clustered around "timescapes," that is context-dependent temporal practices that are tacitly understood. And so in our daily

---

95. Van Dijck, *The Culture of Connectivity,* 5 and 13.
96. Van Dijck, *The Culture of Connectivity,* 16.
97. Van Dijck, *The Culture of Connectivity,* 20.
98. Van Dijck, *The Culture of Connectivity,* 21.
99. Apparently, many people interrupt their sleep to check their smartphones during the night. This new practice is symbolic of the penetration of all aspects of life by digital technologies. See Crary, *24/7.* Nevertheless, birth, aging, and death remain ontological facts.

lives we traverse a multitude of places that come with a wide range of habitual modes of temporal behavior and remind us "that time is inseparable from space, and . . . that context matters."[100] If we recognize that we remain socially embedded in a temporal ecology that involves everyday practices, the conventional clock, biological needs alongside analogue and digital technologies, then we can ask to what extent and how the "information ecology" transforms the very notion of context.[101] For Robert Hassan this new information ecology forms a living amorphous system that is as real as the built environment:

> Contexts may combine and separate in the space of nanoseconds—or last for hours or days or weeks. Contexts traverse geographic space, dissolving it into the virtuality that is the network society. . . . Importantly, this digital environment or ecology is as real as the built environment that comprises the cities and towns and as actual as the natural ecology that provides the building blocks (the contexts) for life on earth.[102]

The intensification of the human-machine interconnectivity is often perceived in terms of the arrival of so-called real time and the cancellation of temporal depth, duration, and latency. But the transfer of real time, a technical term that was originally designed to capture the speed of computing operating systems, to the social sphere is misleading, as it ignores the inherent asynchronicity between the internet and human beings. Network time is defined by "connected asynchronicity," which displaces not so much the ontological condition of our temporal embeddedness but rather the linearity of clock time. "What we experience, albeit in very nascent form," comments Hassan,

> is the recapture of the forms of temporality that were themselves displaced by the clock. What digital networks make possible is the conscious creation of temporal contexts and the freeing of embedded times

---

100. Barbara Adam, *Time* (Cambridge: Polity, 2004), 143.

101. Robert Hassan, "Network Time," in *24/7: Time and Temporality in Network Society*, ed. Robert Hassan and E. Purser (Stanford, CA: Stanford Business Books, 2007), 47.

102. Hassan, "Network Time," 48.

in humans, in nature, and in society that form the timescapes that intersect our lives but that were have been unable to fully experience, appreciate, or understand because of the deadening implacability of the clock.[103]

Scott McQuire discusses "the smart mob" as a potentially "self-organising and self-directed urban multitude" as exemplified in the Arab Spring and the social unrest of disaffected youth in London in 2011.[104] Emily Keightley too argues that both events overturned "comfortable notions of process and ordered duration."[105] The evidence is overwhelming that digital technologies transform the public sphere by creating a society that is always live. For Andrew Hoskins the postbroadcast era has generated a new memory ecology that is characterized by the fluidization of digitized content, new modes of participation in semipublic memory, and the intermedial and transmedial dynamics of old and new media.[106] He introduced the term "connective turn" to capture the shifting dynamic of memory in the digital era.[107] The distinction between production and reception and as such the status of established broadcast media and their power to create and control media events have been eroded. Memory in the digital era is therefore much more diffuse and perhaps harder to pin down. Hoskins concludes that this new memory ecology requires new analytical tools to capture the dynamic of connectivity.

What all this means, then, is that in network society social actors continue to inhabit multiple timescapes, which, rather than immersing them passively in a world of timeless simultaneity, give rise to radical asynchronicities that can be used to very different effect. As long as human beings inhabit multilayered temporal environments that come with different patterns, rhythms, and

103. Hassan, "Network Time," 51.

104. McQuire, "City Times," 132.

105. Emily Keightley, ed., "Introduction," in Keightley, *Time, Media, and Modernity*, 2.

106. Hoskins, "Anachronism of Media, Anachronisms of Memory," 279.

107. Hoskins, "Anachronism of Media, Anachronisms of Memory," 287.

durations, the machine/human interaction will remain inherently asynchronous. As Hassan puts it,

> To be able to achieve true real-time response would mean the ultimate surrender of human agency to digital technology, where latencies have been driven out and where lags no longer occur. This would constitute the militarist dream of absolute power through absolute speed (Paul Virilio 1986) and the capitalist Nirvana where production and circulation function "at the speed of thought" (Gates 1995). Both dreams are destined, however, to be unrealizable because imperfect humans constantly get in the way of perfect systems.[108]

According to Hassan it is far too simplistic to assume that we are blindly headed toward Virilio's dystopian vision of a "digital serfdom" that ushers in a dictatorship of speed. He sees us rather enfolded in a rhizomatic temporality that amounts to "a political and creative reestablishment of social control over time, space and speed."[109]

As a central feature of network society, "connected asynchronicity" has produced a new temporal ecology that is far from flat.[110] Emily Keightley therefore suggests that "a re-evaluation of mediated time" is required "that attends to the interactions between the times of technologies, texts and social contexts in order to move beyond a one-dimensional characterisation in which speed and immediacy monopolise accounts of how time is encountered and lived."[111] Lived time then is an essential notion that holds together multiple timescapes, including clock time, network time, biological time, and social time, which intersect in our daily lives in complex ways.

Precarious Times

Despite vastly differing explanations, it is evident from the discussion so far that the various approaches to the perceived crisis of temporality in the twenty-first century share a diagnostic rhetoric.

---

108. Hassan, "Network Time," 51.
109. Hassan, "Network Time," 58.
110. Hassan, "Network Time," 51.
111. Keightley, "Introduction," 4.

Digital serfdom, dictatorship of speed, stagnation at top speed, point time, atomization of time, timeless time, the broad and never-ending present, the cult of immediacy—these metaphors not only capture the profound impact of digital technologies on our daily lives but also stage a deep crisis of historical time. In the era of globalization world history appears to have become more volatile, fractured, and unpredictable than during the Cold War. The world after 1989–90 can no longer be interpreted in terms of the postwar order, which, with hindsight, some commentators see as a comparatively stable and secure historical epoch. As Tony Judd observes,

> With the passing of the old order many longstanding assumptions would be called into question. What had once seemed permanent and some-how inevitable would take on a more transient air. The Cold-War confrontation; the schism separating East from West; the contest between "Communism" and "capitalism"; the separate and non-communicating stories of prosperous western Europe and the Soviet bloc satellites to its East: all these could no longer be understood as the products of ideological necessity or the iron logic of politics. They were the accidental outcomes of history—and history was thrusting them aside.[112]

While the political revolution of 1989 turned the period from 1945 to 1989 into a kind of prolonged world-historical interim or a "postwar parenthesis,"[113] the date was retrospectively also used to either corroborate or challenge the chronological historical imagination. The fall of the Berlin Wall signaled—in the words of Peter Fritzsche—the "basically impermanent, even unstable nature of all social political constructions; on the other, however, it gave rise to the 'illusion of inevitability.'"[114]

The instantaneous recognition that 1989 marked the end of the established certainties of the postwar period not only prompted the "retrospective illusion of . . . inevitability"[115] but it also gave

---

112. Tony Judd, *Postwar: A History of Europe since 1945* (London: Random House, 2007), 1–2.

113. Judd, *Postwar*, 2.

114. Fritzsche, "1989 and the Chronological Imagination," 18.

115. Fritzsche, "1989 and The Chronological Imagination," 18.

rise to considerable anxiety about the contingent nature of history. In the last analysis, the idea of historical inevitability builds on precisely the type of "chronological imagination" that, by way of its dating systems, advances the grand narrative of history, which is all too often complicit with the historical victors, in this case the Western model of liberal democracy and capitalism. Western "trajectorism," comments Arjun Appadurai, "always assumes that there is a cumulative journey from here to there, or more exactly from now to then, in human affairs, as natural as a river and as all-encompassing as the sky. Trajectorism is the idea that time's arrow inevitably has a telos, and in that telos are to be found all the significant patterns of change, and history."[116] Trajectorism is a way of thinking that habitually eliminates the tentative, fractured, and precarious experience of history that was arguably at the very heart of the unpredictable events of 1989. To be sure, the so-called Monday demonstrators in Leipzig envisioned a radically emancipated future that was meant to leave behind a drab present. The East German protesters articulated the gap between their experience of a stagnating reality and their expectation of a democratic future, thereby attempting to steer history toward a better future. And yet, even though, in the end, the *ancien régime* of the GDR was swept away, in the autumn of 1989 the collapse of socialism had been neither predictable nor intended. From the perspective of the participants, 1989 stands rather for a precarious moment in which hope was interlaced with fear. The pictures that went round the world of jubilant East and West Germans dancing on the Berlin Wall became iconic because they seemed to capture the power of the human spirit in the face of adversity. And yet, the iconicity of these images merely disguises the contingency of the fall of the Berlin Wall. It was contingent because it was the outcome of both free will (as enacted by the GDR demonstrators) and historical chance (as underlined by Günter Schabowski's improvised press conference on 9 November 1989).

---

116. Arjun Appadurai, *The Future as Cultural Fact: Essays on the Global Condition* (London: Verso, 2013), 223.

However, since 1989 this liberating sense of nondetermination seems to have been overtaken by a profound experience of precariousness that also marks the end of the Western politics of time. Globalization, the advance of casino capitalism, the move to the shareholder and so-called knowledge society in Western democracies, and the erosion of the postwar social security systems in both East and West have fueled the experience of "a runaway world."[117] As Richard Sennett has shown, in the first half of the twentieth century social capitalism was so successful not least because it produced "long-term, and incremental and above all predictable time," which was administered by institutions and a bureaucracy that organized the citizens' lives from cradle to grave.[118] "Rationalized time," comments Sennett, "enabled people to think about their lives as narratives—narratives not so much of what will necessarily happen as of how things should happen."[119] The narrative expectation of what ought to happen requires precisely the type of temporal security that has been devalued in the culture of immediacy and in neoliberal society. According to Sennett, the institutional architecture that underpinned the social capitalism of old has been eroded by three factors: the casualization of labor; the delayering of institutional relationships by flexible and fluid structures; and the nonlinear sequencing of tasks, which turns colleagues into competitors as they race against each other in the production of the best result in the quickest time possible.

For Guy Standing, precarization is the child of the neoliberal economy that disembedded the economy from society in order to create global markets. The commodification of all aspects of life undermined the principle of social solidarity that had been at the very core of the Western postwar welfare state. The security of long-term employment was given up in favor of functional flexibility that enabled international corporations to quickly shift or shed

---

117. Giddens, *Runaway World*.
118. Richard Sennett, *The Culture of the New Capitalism* (New Haven, CT: Yale University Press, 2006), 23.
119. Sennett, *The Culture of the New Capitalism*, 23.

their workforce.[120] This resulted in the exponential growth of job insecurity alongside the contractualization of life and the erosion of collective bargaining power in the hands of the trade unions. According to Standing these conditions have produced the precariat as a "class in the making."[121] Unlike the proletariat, whose subordination to the employer was rewarded with labor, the precariat no longer entertains enduring social contracts. "To be precariatised," writes Standing, "is to be subject to pressures and experiences that lead to a precariat existence, of living in the present, without a secure identity or sense of development achieved through work and lifestyle."[122] Social and economic precariousness thus implies an unpredictable future that escapes the practices of self-governance that, ever since the 1800s, have produced the temporally disciplined but sovereign bourgeois subject. In the eighteenth century the upwardly mobile bourgeoisie began to develop a strong sense of temporal sovereignty: while the sphere of work was a sphere of economic expansion and growing influence, the private sphere designated a zone of retreat where meaningful cultural pursuits (such as reading or playing music) cultivated the self. The interdependence of both spheres meant that the bourgeois idea of temporal sovereignty remained tied to the advancement of the self through hard work and education through leisure. Until now *Bildung* (education) and hard work have been the essential contributors to the successful acquisition of social capital. Postwar West Germany was a typical meritocratic society in which the so-called elevator effect ("Fahrstuhleffekt," Ulrich Beck) rewarded social actors for their biographical effort with upward social mobility. Members of postwar society could accrue social capital through investment in their career rather than having to (merely) rely on their inherited family background. In recent decades the "biographical pact" between the

---

120. Guy Standing, *The Precariat: The New Dangerous Class* (London: Bloomsbury, 2014), 62.

121. Standing, *The Precariat*, 11. See also Mona Motakef, *Prekarisierung* (Bielefeld: Transcript, 2015).

122. Standing, *The Precariat*, 28.

state and its citizens has been weakened by an ideology of individualism, innovation, and flexibility. After the fall of the Berlin Wall and German unification, it was middle-aged East German workers who were hit hard by the sudden experience of precariousness: the notion of a cumulative *Lebensleistung* in terms of a meaningful contribution to the common social good was swept from under their feet along with their professional self-esteem. According to Heinz Bude, the social experience of redundancy often leads to the shocking realization that one can no longer formulate a meaningful biographical project.[123]

British filmmaker Ken Loach's film *I, Daniel Blake* (2016) is very relevant in this context: it relates the story of a carpenter in Newcastle who, after a major heart attack, can no longer work. As he is trying to sign on for benefits, he meets and befriends Katie, a single mother from London who has been relocated with her two kids to the northeast because housing for the unemployed is too expensive in London. Faced with a social benefits system in the age of austerity, Dan finds the Kafkaesque bureaucracy humiliating and inhumane: a nonmedical assessor deems him fit to work even though his medical consultant has declared him as far too unwell. As Dan has never been on the web, he finds the online application system—which keeps timing out before he can complete his application for the job seekers' allowance—an ordeal. When he takes issue with the assessor's medical competence, he is told that the Decision-Maker, a figure as powerful and beyond human reach as the judges in Kafka's *The Trial*, will decide his case. As Peter Bradshaw comments, Loach's film exposes a benefits system that "has been repurposed as the 21st century workhouse in our age of austerity: made deliberately grim, to deter or design out all but the most deserving poor."[124]

123. "'Die Überflüssigen': Ein Gespräch zwischen Dirk Baecker, Heinz Bude, Axel Honneth, und Helmut Wiesentahl," in *Exklusion: Die Debatte über die "Überflüssigen,"* ed. Heinz Bude and Andreas Willisch (Frankfurt a. M: Suhrkamp, 2008), 37.

124. Peter Bradshaw, "Ken Loach's Quiet Rage against Injustice." *The Guardian,* 20 October 2016, https://www.theguardian.com/film/2016/oct/20/i-daniel-blake-review-ken-loach-film-benefits-system (accessed 7 November 2016).

The post-2008 recession and the ensuing fiscal austerity across Europe created youth unemployment on a massive scale, particularly in Greece, Spain, Ireland, Italy, and in Portugal, where young people who had gone through the university system were either unemployed or in low-paid precarious jobs or forced to emigrate.[125] In recent years, the emergence of the so-called gig economy has produced new pernicious forms of precarious employment: because workers are classed as independent contractors rather than employees, they lose protection against unfair dismissal, they have no right to redundancy payments and no right to paid holidays or sickness pay. This shift toward freelance or short-term contracts thus exacerbates the sense of existential insecurity.

The growth of the global precariat is further fueled by ongoing warfare and the destabilization of the Middle East and North Africa, which has resulted in the death and displacement of millions of people.[126] Refugees, asylum seekers, and economic migrants are often blamed for driving down wages, burdening the public health and education systems, and exploiting social benefits. The demonization of migrants was particularly toxic in the Brexit debate in the UK in 2016 in which politicians on the far right fanned xenophobic resentment by portraying foreign workers as social security scroungers or cheap laborers responsible for the tribulations of the local workforce.[127] But political parties on the far right have made electoral gains in a wide range of European countries. Included

---

125. By 2010 youth unemployment in Spain was over 40 percent, in Ireland 28 percent, and in Greece 25 percent. Standing, *The Precariat*, 132.

126. According to UNHCR, in 2015 an unprecedented 65.3 million people around the world were forced from home. Among them were nearly 21.3 million refugees, over half of whom were under the age of eighteen. A further 10 million people were stateless, as they had been denied a nationality and access to basic rights such as education, healthcare, employment, and freedom of movement. http://www.unhcr.org/figures-at-a-glance.html (accessed 14 October 2016).

127. A particularly obnoxious example was UKIP's anti-immigration poster, which showed a seemingly endless queue of migrants walking in a long line. The photograph used was of migrants crossing the Croatia-Slovenia border in 2015, with the only prominent white person in the photograph obscured by a box of text. See https://www.theguardian.com/politics/2016/jun/16/nigel-farage-defends-ukip-breaking-point-poster-queue-of-migrants (accessed 14 October 2016).

among them are the Front National in France (even though the party was defeated in the French elections of 2017); UKIP (UK Independence Party) in Britain, which drove the Brexit agenda; the right-wing Law and Justice Party in Poland; and Victor Orban's governing Fidesz party in Hungary. Other European parties on the far right have made great strides, including the Party for Freedom in Holland, the Alternative für Deutschland in Germany (AdF), the Five Star Movement in Italy, and the Freedom Party in Austria— they all reject globalization in favor of a populist identitarian politics that disallows the very notion of otherness.[128] Precariousness undermines solidarity by fueling fear. The Brexit referendum in June 2016, the US election in November of the same year, the huge gains of the AdF in the German elections in 2017 and of the Five Star Movement in the Italian elections of 2018 exemplify the backlash of those who felt abandoned by all established political parties. Right-wing populism successfully channeled the social experience of disenfranchisement into backward-looking nationalistic agendas. "Nation," comments Francis Fukuyama, "almost always trumps class because it is able to tap into a powerful source of identity, the desire to connect with an organic cultural community. This longing for identity is now emerging in the form of the American alt-right, a formerly ostracized collection of groups espousing white nationalism in one form or another."[129] Paradoxically, this angry right-wing nationalism is now an international phenomenon that cleverly exploits the opportunities of social media and information sharing across national boundaries.

Looking beyond Europe, life at the beginning of the twenty-first century is for the majority of the world population an altogether precarious affair. Growing inequality pushes more and more people globally into abject poverty. Jason Hickel quotes reliable figures that demonstrate that today a staggering "4.3 billion people—more

---

128. See "How Far Is Europe Swinging to the Right?," *New York Times*, 5 July 2016. See http://www.nytimes.com/interactive/2016/05/22/world/europe/europe-right-wing-austria-hungary.html?_r=0 (accessed 14 October 2016).

129. Francis Fukuyama, "US against the World?," *Financial Times Weekend*, 12/13 November 2016, Life & Arts, 1.

than 60% of the world's population—live in debilitating poverty, struggling to survive on less than the equivalent of $5 per day. . . . Meanwhile, the wealth of the very richest is piling up on levels unprecedented in human history."[130] In a report published on the occasion of the Davos World Economic Forum in 2017, Oxfam produced the following shocking comparisons:

> Since 2015, the richest 1% has owned more wealth than the rest of the planet. Eight men now own the same amount of wealth as the poorest half of the world. Over the next 20 years, 500 people will hand over $2.1 trillion to their heirs—a sum larger than the GDP of India, a country of 1.3 billion people. The incomes of the poorest 10% of people increased by less than $3 a year between 1988 and 2011, while the incomes of the richest 1% increased 182 times as much. A FTSE-100 CEO earns as much in a year as 10,000 people working in garment factories in Bangladesh.[131]

However, precariousness is not only a socioeconomic category but also a condition that is shared by all life on the planet in the so-called Anthropocene. Precariousness in this literally universal sense affects the fundamental vulnerability of the very category of life, which encompasses plants, maritime life, animals, and humans. Environmental degradation through climate change causes habitat loss and threatens biodiversity and the survival of many species. As a *conditio humana*, precariousness makes us dependent on and involved in the care of others. Precariousness can therefore engender either ethical relations or violence. In her book *Precarious Life*, Judith Butler shows that precariousness is subject to a politics of representation that can dehumanize the Other through triumphalist or degrading images as evident in the media coverage of the Iraq War.[132] Drawing on Emmanuel Levinas's notion of the

---

130. Jason Hickel, *The Divide: A Brief Guide to Global Inequality and Its Solutions* (London: William Heinemann, 2017), 2.

131. Oxfam, "An Economy for the 99%," *Oxfam Briefing Paper*, January 2017, https://www.oxfam.org/sites/. . .oxfam. . ./bp-economy-for-99-percent-160117-en.pdf. (accessed 6 December 2017).

132. Judith Butler, *Precarious Life: The Powers of Mourning and Violence* (London: Verso, 2004).

human face, she explores the ethics of recognizing the Other's life as precarious. For Butler, then, a broader problem consists in the normative schemes of intelligibility, which "establish what will and will not be human, what will be a livable life, what will be a grievable death."[133] Even though Butler does not explicitly address the problem of time, it is apparent that a proper engagement with the Other often requires time, patience, and human resources—that is, a chrono-politics of care.

As already mentioned in the introduction, precariousness gains an aesthetic dimension in the literary, artistic, and filmic narratives that scrutinize and foster diverse modes of asynchronous or achronic time that disrupt or displace the dominant narrative about historical change. In many of the works featured here, 1989 is an uncertain caesura that does not so much signify an enabling historical turning point but rather a historical event that cannot be absorbed into one's biography. In spite of the obvious diversity of media, styles, and themes, the works under discussion in chapters 3 and 4 share one striking feature: the built-in tension between a diagnostic perspective on socio-temporal precariousness in contemporary Germany, on the one hand, and the aesthetic encoding of nonchronological time, on the other. It is precisely this tension between the two levels that opens an alternative space that—like Castells's space of flows—breaks with the linearity of time. However, rather than engendering Castells's "timeless time," the space of flows intersects the temporal anxieties of the digital era with duration. We will see that precariousness in these texts is thus not just a thematic concern and a social condition but a mode of attention that engages the reader in a continually fluctuating move between temporal anxiety, social criticism, and aesthetic attention. While the articulation of anxiety and social criticism lends my corpus a compelling diagnostic tenor, these works simultaneously probe the potential of alternative temporalities to foster or create aesthetic *Eigenzeit*, the self's own time.

---

133. Butler, *Precarious Life*, 146.

Before illuminating artistic and literary responses to the temporal anxieties of our era, chapter 2 returns to the fin de siècle to explore the temporal ambivalence inherent in modernism, especially in the semantic field of acceleration, lateness, and slowness. The analysis of these temporal tropes in texts by Nietzsche, Simmel, Kafka, Thomas Mann, Robert Walser, and Freud reveals a multifaceted experience of modernity, which resists the capitalist doctrine that time is money. By exploring uneconomic temporal behavior, modernist texts often challenge the homogenization of time and the commodification of social experience. Against this backdrop, chapter 3 then illuminates the fragile recuperation of *Eigenzeit* in photography and film.

2

HISTORICAL PERSPECTIVES

Modernism and Speed Politics

Temporality and the Modern Imagination

Cinema, the most innovative medium of the early twentieth century, created a captivating visual imaginary for the energizing yet frightening experience of modern speed politics. Two of the most iconic films of the Weimar period, Walter Ruttmann's *Berlin: Sinfonie der Großstadt* (Symphony of the Big City) and Fritz Lang's *Metropolis*, explored the city as a site of a contradictory modernity: on the one hand, these films celebrate modern technologies, the pleasure of speed, and the visual stimuli unleashed by a world that is constantly in motion; on the other, however, they bring into view the uncontrollable effects of a runaway world in which machines begin to transform human behavior. Released in 1927, both films created a striking visual aesthetic of urban modernity that exploited the technical opportunities of film to new effect.

Set in 2026 in a futuristic and dystopian city that was modeled on Lang's own impressions of New York, *Metropolis* follows the story of Freder, son of the wealthy industrialist Fredersen, who is the Master of the Metropolis, and of Maria, who preaches social peace to the workers in the catacombs underneath the city. Famed for its elaborate set design and special effects, the film's aesthetic incorporates visual elements ranging from modernism and Art Deco to Gothic and biblical imagery. As Andreas Huyssen notes, even though the film was praised for its visual qualities, it was in equal measure condemned for its representation of technology and, above all, the sentimental handling of class conflict as exemplified in the reconciliation of capitalism and labor at the end. For Huyssen, however, this critique is too one-sided, as it ignores the dual representation of technology in the film: while an expressionist strand "emphasizes technology's oppressive and destructive potential and is clearly rooted in the experiences and irrepressible memories of the mechanized battlefields of World War I," a second style evokes the urban landscapes of the *Neue Sachlichkeit* and with it a rational view of technology.[1] For Huyssen it is no coincidence that this conflict about technology involves a female robot: the machine-vamp, argues Huyssen, recasts "the fears and perceptual anxieties emanating from ever more powerful machines . . . in terms of the male fear of female sexuality, reflecting, in the Freudian account, the male's castration anxiety."[2] Even though the film ends with a serene vision of technological progress, it enacts an agonistic struggle that is resolved only by way of the ritualistic exorcism of the machine-woman. And so the burning of the female robot at the stake is a premodern witch hunt launched against the dual threat of an uncontrolled female sexuality and a threatening technology. "It

---

1. Andreas Huyssen, "The Vamp and the Machine: Technology and Sexuality in Fritz Lang's *Metropolis*," *New German Critique* 24/25 (1981/82): 223. Huyssen shows that the conflict between these opposing views of technology is acted out by the machine-vamp, which "embodies the unity of an active and destructive female sexuality and the destructive potential of technology" (Huyssen, 233).
2. Huyssen, "The Vamp and the Machine," 226.

is," comments Huyssen, "as if the destructive potential of modern technology, which the expressionists rightfully feared, had to be displaced and projected onto the machine-woman so that it could be metaphorically purged."[3]

Similar ambivalent perceptions of modernity characterize Ruttmann's quasi-documentary *Berlin: Sinfonie der Großstadt*: tracking a day in the life of modern Berlin from dawn to dusk, Ruttmann creates a montage that offers a totalizing view of the modern city by way of fast-paced intercutting, alternating low and high angles, and the combination of documentation with abstraction. Most critics comment on the famous opening of Ruttmann's film, which sets up a striking visual contrast between slow nature and fast-moving technology. Within the first minute the film moves from the timeless image of rippling water to abstract geometrical shapes before the steam engine shoots into the frame from the left, immediately conjuring up the unstoppable speed of modernity. Shots of the railway tracks and overhead lines are intercut with frames through the train window: as Tony Kaes has argued, Ruttmann's opening thus dramatizes the experience of millions of people who, before and after the turn of the twentieth century, left the countryside to seek work in the big city. Visualizing "the arrival of the migrant to the city," comments Kaes, "the scene's progression from water and organic nature to the fiery speed of the steam engine suggests both birth and separation and the undeniable experience of a primary loss."[4] And so, from the perspective of the forward-moving train,

---

3. Huyssen, "The Vamp and the Machine," 236. In contrast, R. L. Rutsky argues that rather than privileging the *Neue Sachlichkeit* view of technology over an expressionist view, the film envisages precisely the type of mediation that "would restore coherence to an alienated, technologized world split by these dystopian alternatives." In so doing the film works toward a model of organicism that was propagated by Nazism. However, both opposing interpretations emphasize the anxiety about the crippling effects of technology. See R. L. Rutsky, "The Mediation of Technology and Gender: Metropolis, Nazism, Modernism," *New German Critique* 60 (1993): 1.

4. Anton Kaes, "Leaving Home: Film, Migration, and the Urban Experience," *New German Critique* 74 (1998): 186.

the countryside is already marked as a premodern space that is rapidly left behind.[5]

But the train journey by no means constitutes an unambiguous celebration of the accelerating pace of modernity: while the central motif of the train suggests that modernity is on track, the motif of the spinning wheel or spiral that is employed throughout the film is much more ambivalent. On the one hand, the image represents modernity functioning as a gigantic machine—there are numerous images of cogs and wheels; on the other, modernity increasingly appears as a dizzying spiral, signaling lack of control, a sense of vertigo, and the crisis of perception. In Ruttmann's film the visual pleasure of the urban spectacle is interlaced with anxiety that the experience of an unbounded modernity can no longer be processed by the individual, who is bombarded by quickly changing images and sensations. Intercut shots of illuminated advertising, of shop window displays, and sequences of leisurely street life foreground a new urban aesthetic while also exposing the precariousness of the modern subject, who can no longer relate to a stable field of vision. Scenes of congested traffic with cars, cyclists, trams, buses, and horse-drawn coaches crisscrossing each other bring to the fore different speeds and different directions that disrupt the notion of a linear pathway to modernity. Pedestrians are shown stepping into the street and dashing to the other side, always on guard against the unforeseen. The street is a site of continual movement where the lack of urban attention can cause accidents or death. Ruttmann's film thus documents the modern

---

5. Derek Hillard rightly observes that the view from the train window submits the countryside to technology: "The train window marks the countryside as having already been denatured by the camera's technological gaze." Derek Hillard, "Walter Ruttmann's Janus-Faced View of Modernity: The Ambivalence of Description in *Berlin: Die Sinfonie der Großstadt*," *Monatshefte* 96/1 (2004): 82. See also Sabine Hake, "Urban Spectacle in Walter Ruttmann's *Berlin, Symphony of the Big City*," in *Dancing on the Volcano: Essays on the Culture of the Weimar Republic*, ed. Stephen Brockmann and Thomas W. Kniesche (Rochester, NY: Camden House, 1994), 127–37. Analyzing the film's "fetishization of spectacle and specularity," Hake argues that Ruttmann's goal was "visual pleasure, not critical analysis" (128).

city as a pulsating site of fast-paced visual stimuli that produce pleasure and anxiety alongside new modes of urban attention and distraction. In so doing the film contributes to a far-reaching debate on modern subjectivity, which was faced with the threats and thrills of modern speed.

Weimar cinema is the culmination of high modernist engagement with a new politics of speed. From the 1870s, psychologists, philosophers, writers, and artists addressed the urgent question as to whether and how the modern subject would cope with the rate of change and the experience of social and technological acceleration.[6] Attention, distraction, lateness, and slowness emerged as central tropes in a far-ranging discourse that foregrounded the precariousness of modern subjectivity, while also exploring modern reactions and coping mechanisms. Attention became a vital cultural technique that could ward off the danger of too much distraction and ultimately of psychic disintegration. It played a disciplinary function that managed the perpetual production of the new as a striking hallmark of modernity. Distraction as the flip side of attention indicated a noneconomic temporality brought about by the onslaught of overwhelming external stimuli. The third term in the debate is the idea of lateness, which is an epiphenomenon of the modern drive toward the total synchronization of time and the superimposition of a universal time grid. Lateness designates the perceived failure to fulfill a social or economic obligation to arrive on time; it is thus produced by slowness, the fourth term, which in turn can be defined as the self's perceived inability or unwillingness to keep up with the social, economic, and cultural speed of the modern age. As two complementary modes of desynchronization the outcome-oriented notion of lateness and the procedural term slowness emerge in the cultural discourse around 1900 as symptomatic tropes giving expression to various fears about the mal de siècle. As the flip side of acceleration, lateness and slowness

---

6. See Siegfried Kracauer, "Der Kult der Zerstreuung: Über die Berliner Lichtspielhäuser" (1926), in *Das Ornament der Masse: Essays* (Frankfurt a. Main: Suhrkamp, 2014), 311–17.

disrupt the relentless logic of the modernizing project by critiquing the harnessing of attention, which is, as I argue below, a hallmark of modernity's high-speed society.

This chapter touches on diverse articulations of tempo from 1870 to the late 1930s that interrogate modernity and its prioritization of mobility and speed: first, the moral interpretation of lateness as both stigma and a mode of resistance to modernity's valorization of the new (Nietzsche and Mann); second, the psychic view of lateness as a modern condition (Simmel), and, third, as symptom of modern man's inflated sense of autonomy (Kafka). I will then discuss the poetological view of speed, attention, and slowness in the short prose of the Swiss avant-garde writer Robert Walser, whose quirky writings often articulate resistance to and enjoyment of modern speed. The chapter concludes with an analysis of the contribution of psychoanalysis to the modern discourse on time: I will show that Freud turns lateness into a generative principle of cultural change.

Two Visions of Late Culture: Friedrich Nietzsche and Thomas Mann

Anyone writing on lateness cannot overlook the second of Friedrich Nietzsche's *Unzeitgemäße Betrachtungen* (*Untimely Meditations*): his essay *Vom Nutzen und Nachteil der Historie für das Leben* (*On the Uses and Disadvantages of History for Life*), published in 1873, two years after German unification.[7] In characteristic Nietzschean fashion the notion of untimeliness carries two opposing meanings here: in the first instance, it is a mode of critical inquiry that, as the preface explains, runs "gegen die Zeit" in order "auf die Zeit und und hoffentlich zugunsten einer kommenden

---

7. Friedrich Nietzsche, *Vom Nutzen und Nachteil der Historie für das Leben* (Stuttgart: Reclam, 1999); cited as VNN in the text. All English quotations are taken from Friedrich Nietzsche, *On the Uses and Disadvantages of History for Life*, trans. R. J. Hollingdale (Cambridge: Cambridge University Press, 1997); cited as UaD in the text.

Zeit zu wirken" (VNN, 5; "counter to our time and thereby acting on our time and, let us hope, for the benefit of a time to come";
UaD, 60). As a "Zögling älterer Zeiten, zumal der griechischen"
(VNN, 5; "pupil of earlier times, especially the Hellenic"; UaD,
60), Nietzsche claims to have accumulated experiences that make
it possible for him to interrogate the bankrupt spirit of his own
epoch. Such strategic desynchronization appears as a diagnostic tool for the ensuing two-pronged attack on two forms of misguided untimeliness: historicism and the Hegelian conception of a
teleological history. Nietzsche argues that, although diametrically
opposed to one another, both have worked in tandem to produce a
sick culture defined by lateness and an impoverished imagination.
For Nietzsche, nineteenth-century historicism is not an important
scientific achievement of the positivist age, but rather a form of cultural degeneration that, through the promotion of an antiquarian
mind-set, has stifled and mummified life by way of an uncritical
appreciation of all things past. The Rankean historian in particular appears in Nietzsche's essay in the guise of the undiscerning
collector who is driven by "einer blinden Sammelwut, eines ras-
tlosen Zusammenscharrens alles einmal Dagewesenen . . . ; oft-
mals sinkt er so tief, daß er zuletzt mit jeder Kost zufrieden ist
und mit Lust selbst den Staub bibliographischer Quisquilien frißt"
(VNN, 31; "a restless raking together of everything that has ever
existed. . . . Often he sinks so low that in the end he is content to
gobble down any food whatever, even the dust of bibliographical
minutiae"; UaD, 75).

While the antiquarian historian is thus ridiculed in the figure
of the dust-sweeper without judgment, Hegelian philosophy of
history fares no better. For Nietzsche Hegelian world history has
done nothing but mythologize history. Hegelianism mistakes the
limited horizon of the present for all history so that "für Hegel der
Höhepunkt und der Endpunkt des Weltprozesses in seiner eignen
Berliner Existenz zusammenfielen (VNN, 81; "for Hegel the climax
and terminus of the world-process coincided with his own existence in Berlin"; UaD, 104). The historicist and teleological views
of history are nothing but symptoms of a wider cultural malaise
that Nietzsche captures under the heading of "Spätzeit," the late

epoch dominated by the epigone. According to Nietzsche's scathing diagnosis, his own era had thus lost its "plastic power" and the ability to grow. Such plastic power would entail the rejection of the dead ballast of history from the perspective of the living horizon. Modern man is characterized by an emaciated and timid personality that mistakes the poor imitation of historical models for agency:

> Dem, der sich nicht mehr zu trauen wagt, sondern unwillkürlich für sein Empfinden bei der Geschichte um Rat fragt, der wird allmählich aus Furchtsamkeit zum Schauspieler und spielt eine Rolle, meistens sogar viele Rollen und deshalb jede so schlecht und flach. (VNN, 50)

> He who no longer dares to trust himself but involuntarily asks of history 'How ought I to feel about this?' finds that his timidity gradually turns him into an actor and that he is playing a role, usually indeed many roles and therefore playing them badly and superficially. (UaD, 86)

Lateness is thus the condition of modern man who inhabits a culture of imitation. A weakened personality that manifests itself in the split between the outer and the inner self afflicts the modern epigone, in whose personality mere remnants of man's individuality are buried without a chance to assert themselves. Lateness thus designates the condition of a degenerate and emaciated culture that has lost all vigor and power of renewal.

Nietzsche's critique of his epoch in terms of a malignant lateness is echoed up to a point in Thomas Mann's *Buddenbrooks* (1901) where the family's rise and fall proceed through a chain of four generations.[8] Old Johann Buddenbrook who switches easily between High German, Platt, and cosmopolitan French and conducts his business without anxiety represents the first generation's vigorous entrepreneurship yet local rootedness. In the second generation, the mix of business ruthlessness with sentimental Pietism in old Johann's son Consul Johann Buddenbrook suggests growing tensions. While the process of erosion is only subliminally present in the second generation, members of the third and fourth generations are increasingly marked by a debilitating moral consciousness

---

8. Thomas Mann, *Buddenbrooks: Verfall einer Familie* (Frankfurt a. Main: Fischer, 1997).

that induces a sense of guilty failure when they attempt but fail to move with more ruthless times. The latter traits are embodied by Christian Buddenbrook, on the face of it, a walking annotation of the Nietzschean degenerate. Christian combines the Nietzschean gift for satirical imitation with a hypochondriac personality obsessed by the smallest bodily malfunction. Throughout the novel Christian represents the inept cultural latecomer, whose various attempts to engage in global business do not indicate expanding horizons but lack of solidity, as his failing import-and-export business witnesses. However, it turns out that his responsible brother Thomas who rises to the rank of senator is also afflicted by the malaise of cultural exhaustion: his increasing failure as a businessman is accompanied by a nervous fastidiousness that requires him to spend an hour and a half on his morning toilette.[9] The fourth link in the chain, Hanno, is from birth marked by an effeminate weakness that makes him unfit for life in the new age. His musicality is at once a creative gift, never to be realized, and the symptom of a denial of life: Hanno's inability to keep time with changing times comes out psychosomatically in his affliction by typhoid fever, which, in the end, is the physical cause of a death that he also chooses. Of course the subtle perspectivistic narration in *Buddenbrooks* leaves opens the possibility that the later family members cannot keep up with the ideal of masculinity prevalent in the new Germany, born in military victory after the French capitulation in the Franco-Prussian War and German unification in 1871. Their look backward at family traditions no longer provides valid points of orientation. In this way, Mann simultaneously sets up and undercuts the Nietzschean version of late culture.

Thomas Mann radicalized his analysis of the pathology of time in his monumental novel *Der Zauberberg* (*The Magic Mountain*, 1924), which, as many critics have observed, engages with various philosophies of time, from Schopenhauer, Nietzsche, and Bergson to Asiatic conceptions of time.[10] Besides offering a philosophically

---

9. Mann, *Buddenbrooks*, 631.

10. See Ruprecht Wimmer, "Zur Philosophie der Zeit im *Zauberberg*," in *Auf dem Weg zum Zauberberg: Die Davoser Literaturtage 1996*, ed. Thomas Sprecher

rich discourse on diverse conceptions of time and history, the novel is, as Joshua Kavaloski rightly emphasizes, extremely performative in its handling of the relationship of narrative time and narrated time.[11] In his foreword the omniscient narrator declares: "Geschichten müssen vergangen sein und je vergangener, könnte man sagen, desto besser für sie in ihrer Eigenschaft als Geschichten und für den Erzähler, den raunenenden Beschwörer des Imperfekts."[12] ("Stories as histories must be past, and the further past, one might say, the better for them as stories and for the storyteller, that conjurer who murmurs in past tenses.")[13] However, instead of adopting the epic preterite and maintaining his ironic distance from Castorp, the narrator regularly focalizes Castorp's subjective and, indeed, pathological experience of a timeless present that is seemingly divorced from historical time. The entire first chapter is dedicated to the few hours after Hans Castorp's arrival at the Swiss sanatorium. After a flashback in chapter 2 that deals with Castorp's family background, the remaining narrative proceeds chronologically. What may look like a conventional story arc is, however, dislodged by the slow narrative pace: while the conversations between the various patients approximate narrative time and narrated time, the extensive and microcosmic descriptions of the sanatorium and its environs create a time-space that is overlaid by Castorp's subjective perceptions, impressions, and subconscious desire.[14] Chapter 3, which is over

---

(Frankfurt a. M.: Klostermann, 1997), 251–72; Beate Pinkerneil, "Ewigkeitssssuppe kontra schöpferisches Werden: Zum Thema Thomas Mann—Bergson," in *Thomas Mann und die Tradition*, ed. Peter Pütz (Frankfurt a. M.: Athenäum, 1971), 250–81; Borge Kristianson, "Thomas Mann und die Philosophie," in *Thomas Mann Handbuch*, ed. Helmut Koopmann, 3rd ed. (Stuttgart: Kröner, 2001), 259–83.

11. Joshua Kavaloski, "Performativity and the Dialectics of Time in Thomas Mann's *Der Zauberberg*," *German Studies Review* 32/2 (2009): 319–42.

12. Thomas Mann, *Der Zauberberg* (Frankfurt a. Main: Fischer, 1979), 5; cited as DZ in the text.

13. Thomas Mann, *The Magic Mountain*, trans. John E. Woods (New York: Everyman's Library, 2005), n.p.; cited as MM in the text.

14. For a highly nuanced critique of the so-called spatial turn and a subtle reexamination of space and time in modernist narrratives, see Erica Wickerson, *The Architecture of Narrative Time: Thomas Mann and the Problems of Modern Narrative* (Oxford: Oxford University Press, 2017).

sixty pages long, offers a full account of Castorp's first day; and
chapter 4, which is more than a hundred pages, depicts the first
three weeks of Castorp's sojourn. As Kavaloski observes, "The
congruity of narrative time and story time demonstrates that the
storyteller seeks to translate Hans Castorp's temporal experience
into narrative practice."[15] In the world of the Berghof the linearity of time is suspended in favor of an extremely slow therapeutic
schedule that revolves around sleep, meals, walks, medical exami-
nations, conversations, and special occasions. In this microcosm,
the smallest temporal unit is, as Settembrini explains to the nov-
ice Castorp, a month: "Unsere kleinste Zeiteinheit ist der Monat.
Wir rechnen im großen Stil, das ist der das Vorrecht der Schatten"
(DZ, 63; "Our smallest unit of time is the month. We measure on
a grand scale—it is one of the privileges of shades"; MM, 67). At
the end of his first day Castorp is already infected by the inability
to keep time: barely able to remember his own age, he explains
that his first day was simultaneously "kurzweilig and langweilig"
("diverting and dull") and claims to feel considerably older and
wiser (DZ, 91; MM, 100). Alarmed at the infectious spread of the
temporal disorder that marks the patients on the magic mountain,
Settembrini, the representative of the enlightenment spirit, commands Hans to pack his bags and catch the first train back to the
real world:

> Da der Aufenthalt Ihnen nicht zuträglich zu sein scheint, da Sie sich
> körperlich und, wenn mich nicht alles täuscht, auch seelisch nicht wohl
> bei uns befinden,—wie wäre es denn da, wenn Sie darauf verzichteten,
> hier älter zu werden, kurz, wenn Sie noch heute nacht wieder aufpack-
> ten und sich morgen mit den fahrplanmäßigen Schnellzügen auf-und da-
> vonmachten? (DZ, 92)

> Since your stay here appears not to be good for you—neither physically
> nor, if I am not mistaken, mentally—how would it be, if you were to
> forego the pleasure of growing older here, in short, if you were to pack
> your things tonight and be on your way with one of the scheduled ex-
> press trains tomorrow morning? (MM, 101)

---

15. Kavaloski, "Performativity and the Dialectics of Time," 325.

Castorp's temporal condition, however, has already disconnected him from such modern regimentation by the clock and, above all, from the future as the bourgeois self's horizon of self-realization. Under the spell of the Berghof's "großzügige Zeitwirtschaft" (DZ, 202; "generous time management"), he completely abandons the modern ideology of temporal discipline in favor of an empty duration that, as the omniscient narrator explains, paradoxically dissolves large units of time "bis zur Nichtigkeit" (DZ, 110; "until they seem nothing"; MM, 122). The complete abrogation of chronological time later manifests itself in Castorp's "lästerliche Gewohnheit . . . , statt 'Vor einem Jahre': 'Gestern und 'Morgen' für 'Übers Jahr' zu sagen" (DZ, 573) ("disgraceful habit . . . of saying 'yesterday' for 'a year ago' and 'tomorrow' for 'a year from now'"; MM, 674). Castorp's temporal crisis reaches its dramatic climax in the famous snow chapter, where his idyllic vision of a harmonious relationship between man and nature flips over into a nightmarish scene with two half-naked old women ripping apart a baby and devouring its limbs. This frightening hallucination of debauched barbarism, a mix of classical Bacchic frenzy with the Germanic witches, goes hand in hand with a crisis of temporality. On waking up in the snow Castorp checks his watch and finds that barely ten minutes have passed even though his nightmare appears to have lasted forever. As Kavaloski comments, "The temporal perception by the main character vastly outstrips story time and suggests an incompatibility between subjective and objective temporality."[16] When, at the end of the novel, the news about mobilization and first declarations of war reach the Berghof, the enchantment is finally broken, and Castorp feels set free "von elementaren Außenmächten" (DZ, 752; "by elementary external forces"; MM, 848). The outbreak of the war not only accelerates time, catapulting all the inhabitants of the magic mountain down to the flatland, but it replaces the temporal disorder of lateness with a global maelstrom that, in all likelihood, will swallow up Castorp. The thunderbolt of the First World War abruptly ends the temporal disorder of the

---

16. Kavaloski, "Performativity and the Dialectics of Time," 331.

magic mountain only to replace it with a new temporal pathology: that of a barbaric chrono-mania, as evident in the frenzied race for imperial power among European states in the run-up to the First World War. While Mann's novel thus echoes Nietzsche's critique of a late culture that has lost the plastic power to shape the future, he is careful not to advocate the modern power politics of competing nations and above all the relentless valorization of a new and better time that is projected onto the future. Even though the empty duration on the magic mountain drained Castorp of all vitality, the novel proposes an aesthetics of slowness that resists modernity's subjugation of subjective time to historical time.[17]

Attention, Distraction, and the Modern Conditions of Perception: Georg Simmel and Franz Kafka

Georg Simmel, who lived almost his entire life in Berlin, has been aptly described as "the first sociologist of modernity,"[18] because he had a pronounced sensibility for the new and the modern. His famous essay "Die Großstädte und das Geistesleben" ("The Metropolis and Mental Life," 1903) "seeks out the fleeting, transitory and contingent elements of modernity" by mapping out the mobility of urban street life, which engenders a rich variety of contacts, dynamic encounters, and visual impressions that can no longer be processed in their totality by the individual.[19] Simmel's essay must be seen in the context of a widespread debate on attention at

---

17. For a discussion of the novel as a document of the era leading up to World War I, see T. J. Reed, *Thomas Mann: The Uses of Tradition*, 2nd ed. (1973; Oxford: Clarendon, 1996); Ulrich Karthaus, "*Der Zauberberg*—ein Zeitroman (Zeit, Geschichte, Mythos)," *Deutsche Vierteljahrsschrift für Literaturwissenschaft und Geistesgeschichte* 44 (1970): 269–305; Paul Michael Lützeler, "Schlafwandler am Zauberberg: Die Europa-Diskussion in Hermann Brochs und Thomas Manns Zeitromanen," *Thomas-Mann-Jahrbuch* 14 (2001): 49–62; Peter Pütz, "Thomas Mann und Nietzsche," in Pütz, *Thomas Mann und die Tradition*, 225–49.

18. David Frisby, *Fragments of Modernity: Theories of Modernity in the Work of Simmel, Krakauer, and Benjamin* (Cambridge, MA: MIT Press, 1986), 39.

19. Frisby, *Fragments of Modernity*, 46.

the fin de siècle. By the end of the nineteenth century, the collapse of classical models of vision and of the stable subjects these models had presupposed, motivated an empirical-scientific approach to the notion of human sensation, which was now produced, controlled, and observed in the laboratory environment. For psychologists such as Wilhelm Wundt or Alfred Binet, attention became the single most important category that was deemed to guarantee unity of consciousness and perception.[20] The Viennese philosopher Ernst Mach captured the modern self in the impressionistic metaphor of the "Elementenkomplex," a complex of elements.[21] Mach dissolved both the subject's unity and the external world, which, in his analysis, was nothing but an effect of floating perceptions that were no longer integrated by Kant's transcendental unity of apperception. The potential threat this disintegration of perception through distraction posed to social order therefore required containment by way of attention as a regulatory tool.[22] Attention was meant to contain the danger of an urban environment that posed the threat of too much distraction and ultimately of psychic disintegration. However, it also allowed for the rapid switching of attention from one object to the next.[23] It thus played a disciplinary function that managed the perpetual production of the new as one of modernity's hallmarks. The issue of attention was deemed to be particularly important in the context of the urban experience of accelerating modernity that had produced a confusing field of vision that made modern subjectivity precarious und unstable.

---

20. Jonathan Crary, *Suspensions of Perceptions, Attention, Spectacle, and Modern Culture* (Cambridge, MA: MIT Press, 1999), 38.

21. Ernst Mach, *Die Analyse der Empfindungen und das Verhältnis des Physischen zum Psychischen*, 9th ed. (Jena: Fischer, 1922; repr., Darmstadt: Wissenschaftliche Buchgesellschaft, 1991).

22. Siegfried Kracauer addresses the problem of distraction and attention in "Der Kult der Zerstreuung" (1926), in *Das Ornament der Masse: Essays* (Frankfurt a. Main: Suhrkamp, 1977), 311–17.

23. See also Georg Franck, *Ökonomie der Aufmerksamkeit: Ein Entwurf* (Munich: Hanser, 1998); Franck, *Mentaler Kapitalismus: Eine politische Ökonomie des Geistes* (Munich: Hanser, 2005).

In his seminal essay on the problem of attention, Simmel firstly contrasts the steady rhythm of rural life with the speed of the modern metropolis, then describes how the metropolitan self is continually bombarded by quickly changing stimuli and fractured sensations that succeed each other in sharp discontinuity.[24] According to Simmel, such dramatic "Steigerung des Nervenlebens" (GG, 228; "intensification of nervous stimulation"; MML, 175) requires the development of a protective mechanism against this onslaught. In reaction to the city environment and its demands on the nervous system, the modern city dweller adopts a highly intellectualized outlook that disconnects the individual from the depth of feelings. The implication here is that in his perpetual engagement with exchange values and fleeting surfaces modern man becomes a hardened self, indifferent "gegen alles eigentlich Individuelle" (GG, 229; "to all genuine individuality"; MML, 176). Hence his propensity to adopt a blasé attitude: as a cultivated form of indifference, this is an essential strategy that allows the individual to ignore the meaning and differing value of things. For Simmel this refusal of the nerves to react to external stimulation is thus a protective technique developed by the modern individual in response to a potentially overwhelming and threatening exposure to stimuli (GG, 233; MML, 179). Evidently, in this essay Simmel does not conceive of the city as an enjoyable spectacle with enormous aesthetic potential, but sees it rather in terms of a threatening environment against which individuals need to defend themselves by means of a psychic economy that ranges from modern man's blasé attitude, on the one hand, to his striking intellectualism, on the other. It is therefore only logical that metropolitan life requires temporal organization by means of an impersonal timetable that synchronizes modern life:

> Wenn alle Uhren in Berlin plötzlich in verschiedene Richtung falschgehen würden, auch nur um den Spielraum einer Stunde, so wäre sein

---

24. Georg Simmel, "Die Großstädte und das Geistesleben," in *Gesamtausgabe*, ed. Rüdiger Kramme (Frankfurt a. Main: Suhrkamp, 1995), 7:227–42; cited as GG in the text. Simmel, "The Metropolis and Mental Life," in *Simmel on Culture*, ed. David Frisby and Mike Featherstone (London: Sage, 1997), 174–85; cited as MML in the text.

ganzes wirtschaftliches und sonstiges Verkehrsleben auf lange hinaus zerrüttet. Dazu kommt, scheinbar noch äußerlicher, die Größe der Entfernungen, die alles Warten und Vergebenskommen zu einem gar nicht aufzubringenden Zeitaufwand machen. So ist die Technik des großstädtischen Lebens überhaupt nicht denkbar, ohne daß alle Tätigkeiten und Wechselbeziehungen aufs Pünklichste in ein festes übersubjektives Zeitschema eingeordnet würden. (GG, 231)

If all clocks and watches in Berlin would suddenly go wrong in different ways, even if only by one hour, all economic life and communication of the city would be distracted for a long time. In addition, an apparently mere external factor—long distances—would make all waiting and broken appointments result in ill-afforded waste of time. Thus the technique of metropolitan life is unimaginable without the most punctual integration of all activities and mutual relations into a stable and impersonal time schedule. (MM, 177)

Punctuality is thus not just a moral virtue of the bourgeois self but, much more importantly, another essential cultural technique that manages the accelerated pace of modern life through a high degree of synchronization. Although Simmel does not write explicitly about lateness, the implication here is that lateness is a mode of distracted desynchronization and an expression of the individual's exposure to constantly changing stimuli.

A salient example of the connection between lateness and distraction can be found in Kafka's first novel, *Der Verschollene* (*The Man Who Disappeared*, 1912), which is better known as *Amerika*.[25] The America in this novel is the place of modernity par excellence where the temporal slackness that still marks Europe has been harnessed by Taylorian time efficiencies. The protagonist Karl Roßmann is a young European immigrant who, on his arrival in New York, meets an unknown uncle, the living embodiment of the rags to riches myth, who takes him under his wing. Uncle Jacob is driven by modern chrono-mania: he not only introduced the Taylorian time practices in his business but also applies them

---

25. Franz Kafka, *Der Verschollene: Roman in der Fassung der Handschrift* (Frankfurt a. Main: Fischer, 1994); cited as DV in the text. For an English translation, see Franz Kafka, *Amerika (The Man Who Disappeared)*, trans. Michael Hofmann (London: Penguin, 1996); cited as A in the text.

to his nephew, who becomes the victim of his disciplinary time regime.[26] At first, however, Uncle Jacob acts as Roßmann's savior and educator, submitting the young Roßmann to a structured timetable that includes English and piano lessons, riding lessons, and a step-by-step introduction to the American world of business. In the second chapter we find Roßmann standing on the balcony of his room in New York, admiring the vibrant city below with its incessant traffic patterns:

> Und morgen wie abend und in den Träumen der Nacht vollzog sich auf dieser Straße ein immer drängender Verkehr, der von oben gesehen sich als eine aus immer neuen Anfängen ineinandergestreute Mischung von verzerrten menschlichen Figuren und von Dächern der Fuhrwerke aller Art darstellte, von der aus sich noch eine neue verfielfältigte wildere Mischung von Lärm, Staub und Gerüchen erhob, und alles dieses wurde erfaßt und durchdrungen von einem mächtigeren Licht, das immer wieder von der Menge der Gegenstände zerstreut, fortgetragen und wieder eifrig herbeigebracht wurde. (DV, 46)

> In the morning and evening, and in his dreams at night, that street was always full of swarming traffic. Seen from above, it appeared to be a swirling kaleidoscope of distorted human figures and the roofs of vehicles of all kinds, from which a new and amplified and wilder mixture of noise, dust and smells arose, and all this was held and penetrated by a majority of light, that was forever being scattered, carried and eagerly returned by the multitudes of objects, and that seemed so palpable to the confused eye that it was like a sheet of glass spread out over the street that was being continually and violently smashed. (A, 28–29)

---

26. On the representation of America in this novel, see Mark Harman, "Wie Kafka sich Amerika vorstellte," *Sinn und Form* 60 (2008): 794–804; Dieter Heimböckel, "'Amerika im Kopf': Franz Kafkas Roman *Der Verschollene* und der Amerika-Diskurs seiner Zeit," *DVjs* 77 (2003): 130–47; on Kafka's sources, see Hans Peter Rüsing, "Quellenforschung als Interpretation: Holitschers und Soukups Reiseberichte über Amerika und Kafka's Roman *Der Verschollene*," *MAL* 20 (1987): 1–38. On patriarchal power, Elizabeth Boa, "Karl Rossmann and, or the Boy Who Wouldn't Grow Up: The Flight from Manhood in Franz Kafka's *Der Verschollene*," in *From Goethe to Gide: Feminism, Aesthetics, and the French and German Literary Canon, 1770–1936*, ed. Mary Orr and Lesley Sharpe (Exeter: University of Exeter Press, 2005), 168–83; Anne Fuchs, "A Psychoanalytic Reading of *The Man Who Disappeared*," in *The Cambridge Companion to Kafka*, ed. Julian Preece (Cambridge: Cambridge University Press, 2002), 25–41.

This wild mixture of impressions and stimuli blurs olfactory, visual, and audible stimuli to such an extent that Roßmann no longer has the ability to perceive any object clearly. In the eyes of his uncle, Roßmann represents the dazzled newcomer to the United States who has not yet internalized the modern self-regulation that wards off the danger of too much distraction. Even though this simultaneously fascinating and confusing concoction of sounds, smells, and dust represents precisely the conditions of the metropolitan modernity as described by Simmel, the lack of a temporal and spatial order in the above scene poses a threat to a modernity that aims to harness such "ill-afforded waste of time," to use Simmel's terms. This is precisely the context for Uncle Jacob's admonition that Karl should not waste his time on the balcony like so many immigrants who stare at the streets below them like lost sheep rather than dedicating their attention to planning their future (DV, 46). Kafka spells out the connection between distraction and Roßmann's lateness even more openly in the chapter "Ein Landhaus bei New York" ("A Country House near New York"), where his host's daughter, Klara Pollunder, distracts Karl. At the end of the chapter Karl is given a letter in which his uncle explains that Karl has offended a basic principle by accepting Herr Pollunder's invitation: accordingly, he punishes Karl by withdrawing his guardianship. Interestingly, the act of expulsion is synchronized with a timetable that Karl is unaware of. The envelope states: "An Karl Roßmann. Um Mitternacht persönlich abzugeben, wo immer er angetroffen wird" (DV, 96; For Karl Roßmann. To be handed to him personally at midnight wherever he may be found). In the context of such punitive regimentation of social time, it is doubtful that the sequence in the Teater von Oklahama (*sic*) really envisages an alternative temporality: even though the biblical imagery of the trumpet-blowing angels evokes the notion of eternal salvation, the bureaucracy of the registration process and the ominous announcement that the identity papers of all theater applicants will be checked on arrival in Oklahoma thwart this seemingly utopian vision.

Modern Man and the Trouble with Time:
Franz Kafka's *Der Proceß*

In his American novel, which was also his first, Kafka made late-ness an effect of the distracted modern individual, who cannot process his environment in accordance with the rigid timetable of modernity. In his second novel, *Der Proceß* (*The Trial*, written in 1914–15, posthumously published in 1925), he gave lateness a metaphysical twist.[27] Here the protagonist's trouble with time no longer concerns merely its crippling effects on the self but rather the ethical ramifications of a time consciousness that is oblivious to any meaningful notion of care for the Other. Josef K. is the pro-verbial modern Western man whose routinized schedule underlines the functionalization of all human relations. His weekly schedule revolves around work in the bank until 9:00 p.m., followed by a short walk that takes him to a public house where he spends the evening in the company of older and professionally important men until 11:00 p.m. This habitualized timetable is complemented by a weekly visit to Elsa, a waitress who also works as a prostitute, and on weekends he accepts the odd invitation by his boss (DP, 26). The striking absence of proper friends, family, and intimate rela-tions in K.'s life accentuates the lack of nonutilitarian time in his life: even his leisure time is dominated by calculated considerations and exploitative relations. In the pursuit of his case, K. is then con-fronted with a dyschronic and ultimately metaphysical schedule that paradoxically makes use of clock time only to invalidate its rule. And so even though Kafka equipped the narrative with a clear timeline—it begins on K.'s thirtieth birthday and ends one year later on the eve of his thirty-first birthday—the novel enacts tem-poral dyschronia to stage the crisis of modern time consciousness.

The narrative opens with an incident that overturns the rou-tinized time structures of the protagonist's everyday life: on the

---

27. Franz Kafka, *Der Proceß: Roman in der Fassung der Handschrift* (Frank-furt a. Main: Fischer, 1995); cited in the text as DP. Franz Kafka, *The Trial*, trans. Breon Mitchell (New York: Schocken, 1998); cited as TT in the text.

morning of his thirtieth birthday, K. wakes up only to be arrested
in his bedroom.[28] K. immediately attempts to rectify this disruption by asking authoritatively for his breakfast, which is normally served before 8:00 a.m. by the servant girl, Anna. But on
his thirtieth birthday his request is merely met by a sniggering
response that appears to emanate from the room next door. K.'s
authority as a male bourgeois subject is thus challenged by the
invasion of his privacy, the discontinuation of his daily routine,
and the erosion of his authority as a man.[29] When K. demands an
explanation, he is told that he is arrested and that he must return
to his room and wait: "Das Verfahren ist nun einmal eingeleitet
und Sie werden alles zur richtigen Zeit erfahren," explains one of
the wardens (DP, 11; "Proceedings are underway and you'll learn
everything in due course"; TT, 5). The trial, so it seems, is a process that will unfold according to a radically alternative notion of
time that has nothing to do with the type of temporal order that
defines bourgeois male identity.

The trial involves a battle between opposing time regimes: with
its rational division into a public time and a harnessed private time,
the linearity of modern time is cut through by a nonchronological
and ultimately metaphysical "other" time that invalidates the type
of functionalized human agency that K. represents. The dyschronic
nature of the world of the court is a constant theme: even though
K. is called to his first hearing by telephone, he is not given a time
for this appointment. The rule of this "other time" is given full-
est expression in two paradigmatic episodes. One day K. opens
the door of a junk room at his workplace, the bank, and finds the
wardens Franz and Willem being flogged because he had made a
complaint about them. When K. passes the junk room the next day
he opens the door again and, to his horror, finds the same scenario

---

28. On the opening, see Elizabeth Boa, *Kafka: Gender, Class, and Race in the
Letters and Fictions* (Oxford: Clarendon, 1996), 188.

29. "Domestic arrangements," comments Boa, "are intrinsically trivial; part of
the unchanging, natural order of things, they are beneath notice. But by the same
token, they belong to the very basis of patriarchy." Boa, *Kafka: Gender, Class, and
Race*, 189.

as on the previous evening: the whipper is still there with his cane and the two wardens, still undressed, who beg him for help, as on the previous day.[30] The second episode concerning other time is the legend of the doorkeeper, which the prison chaplain relates to illustrate how deluded K. has been about the court.[31] This famous parable is shot through with temporal adverbs that evoke expectations steeped in linear time. By telling the man from the country that he cannot let him into the law right now, the doorkeeper gestures to the future as a time when the law might be reached. Accordingly, the man from the country inquires whether he may gain access later, to which the doorkeeper responds that it is possible but not now. The illocutionary and temporal logic of "now"—"not now"—"later" misleads the man from the country to waste his life waiting for the permission to enter the law. While these adverbs gesture to the modern concept of linear time, in reality they set in train a dyschronic mode of deferral that, in the end, fails to reward the man from the country and also leaves the reader unsatisfied. After longwinded attempts at exegesis, the chapter concludes with the chaplain pointing to the nonchronological temporality of the court: "Es nimmt dich auf, wenn du kommst und es entläßt dich wenn du gehst" (DP, 235; "It receives you when you come and it dismisses you when you leave"; TT, 224).

Kafka employs three temporal tropes that map K.'s growing inability to time his life: when it really matters K. is either tired,

---

30. On the temporal structure of the novel and the whipper scene in particular, see Beda Allemann, "Noch einmal Kafkas *Process*," in *Zeit und Geschichte im Werk Kafkas* (Göttingen: Wallstein, 1998) 104–5.

31. On this much-interpreted parable, see Hartmut Binder, *Vor dem Gesetz: Einführung in Kafkas Welt* (Stuttgart: Metzler, 1993); Aage Hansen-Löve, "Vor dem Gesetz," in *Interpretationen—Franz Kafka: Romane und Erzählungen*, ed. Michael Müller (Stuttgart: Reclam, 1994), 146–58; Bernd Auerochs, "Innehalten vor der Schwelle: Kafkas 'Vor dem Gesetz' im Kontext der traditionellen Parabel," in *Grenzsituationen: Wahrnehmung, Bedeutung und Gestaltung in der neueren Literatur*, ed. Dorothea Lauterbach, Uwe Spörl, and Ulrich Wunderlich (Göttingen: Vandenhoeck & Ruprecht, 2002), 131–50; Wolf Kittler, "Burial without Resurrection: On Kafka's Legend 'Before the Law,'" *Modern Language Notes* 121/3 (2006): 647–78.

late, or too distracted to pay attention. On the one hand, these temporal disorders indicate that K. is falling out of step with modernity's time regime as he is increasingly consumed by his case; on the other, they also symptomatically disclose the lack of proper *Eigenzeit* in his life. K.'s rigid schedule, as sketched above, left no room for a nonfunctional experience of time. From a temporal perspective, then, it is the lack of *Eigenzeit* in K.'s life that makes him increasingly desynchronized with all aspects of time, including his daily life and the timing of the court. Precisely because K. never took time to properly care for nonutilitarian relations between the self and the Other does he end up as a time-troubled man who is out of sync with all modes of temporality.

At the beginning of chapter 3 K. is informed by telephone that there will be a small hearing concerning his case the following Sunday. He is made aware that these cross-examinations will follow one another regularly, perhaps not every week but quite frequently. Upon hanging up the telephone receiver, K. realizes that he has not been given a precise time for the hearing and decides to get there by 9:00 a.m.. On the Sunday in question he nearly oversleeps because he had stayed out drinking until late in the night. Rushing out without breakfast to make up for lost time, he then decides to walk to the hearing because he does not want to be too punctual. However, he ends up running the last stretch so that he will get there by 9:00 a.m. (DP, 43). As he reaches his destination, he slows down again, "als hätte er nun schon Zeit oder als sähe ihn der Untersuchungsrichter aus irgendeinem Fenster und wisse also daß sich K. eingefunden habe. Es war kurz nach neun" (DP, 44; "as if he had plenty of time now, or as if the examining magistrate had seen him from some window and therefore knew that K. had arrived. It was shortly after nine"; TT, 39). K's contradictory thought process points to a clash between the modern subject's assertion of autonomy, on the one hand, and a higher order that challenges such sovereignty, on the other. When the sitting magistrate tells K. on his arrival that he is precisely one hour and five minutes late, K. therefore demonstratively refuses to apologize: "Mag ich zu spät gekommen sein, jetzt bin ich hier" (DP, 49; "I may have arrived late, but I'm here now"; TT, 43). K.'s deliberate lateness and his supposed time scarcity are complementary modes of behavior that are meant to make manifest his sense of authority and control over his life.

In the course of the novel he becomes a time gambler whose games with time are always misguided: for example, when his concerned uncle takes him to Advokat Huld for a first consultation— instead of availing himself of the opportunity to discuss his case with Huld and the Kanzleidirektor, who happens to be present— K. is distracted by Leni, who takes him to the kitchen, where he loses his sense of time in an eerie scene of rising sexual tension. When he finally leaves Huld's house, his uncle leaps out of the car, reproaching him for his inconsiderate conduct toward the lawyer and the office director, who were waiting in vain for K. to return and discuss his case. The aggrieved uncle concludes: "Und mich deinen Onkel läßt Du hier im Regen, fühle nur, ich bin ganz durchnäßt, stundenlang warten." (DP, 117; "And you leave me, your uncle, waiting here in the rain for hours: just feel, I'm soaked clear through"; TT, 110). In his conversation with Kaufmann Block the topic of waiting comes up once more when K. discovers that he had already met Block among the waiting clients in the corridor of the courtrooms where he got so violently sick. When K. says that it seemed pointless for them to be waiting in that way, Block responds: "Das Warten ist nicht nutzlos . . . , nutzlos ist nur das selbständige Eingreifen" (DP, 185; "Waiting is not pointless . . . , the only thing that's pointless is independent action"; TT, 176). Later on in the chapter, K. demonstrates once more that, as the proverbial modern man, he feels entitled to capitalize on the time of others without any regard for timeliness. Leni rightly observes that he does not seem in the slightest surprised that the lawyer, despite being ill, is willing to receive him at 11:00 p.m. at night: "Du nimmst das, was deine Freunde für dich tun, doch als zu selbstverständlich an" (DP, 190; "You take what your friends do for you too much for granted"; TT, 181).

Both K.'s ill-judged choice to let others wait and his inability to wait for others underline his poor timing: as the warden Willem already observed in chapter 1, he has no sense of the "richtigen Zeitpunkt," the right time. Prior to the trial his life was ruled by a rigid and utterly functional timetable that left no room for nonalienated relations and meaningful human interactions. In the course of the trial K.'s modern belief in self-determination is then gradually eroded: he turns from a temporal control freak into an untimely man who is out of sync with the timing of the court as well as the modern time regime that produced his type.

And so in Kafka's novel K.'s lack of presence symbolizes his loss of authority and growing sense of alienation from his habitual world. A salient example in this regard is his visit to the court offices in the company of the court usher the Sunday after his first hearing. As he is being led though the corridor of the attic rooms of the court, K. is overcome by an overwhelming sense of tiredness, which makes him implore the court usher to take him immediately back to the exit. Astonished that K. has already lost his sense of orientation, the court usher explains that he will have to wait until he has delivered a message. But we already know that K. is notoriously unable to wait for others. As a young woman fetches an armchair for K., another court employee who turns out to be the information man joins her. Even though the young woman points out that the information man has an answer to all questions, K. can barely follow this intermediary's explanations about the workings of the court. While such moments have often been read in terms of the protagonist's moral flaw, they also highlight the precariousness of the modern subject, who can no longer mobilize his attention from a stable subject position.[32] Looked at from this angle, the failure of Kafka's protagonists to stay attentive when it really matters has little to do with a moral flaw but much with the fact that distraction is "an effect of the many attempts to produce

32. On the question of guilt, see Hans H. Hiebel, "Schuld oder Scheinbarkeit der Schuld? Zu Kafkas Roman *Der Proceß*," in *Das Schuld-Problem bei Franz Kafka*, ed. Wolfgang Kraus and Norbert Winkler (Klosterneuburg: Böhlau, 1993), 95–117; Ritchie Robertson, "Reading the Clues: Franz Kafka, *Der Proceß*," in *The German Novel in the 20th Century: Beyond Realism*, ed. David Midgley (Edinburgh: Edinburgh University Press, 1993), 59–79; Klaus-Peter Philippi, "'K. lebte doch in einem Rechtsstaat': Franz Kafkas *Der Proceß*—ein Prozeß des Mißverstehens," in *Aufklärungen: Zur Literaturgeschichte der Moderne*, ed. Werner Frick (Tübingen: Niemeyer, 2003), 259–82.

attentiveness in human subjects."[33] Kafka employs the metaphor of a ship during a violent storm to give expression to K.'s crisis of orientation: he feels as if he were suffering seasickness on a rough sea and as if crashing waves were hitting against the wooden walls with thunder swelling up from the depths of the corridor (DP, 84). Having been led to the exit propped up by the young woman and the information man, K. is deprived of his sense of autonomy and violently made aware of his bodily reality, which appears to cause him a second trial (DP, 85). On the one hand, dyschronia gives expression to the crisis of the modern time regime that, in Kafka's world, can no longer guarantee control over the future. On the other hand, K.'s lack of presence of mind indicates a new temporal modality that, in the end, attunes him to the alternative unfolding of his trial.[34]

In sharp contrast to the opening scene, in which K. was surprised by his arrest, at the very end he awaits his executioners, who arrive about 9:00 p.m., the evening of his thirty-first birthday. Even though he was not notified that they would be coming, he sits in a chair near the door, dressed in black, slowly putting on new gloves and behaving as if he were expecting visitors. When his executioners arrive, he immediately stands up and asks whether they have come for him (DP, 236). K.'s timing at the end indicates his submission to a higher force. But this synchronization of clock time and metaphysical time that culminates in K's horrifying execution "like a dog" (as he himself describes it) stands for a brutal new order in which temporal efficiency services archaic practice.

---

33. Crary, *Suspensions of Perceptions*, 49.

34. This also explains why the novel no longer unfolds in the paradigm of the Bildungsroman (developmental novel) with its teleological biographical script but rather as a "Folge von Probeläufen" (a sequence of trial runs), which, as Gerhard Neumann observes, continually rewrites the opening scene. Gerhard Neumann, "Der Zauber des Anfangs und das 'Zögern vor der Geburt'—Kafkas Poetologie des 'riskantesten Augenblicks,'" in *Nach erneuter Lektüre: Franz Kafkas "Der Proceß,"* ed. Hans Dieter Zimmermann (Würzburg: Königshausen & Neumann, 1992), 128. Also Neumann, "'Blinde Parabel' oder Bildungsroman? Zur Struktur von Franz Kafkas *Proceß*-Fragment," in *Franz Kafka: Experte der Macht* (Munich: Hanser, 2012), 101–36.

Speed Politics in Robert Walser's Short Prose

In his study *Reading Berlin 1900*, the historian Peter Fritzsche analyzes the emergence of Berlin as a text-producing and text-consuming metropolis. By the turn of the century, the city had morphed from a provincial backwater into a modern metropolis, as the substantial growth of its population (from 400,000 inhabitants in 1848 to 2 million in 1905), the expansion of the city boundaries, and the development of a modern transport system and infrastructure make evident. "A rich stream of texts," comments Fritzsche, "guided and misguided its inhabitants, and, in large measure, fashioned the metropolitan experience."[35] On their daily journeys through the bustling city, Berliners encountered a myriad of print forms and images, in mass circulation newspapers, posters, advertisements on the omnipresent *Litfaßsäulen* (advertising pillars), schedules, announcements, and traffic signs, which, in Fritzsche's words, brought forth a "word city" that overlaid the built city with heteroglossic text.[36] New print technologies had boosted the newspaper industry in Imperial Germany: in the period from 1881 to 1897 the market expanded from 2,437 printed daily papers to 3,405,[37] and in Berlin alone approximately ninety newspapers were in circulation.[38] By 1920 the three main publishers—Ullstein, Scherl, and Mosse—all published midday, evening, and night editions on top of their regular morning editions of the *Berliner Morgenpost*, the *Berliner Lokal-Anzeiger*, and the liberal *Berliner Tagblatt*, in which the Swiss modernist writer Robert Walser published his feuilletons and short prose sketches.[39] The metropolitan city thus constituted itself through a continually evolving

---

35. Peter Fritzsche, *Reading Berlin 1900* (Cambridge, MA: Harvard University Press, 1996), 1.

36. Fritzsche, *Reading Berlin 1900*, 5.

37. Werner Faulstich, *Medienwandel im Industrie- und Massenzeitalter 1830–1900* (Göttingen: Vandenhoeck & Ruprecht, 2004), 31.

38. Christian Jäger and Erhard Schütz, *Städtebilder zwischen Literatur und Journalismus: Wien, Berlin und das Feuilleton der Weimarer Republik* (Wiesbaden: Deutscher Universitätsverlag, 1999), 9–10.

39. Fritzsche, *Reading Berlin 1900*, 29.

text world that orchestrated the exciting and unnerving dynamic of modernity through a polyphony of dissonant voices.

The prime locus for the continual traffic between the city as lived texture and published text was the literary feuilleton, that is, short prose piece, which appeared "unter dem Strich" (below the line), topographically separated from the more important news items.[40] By around 1900 the feuilleton had established itself as a modern genre that was especially suited to capturing the fast-paced dynamic of modernity. It secured its place in the newspaper by taking care of seemingly nonpolitical affairs, including articles on fashion, art, and culture, and everyday observations and subjective impressions about modern life.[41] Precisely because it seemed so marginal to mainstream political news coverage, it became an experimental field where the boundaries between fiction and autobiography, reality and imagination, and the city as material environment and the city as text were constantly crossed. As a lively forum for cultural commentary, the feuilleton thus occupies a central role in the archive of modernity's cultural history, tracking, as Christian Jäger and Erhard Schütz put it, "the self-perception of the age."[42] As a "genre beyond established genre boundaries,"[43]

---

40. See Günter Oesterle, "'Unter dem Strich': Skizze einer Kulturpoetik des Feuilletons," in *Das schwierige neunzehnte Jahrhundert: Germanistische Tagung zum 65. Geburtstag von Eda Sagarra im August 1998*, ed. Jürgen Barkhoff et al. (Tübingen: Niemeyer, 2000), 235.

41. The author of a detailed history of the *Frankfurter Zeitung*, published in 1911, highlights the enhanced importance of the feuilleton as a dynamic form that now competed with the *Leitartikel* (the lead article) for the reader's attention. *Geschichte der Frankfurter Zeitung von 1856 bis 1906*, ed. Verlag der Frankfurter Zeitung (Frankfurt a. M.: August Osterrieth, 1911), 919.

42. Christian Jäger and Erhard Schütz, eds., *Glänzender Asphalt: Berlin im Feuilleton der Weimarer Republik* (Berlin: Fannei & Waltz, 1994), 336. In the same vein Andreas Huyssen observes that "the modern miniature as a specific mode of writing may indeed be more central to the new in literary modernism than the novel or poetry." Andreas Huyssen, "Modernist Miniatures: Literary Snapshots of Urban Spaces," *PMLA* 122/1 (2007): 29.

43. Thomas Althaus, Wolfgang Bunzel, and Dirk Göttsche, "Ränder, Schwellen, Zwischenräume: Zum Standort Kleiner Prosa im Literatursystem der Moderne," in *Kleine Prosa: Theorie und Geschichte eines Textfeldes im Literatursystem der Moderne*, ed. Thomas Althaus, Wolfgang Bunzel, and Dirk Göttsche (Tübingen: Niemeyer, 2007), ix. See also Dirk Göttsche, *Kleine Prosa in Moderne und Gegenwart* (Münster: Aschendorff, 2006).

the miniature prose sketch defined itself programmatically through a heightened self-reflexivity that accentuated the subjective experience of modernity. For Thomas Althaus, Wolfgang Bunzel, and Dirk Göttsche the genre's intrinsic marginality is its driving engine: by combining cultural analysis with fleeting everyday observations and a heightened self-reflexivity the genre became the playing field par excellence for literary innovation in German modernism.[44]

Beyond such poetological considerations, the boom of modern short prose around 1900 has to be understood as "a reflection of an accelerated pace of life in the fragmented post-metaphysical universe of modernity—and as a critical response to this very experience: an antidote to the temporal logic of modernity that reappreciates the living moment (Augenblick)."[45] Between 1900 and the 1930s, the feuilleton and the genre of short prose became a playing field for an exploration of the aesthetic possibilities of both acceleration and desynchronization through slowness or lateness. While an accelerated mode of being was celebrated as a way of energizing one's subjectivity through the exposure to a new intensity of stimuli, lateness and slowness were simultaneously discovered as authentic expressions of an autonomous subjectivity that had salvaged the ability to step outside the demands of the relentless modern timetable.

Robert Walser, the Swiss avant-garde author and writer of short prose par excellence, moved to Berlin in 1905, where he produced more than 100 short prose pieces, which appeared in leading newspapers and journals, including *Die Schaubühne*, *Die Neue Rundschau*, and the *Berliner Tagblatt*.[46] These pieces cover a broad

---

44. Althaus, Bunzel, and Göttsche, "Ränder, Schwellen, Zwischenräume," xx.

45. Dirk Göttsche, "Epistemology, Poetics, and Time in Modernist Short Prose around 1900," in *Time in German Literature and Culture, 1900–2015: Between Acceleration and Slowness*, ed. Anne Fuchs and Jonathan Long (Basingstoke: Macmillan Palgrave, 2016), 72.

46. His brother Karl, who had already made his name as a stage designer for Max Reinhardt, introduced him to the literary and cultural elite, including the publishers Bruno Cassirer and Samuel Fischer and the head of the Berlin Secession Max Liebermann. Karl Walser produced the set for Reinhardt's production of *A Midsummer Night's Dream*, which used a revolving stage for the first time. See Bernhard Echte and Andreas Meier, eds., *Die Brüder Karl und Robert Walser: Maler und Dichter* (Zurich: Rothenhäusler Verlag Stäfa, 1990), 178–82.

territory, ranging from fictionalized literary portraits, unconventional reviews of theatrical productions, short dialogic sketches, reimaginings of literary characters, and sketches about food and fashion to topographical explorations of the city environment. Walser was particularly interested in Berlin as a site of an astonishing and fast-paced modernity. In pieces such as "Aschinger," "Tiergarten," "Gebirgshallen," and "Berlin W" he experimented with an ephemeral aesthetics that took its cue from impressionism and the figure of the flâneur. A typical example is his prose piece "Friedrichstraße," which appeared in *Die Neue Rundschau* in August 1909 and depicts the buzzing street life from the perspective of the pedestrian. The piece opens with a vertical upward perspective that is drawn toward large-lettered advertisements at roof level before zooming in on the street as metropolitan site of a ceaseless flow of movement. Walser's description combines elements of a metropolitan modernity that is designed to create visual spectacle with a nature imagery that captures an invigorating vitality:

> Bis zu den Dächern hinauf und über die Dächer noch hinaus schweben und kleben Reklamen. Große Buchstaben fallen in die Augen. Und immer gehen hier Menschen. Noch nie, seit sie ist, hat in dieser Straße das Leben aufgehört zu leben. Hier ist das Herz, die unaufhörlich atmende Brust des großstädtischen Wesens. Hier atmet es hoch auf und tief nieder, als wenn das Leben selber über seinem Schritt und Tritt unangenehm beengt wäre. Hier ist die Quelle, der Bach der Fluß und das Meer der Bewegungen.[47]

> Right up to roof level and even beyond advertisements hover and cling. Large lettering catches the eye. And people incessantly walk along. Never since this street has existed has life come to a standstill here. It is the heart, the continually breathing bosom of metropolitan organism. Here life itself breathes deeply in and out as if it were uncomfortably restricted on every step of the way. Here is the source, the stream the river and the sea of all movement.

The typically Walserian anthropomorphism evokes the street as a theater of a vibrant totality of life. In "Friedrichstraße" social

---

47. Robert Walser, *Sämtliche Werke in Einzelausgaben*, ed. Jochen Greven (Frankfurt a. Main: Suhrkamp, 1986), 3:76; cited as SW in the text. All translations of Walser's prose pieces are mine unless otherwise indicated.

antagonisms and differences are neutralized by way of an organic proximity of people and things. For Walser the choreography of crowd movement on the street produces a new form of social tolerance and acceptance, "weil jeder einzelne, durch den Zwang des zusammengeknebelten Verkehrs genötigt, ohne Zaudern alles, was er hört und sieht, billigen muß" (SW 3:77; because by force of the tightly controlled and gagging traffic everyone must willynilly tolerate everything that he hears and sees). The intensity and speed of the traffic enforces new forms of mutual toleration in the public domain: "Jeder Bettler, Gauner, Unhold usw. ist hier Mitmensch und muß einstweilen, weil alles schiebt, stößt und drängt, als etwas Mithinzugehöriges geduldet werden." (SW 3:78; Each beggar, crook or ogre is a fellow creature here and because everybody keeps pushing, elbowing and shoving has to be tolerated for the time being as part of the crowd.) Rather than a locus of anonymity and alienation, the street is the true "Heimat der Nichtswürdigen, der Kleinen" (SW 3:78; home of the undeserving, the little people). It is not moral conviction or political consensus that inspires this new form of tolerance but merely the steady footfall of rushed pedestrians and traffic flow patterns. The small form is particularly suited to paying attention to the little people even in their metropolitan massification.

At the same time the production of a specifically metropolitan code of toleration also comes with new modes of self-discipline and uniformity that ache for release. Friedrichstraße is thus shown to morph at night into a titillating stage for entertainment, unleashing pent-up passions. As people chase their unfulfilled desires, "ein wollüstig auf und nieder atmender Körpertraum" (SW 3:79; a sensual bodily dream, breathing up and down) descends on the street. With this final and strikingly anthropomorphic image Walser envisages the urban street as a vital organism pulsing with the flow of desire and life.

While "Friedrichstraße" unfolds a chronological schedule that takes the reader from daytime activity to the electrifying nightlife, "Guten Tag, Riesin!" (Good Morning, Giant!) delves into the polychronicity of urban life in the early morning hours: here, the pathways of blue-collar workers, small salesmen, early travelers, and girls from all walks of life cross with an assortment of late night revelers who are being catapulted out into the streets (SW 3:65). Such dissonances invite fleeting engagement that favors the fragmentary detail over the totalizing panoramic view:

> Immer gehst du und flüchtige Blicke für alles, für Bewegliches und Feststehendes, für Droschken, die träge fortrumpeln, für die Elektrische, die jetzt zu fahren beginnt, von der herab Menschen dich ansehen, für den stupiden Helm eines Schutzmannes, für einen Menschen mit zerrissenen Hosen . . . , für alles, wie du selber für alles ein flüchtiges Augenmerk bist. (SW 3:65)

> You are always walking along fleetingly noting everything that moves or stays still, coaches that sluggishly rumble along, people looking down at you from the tram which is just starting up, the stupid helmet of the policeman, a man with torn trousers . . . , everything, as you yourself are for the others, only a fleeting glance.

The impressionistic annotation of a world in flux takes the place of the authoritative description of a stable urban physiognomy. As Peter Fritzsche comments, the feuilletonists of the early twentieth century "did not nail down city matters but merely alerted readers to detail and fluctuation. As a result, the city became equally unknowable and equally astonishing to all its readers."[48]

"Guten Tag, Riesin!" singles out the observing self in the crowd by addressing this self in the second-person singular. By contrast, Walser's prose piece "Auf der Elektrischen" (On the Tram) adopts the perspective of the impersonal "man" (one) to foreground the experience of urban massification. The piece, which describes the "billiges Vergnügen, Elektrische zu fahren" (the cheap pleasure of a tram ride), appeared in the morning edition of the *Berliner Tagblatt* on 28 April 1908: in all likelihood, it was placed in the early edition to catch the attention of commuters traveling to work.[49] Walser's narrative perspective alternates here between identifying collective

---

48. Fritzsche, *Reading Berlin 1900*, 94.
49. Robert Walser, "Auf der Elektrischen," in *Kritische Ausgabe sämtlicher Drucke*, ed. Wolfram Groddeck and Barbara von Reibnitz, vol. 3.1: *Drucke im Berliner Tagblatt*, ed. Hans-Joachim Heerde (Basel: Stroemfeld/Schwabe, 2013), 22; cited as AdE.

patterns of behavior among the passengers and the self's ultrasubjective perception. The piece mimics a tram journey by depicting how the tram arrives and the passengers, including the narrating self, board the carriage: the self immediately adopts the mask of everyman by employing the impersonal "man" (one) throughout. However, this anthropological perspective is soon disrupted when the self announces that he is musically gifted because melodies and songs are playing inside his head and, indeed, that he may have morphed into a new Mozart. Evidently, Walser adopts an ironic tone here that highlights the gap between urban sameness, on the one hand, and a heightened individuality in the city environment, on the other. The ensuing description of the tram journey emphasizes, first, the uniformity of the experience: standing on the platform at the back of the tram, the self is shown to look straight ahead like most passengers. The journey is lacking in excitement because of its length and the passengers' immobile position: feeling increasingly bored, the self is actively looking for distractions by studying the face of the conductor before gazing straight ahead: "Ich muß bekennen: im Gradausschauen habe ich es bereits bis zu einer gewissen technischen Vollendung gebracht." (AdE, 23; I must admit, I have developed a certain technical perfection in gazing straight ahead.) As a mechanical means of public transportation the tram dictates a quasi-Taylorian disciplinary mode of engagement with the environment: it enforces the forward-looking perspective of the age of mechanical acceleration. Faced with such enforced uniformity, Walser's self then attempts to regain a sense of autonomy by breaking the rules and engaging the conductor in conversation or by embarking on "eine kleine Rundreise mit den Augen" (a short round trip with the eyes) on the lookout for visual distractions (AdE, 24). Walser's piece about the tram ride undercuts the common association of new technologies with titillating speed: even though the tram was a relatively fast means of transportation around the turn of the twentieth century, here it engenders a sense of boredom. The uniform practice of *Gradausschauen* mobilizes resistance in the traveling self, who, by undertaking a round trip with his eyes, discovers interesting everyday details that, in turn, engender further visual exploration of the urban environment in flux.

Besides delving into urban modes of behavior, Walser's prose
pieces explore the transformative effects of modern speed politics
in other settings. In Walser's great prose narrative *Der Spaziergang*
(*The Walk*) of 1917, the reader encounters a perambulating self
whose leisurely excursion into the suburbs of an unnamed Swiss
town is replicated by a meandering narrative voice that is evidently
unperturbed by the economy of speed.[50] Surrounded by a working
population that has internalized the time management of modern
life and is therefore quite hostile to this walking misfit, the Walserian peripatetic self stimulates his poetic imagination through
deliberate desynchronization. When a passing worker on a bicycle
accuses him of being out for a walk again during regular working
hours, the self waves to him, calmly walking on "ohne mich im Ger-
ingsten über das Ertapptwerden zu ärgern" (SW 5:18; "without the
least annoyance at having been found out"; TW, 62). And when
the tax inspector later challenges his application for tax exemption
because he is always out for a walk, he delivers a theatrical speech
that defends the principles of poetic perambulation (SW 5:50; TW,
85). The Walserian self emphasizes the emotional connectedness
with the living world that is brought about by an intrinsically democratic mode of perception that aims to do justice to all phenomena, be they small or large. However, it would be a mistake to read
Walser's perambulations in terms of an antimodern turn: instead
of relating the measured walk that he promised at the outset (SW
5:15), the narrator-walker strategically employs digression, mise en
abyme, and a narrative pace that, at significant moments, mimics
urban behavior and modes of perception. Toward the end of his
walk, the Walserian self enumerates the things that make up the
exterior world:

Ferner an Läden: Papier-, Fleisch-, Uhren-, Schuh-, Hut-, Eisen-,
Tuch-, Kolonialwaren-, Spezerei-, Galanterie-, Mercerie-, Bäcker- und

---

50. Robert Walser, *Der Spaziergang*, in SW 5:7–77. A slightly edited version
appeared in *Seeland*. See SW 7:83–151. For an English translation of the first edition, see Robert Walser, *The Walk and Other Stories*, trans. Christopher Middleton (London: Serpent's Tail, 1992), 54–104; cited as TW in the text.

Zuckerbäckerläden. Und überall, auf allen diesen Dingen, liebe Abend-sonne. Ferner viel Lärm und Geräusch, Schulen und Schullehrer, letz-tere mit Gewicht und Würde im Gesicht, Landschaft, Luft und etliche Malerei. Ferner nicht zu übersehen oder zu vergessen: Aufschriften und Ankündigungen, wie "Persil" oder "Maggis unübertroffene Suppenrol-len" oder "Continental-Gummiabsatz enorm haltbar" oder "Grund-stück zu verkaufen" oder "Die beste Milchschokolade" oder ich weiß wahrhaftig nicht, was sonst noch alles. Wollte man aufzählen, bis alles getreulich aufgezählt wäre, so käme man an kein Ende. (SW 5:70)

Further, in the way of shops; paper, meat, clock, shoe, hat, iron, cloth, grocery, spice, fancy goods, millinery, bakery, and confectionary shops. And everywhere on all these things delicious evening sun. Further, much noise and uproar, school and schoolteachers, the latter with weighty and dignified faces, an air and much else that is picturesque. Further, not to be overlooked or forgotten: signs and advertisements, as "Per-sil," "Maggi's Unsurpassed Soups," or "Continental Rubber Heels Enormously Durable," or "Freehold Property for sale," or "The Best Milk Chocolate," and I honestly don't know what else. If one were to count until everything had been accurately enumerated, one would never reach the end. (TW, 99–100)

Instead of delivering "tiefsinnige Landschaftsschilderungen" (SW 5:68; "profound landscape descriptions"; TW, 102) the walker-narrator creates here a list of all kinds of things, ranging from ma-terial objects to auditory impressions, that are no longer integrated into a coherent whole. While this enumeration parodies the mod-ern preoccupation with taxonomies of knowledge, the passage also gestures to the capitalist economy of attention that transforms the walker willy-nilly into a potential consumer: even though he ad-vocates a quasi-mystical union with the smallest things (SW 5:51), here he succumbs to the fetishist appeal of the consumer product. In the end, it is no longer the romantic sunset but the advertisement billboards that captivate his attention.

Walser's fascination with modern speed politics is particularly striking in his prose pieces that place his perambulating self inside railway stations. In "Bahnhof II," which was written during his Bern years in the 1920s, the railway building is introduced as a space "der das Maschinenzeitalter veranschaulicht und etwas Internationales verkörpert" (SW 20:76; which represents the machine age and embodies internationalism). As a node in "einem weitverzweigte(n) Bildungs- und Zivilisationsnetz" (SW 20:76; in

a branched-out network of education and civilization) it intercon-
nects the province with European metropolitan centers. A busy and
modern transport hub, the railway station is the right setting for
the performance of autonomy through the self's leisurely perambulation. In "Bahnhof I" the self describes how he enjoys stroll-
ing among the crowd of hurried travelers before embarking on an
imaginary trip:

> Ich war der Meinung, der Bahnhof eigne sich zum darin Spazierenge-
> hen gut, und was eine Reihe von Plakaten betraf, an denen ich vor-
> beidefilierte, fand ich den Vierwaldstättersee vor, den anmutige, duftige
> Ufer auszeichnen. Die Stadt Wiborg war samt ihren Altertümlichkeiten
> wirkungsvoll abgebildet, Luzern bei Nacht mit Tausenden von Lichtern
> ergab ein anschauenswertes Bild. Einer Kathedrale in England widmete
> ich mit Vergnügen meine achtungspendende Aufmerksamkeit. Eine
> französische Stadtwiedergabe ließ mich an die Vortrefflichkeit gewisser
> bürgerlicher Romane denken. (SW 20:73)

> I was of the opinion that the railway station is a great spot for per-
> ambulating, and as regards a series of posters that I was passing by,
> I saw Lake Vierwaldstätter with its charming balmy shores. The city
> of Wiborg was depicted well with all its antiquities; Lucerne at night
> presented a most pleasant view. I dedicated with great pleasure my re-
> spectful attention to a cathedral in England. The representation of a
> French city made me think of the greatness of some bourgeois novels.

This imaginary encounter with tourist sites supersedes here the need
for a real trip to new places. It is striking how the passage transfers the bipedal mobility of *Der Spaziergang* and other peripatetic
texts onto the mobility of the flâneur's eyes, which travel swiftly from
poster to poster in a brief package tour inside the railway station. It
is precisely the flâneur's decelerated movement around the railway
station that makes possible an accelerated journey through Europe.
While the ironic description of the tourist sites that are displayed on
these posters points to the commodification of the desire for authenticity in modern tourism, as analyzed by Hans Magnus Enzensberger,
Walser deconstructs the opposition between kitsch and authenticity.[51]

---

51. Hans Magnus Enzensberger, *Eine Theorie des Tourismus* (1958), in *Einzelheiten I & II* (Hamburg: Spiegel Verlag, 2006), 177–203.

And so the posters of various tourist sites fulfill the same function
as the idyllic landscape descriptions in *Der Spaziergang* and other
Walser texts: they give expression to the desire for a timeless otherness that, however, remains unattainable precisely because the movement of this mobile subjectivity is under the spell of modern speed
politics.

From Lateness to Latency: Sigmund Freud

In the texts discussed so far lateness and slowness feature not only
as reactive temporal modes that aim to correct the modern intoxication with speed. They are also manifestations of a broader aesthetic intervention that disrupts modern speed politics and the
linearity of time by bringing to the fore alternate trajectories and
temporalities. A qualitatively new understanding of the problematic of lateness emerges with psychoanalysis. Freud removed the
debate on lateness from its specifically modern context by turning
it into a universal category of both onto- and phylogenetic development. The idea of lateness in Freud's work develops alongside
his theory of sexuality. In *Drei Abhandlungen zur Sexualtheorie*
(*Three Essays on Sexuality*, 1905) Freud argued that the Oedipal
phase is normally superseded by a latency period in which the early
sexual drives of the small child are divested of their sexual object in
favor of a rechanneling of these energies toward new aims.[52] A process of sublimation, which helps to put in place the ethical restric-
tions that are governed by the superego, accompanies this period
of latency. Lateness and its topological equivalent, latency, act as
powerful psychological drivers of the integration of the primary
drives under the command of a higher censor, the superego. However, while latency thus plays a major role in the process of indi-
viduation, it gains an even more pronounced function in Freud's
trauma theory. In their *Studien über Hysterie* (*Studies on Hysteria*,
1895) Freud and Breuer had first traced the condition of hysteria

---

52. Sigmund Freud, *Drei Abhandlungen zur Sexualtheorie*, in *Gesammelte
Werke*, ed. Anna Freud et al. (Frankfurt a. Main: Fischer, 1999), 5:27–145.

back to experiences that had a traumatic effect rather than to physiological causes.[53] Although in his early work Freud adhered to the seduction theory based on a real sexual event in early childhood, even at this point he maintained that trauma was the effect of a latency period.[54] For Freud it was not the events as such, but rather the delayed recall of a first event through a later memory trigger that created the conditions for trauma. Latency is simultaneously the precondition for the manifestation of a traumatic disorder and a protective mechanism that allows individuals to cope with undigested experiences and legacies. Only once individuals have reached adolescence can they understand the sexual meaning of early childhood experiences. And so that latency carries within it a temporal structure that makes one's past accessible only through deferred and retrospective acts of interpretation. By ascribing such a significant role to the notion of an incubation period in the etiology of trauma, Freud implicitly challenged the prevalent culture of immediacy with its strong attraction to surfaces and spectacles, as expressed in much of fin de siècle culture.[55] For Jonathan Crary the dismantling of the separation of appearance and reality was one of the price tags of a modernity that invested hugely in the titillating immediacy of fleeting sensations. Freud, however, confronts such cultural fascination with immediacy by interpreting all present appearances as mere symptoms of a buried past. "Nachträglichkeit," a term that is difficult to translate (often rendered in French as "après-coup" and in English as "deferred action"), is thus an

---

53. Sigmund Freud, *Studien über Hysterie*, in *Gesammelte Werke*, 1:75–312.

54. "According to the temporal logic of what Freud called *Nachträglichkeit*, or 'deferred action'," comments Ruth Leys, "trauma was constituted by a relationship between two events or experiences—a first event that was not necessarily traumatic because it came too early in the child's development to be understood and assimilated, and a second event that also was not inherently traumatic but that triggered a memory of the first event that only then was given traumatic meaning and hence repressed." Ruth Leys, *Trauma: A Genealogy* (Chicago: University of Chicago Press, 2000), 20.

55. On the staging of reality as spectacle without depth and the commodification of attention, see Jonathan Crary's excellent interpretation of Seurat's painting *Parade de Cirque*. Crary, *Suspensions of Perceptions*, 150–279.

indication of an inescapable connectedness with the depth of one's personal history.[56]

Over time, Freud developed the notion of latency into a generative principle that drives cultural development and the process of civilization.[57] This is most evident in his last and perhaps most problematic book, *Der Mann Moses und die monotheistische Religion* (*Moses and Monotheism*, 1939), which was written in the context of the National Socialist persecution of the Jews and his own exile.[58] Debating the question of anti-Semitism by way of a highly speculative examination of the emergence of monotheism, Freud argued that Moses was an Egyptian and a follower of the Aton religion, a strict form of monotheism that the Egyptian people rejected because of its ethical harshness. Leaving Egypt, Moses imposed monotheism and the rite of circumcision on the Jewish people, whom he led to Canaan. In Freud's dramatic narrative the Jews then killed their overly demanding father figure, before joining up with related tribes and accepting the worship of the God Yahweh. Although the memory of Moses was submerged for generations after the murder, it survived latently among the Levites, the people of Moses. By keeping Mosaic traditions alive, they tried to forget their feelings of guilt. For generations, the Mosaic tradition existed only in repressed form, but continued to exercise latent influence over the cult of Yahweh, which eventually collapsed into the Mosaic God. Freud lends additional urgency to his model of cultural development by arguing that the three steps—the

---

56. See Sigrid Weigel, "The Symptomatology of a Universalized Concept of Trauma: On the Failing of Freud's Reading of *Tasso* in the Trauma of History," *New German Critique* 90 (2003): 85–94.

57. See Anne Fuchs, "Defending Lateness: Deliberations on Acceleration, Attention, and Lateness, 1900–2000," in "Figuring Lateness," ed. Karen Leeder, special issue, *New German Critique* 125/42 (2015): 31–48.

58. Sigmund Freud, *Der Mann Moses und die monotheistische Religion*, in *Gesammelte Werke*, 16:101–246. On Freud's method of speculation and his original denomination of the essay as a historical novel, see Yosef Hayim Yerushalmi, *Freud's Moses: Judaism Terminable and Interminable* (New Haven: Yale University Press, 1991). On monotheism, see Jan Assmann, *Die mosaische Unterscheidung oder der Preis des Monotheismus* (Munich: Hanser, 2003).

killing of Moses, followed by a latency period and the return of the repressed—had repeated an earlier trauma concerning all humankind: the killing of the primal father by his sons in the primal horde, a thesis that he had already put forward in *Totem und Tabu* (*Totem and Taboo*, 1912). By making the murder of Moses a symptomatic return of the repressed killing of the primal father, Freud converts history into myth or anthropology. On the one hand, this eclipsed history at the very moment when Jews were being persecuted. Freud's hesitant style and his tortured prefaces in *Der Mann Moses* indicate a heightened sense of anxiety about the direction of this project. On the other hand, the idea that the killing of Moses was a collective and subconscious act of repetition introduces the notion of the *longue durée* of traumatic memory as a driving force in history. Freud thereby turned latency into a dormant deposit account with massive transgenerational interest. Repression and repetition are the key devices that pass down the memory of earlier experiences to later generations. As Jan Assmann has pointed out, repression achieves an encryption of this legacy, forestalling a simple working-through; repetition complements this by ensuring the transgenerational transmission of trauma. In this way, Freud's speculative narrative about Moses highlighted the cultural function of guilt, repression, and remembrance in the history of religion and in the history of civilization.[59]

Freud's theoretical elaborations resonate across a wide range of literary texts that profile latency and the return of the repressed. Two outstanding examples in this regard published around the time of *Totem und Tabu* are Robert Musil's *Die Verwirrungen des Zöglings Törleß* (*The Confusions of Young Törless*, 1906) and

---

59. Jan Assmann, *Religion and Cultural Memory: Ten Studies*, trans. Rodney Livingstone (Stanford, CA: Stanford University Press, 2006), 233. Assmann's view diverges from Freud's in one important respect: unlike Freud, who views all cultural objectifications in terms of symptomatic disguise of a latent and repressed reality, Assmann argues that writing itself can be a locus of latency. He writes: "It becomes a place of refuge to which the repressed and the inopportune can retreat, and a background from which what is forgotten can re-emerge, a place of latency" (99).

Thomas Mann's *Der Tod in Venedig* (*Death in Venice*, 1912).[60] In both narratives the protagonists' personal transgressions flow from dark cultural undercurrents, which, as a return of the repressed, haunt Europe's modernizing project. Both narratives employ what one might call "a geography of latency," which punctures the surface appearance of all things.[61]

In fin de siècle discourse lateness emerges as a flexible trope that allows for extremely divergent evaluations of compressed time as modernity's main resource. Freud departed from this paradigm by decoupling lateness from its modern currency and transforming it into the notion of latency. With this decisive step, Freud remodels lateness from a category of desynchronized time into a generative principle of cultural development. While the modernizer eagerly embraces accelerated speed as a means of achieving technological and cultural progress, Freud's reading suggests that it is above all the *longue durée* of culture that fuels the process of civilization. Lateness is neither a moral failure nor a psychic mechanism for the achievement of an autonomous subjectivity, but rather a very powerful, subconscious mode of cultural encryption that creates diachronic connectivity with the past.

Conclusion

My analysis of a wide range of temporal positions in German cultural discourse from the 1870s into the late 1930s when Freud wrote his last major work shows that, despite the modern

---

60. Thomas Mann, *Der Tod in Venedig und andere Erzählungen* (Frankfurt a. Main: Fischer, 1987); Robert Musil, *Die Verwirrungen des Zöglings Törless*, in *Gesammelte Werke in neun Bänden*, ed. Adolf Frisé (Reinbek: Rowohlt, 1981), 6:7–140.

61. Musil connects the uncanny doubleness of all things with Indian Buddhism. Likewise, in *Death in Venice*, a web of uncanny symbols unfolds that is associated with the sirocco, the wind that travels up the south/north axis but carries Indian cholera. For a nuanced analysis of Mann's cultural geography, see Elizabeth Boa, "Global Intimations: Cultural Geography in *Buddenbrooks*, *Tonio Kröger*, and *Der Tod in Venedig*," *Oxford German Studies* 35 (2006): 21–33.

investment in the future as the horizon of man's self-realization, this period is by no means solely in the grip of speed. To be sure, the established view of modernity rightly emphasizes the transformation of the modern temporal experience in terms of a seismic paradigm shift that, facilitated by a wave of technological revolutions, replaced a cyclical temporal consciousness with the idea of linear temporal progression. While the former drew on the past to make sense of the imminent future, which was not yet separated from the present, the latter devalues the past in favor of a radically different future that leaves behind both past and present. Reinhart Koselleck has shown that the experience of time needed to be denaturalized before a modern historical consciousness could emerge that then understood history as taking place in the space between the past and the future.[62] Modern temporal consciousness differs from earlier notions of temporality because it projects progress onto a radically different future that requires urgent intervention and planning. "The shortening of the time spans necessary for gaining new experiences that the technical-industrial world forces upon us," explains Koselleck, "can be described a historical acceleration."[63] Dirk Göttsche emphasizes the rich metaphoric of time that marks German literary and intellectual discourse from around 1800: terms such as *Zeitgeist, Zeitangst, Zeitgeschichte, Zeitnot*, and so on entered public discourse,[64] articulating a new historical consciousness that registered its own contemporaneity "in terms of a qualitatively new, self-transcending temporality."[65] Capitalism was the main driver in this new economy of time, which, as Marx observed, annihilated space with time. And so speed became what Enda Duffy calls "the desire par excellence in Western culture."[66]

---

62. Koselleck, "Time and History," 100–114.

63. Koselleck, "Time and History," 113.

64. Göttsche, "Introduction," 4. See also Dirk Göttsche, *Zeit im Roman: Literarische Zeitreflexion und die Geschichte des Zeitromans im späten 18. und im 19. Jahrhundert* (Munich: Wilhelm Fink, 2001).

65. Osborne, *The Politics of Time*, 15.

66. Duffy, *The Speed Handbook*, 35.

Speed was "fostered and tolerated to reconcile human subjects to their lot as actors in a 'dynamic' capitalist economic milieu. Speed, intimately woven into a new paradigm of the modern subject's nexus of desires, becomes the new opiate and the new (after)taste of movement as power."[67]

Against this backdrop, this chapter analyzed how modernist authors, intellectuals, and filmmakers articulate, dissect, and displace the modern fascination with speed, even when they overtly celebrate its thrills. To be sure, the *Zeitroman* of the nineteenth century already explored the sociopolitical consequences of modern temporalization. But the aesthetic potential of modern time consciousness was only fully discovered through modernist experiments with all kinds of (narrative) speeds and modes in different settings and through different genres. The double encoding of technology in Fritz Lang's *Metropolis* and the filmic representation of the spectacle of speed alongside the anxiety-inducing images of cogs and wheels in Walter Ruttmann's *Berlin: Sinfonie der Großstadt* are cases in point: while both aesthetically celebrate technologically enabled new visual pleasure, they simultaneously enmesh anxiety about the uncontrollable effects of technology with the thrilling experience of speed. In the domain of literature then the modern fascination with and ambivalence toward modern time finds expression in two genres: the modernist novel and modern short prose. Whereas the first gravitates toward length and fairly plotless narration, as in the great modernist writers from Woolf, Joyce, and Proust to Musil and Mann, the latter attempts to capture the ephemeral experience of a reality in flux. I touched on Mann's *Zauberberg* because this monumental novel articulates Castorp's subjective and increasingly pathological experience of circular or stagnant time through an extreme aesthetic of slowness that approximates narrative time and narrated time. Long dialogues, extensive descriptions, and analeptic renditions of

---

67. Duffy, *The Speed Handbook*, 35.

memories create a slow-motion effect that suspends the politics of speed in the faraway flatland. From a Nietzschean perspective, the retarded movement and slow speed in the world of the Berghof would be symptomatic of a crippling lateness that for Nietzsche had emaciated modern culture. At the end of the novel, historical time then reasserts itself violently with the outbreak of the First World War. Besides Nietzsche it was Freud who provided the theoretical scaffolding for this modern pathology of time: from Freud's perspective, the outbreak of war marks the return of the repressed after a period of latency.

It is essential to emphasize, however, that the modernist engagement with these temporal tropes remains profoundly ambivalent: Castorp's absorption into the world of the Berghof may be pathological from the perspective of the disciplinary modern time regime. However, on the level of discourse it leads to a mode of narration that foregrounds how space and time are filtered through consciousness. Besides continually evaluating Castorp's experience of time and space from an omniscient perspective, the narrator immerses the reader in Castorp's subjectivity through a focalized perspectivism that brings into view a composite reality that is overlaid by memories, reflections, and desire. The narratologically produced experience of *ästhetische Eigenzeit* pushes against the linearity of modern time. A similar ambivalence characterizes Kafka's exploration of time in *Der Verschollene* and *Der Proceß*: at plot level Kafka's protagonists are always punished for their inability to keep time; on the level of discourse, however, their apparent distractions can bring forth glimpses of fulfilled time or *Eigenzeit*. Rossmann's absorption by the never-ending traffic patterns of New York City or Josef K.'s theatrical reenactment of his arrest in front of Fräulein Bürstner exemplify such rare moments. In *Der Proceß* Kafka employs a mode of narration that overlays the overt realism with symbolic meaning. The guards, lawyers, and judges that make up the world of the court are simultaneously representatives of the modern bureaucracy as well as mediators of an absolute metaphysical order beyond human control. And so it is that Josef K. (and the reader) keeps misreading these doubly encoded signs. Besides staging the clash between the modern and the metaphysical, Kafka also exposes the inherently contradictory effect of modern time: on the one hand, it subjugates the modern self under the rule of the clock, thereby producing the type of utilitarian and impoverished human relations that prevail in Josef K.'s life. On the other, it equips modern man with a false sense of autonomy and hubris, which the trial then exposes as unfounded in the most cruel way.

The texts discussed in this chapter all employ tropes of attention and distraction to explore new conditions of subjectivity in the context of accelerating modernity. The fragmentation of the visual field emerged as a major problem in philosophy, sociology, psychology, pedagogy, and the medical disciplines.[68] By the end of the nineteenth century the problem of attention had become "part of a dense network of texts and techniques around which the truth of perception was organized and structured."[69] In Simmel's discussion, modern subjectivity adapts to the relentless onslaught by external stimuli in the metropolitan environment via a selective attentiveness that protects the self from being overwhelmed. For Simmel attention is both a social and a psychic technique that gives birth to the blasé metropolitan self. In contrast to this disciplinary effect of attention on the impersonal modern subject, writers of modern short prose often stage the dialectic interplay between attention and distraction to foreground a mercurial and highly mobile modern subjectivity. Robert Walser's short prose pieces from his time in Berlin, and his Biel and Bern years, reclaim individuality through a choreography of mobility that exploits the aesthetic possibilities of modern speed politics. In Walser's prose pieces both speed and slowness can give rise to ultrasubjective perceptions of the environment, regardless of whether the context is urban or not. Walser's grammar of mobility articulates both the exhilarating experience of modernity and the commodification of perception by capitalism.

---

68. See Crary, *Suspensions of Perceptions*, 17–46.
69. Crary, *Suspensions of Perceptions*, 22.

What this chapter shows then is not so much the one-sided fascination of modernist writers with speed but rather with temporal desynchronization. Slowness, lateness, attention, and distraction have emerged here as central tropes in a multifaceted discourse on time that accentuates the precariousness of modern subjectivity. Slowness, attention, distraction, and lateness are tactical and provisional positions of a precarious modern self. On the level of form, however, these tropes give rise to experiments with form that generate *ästhetische Eigenzeit* in the interaction between text and reader.

3

Contemporary Perspectives

Precarious Time(s) in Photography and Film

Slow Art

The previous chapter foregrounded lateness, slowness, and attention as central tropes in a dissonant modernist discourse that
pursued vastly different temporal itineraries. Technological and
infrastructural innovations, above all the development of a modern urban transport system with buses, trams, and underground
trains, accelerated urban living in all major European cities long
before the motorcar became affordable after World War II. The
Futurist glorification of unruly speed articulated an exaggerated
love affair with the accelerating tempo of modern life. The flip
side of this celebration of speed was a deep engagement with lateness and slowness as two complementary modes of desynchronization, which, aesthetically and temporally, disrupted the project
of unflinching modernization. Chapter 2 also showed that lateness and slowness themselves are not homogeneous: in modernist

discourse they are evaluated along very different lines, as can be gleaned from Nietzsche's scathing attack on his own late culture, Kafka's exploration of lateness as a mode of resistance to power, or Freud's interpretation of latency and lateness as anthropological conditions. In the light of the overwhelming evidence of the modern fascination with vastly different times and modes of temporality, Lutz Koepnick "urges us to reconsider monolithic definitions of the modern and postmodern," which he sees as a continuum rather than in terms of a binary.[1]

For Koepnick contemporary art radicalizes the modernist interest in time through an aesthetic of slowness that exploits all kinds of technologies, both analogue and digital. In similar fashion, Urs Stäheli emphasizes that contemporary art is profoundly concerned with the exploration of time as an aesthetic experience. Stäheli is particularly interested in modes of slowness that rely on procedural practices and scripts of disengagement.[2] A prominent and very early example in this regard is the American artist Lee Lozano's *General Strike Piece* of 1969 in which the artist instructed herself as follows:

> GRADUALLY BUT DETERMINEDLY AVOID BEING PRESENT AT OFFICIAL OR PUBLIC "UPTOWN" FUNCTIONS OR GATHERINGS RELATED TO THE ART WORLD IN ORDER TO PURSUE INVESTIGATION OF TOTAL PERSONAL & PUBLIC REVOLUTION.[3]

Lozano then realized her manifesto through a gradual process of disengaging with the hyped-up New York art scene, by, for example, avoiding appearances at the opening of art exhibitions. The project culminated in the so-called *Dropout Piece* in the early 1970s when Lozano locked up her studio and left New York for good. Before her death in 1999, she chose an unmarked grave outside Dallas for her burial as the culmination of her dropout project.

---

1. Koepnick, *On Slowness*, 11.
2. Urs Stäheli, "Entnetzt euch! Praktiken und Ästhetiken der Anschlusslosigkeit," *Mittelweg* 36/22 (August/Sept. 2013): 24.
3. Reproduced in Stäheli, "Entnetzt euch!," 17.

As Stäheli notes, what makes this performance so remarkable is the absence of documentation of an act that was planned but, for a long time, went unrecognized.[4] Here the script of disappearance entailed the erasure of that very script in the completion of the project. As in Kafka's story of the disappearing mouse singer, *Josefine, die Sängerin*, Lozano's disappearance from an art scene that craves high visibility and celebrification received attention only retrospectively. Both Kafka's story and Lozano's performance pieces are about resonance through absence or disconnectedness.

Whereas Lozano orchestrated the slow disappearance of the artist from the contemporary art scene, Marina Abramović staged artistic presence in her slow performance piece *The Artist Is Present*, which was part of a comprehensive retrospective of her work at the Museum of Modern Art in New York in 2010.[5] Besides video installations and photographs, the exhibition also included a live restaging of five of the exhibited performances. However, what turned the exhibition into a spectacle that attracted roughly 700,000 visitors was Abramović's daily performance of *The Artist Is Present* in the museum's atrium. From 14 March to 31 May 2010 she sat for six days a week and seven hours a day motionless and silent in a chair facing individual members of the public who were allowed to sit in a chair opposite her, equally motionless and silent, for as long

---

4. Stäheli, "Entnetzt euch!," 18.

5. The Serbian-born performance artist is internationally known for her extreme physical exploration of pain and power in *longue durée*. For example, in her early piece *Rhythm 10* (1973), she used twenty knives to quickly stab at the spaces between her outstretched fingers. Whenever she pierced her skin, she selected another knife from those laid out in front of her. She described her performance as follows: "Performance: I switch on the first cassette recorder. I take the knife and plunge it, as fast as I can, into the flesh between the outstretched fingers of my left hand. After each cut, I change to a different knife. Once all the knives (all the rhythms) have been used, I rewind the tape. I listen to the recording of the first performance. I concentrate. I repeat the first part of the performance. I pick up the knives in the same sequence, adhere to the same rhythm and cut myself in the same places. In this performance, the mistakes of the past and those of the present are synchronous. I rewind the same tape and listen to the dual rhythm of the knives. I leave." See http://www.medienkunstnetz.de/works/rhythm-10-2/ (accessed 3 January 2017).

as they wanted. In between these sitters Abramović closed her eyes to refocus on the new person sitting opposite her. In terms of her appearance, she alternated between three dresses, a red, a white, and a dark blue gown with a long train. With her posture slightly bent forward, her hair in a braided plait pulled over her left shoulder and her hands on her knees she gazed silently straight ahead. The effect of this theatrical arrangement was a still life that minimized the dramaturgy of performance to the brief intervals when the sitters opposite Abramović were changing. Visitors became witnesses to the passage of time: the artist's presence created a space of stillness in an otherwise bustling and noisy environment. The enactment of aesthetic *Eigenzeit* in the here and now thus depended on a spatial arrangement that separated Abramović from the museum space. Only because she was physically set apart from her audience, could she exude an aura that enacted aesthetic *Eigenzeit*.

By holding the sitter's gaze, Abramović enacted a form of heightened attentiveness that dispensed with the unawareness of the flow of time in everyday life. Evidently, *The Artist Is Present* was about the deliberate enactment of slow and equal time: Abramović looked at all sitters with the same focused intensity. However, the performance also brought forth time as sheer weight by emptying it of all action and content. In the first two months a table separated Abramović and her sitters; in the latter part of the performance the table was removed to emphasize the intensity of the encounter between artist and sitter in the present. Indeed, this performance of presence engendered a highly emotional connectedness between Abramović, the onlookers, and the sitters, who, as result of the intensity of her gaze, often broke out into tears. It also encouraged the onlookers as well as the sitters to question the experience and expectations of looking. Perhaps it is not surprising then that, with the passage of time, the lines of people waiting outside MoMA for their slot became longer and longer.[6]

---

6. The MoMA retrospective and Abramović's central performance were also the subject of the celebrated and award-winning documentary *Marina Abramović: The Artist Is Present* (dir. Matthew Akers, Jeffrey Dupre, 2012), which received the Sundance Film Festival Award (2012) , the Berlin Film Festival Audience Award (2012),

Slowness as an aesthetic practice and a mode of reception features prominently in much contemporary photography and film, defying the fast-paced entertainment conventions and the capitalist commodification of time, as are evident, for example, in recent blockbusters. Mainstream cinema's affirmation of the thrill of speed goes hand in hand with "cinematographic techniques and editing practices that emphasize pace and energy in ways that are sometimes seen as antithetical to narrative coherence and spatiotemporal continuity."[7] While these films favor fast-paced cutting, jerky and unfocused panning, or hectic zooming, slow cinema and slow photography embrace grammars of minimalism to interrupt the cult of speed. Slowness in this sense is more than a binary term in opposition to speed: it is an aesthetic art practice that may include the employment of digital or analogue technologies; slow diegesis and slow narrative; the gallery or cinema as a contemplative exhibition or reception space; and a responsive spectatorship. Often used synonymously with art house cinema, slow cinema favors the long take, minimalist plotlines, sparse dialogue punctured by pauses, and opaque narratives with hesitant or slowly moving protagonists who squander time. As Karl Schoonover has put it, in slow cinema "seeing becomes a form of labor" that requires effort and an attentive viewing practice on the part of the spectator, who may experience anxiety about the waste of onscreen and offscreen time.[8] "Art

---

and the Special Jury Award of the Sheffield Doc/Fest (2012). The film follows the narrative conventions of the documentary: interviews with Abramović frame a loosely biographical story line that leads up to her performance at MoMA in the spring of 2010. Interspersed are interviews with various art critics, Abramović's gallerist Sean Kelly, the curator of the MoMA exhibition Klaus Biesenbach, her former lover and collaborator Ulay, and Abramović herself. The film converts the embodiment of slow presence into a fast-paced, edited, and narrativized spectacle in a documentary format.

7. Tinda Kendall, "Staying on, or Getting off (the Bus): Approaching Speed in Cinema and Media Studies," *Cinema Journal* 55/2 (2017): 114. Timothy Corrigan discusses the "frenetic global espionage game" of the *Bourne* films as emblematic in this regard. See Timothy Corrigan, "Still Speed: Cinematic Acceleration, Value, and Execution," *Cinema Journal* 55/2 (2016): 120.

8. Karl Schoonover, "Wastrels of Time: Slow Cinema's Labouring Body, the Political Spectator, and the Queer," *Framework: The Journal of Cinema and Media* 51/1 (2012): 66.

cinema," comments Schoonover, "exploits its spectator's boredom, becoming as much a cinema of expectancies as one of attractions. It turns boredom into a kind of special work."[9] For Tiago de Luca slow cinema needs the big screen "to facilitate a sustained perceptual engagement with the audio-visual elements on-screen."[10] De Luca suggests that the slow style "diverts attention away from the screen and onto the space of the film theatre itself, thus illuminating the viewing situation as a collective situation from the historically privileged perspective of today's spectator."[11] In so doing, it invites reflection on the very idea of collective spectatorship in the context of ever more fragmented modes of multiple screen viewing.

In the following I discuss a selection of works by photographers and filmmakers who employ aesthetics of slowness that disrupt not only the politics of speed but also the chronological imagination that invests in historical turning points. Exemplary in this regard is German photographer Michael Wesely, who was born in Munich in 1963: his photographs of railway stations in Europe in the early 1990s, of the rebuilding of Berlin's Potsdamer Platz in the late 1990s, and of East Germany after the millennium defy the very premise of the photographic medium, namely, that the photograph freezes a single moment in the flow of time. His experiments with exposure time not only capture extended periods of time in a single image, but these images create a new visual representation of time as a layered experience. The aesthetic experience of Wesely's time works is precarious precisely because it destabilizes linear and chronological time. Ulrich Wüst was born in Magdeburg in the GDR in 1949: his photobook *Später Sommer/Letzter Herbst* (Late Summer/Final Autumn, 2016) both draws on and overturns the conventions of the photobook to stage the dramatic events of 1989 as empty time and empty space. Covering various East German locations and a trip to Moscow in 1989, Wüst's photobook foregrounds the contingency of everyday life at the very moment when history was about to assert

---

9. Schoonover, "Wastrels of Time," 70–71.

10. Tiago de Luca, "Slow Time, Visible Cinema: Duration, Experience, and Spectatorship," *Cinema Journal* 56/1 (2016): 26.

11. De Luca, "Slow Time, Visible Cinema," 38.

itself. These photographs are grainy, distanced, and difficult to read; they displace the common view of 1989 as an electrifying historical moment with a sense of historical precariousness. Christian Petzold was born in the Federal Republic in 1960: his film *Barbara* (2012) is set in the provincial GDR in the 1980s and explores the weight of slow time before the fall of the Berlin Wall. My discussion focuses on the crucial role of diegetic sound in a film that aims to recreate the "acoustic space" of the GDR. Ulrich Seidl was born in Vienna in 1952: his film *Paradise: Faith* (2012) is set in present-day Vienna and explores the return of religion against the backdrop of the dislocating effects of globalization. Like Petzold, Seidl employs a strikingly slow filmic aesthetics that works with long takes, static shots, and extreme forms of symmetry to capture the quest for *Eigenzeit*. The chapter concludes with a discussion of Maren Ade's acclaimed tragicomedy *Toni Erdmann* (2016): set in the neoliberal era of global capitalism, the film explores generationally inflected notions of the good life through the relationship of Winfried, a retired music teacher and a representative of the 1968 generation, with his daughter Ines, who represents a new professionally ambitious generation without any political ideals. While the film is not an example of slow cinema in the strict sense of cinematography, it is included in this chapter because of the filmic exploration of two diametrically opposed notions of performance that engender different speeds and opposing politics of time. Even though the artistic practices and media discussed here are very divergent, they all investigate the precariousness of our embeddedness in time and space. The works under discussion can be classed as "time works"—to appropriate the title of one of Michael Wesely's photobooks—because they experiment with modes of temporality that tentatively recuperate *Eigenzeit*.

The Disruption of Linear Time: Michael Wesely's Time Photography

West German photographer Michael Wesely's fascinating time photography of the built and natural environment challenges the very premise of the photographic medium: that its singularity derives from its ability to wrest a particular moment in time from life. For Roland Barthes the indexicality of the photograph was irrefutable because analogue photography always captured a singular and non-repeatable moment. In his classic book *Camera Lucida* he argued that photography's ontological status resides in the indisputable "has-been-ness" of the photograph, which in turn provokes the unsettling experience of the "punctum," that is, of a moment when the observer is disturbed by a detail in the image that she cannot account for.[12] Susan Sontag too famously argued that

> a photograph passes for incontrovertible proof that a given thing happened. The picture may distort; but there is always a presumption that something exists, or did exist, which is like what's in the picture. Whatever the limitations (through amateurism) or pretensions (through artistry) of the individual photographer, a photograph—any photograph—seems to have a more innocent, and therefore more accurate, relation to visible reality than do other mimetic objects.[13]

In his famous essay "The Ontology of the Photographic Image" (1945) André Bazin compared film with photography, claiming that while cinema produces images of objects in duration, photography embalms time.[14] Whereas film unfolds in our time and space, photography can only offer images of a frozen past.

In the digital age, the conventional polarization of film and photography and of past and present in the two media has collapsed. There is a high degree of convergence between film and photography: the same digital camera can be used to take film shots and photographs or to arrest, repeat, or slow down filmic images. Martin Lister distinguishes between the "time in a photograph" and

---

12. Roland Barthes, *Camera Lucida: Reflections on Photography*, trans. R. Howard (New York: Vintage Classics, 1993), 43.

13. Susan Sontag, *On Photography* (New York: Doubleday, 1973), 5–6.

14. André Bazin, "The Ontology of the Photographic Image," in *Classic Essays on Photography*, ed. A. Trachtenberg, trans. H. Gray (New Haven, CT: Leete's Island Books, 1980), 237–44. For a historical survey of the debate on time and photography, see Hilde van Gelder and Helen Westgeest, *Photography Theory in Historical Perspective: Case Studies from Contemporary Art* (Oxford: Wiley-Blackwell, 2011), 64–111.

the "time of a photograph": while the first flows from technology and refers to the exposure time as well as "the peculiar temporality which invests a photograph at the time of its making," the latter captures the meanings and uses of photographs that are engendered in the process of reception.[15] "Once the image is inscribed," comments Lister, "it opens up to our cultural, our imaginative and intellectual investments in photography—especially with regard to how we conceive of time, the relations of past, present and future, and hence to matters of historical time and the temporality of memory."[16]

Our relationship to time is a key concern of Michael Wesely's photography. At the very moment when the technical possibilities of the digital era made the manipulation of photographs so simple, Wesely returned to the pioneering era of photography in the nineteenth century. When he was a student at the Bayerische Staatslehranstalt für Fotografie in Munich in the late 1980s, Wesely was given a portrait assignment. He realized that he could not arrest the character of a person in a tiny fraction of the shutter closure. Hence he began to experiment with extremely long exposure times by, for example, constructing pinhole cameras with filters and extremely small apertures to reduce the amount of light striking the film. However, in the end the pinhole camera was not capable of achieving the desired level of photographic detail and sharpness: Wesely therefore built his own camera housing for large-format lenses, using 13/18 and 9/12 cm sheet films.[17] By the 1990s he had managed to lengthen his exposure time up to several months, and ten years later up to several years. All fleeting or rapid movement is eliminated in these images because it cannot be picked up by the film: while enduring elements that remain unchanged for the duration of exposure time are in focus, recurring movement over time appears as a blur or imprints of impermanence. For the

15. Martin Lister, "The Times of Photography," in *Time, Media, and Modernity*, 49.
16. Lister, "The Times of Photography," 55.
17. Michael Wesely, email message to author, 1 August 2018.

same reason we cannot identify a particular season or differenti-
ate between day and night: these photographs produce a strange
quality of light that captures extended time.[18] By employing these
extraordinary exposure times Wesely creates layered images in
which different temporal states are copresent: he thus not only
challenges the very premise of the medium, namely, that it provides "incontrovertible proof that a given thing happened," but he
also makes us think afresh about the passage of time and the relationship of the visible world to time. These photographs no longer
assert the single and nonrefutable moment and with it Barthes's
has-been-ness as the ontological signature of photography. Wesely
emphasizes: "Für mich wichtig sind die vielen unscharfen Details,
in denen sich die Veränderungen andeuten, An- und Abwesenheit
sich die Hand reichen."[19] (It is important for me to capture the
blurred details, which indicate change and in which presence and
absence are conjoined.)

The spectral effect of this technique is particularly pronounced
in his photographs of European railway stations: having set up
his cameras in various stations around Europe in 1992, Wesely
opened the shutter of his camera exactly when a train left the
station, and he closed it at the scheduled arrival time.[20] From
a temporal perspective the project is fascinating: formally it
adheres to the logic of the synchronized timetable because the
exposure time is determined by the departure and arrival times of
the various trains. Synchronized time was a relatively late invention of the nineteenth century in response to the rapid expansion
of the railway system. The introduction of Greenwich mean time

---

18. See William Firebrace, "Slow Spaces," in *Camera Constructs: Photography,
Architecture, and the Modern City*, ed. Andrew Higgott and Timothy Wray (Farnham: Ashgate, 2014), 250.

19. Wesely, email to author, 1 August 2018.

20. This photographic scenario may also be seen to reference the (much-
mythologized) "primal scene" of cinema, the Lumière brothers' *The Arrival of a
Train in La Ciotat* (1895). The fifty-second film shows the arrival of a train that is
pulled by a steam locomotive at the French town La Ciotat in one single unedited
take. Arguably, this is one of the (media) spectacles that is evacuated from Wesely's
railway scene.

coordinated hitherto local time zones by way of a universal grid, which then enabled the smooth running of increasingly complex transport networks. In this way time lost its primary attachment to locality and became a global unit of measurement that also facilitated capitalist enterprise and imperial ambitions.[21] With this in mind, we can now see how Wesely's photography overturns the logic of the railway system, which led to time-space compression by means of a network that interconnected European cities on high-speed routes. By setting up his camera at central railway stations, Wesely foregrounds the time-space interdependency that marked modern capitalist expansion: unlike the rural stop on a secondary line, the central railway station is a busy transport hub and as such a major traffic node in an international network that stands for rapacious acceleration. But in Wesely's photographs the central railway stations appear as eerie and empty places. For example, when Wesely photographed Prague railway station in 1992, he opened the shutter at 15:10 when the train departed and closed it at 20:22 when it reached its destination in Linz (fig. 1). Even though the departure and arrival times determined the exposure time, the decisive moments of departure and arrival are canceled in this photograph. Instead of passengers alighting from and boarding the trains, we can barely see the ghostly contours of people sitting on a bench on the platform. On either side of the platform we see blurred lines that are created by the incoming and outgoing trains. The "still" photograph thus does capture movement through space, which, historically, was the concern of photodynamism at the beginning of the twentieth century.[22] In

---

21. On the loss of local time as a result of the expansion of the railway network, see Wolfgang Schivelbusch's classic study *Geschichte der Eisenbahnreise: Zur Industrialisierung von Raum und Zeit im 19. Jahrhundert*, 5th ed. (Frankfurt a. Main: Fischer, 2011).

22. The Italian Bragaglia brothers attempted to capture the passage of movement through extended exposure times. Anton Giulio Bragaglia published the manifesto *Fotodinamismo futurista* in 1913. See Anton Giulio Bragaglia, "Excerpts from Futurist Photodynamism," in *Photography in the Modern Era: European Documents and Critical Writings, 1913–1940*, ed. C. Phillips (New York: Metropolitan Museum of Modern Art, 1989), 287–95.

Figure 1. Michael Wesely, *Praha 15.10—Linz 20.22* (1992).
© Michael Wesely, Bild-Kunst Bonn/IVARO Dublin, 2018.

Wesely's image the rolling stock appears even more dematerial-
ized than the ghostly passengers on the platform. Speed is directionless here and thus without velocity, as we cannot determine
whether the blurred lines record movement into or out of the station or both. On another level, the German railway stations and,
by extension, the Central European rail network altogether, are
particularly burdened sites of memory: seen from this perspective, the train stations with these phantom figures on the platform
may evoke memories of the Holocaust.

In contrast to all fleeting phenomena, the industrial architecture of the different railway stations remains unaffected by the
long exposure: the iron supports and glass domes arching over
the tracks accentuate the ambitious architectural aspirations of the
industrial era, which had invented the glass dome as a secular version of the cathedral. However, this impression of industrial solidity and permanence is overlaid by the eeriness of the platforms and

tracks.[23] Wesely's photographs are so ghostly precisely because the uncanny simultaneity of past, present, and future creates a profoundly anachronic temporality that dislodges linear temporal orientation. Instead of placing us in a dynamic transport hub full of life, these images appear strangely dislocated from time and from anchorage in a precise location.[24]

When Potsdamer Platz was rebuilt in Berlin in the late 1990s, Wesely left the shutter of his camera open for two entire years: as with his previous long-exposure photographs, he used a self-built camera with large-format lenses and sheet films.[25] Instead of a series of momentary snapshots taken over time, the viewer is confronted with layered images that not only unfreeze photography but also collapse the linearity of time. While these photographs capture different stages of the various building projects, they do not obey the chronological imagination that sustains dating systems and systems of periodization: instead of symbolically

---

23. Writing about Wesely's clocks, which, in other images, show no hands, Koepnick observes: "The clock's missing hands . . . are the sundials of a history in whose wake neither the industrial city nor the nation nor the political blocs of the cold war offer defining limits and may anchor the itineraries of everyday life within the topographies of the present. All numbers, and yet unable to tell us the time, Wesely's uncanny clocks are witness to a historical moment in which insular notions of the local—of unified identities, demarcated territories, and distinct presences—no longer appeared viable because, after the collapse of the Soviet Empire, the open and fast-paced form of the network emerged as the perhaps dominant structure of communication, collaboration, and cultural production." Koepnick, *On Slowness*, 70.

24. Here I deviate from Koepnick's reading; Koepnick follows Doreen Massey, arguing that space in Wesely's open shutter photography gives expression to a "dynamic simultaneity." Koepnick, *On Slowness*, 73. In contrast I argue that the copresence of different times in one shot produces surreal still lifes without any movement.

25. Critics tend to claim that these photographs were taken with the pinhole camera. See, for example, Koepnick, *On Slowness*, 71. Wesely writes: "In der Tat habe ich viel mit Lochkameras gearbeitet, schlussendlich aber diesen Apparat nicht für die Langzeitbelichtungen verwendet. Bereits die erwähnten Portraits wurden mit Grossformat-Objektiven gemacht." (It is true that I have often worked with the pinhole camera, but in the end I did not use it for the long exposures. Even the aforementioned portraits were shot with large-format lenses.) Wesely, email to author, 1 August 2018.

confirming the end of Germany's division and the beginning of a new era of confidence as represented by architecture, these photographs offer a visual representation of the copresence of past, present, and future. When we look at the photograph taken between 4 April 1997 and 4 June 1999 we can see how the apparent solidity of the built environment dissolves (fig. 2). It is interesting to note that the trees in the foreground actually appear more enduring than the built environment. The trees (which also feature in other pictures of the Potsdamer Platz series) introduce a temporal chasm between a seemingly immutable and strangely static nature and the man-made transformations of the environment, which appear ephemeral and transitory. And so the photograph creates an uncanny and ghostly effect that makes the emerging buildings look like phantoms of a past that, in spite of the rapacious rebuilding process, remains irrepressible.

Figure 2. Michael Wesely, *4.4.1997—4.6.1999, Potsdamer Platz, Berlin: "Long Exposures"* (1999). © Michael Wesely, Bild-Kunst Bonn/IVARO Dublin, 2018.

The Potsdamer Platz series thus marks a further radicalization of Wesely's time photography: neither time nor space functions here as a stable point of orientation. One could say that these photographs have a "prospective archaeological effect," as they track a process of construction that involves transitory stages of construction and demolition. But we shouldn't stretch this analogy too far: archaeology is keen to piece together fragments from the past with a view to salvaging material objects that it then places in a temporal sequence and order. By contrast, Wesely takes an image of a temporal whole that pulverizes the chronological imagination and brings into view an uncanny anachronicity, which probes the progressive transformation of Berlin after German unification. It is perhaps not surprising that Wesely himself describes his photography through an analogy with John Cage's music: "Mir liegt immer der Vergleich mit John Cage nahe. Er sagt, Musik sei: 'Fenster auf'!, er nimmt in einem Zeitfenster alles was kommt, er öffnet sich hin dazu, alles zu akzeptieren. Meine Bilder leben genau mit dieser Notwendigkeit das Ergebnis zu akzeptieren."[26] (I am always reminded of John Cage. He says that music is an "open window"!; he incorporates everything that is happening in this time window; he is open to accepting absolutely everything. My pictures live exactly off the very necessity to accept the outcome.)

Wesely's photography could be held to offer an artistic representation of Hans Ulrich Gumbrecht's idea of an extended present. But whereas Gumbrecht is fearful of such an unbounded sea of simultaneities, Wesely exploits extended exposure times to create a hitherto unseen image of copresence. The spectral effect of his images is undeniable; it forces the viewer to reconsider the meaning of being connected to the world in the here and now.

Wesely's long-term exposures have a very different effect when applied to the natural environment. His photobook *Ostdeutschland* (East Germany) appeared in 2004, fourteen years after unification, and contains fifty-three color photographs from different locations that were shot with a pinhole camera in which the aperture of the

---

26. Wesely, email to author, 1 August 2018.

pinhole was replaced by a narrow slit. Wesely explains the technical dimension of his approach as follows:

> Wenn man die Kamera mit dem Spalt horizontal auf Landschaft richtet, entsteht über die Vertikale gesehen, ein Bild, das korrekte Proportionen aufweist. Horizontal werden die Farb- und Helligkeitswerte zusammengetragen, aufaddiert und alle vertikalen Strukturen gebrochen, praktisch aufgelöst.[27]

> When you direct the camera with the slit horizontally at the landscape, from the vertical perspective you get an image that has the correct proportions. Color and brightness are produced and added up horizontally so that all vertical structures are broken down and practically dissolved.

The captions identify the various East German locations in very general terms—for example, "Lausitzer Bergland" (Mountainous Landscape near Lausitz), "Blick in Pirna auf die Elbbrücke" (View in Pirna from the Elbe Bridge), "Sonnenblumenfelder bei Niesky" (Sunflower Fields near Niesky), and "Lavendelfelder bei Großleuthen" (Lavender Fields near Großleuthen). What we see here are painterly images of horizontal bands of color that, at first sight, appear to bear no mimetic relation to any real place. For example, in "Ackerland bei Gusow" (Farmland near Gusow) the image is composed of a broad and dark band of the color brown, which then gives way to a lighter brown before a narrow darker line divides the bottom half from the top half, where a whitish hue then turns into a dark blue. While we can translate these colors into the representation of a field melting into the blue sky along the line of the horizon, there are no distinctive topographical features that suggest a particular place and time or that interrupt the flatness of the lines. It is possible to associate "Ackerland bei Gusow" with industrial agricultural production on a massive scale. However, the flatness of these images undermines the connection to real places: are we really looking at cultivated land that has been dug over for centuries? Or is this the kind of extraterrestrial perspective that catapults the viewer into a nontemporal sphere? In any case, it is

---

27. Wesely, email to author, 1 August 2018.

evident that the human relationship to the land is elided from a series of photographs that are more reminiscent of modern abstract painting than of photography.

While images like "Ackerland bei Gusow" still maintain a generic representational dimension, this link is far more tenuous in those pictures that were taken near towns or landmarks that resonate with the history of the GDR and the Cold War period. A prominent example in this regard is "Blick von der Glienicker Brücke auf Schloss Babelsberg" (View from Glienicke Bridge to Schloss Babelsberg). Glienicke Bridge is the bridge across the river Havel that connects Berlin-Zehlendorf with Potsdam. Originally a wooden bridge, then a stone bridge designed by the Prussian court architect Karl Friedrich Schinkel, it was rebuilt as a modern steel bridge at the beginning of the twentieth century to increase the shipping capacity of the Havel and the Teltow Canal. In the final days of World War II the bridge was badly damaged. Rebuilding began in 1947, and the bridge was reopened in December 1949, three months after the foundation of the GDR. Even though it was renamed Brücke der Einheit (Bridge of Unity), a line across the middle of the bridge was drawn to demarcate the so-called inner-German border. From 1952 cars driven by civilians could no longer cross, and pedestrians needed a special permit; one year later the bridge—by now one of the last remaining bridges connecting East and West—was completely closed to all civilians. In the period between 1962 and 1986 the bridge was known as the Bridge of Spies because it was used for the exchange of Eastern and Western spies and Eastern dissidents.[28] On 10 November 1989, one day after the fall of the Berlin Wall, the bridge was finally reopened to general traffic. A metal strip on the footpath across the bridge reminds pedestrians of the division and unification of Germany. In

---

28. See Thomas Blees, *Glienicker Brücke: Schauplatz der Geschichte* (Berlin: Berlin Edition, 2010); Giles Whittell, *Bridge of Spies—A True Story of the Cold War* (London: Simon & Schuster, 2011); See also *Operationsgebiet DDR: Endstation Glienicker Brücke*, a documentary by Jürgen Ast and Martin Hübner; first screening, 23 November 2004. For a review, see http://www.mdr.de/doku/1311404-hintergrund-1311163.html.

1998, the Deutsche Post issued a special stamp commemorating the bridge as a significant *lieu de mémoire* in German history.[29]

In sharp contrast to the cartographic symbolism of the stamp, Wesely's photograph from the bridge across the Havel to Schloss Babelsberg carries no imprints at all of the location's fractured history (fig. 3 and color pl.). The upheavals of twentieth-century German history are absent from a picture that shows once again horizontal bands of color that change from a moss green to a grayish blue, then into

Figure 3. Michael Wesely, *'Blick von der Glienicker Brücke auf Schloss Babelsberg,' Ostdeutschland* (2004). © Michael Wesely, Bild-Kunst Bonn/IVARO Dublin, 2018.

29. Schloss Babelsberg too resonates with historical significance: situated in a park outside Potsdam, Schloss Babelsberg served in the nineteenth century as the summer residence of Prince Wilhelm, later Emperor Wilhelm I. The palace and garden were the very site where Wilhelm and Bismarck conducted talks in 1862 that led to Bismarck's appointment as prime minister and foreign minister.

Michael Wesely, *'Blick von der Glienicker Brücke auf Schloss Babelsberg,' Ostdeutschland* (2004). © Michael Wesely, Bild-Kunst Bonn/IVARO Dublin, 2018.

a strip of brown and blue that gives way to the grayish blue of the lower half before fading into the light blue of the sky. With its long exposure time, Wesely's camera erases all topographical markers and geographical landscape features as mere epiphenomena of a pure landscape that is composed of gradations of color and light.

Rather than inviting historical reflection, the photograph from Glienicke Bridge may be placed in the tradition of Jacob van Ruisdael and Caspar David Friedrich whose landscapes emphasize the horizon and the sublime. In Kantian philosophy, the sublime is a state of mind entered into by an encounter with a representation of the infinite or boundlessness.[30] It involves a movement of the mind that destroys time. But these images are perhaps also visually reminiscent of the landscape photography by Andreas Gursky. The Leipzig-born photographer digitally manipulates his large-scale photographs, retouching them and joining up segments of different photographs into a landscape montage that appears to be untouched by human intervention.[31] For example, *Rhein II* (Rhine II, 1999), the second of a set of six Rhine photographs, is a large-scale composition (190 cm by 360 cm) of color and geometry: while the original image captured a factory complex on the far side of the river, the manipulated photograph completely elides any reference to industry. In the foreground we see a narrow and horizontal band of green and a gray cycling path; in the middle ground the green embankment and the river Rhine, which flows horizontally across the field of view, and another band of green on the far side of the river under the overcast sky. Overall Gursky's work is more topographical than Wesely's in that we do recognize these landscape features. However, the overriding effect is not dissimilar to Wesely's time photography:[32] in both instances photography

---

30. Rudolf Makreel, "Imagination and Temporality in Kant's Theory of the Sublime," *Journal of Aesthetics and Art Criticism* 42/3 (1984): 303–15.

31. He studied at the Staatliche Kunstakademie Düsseldorf under Bernd and Hilla Becher where he started with black-and-white photography before switching to color.

32. However, it is important to note that Gursky's work is characterized by the tension between extreme detail, on the one hand, and the creation of a painterly transcendental effect, on the other.

achieves an intermedial effect that gestures to landscape painting. On the other hand, Wesely's landscape photographs have a more abstract effect: with their colored and layered strips, one could also view them as scientific representations of geological strata. When viewed in this way, the image also brings into view a transhuman dating system that exceeds human time.

Whether viewed as abstract landscapes or as quasi-scientific images, they are evidently stripped of any concrete historical and topographical reference points that could assign them a place in German history and the chronological imagination. And so the East Germany in Wesely's photobook is no longer a site of ideological contestation but the springboard for an imagination that employs the technical media to ultrasubjective effect. The images capture a timelessness that seems to have escaped the assault of history. When seen against the backdrop of the heated postunification debate about the place of the GDR in German history that dominated the 1990s, these images gain an acute historical index: they overwrite the Western idea of the drabness of East Germany with astonishing pictorial splendor.

The Disruption of Historical Time: Ulrich Wüst's Photobook *Später Sommer/Letzter Herbst*

The title of Ulrich Wüst's photobook *Später Sommer/Letzter Herbst* (Late Summer/Final Autumn, 2016) immediately conjures up the trope of lateness, which, as we saw in chapter 2, figured so prominently in fin de siècle discourse.[33] Just two years after German unification in 1871 Nietzsche diagnosed lateness as the defining sickness of modern culture. Nietzsche's *Untimely Meditations* punctured German nationalist fervor through a scathing attack on the contemporary era, which he described as a malignant *Spätzeit*, a late epoch under the spell of the epigone and dandy. For Nietzsche modern life had lost its creative power to an antiquarian mind-set,

---

33. Ulrich Wüst, *Später Sommer/Letzter Herbst* (Heidelberg: Kehrer, 2016).

which had led to the uncritical appreciation of all things past that, for Nietzsche, crippled his own era.

My association of Nietzsche with the works of East German photographer Ulrich Wüst may seem idiosyncratic. It is, however, motivated by the striking untimeliness of Wüst's photobook, which was published in conjunction with an exhibition at the CO Photographic Gallery in Berlin in 2016. The photos included in the exhibition and in the book were taken in the run-up to the fall of the Berlin Wall in August, September, and October 1989. Wüst's photobook is untimely in Nietzsche's sense: its belated appearance more than twenty-five years after German unification creates reflective distance and an alternative view of history that displaces the global iconicity of 1989. His photo narrative does not depict the usual images of the Monday demonstrators in Leipzig, of ecstatic East Berliners arriving in the West or of jubilant Westerners making their way into the unknown East, of lines of pastel-colored Trabants at the open border, of bewildered and bemused GDR officials, but rather a series of impressions that, with a few exceptions, appear as nonevents.

Before analyzing the thematic and temporal structure of the book, it may be useful to briefly touch on the genre of the photobook and its history. In terms of scale and diversity, the photobook is an important genre that has accompanied the history of photography ever since the nineteenth century when Henry Fox Talbot's *Pencil of Nature* and *Sun Pictures in Scotland* appeared in the mid-1840s. Talbot's *Sun Pictures in Scotland* responded to the Victorian craze for all things Scottish and the apotheosis of Sir Walter Scott: the twenty-three plates of Scottish landmarks and sites of memory "comprise a visual anthology of subjects connected to Scott."[34] The book thus stands at the beginning of a rich genre that, in spite of its apparent diversity, is characterized by an overarching narrative and aesthetic concern that place each individual photograph in a

---

34. Graham Smith, "H. Fox Talbot's 'Scotch Views' for *Sun Pictures in Scotland* (1845)," in *The Photobook: From Talbot to Ruscha and Beyond*, ed. Patrizia Di Bello, Colette Wilson, and Shamoon Zamir (New York: I.B. Tauris, 2012), 20.

broader context. In their seminal *The Photobook: A History* Martin Parr and Gerry Badger insist that a photobook must be more than a collection of images in book form. For Parr and Badger it is essential that the photobook give expression to a coherent photographic idea, a particular aesthetic, or a definable thematic interest: "The sum, by definition," writes Parr, "is greater than the part."[35] As Patrizia Di Bello and Shamoon Zamir observe with reference to Talbot's Victorian publications and Ed Ruscha's conceptual *Twentysix Gasoline Stations* (1962), which has gained iconic status in the history of the genre, photobooks are often concerned

> with the relations between place, history and nationhood. Both [Talbot and Ruscha] explore, whether romantically or ironically, places which have become weighted with cultural memory and myth. . . . Both are also books of travel, the photobook not merely as a record but also in some way an enactment of journeying, and kinds of autobiography or memoir by indirection.[36]

In Germany the photobook came to prominence in the mid-1920s when interest in montage aesthetics coincided with the exploration of photography's representational practices and potential. "What distinguished the photobook," comments Patrizia McBride, "is not simply that it provided accounts of the world that privileged visual over literary strategies. Rather, its images were endowed with a performative quality; that is, they were meant to demonstrate the representational strategies proper to the photographic medium, which the photobook sought to foreground and reflect on."[37] McBride's analysis focuses on the construction of visual meaning in the work of the Dada artist Hannah Höch, who, in the early 1930s, produced a scrapbook that comprises several

---

35. Martin Parr, "Preface," in Martin Parr and Gerry Badger, *The Photobook: A History* (London: Phaidon, 2004), 1:7.

36. Di Bello and Zamir, "Introduction," in *The Photobook: From Talbot to Ruscha and Beyond*, 6–7.

37. Patrizia McBride, "Narrative Resemblance: The Production of Truth in the Modernist Photobook of Weimar Germany," *New German Critique* 115/39 (2012): 182.

hundred images that she took from various illustrated magazines, pasting them onto two issues of the Weimar women's magazine *Die Dame*.[38] Analyzing the complex analogical networks that are created by the dizzying montage of the photographs in a grid layout, McBride demonstrates that Höch's scrapbook overturns the mimetic relationship between the photographic image and its referent. It challenges photography's investment in verisimilitude and illusionism by way of a montage technique that calls for analogical comparisons between seemingly unrelated images. In this way Höch's work initiates a "performative investigation of photography's narrative and rhetorical power."[39]

McBride's astute observations about the performative potential of the photobook are highly relevant for the discussion of Wüst's *Später Sommer/Letzter Herbst*, which complicates the relationship between place, history, and nationhood. In effect, the anti-illusionist representational practice of *Später Sommer/Letzter Herbst* negates the foundational myth that 1989 marks the beginning of the reunification of the divided German nation. While Wesely's *Ostdeutschland* erases all traces of human history, Wüst's photobook obliterates the very category of history by foregrounding the contingency of life. His black-and-white photo narrative opens with a title page that shows a screen shot of a television set displaying the West German news program *Tagesschau* on 3 October 1989. A female news presenter is reading the news against the backdrop of a map that shows West Germany, the GDR, Czechoslovakia, and Poland with their respective capital cities, Bonn, East Berlin, Prague, and Warsaw. On the bottom left of the screen the strapline reads: "DDR-Flüchtlinge können jetzt ausreisen" (GDR refugees are now allowed to leave). While this opening screen shot of a highly mediatized news event draws attention to the dramatic build-up leading to the fall of the Berlin Wall, the ensuing photobook undercuts the chronological imagination that has accompanied the

---

38. McBride, "Narrative Resemblance," 183. A facsimile volume has been published by Gunda Luyken: *Hannah Höch Album* (Ostfildern-Ruit: Cantz, 2004).

39. McBride, "Narrative Resemblance," 196.

narrative of 1989. The image of *Die Tagesschau* is not indicative of a photojournalistic perspective; Wüst rejects the type of visual strategy that stages history as a series of electrifying moments and dramatic turning points that symbolize human agency. Rather, his photography exposes "the dialectic between alleged objectivity and subjective-subversive attention to detail."[40]

Wüst's photobook is divided into a prologue, five central photo series, and an epilogue. Each section carries a brief title, date, and place-names.[41] The photographs are arranged either as a single photograph per page or as developed contact strips or sequences of negatives: four photographs with perforation holes run across and over the edge of the double page. The perforated roll film foregrounds the materiality and historicity of analogue photography: roll film not only massively helped to speed up exposure times but also recorded the chronological occurrence of the photographs. Wüst overturns these conventions: his pictures neither capture the acceleration of history in 1989 nor do they allow the viewer to produce an "order of time" through chronological sequencing. Even though the photobook records journeys undertaken by Wüst in 1989, these journeys appear uneventful and inconclusive.

The prologue comprises five disparate photographs that are not interconnected by any explanatory narrative or captions: on the left-hand page we see a close-up of two T-shirts with a picture of Gorbachev and Russian inscriptions about perestroika, democracy, and glasnost; on the right-hand side there is a photograph of the exterior of a building with various graffiti: someone sprayed "D Jetzt" (democracy now) underneath an old-fashioned and faded

---

40. Felix Hoffmann, "Leporello/Time/Memory: On Ulrich Wüst and His Leporello *Später Sommer/Letzter Herbst*," in Wüst, *Später Sommer/Letzter Herbst*, 87.

41. "Stadtflucht Berlin Prenzlau" (Escape from Berlin Prenzlau) and "Sommernacht Prenzlauer Berg" (Summer Night Prenzlauer Berg) were shot in August 1989; "Spätsommer Kühlungsborn" (Late Summer Kühlungsborn) in September 1989; "Oktober (1)" was shot in Leipzig in September, "October (2)" in Berlin on 6 and 7 October, that is, shortly before and on the fortieth anniversary of the GDR. While "October (3)" was shot in Leningrad and Moscow in October, the epilogue carries no dates or locations at all: it contains two photographs of a GDR flag hanging from a domestic radiator underneath a net curtain with a floral pattern.

advertisement for "Rohprodukte" (raw materials). This photograph carries the cryptic caption "(P.S.)" (post scriptum), which dislodges the imperative gesture of the "democracy now" slogan. The sense of uncertainty about what precisely we are looking at, or when, is carried over to the next double page: on the left-hand page we see two Russian guards in front of a national shrine. The Russian inscription over the entrance allows the reader to identify Lenin's mausoleum in Moscow; on the right-hand page we see the silhouettes of two people, possibly Russians, on top of a wide set of steps that appear to lead to some grand memorial. The prologue concludes with a sparse shop window display with a sport trophy in the middle, a poster of a GDR sprinter in a race on the left, and a newspaper cutting at the bottom about the success of the GDR women's team at the World Cup. The prologue adopts an associative rather than a chronological perspective: while some of the images can be read as iconic expressions of the grassroots movement of 1989, others do not fit this template. Is Lenin's mausoleum an icon of the greatness of the Russian Revolution or a representation of a dead idea? Does the image of the peculiar shop window display offer an ironic view of the GDR's race against the West? Or is it a representation of the difficulty of capturing movement in photography?

However the viewer deals with these questions, this prologue clearly at once fulfills and undermines the prime function of a prologue to provide the context for the ensuing drama or narrative. In keeping with this strategy of decontextualization, the first series, "Stadtflucht Berlin Prenzlau" (Escape from Berlin Prenzlau), which was taken in August 1989, consists of a developed strip of negatives of extremely grainy photographic shots that appear to have been taken from a train that was traveling through the industrial landscape on the urban periphery north of Berlin, passing highways, bridges, massive overland heating pipes, weekend dachas, a coal-powered station or storage facility, electricity pylons, and a harvester (fig. 4).

The sequentiality of what appears to be a contact strip evokes movement through time and space, but the individual images appear strangely static and frozen in time, an effect that is heightened by the black border that separates the images. Presented as filmstrips or contact prints they produce an aesthetics of the

Figure 4. Ulrich Wüst, "Stadtflucht Berlin Prenzlau," *Später Sommer/ Letzter Herbst* (1989). © Ulrich Wüst, Kehrer Verlag 2016.

unfinished. The absence of captions magnifies the sense that these images are not about wresting a particular moment in time from life. They don't seem to capture the singular and nonrepeatable moment that, for Roland Barthes, defines photography's ontological status. By depicting a journey through a frozen industrial landscape in which humans are either absent or barely recognizable, they stage the summer of 1989 as nonevent.

Such defiance of the chronological imagination structures the book as a whole: the next series is entitled "Sommernacht Prenzlauer Berg" (A Summer Night, Prenzlauer Berg) and dated August 1989. Prenzlauer Berg lies in the district of Pankow in East Berlin and was home to numerous East German dissidents, countercultural artists, and illegal movements (including squatters) during GDR times. Within its boundaries are two key sites of the peaceful revolution: the Zion Church, which allowed activists to use its facilities to print illegal magazines and flyers in 1989; and the Gethsemane Church, which became a hot spot for protests in the lead-up to the fall of the Berlin Wall. Wüst, however, does not engage with any *lieux de mémoire* at all: his Prenzlauer Berg series contains nine close-ups of urban pavement with various objects on the ground, including a single shoe, a shovel, a branch broken off a tree, a cord with empty cotton bags tied to its end, and a fallen-over metal pole. The close-ups do not help but hinder interpretation: we are looking at a series of details that are as hard to understand as the industrial landscapes of the previous series.

The title "Sommernacht Prenzlauer Berg" may be seen to evoke the idea of a romantic encounter that has little to do with these pictures of debris. While the previous series showed images in flux that look static, the Prenzlauer Berg photographs consists of close-ups that provide unreadable images. Both series thus archive places and times that resist integration into any meaningful historical narrative. Like the Weimar artist Hannah Höch, Ulrich Wüst disrupts the mimetic relationship between the photographic image and the referent: we do not recognize what we see in these photographs. Recognition of the referent is replaced here by analogical comparisons between similar images that cannot be narrativized. Wüst's photobook thus draws the viewer's attention to photography's representational strategies and rhetorical power. Neither the time *in* the photograph nor the time *of* the photograph—to use Martin Lister's terminology—can be established with any degree of certainty.

"Spätsommer Kühlungsborn" (Late Summer, Kühlungsborn) is the central and perhaps most intriguing section, as it seems to return to the conventional idea that the photograph has "a more innocent, and therefore more accurate, relation to visible reality than do other mimetic objects."[42] This series consists of nine images that, as the caption informs us, were taken in September 1989 near Kühlungsborn, a popular holiday resort on the Baltic coast of the GDR. Seven of the nine photographs show rear views of individuals or groups of two or three people looking out at the sea or the beach in front of them. The viewer forms the impression that these people are paying their final visit to the beach before returning home—they are all dressed, and many carry their luggage with them. The German viewer in particular is likely to interpret these images as expressions of the desire for a more open country without the legally punishable offence of *Republikflucht* (desertion from the republic, i.e., the GDR). We will see that such beach scenes on the Baltic are a recurring motif in narratives about 1989: it occurs in Petzold's film *Barbara* when the eponymous protagonist helps a teenager to

---

42. Sontag, *On Photography*, 5–6.

escape from the GDR while she returns to her job as a doctor in a provincial hospital. Wüst's figures in the Kühlungsborn series could also be straight out of the world of Lutz Seiler's acclaimed novel *Kruso* (2014), which is set on the small Baltic island of Hiddensee, west of Rügen, which even during GDR times was a haven for dissidents and intellectuals. Edgar Bendler, the protagonist, who has just arrived on the island, goes down to the beach where he is overcome by the view of the sea: "Der Anblick des Meeres! Ed fühlte die Verheißung. Und nichts anderes war es doch, wonach er sich sehnte, eine Art Jenseits, groß, rein, übermächtig."[43] (The view of the sea! Ed felt the promise of it. And he longed for nothing else, only a sort of beyond, great, pure, and all-powerful.)

Returning to Wüst's series: the first photograph, "Spätsommer Kühlungsborn," shows a small group that could be a family: a woman dressed in a light overcoat with a large handbag hanging from her shoulder is about to place a black suitcase on the beach (fig. 5). She is flanked by two men to her left and right:

Figure 5. Ulrich Wüst, "Spätsommer Kühlungsborn, September 1989," *Später Sommer/Letzter Herbst* (1989). © Ulrich Wüst, Kehrer Verlag 2016.

43. Lutz Seiler, *Kruso* (Berlin: Suhrkamp, 2014), 75.

the middle-aged man on her left wears a black leather jacket and a light pair of trousers; he carries a small suitcase while looking out at the sea. The young man on the right—perhaps the couple's son—has rolled up his dark trousers above his ankles; in his right hand he holds a small travel bag with a white pair of trainers tied to its handle. He too is gazing at the sea.

Unlike in the other series included in the photobook, the location, date, and subject matter of these photographs seemingly accentuate their anchorage in historical time. As Susan Sontag observed, "All photographs are *memento mori*. To take a photograph is to participate in another person's (or thing's) mortality, vulnerability, mutability. Precisely by slicing out this moment and freezing it, all photographs testify to time's relentless melt."[44] The *punctum* of the particular moment, when the woman is about to place her suitcase on the beach, occurs within an iconography that evokes transcendence. For the German viewer the composition of this photograph is perhaps reminiscent of Caspar David Friedrich's *Der Mönch am Meer* (*The Monk by the Sea*, 1808–10). Friedrich's epochal painting depicts a single figure in a long garment in rear view on a dune overlooking the sea and the vast expanse of the horizon.[45] The symbolism of Friedrich's painting derives from the vastness of the sky (which takes up more than three-quarters of the picture) and the small scale of the human figure—the only vertical element in an otherwise horizontal composition. Wüst's photograph, too, makes do with only a small number of compositional elements. Apart from the beach, the sea, the sky, and the three figures, only a pair of seagulls are to be seen, one resting on a post at the edge of the picture on the left, the other bobbing in the water to the right of the center of the picture. As in the case of Friedrich's painting, Wüst's photograph is composed of strict horizontal layers: the sky

---

44. Sontag, *On Photography*, 15.

45. Anselm Kiefer is another artist who has reworked Friedrich's Romantic paintings: his series *Besetzungen* (Occupations) of the late 1960s contains the photograph of a man in riding boots standing on the foaming seashore extending his arm out to the sea in Hitler salute. The composition of the photograph combines elements from Friedrich's *The Monk by the Sea* and his *Wanderer above the Sea of Fog* (1818).

is separated from the bottom half of the picture by the sharp line of the horizon. Aside from the emptiness of the picture, what is apparent is the lack of any perspective depth. Wüst's figures stare at a horizon that, despite its breadth, appears opaque.

The Kühlungsborn series ends with a double page that draws attention to the sequential nature of the leporello. On the left-hand edge of the picture, a man, who is also carrying two bags, looks, from a rocky outcrop or wall, out onto the sea, which lies approximately a meter below. Two vertical posts that rise from the water underscore the horizontal composition of beach, sea, and sky. The last picture, on the double page on the right-hand side, shows the identical scene without the male figure: all the people who looked so longingly out at the sea have now left. Wüst's Kühlungsborn series can be read as an allegorical view of the longing for emigration and political freedom at the very moment when this was about to become possible. And so the "time of the photograph" is intensely historical because viewers superimpose their knowledge of subsequent events. By sharp contrast, "the time in the photograph" captures a stagnating and extended present without a future horizon under the conditions of GDR socialism.

There is only one series in Wüst's photobook that seemingly reinstates the chronological imagination and historical time: the photos of the series "October 2" were taken on 6 and 7 October 1989 in Berlin, that is, on the fortieth anniversary of the foundation of the GDR. As the East German leadership prepared bombastic celebrations with a military parade, the seeds of its imminent collapse had already been sown. Thousands of citizens had fled via Hungary and Czechoslovakia, while others stayed and tried to change the system from within, forming protest groups and organizing peaceful demonstrations. But despite this crisis of legitimacy, the politburo in East Berlin refused to engage with this grassroots movement. The brutal crackdown on Chinese pro-democracy protestors in Tiananmen Square a few months before fueled the fear that the GDR regime could resort to similar measures. The GDR's guest of honor was Gorbachev, whose calls for perestroika were ignored by Honecker and his leadership. But as Gorbachev made his way toward the Palast der Republik (Palace of the Republic), the seat of the East German Volkskammer (Parliament), crowds lined the street shouting, "Gorbi, Gorbi."[46]

Like the prologue, Wüst's photo series "October 2" opens with a shot of a television screen showing a very grainy picture of the fortieth-anniversary celebrations in a large assembly or concert hall, presumably in the Palast der Republik. In the foreground, we see the audience standing up in an orderly manner while a choir and orchestra appear to be performing on stage. A dark curtain in the background is adorned with the dates 1949 and 1989 and the GDR symbol of hammer and compass surrounded by a garland of corn. Because of the poor quality of the picture, it is impossible to identify any historical actors who participated in the official events.

The ensuing series then consists of a contact strip that shows street views before and during the main military parade: soldiers and other official groups are photographed in profile marching along the parade route in East Berlin with onlookers lining the streets. Two photographs disrupt the sequentiality of the series: a first full-page photograph shows musicians on a stage with five people in the foreground who seem to be listening to a lackluster rehearsal. A second full-page image depicts crowds lining Schön-hauser Allee behind barriers; a military band is playing while the parade appears to be approaching (fig. 6). There is a sense of collective expectation, as the heads of the onlookers are turned to the left. This full-page photograph thus foregrounds the staged character of a choreography that turned citizens into passive onlookers on a spectacle that aimed to legitimize the GDR. The next strip shows marching bands who are at distance from the crowd: what is most striking about these images is the amount of empty space and the large gaps between participating groups (fig. 7). Empty space is an index of the empty and depleted time of the GDR leadership, which is holding onto hollow rituals of power in the face of change.

---

46. For a video of the official coverage of the military parade and celebrations, see http://www.the-berlin-wall.com/videos/gorbachev-at-gdrs-40th-anniversary-722/ (accessed 22 November 2016); http://www.amara.org/en/videos/cK6YPytFY rgF/info/40-jahre-ddr-40-years-of-gdr-military-parade-full-ceremony/ (accessed 23 November 2016).

Figure 6. Ulrich Wüst, "Oktober 2: 6.–7. Oktober," *Später Sommer/ Letzter Herbst* (1989). © Ulrich Wüst, Kehrer Verlag 2016.

Figure 7. Ulrich Wüst, "Oktober 2: 6.–7. Oktober," *Später Sommer/ Letzter Herbst* (1989). © Ulrich Wüst, Kehrer Verlag 2016.

This series thus highlights how the GDR leadership orchestrated power in public space; it also exposes the ritualistic character of an utterly cheerless spectacle that symbolizes the *Spätzeit* or the end game of the GDR. Overall, the series makes visible an antiquarian scenography that, in a futile gesture, converted public space into a stage for the hollow performance of authoritarian power.[47]

By interweaving strips of negatives with individual photographs that are displayed on one page, Wüst adopts a technique that disrupts the kind of photographic illusionism that points to the historical referent outside the image. Instead of dramatizing a historical moment, the photo narrative creates a network of visual analogies that attune the viewer to resemblances and differences that remain, however, ultimately unreadable. The overall effect of this analogical representational strategy is a radical de-dramatization of the political moment of 1989. *Später Sommer/Letzter Herbst* offers us an ironic and melancholy view of the GDR as a ghostly and emaciated *Spätzeit*.

In the Acoustic Space of the GDR: Christian Petzold's *Barbara*

Christian Petzold is one of the most acclaimed directors of the so-called Berlin School who made his name at the Berlinale in 2005 with *Gespenster* (Ghosts), the second part of his trilogy, which is characterized by a strikingly spectral cinematography that showcases the Berlin Republic as haunted by ghosts.[48] By contrast to the earlier Ghost trilogy, his feature *Barbara* (2012) appears as a fairly realistic history film that offers a nuanced representation of life in the GDR in the early 1980s from the perspective of its eponymous protagonist. Barbara Wolff is a dissident medical doctor who, after a prison sentence, is banished from the prestigious Charité in Berlin to a provincial hospital near the Baltic Sea. She must work under Dr André Reiser, who, as Barbara knows very well, is reporting on

47. On this issue, see Anne Fuchs, *After the Dresden Bombing: Pathways of Memory, 1945 to the Present* (Houndmills: Palgrave Macmillan, 2012), 104–10.

48. The other films are *Die innere Sicherheit* (*The State I Am In*) and *Yella* (2007). On hauntology as a signature of Petzold's work, see Andrew J. Webber, "Topographical Turns: Recasting Berlin in Christian Petzold's *Gespenster*," in *Debating German Cultural Identity since 1989*, 67–81.

her to the local Stasi man, Klaus Schütz. Arriving in the province, Barbara is already plotting her escape with the help of her West German boyfriend, a businessman, who provides her with money and an escape plan. There are two meetings of the West German lover and Barbara: the first time in a forest setting where they engage in hurried sex before the lover is driven off by his Western colleague in a shiny Mercedes Benz. The second furtive rendezvous takes place in an Interhotel where Barbara's lover is called to a business meeting before they have sex. During their conversation, Barbara's lover assures her that she will not need to work in the West because he is earning a good income. This unwanted assurance has an unsettling effect on Barbara who does not share his patriarchal vision of the good life in the West.[49] Over time, Barbara becomes increasingly absorbed by her work in the hospital, taking care of the patients in tandem with André. The film ends with Barbara's return to the hospital after helping Stella, an unhappy young girl who is pregnant and has run away from a youth penal center in Torgau, to escape in her place. Hailed by reviewers as a sort of love story, the film eschews the conventions of melodrama: even though the plot has the makings of a melodrama—a woman is caught between two men who represent two opposing ideological systems—the film abstains from a conventional grammar of passion. As Nick Hodgin comments, "Barbara disrupts generic expectations by consciously undermining the very genre it invokes. Passion is largely absent; at best underplayed, interrupted."[50]

Visually, Petzold's film breaks with the conventional image of the mousy-gray GDR by employing a strikingly warm color palette.[51]

---

49. When the girl from the adjoining hotel room shows her pictures of various rings in the *Quelle* catalogue—an icon of the downward distribution of wealth in the capitalist West—Barbara plays along without any real enthusiasm.

50. Nick Hodgin, "East Germany Revisited, Reimagined, Repositioned: Representing the GDR in Dominik Graf's *Der rote Kakadu* (2005) and Christian Petzold's *Barbara*," in *East, West, and Centre: Reframing Post-1989 European Cinema*, ed. Michael Gott and Todd Herzog (Edinburgh: Edinburgh University Press, 2015), 247.

51. See *The Making of Barbara*, pt. 2, Hans Fromm, Anette Guther, and K. D. Gruber in conversation with Hans-Christian Boese, 0:15–0:45; Christian Petzold, dir., *Barbara* (2013), DVD.

The retro "Kodak look" of the mise-en-scène does not so much induce nostalgia as a sense of historical distance from a bygone world in which technologies are largely absent or antiquated. The state's obsession with controlling its citizens is set in a low-tech context, which features in the establishing sequence in the guise of an old-fashioned tram that transports Barbara to the province. The Trabants and Wartburgs that are used to observe and hassle Barbara symbolize the hopeless backwardness of the GDR. And yet, even though this regime of surveillance appears anachronistic when compared with the technologies of the West, it is no less intrusive and intimidating in its slow and deliberate execution of power.

The competition over speed between East and West features directly in the forest sequence, which includes an encounter between a West German who drives a slick Mercedes Benz that can do 200 kilometers per hour and an East German Trabant owner who laments that he had to wait eight years for his car. For Nick Hodgin the direct juxtaposition of the Trabant to the Mercedes is so clichéd that it becomes parodic, drawing attention to the overworked visual grammar of postunification discourse.[52] The scene ends with the Trabi driving past the Mercedes, which is shown to reverse back on the woodland road. As Andrew Webber observes, the "cartoon form" of speed politics in this scene casts "its more general and subtle ideological freighting in the rest of the film into relief."[53] It is important to emphasize that the film does not merely feature slow speed diegetically as a symbol of backwardness; it also employs an arresting aesthetics of slowness that recuperates *Eigenzeit* under the conditions of surveillance.

In his illuminating essay on Petzold's film, Andrew Webber demonstrates that in *Barbara* the three principal levels of speed in film are slowed down: firstly, the movements of people and things in the filmic space appear as studies in time and motion. Secondly, the motion of the camera is slow; it often favors "a distinctive

---

52. Hodgin, "East Germany Revisited," 248.
53. Andrew J. Webber, "'Good Work': Speed, Slowness, and Taking Care in Christian Petzold's *Barbara*," in *Time in German Literature and Culture*, 177.

attention to the framed image and iconographic organisation."[54] Thirdly, the editing and cutting "is designed to hold action back": even though there are more cuts in *Barbara* than in earlier works by Petzold, the film uses this device to heighten the intensity of the encounter between its principal characters.

Webber's main concern is Petzold's "dynamics of carefulness,"[55] which finds paradigmatic expression in a scene devoted to the contemplation and discussion of Rembrandt's famous painting *The Anatomy Lesson of Dr Nicolaes Tulp* (1632). André has invited Barbara to visit a laboratory, which he has assembled in the hospital so that he can carry out diagnostic tests on location. As Barbara is using the microscope to verify an earlier diagnosis, André observes her while standing at the window, a position that, in the topology of the film, is linked with the theme of surveillance. The establishing sequence represented Barbara's arrival from the point of view of André, who is shown to observe her from a hospital window in the company of the Stasi man, Schütz. Barbara's deliberate behavior in the establishing scene—sitting down on a bench, she lights a cigarette to avoid arriving a minute too early—is a calculated demonstration directed at the Stasi informers. When in the later lab scene Barbara compliments André on his good work (23:59), he seizes the opportunity to gain her confidence by offering her the use of the laboratory. But Barbara remains on her guard because his real role is "Aufpassen, dass sich niemand separiert" (to make sure that nobody segregates themselves) from the GDR. Her comment is an ironic repetition of André's early advice that Barbara should not "segregate" herself from her colleagues in the hospital. Petzold's use of the fast-paced shot-reverse technique in this exchange enhances the tension between the protagonists: their mutual sexual attraction remains shadowed by the political question as to whether trust can be established under the conditions of surveillance. It is at this point that André offers an interpretation of Rembrandt's painting. As Webber demonstrates, his description

---

54. Webber, "Good Work," 180.
55. Webber, "Good Work," 174.

of the painting—a reproduction of it is hanging on the lab wall—is an intertextual citation of the elaborate ekphrastic description of the same painting in W. G. Sebald's *Die Ringe des Saturn* (*The Rings of Saturn*, 1995). I have argued elsewhere that Sebald's own interpretation aims to challenge the disastrous consequences of modern biopolitics, which, for Sebald, was brought about by the Cartesian split between body and mind in early modernity.[56] André follows in the footsteps of the Sebaldian narrator by offering a forensic interpretation of the misrepresentation of a significant detail in the picture: the dead man's dissected hand is anatomically wrong. Both Sebald's narrator and André suggest that the misrepresentation of the hand in a painting that is exemplary of Renaissance realism is symbolic of Rembrandt's partisanship with the victims of history: the body of the dead thief, which is exposed on the slab for the surgeons and viewers to see, is being subjected to retributive punishment even after death by hanging. Webber points out that both Sebald's narrator and André produce readings that engage in the very instrumentalization that they overtly criticize: as André claims that all doctors in Rembrandt's picture have their eyes on the anatomy atlas rather than on the pale body of the dead man, the camera zooms in on one figure in the painting who is gazing at us, the viewers, and not at the anatomy atlas. For Webber this raises the question as to whether this is simply a continuity error or a deliberate device designed to make us even more suspicious of André's manipulation of Barbara. Webber suggests that the scene represents "a broader reflection upon the epistemological—and thereby ontological—status of acts of reading and misreading, of witnessing and interpretation, of situations and behaviours in the film."[57] The incorporation of the painting allows the viewer "to look slowly and carefully at what is hidden in full view."[58]

Building on Webber's insights about Petzold's slow cinematography and the politics of looking in this film, I will examine the use

---

56. Anne Fuchs, "W. G. Sebald's Painters: Some Reflections on Fine Art in W. G. Sebald's Prose Works," *Modern Language Review* 101/1 (2006): 172–74.
57. Webber, "Good Work,"187.
58. Webber, "Good Work," 188.

of diegetic sound. Diegetic sound plays a crucial role in a film that explores the conditions for intimacy and *Eigenzeit* in the context of state surveillance. Rather than using extradiegetic music to underscore emotional intensity in Hollywood fashion, the sound in the film is, in the main, diegetic: we hear wind picking up when Barbara is cycling through a threatening landscape, birdsong, barking dogs, engines of cars, trams, and the ordinary clatter of noise in everyday life.[59] In an interview, Petzold explained that he had recorded the diegetic sound before filming so that his actors could hear it on the set: "The reaction of the actors to the sound has to be natural. It's the ambiance. The ambiance must be the acoustic room of the German Democratic Republic, 1980."[60]

Diegetic sound does not just support the naturalistic representation of the exterior world; it creates an "acoustic space"—to appropriate Petzold's suggestive term—in which all sound is potentially indicative of a menacing intrusion into privacy and the disruption of *Eigenzeit*. Examples of symbolic sound include the sizzling of a defective socket in Barbara's flat, barking dogs, ticking clocks, and the loud ringing of the doorbell, which is a recurring motif. The first time we see Barbara in her flat, she is shown sitting in her bathroom in a white dressing gown smoking a cigarette. Evidently she has just had a bath and is enjoying a small moment of intimacy when she hears a barking dog in the distance followed by a car engine. A furtive look from the window confirms that she is under observation by the Stasi. A further disruption of *Eigenzeit* occurs when the doorbell rings three times. Barbara approaches the door hesitantly but opens it after further knocking: it is not the Stasi but the nosy female caretaker who demands that Barbara accompany

---

59. We also hear parts of a radio broadcast of the overture of Carl Maria von Weber's *Freischütz* (1820)—the paradigmatic German Romantic opera—when Barbara repairs the bicycle tire in her bathroom, and later on, the live transmission of a race in the 1980 Moscow Olympics, which anchors the film in a precise historical context.

60. Petzold employs the phrase "acoustic room" rather than "acoustic space." I employ the latter term to capture the idea of a space of surveillance that produces aural alertness. Daniel Kasman, "Spatial Suspense: A Conversation with Christian Petzold," *Notebook* 16 (2012), https://mubi.com/notebook/posts/spatial-suspense-a-conversation-with-christian-petzold (accessed 19 January 2017).

her immediately to inspect the cellar. Still in her bathrobe, Barbara inquires whether this cannot wait until tomorrow, but the caretaker responds: "Nein. Morgen hab' ich keine Zeit." (8:54; No. Tomorrow I won't have time.) The doorbell is a leitmotif symbolizing the enactment of the type of temporal authoritarianism that strategically disrupts rare moments of intimacy and *Eigenzeit*. As Barbara and the hostile caretaker descend into the dungeon-like cellar, the cinematography employs the suspense techniques of horror movies without, however, overlaying the scene with an extradiegetic soundtrack: standing in the cellar, Barbara notices the barking dog in the distance. The disjuncture between the cinematography and the sound in this scene throws into relief the displacement of fear: the cellar is not the locus of a monstrous threat but a storage facility for coal and the place where Barbara finds the bicycle that enables her to embark on her furtive excursions.

The invasion of intimacy and *Eigenzeit* occurs in the main in the domestic setting. Petzold describes the scene where the Stasi men are searching Barbara's apartment as a deliberately quiet, unrushed, and systematic intrusion:

> Die beiden Männer. Jetzt in Barbaras Wohnung. Einer der beiden, Schütz, sitzt in einem Sessel. Der andere durchsucht die Wohnung. Schweigend, langsam und genau. Arbeitsteilung. Schütz betrachtet Barbara.[61]

> The two men, now in Barbara's flat. One of them, Schütz, is sitting in an armchair. The other one is searching her flat. Silently, slowly, and methodically. Division of labor. Schütz is studying Barbara.

In the acoustic space of the GDR, both stillness and sound can exude threat. The first search scene concludes with the doorbell ringing and a woman entering. She demonstratively puts on a pair of clinical rubber gloves before requesting that Barbara follow her into another room for a strip search.[62] After the house search,

---

61. Christian Petzold, *Barbara: Ein Drehbuch*, ed. Fred Breinersdorfer and Dorothee Schön (Berlin: Deutsche Filmakademie, 2012), 29.
62. While in this scene the body search is conducted offscreen, the later repetition of the search scene shows Barbara's degradation as she is forced to bend over so that the woman can execute a penetrative body search.

Barbara is curled up on her bed when the doorbell rings again: this time it is André, who has come to tell her that the much-awaited serum has arrived and that she is needed to administer it to Stella. Barbara's first reaction to his unplanned visit—"Ich weiß, ich bin zu spät. Können Sie melden." (18:57; I know I am late—you can report me.)—accentuates the Pavlovian function of the doorbell: whenever it rings, Barbara expects the invasion of her privacy.[63] And so Barbara develops a heightened state of alertness and vigilance vis-à-vis the threat of intrusion. She registers André's unannounced visit or the sudden appearance of the piano tuner on her doorstep as unwelcome intrusions because they occur in the same acoustic space of surveillance as the visits by the nasty caretaker or the searches by the Stasi. It is for this reason that Barbara remains on her guard, assuming a somewhat mannered posture that always anticipates surveillance and all kinds of intrusion.

Her vigilance is, however, balanced by the rhythm of her movement through space: this is particularly so when she is shown walking. Barbara's posture and gait are coded as a practice that establishes *Eigenzeit* as biorhythm. The enabling effect of her bodily rhythm can be gleaned from the short scene in which Barbara walks to her flat down a little lane in the village. To fully appreciate the symbolism of this short scene, we need to place it in a longer sequence of events. At the end of her first day, Barbara is waiting at the bus stop in front of the hospital when André passes her in his Wartburg before stopping and reversing to offer her a lift. Accepting his offer rather reluctantly, Barbara opens the door and quickly gets inside. The ensuing conversation during the car ride reveals the asymmetrical power that governs their relationship. André advises Barbara that she should not segregate herself from her colleagues in the hospital because they might feel provincial and second class. His rebuke refers to their lunch break in the staff restaurant: André and his team are discussing a case over lunch,

---

63. It is interesting to note that in the script, André is knocking on the door; during filming Petzold replaced the knocking with the doorbell to underscore its Pavlovian effect.

when he notices Barbara walking toward them with her tray. As he is turning his head to invite her to join their group, she cuts him off by wishing them "Mahlzeit" (an enjoyable lunch) while walking on to a different table. During the car ride she responds to André's reprimand by mocking his choice of the Latin-derived verb "separieren" (to segregate) instead of the more common "absondern" (to set apart). She suggests that his stilted formulation may be symptomatic of his own fear of being second class. When André turns left at a junction without asking for any directions, Barbara brings his complicity with the system and their asymmetrical relationship into the open: he did not need to ask where she is living or why she ended up in the province because he had already been "prepared" by the authorities: "Sie sind doch prepariert! Und ich separiere mich jetzt." (5:57; You have surely been prepared! And now I am going to segregate myself!) By repeating the loaded term "separieren," Barbara rejects André's pitch. Asking him to stop the car, she gets out and walks away from him down the rural lane. Their bristling exchange in the confines of André's car lends Barbara's short walk symbolic significance: it reenacts precisely the type of segregation from the collective identity that had provoked André in the restaurant scene. The rhythmic sound of her footfall accentuates her defiant individuality.

Petzold's film explores the politics of *Eigenzeit* in the context of divided Germany. While the Stasi terrorizes Barbara with its strategy of surveillance and intrusion, André works toward reconciling her to a life in the socialist collective through collaborative work as medical clinicians. His growing attraction adds complexity to his character, thereby avoiding a purely negative representation of the GDR.[64] André offers the prospect of a useful and fulfilling life that makes its peace with the Stasi and the repressive state. The West German lover promised a seemingly free and unburdened life in the West that, however, comes with new strings attached. Because

---

64. On this issue, see Debbie Pinfold, "The End of the Fairy Tale? Christian Petzold's *Barbara* and the Difficulties of Interpretation," *German Life & Letters* 67/2 (2014): 280–300.

his deep-seated patriarchal attitudes would turn her into a priceless asset, Barbara rejects this commodified version of freedom. However, her return to the hospital at the end of the film is deliberately anticlimactic and highly ambivalent: sitting at the bedside of a youngster who attempted to commit suicide, she is facing André, who is her colleague, a Stasi informer, and a potential lover. The silence in the final scene is laden and heavy with uncertainty. It is left completely open how Barbara will fare in the GDR before the fall of the Berlin Wall.

Petzold's slow cinematography creates an acoustic space in which diegetic sound often heralds the methodical intrusion into privacy and the disruption of *Eigenzeit* by agents of the state. The ringing doorbell, the running car engines, ticking clocks, and so forth produce a grammar of interruption that, in its very predictability, is extremely threatening. Responding to the politics of intrusion by the agents of the state, Barbara develops and fine-tunes a form of vigilant attentiveness that always anticipates her opponents' next move. Under such conditions Barbara's quest for *Eigenzeit* will remain precarious.

The Longing for Transcendence: Ulrich Seidl's *Paradies: Glaube*

According to Thomas Luckmann, the widely shared assumption that the Western project of modernization inevitably involves a process of secularization, understood as the shrinking and eventual disappearance of religion from the modern world, is mistaken. As modern society evolved, Luckmann argues, it could not maintain "the social universality of an essentially religious world view oriented to the supremacy of a salvational articulation of the great transcendences."[65] But the emancipation of a secular domain did not remove religion from modern life altogether; rather, it relegated

---

65. Thomas Luckmann, *The Invisible Religion: The Problem of Religion in Modern Society* (New York: Collier-Macmillan, 1967), 132.

it to the private domain where it became a matter of individual choice. In modernity the compulsory sacred world view gave way to a variety of competing belief systems from which individuals could pick themes to combine and build them into "a private system of ultimate significance."[66] For Luckmann the privatization of religion also diminishes the "span of transcendence": the longing for the great transcendence of doctrinal religion transmutes into the search for "intermediate" or even "minimal" notions of transcendence that respond to the individual's needs.[67] Luckmann does not explicitly highlight an important side effect of this currency conversion: as the great transcendence is exchanged for more attainable little transcendences, the notion loses its transtemporal quality, that is, its association with eternity as a time that encompasses past, present, and future. At the beginning of the twenty-first century, the search for attainable transcendences also points to the precariousness of social relations. Religious sects and sectarianism have flourished in recent decades, not least because they promise certainty and salvation in an era that is characterized by profound economic, social, technological, and environmental upheaval.

A recent example of artistic engagement with the quest for attainable transcendence in the age of precariousness is Austrian filmmaker Ulrich Seidl's *Paradies: Glaube* (Paradise: Faith), which was released in 2012. The film is the middle part of Seidl's Paradise trilogy, which offers an ironic exploration of three different versions of paradise in the twenty-first century.[68] The trilogy foregrounds the precariousness of happiness in the twenty-first century by covering the same period of time in the lives of three female protagonists who are members of the same family but embark on individual holidays in search of their private paradise. As in previous films, Seidl allowed the narrative to develop during the shooting in interaction with his cast of lay and professional actors: his script

---

66. Luckmann, *The Invisible Religion*, 134.

67. Luckmann, *The Invisible Religion*, 135.

68. The subtitles are derived from Ödon von Horvath's play *Glaube Liebe Hoffnung* (Faith Love Hope, 1932). Originally conceived as one feature film, Seidl decided to make three full-length feature films.

contains no written dialogue, as he believes that dialogue should evolve in the filming process. The first part, *Paradies: Liebe* (Paradise: Love), tells the story of fifty-year-old Teresa (Margarete Tiesel), a single mother, who travels to Kenia in search of sex. On the beach of her resort she meets Mungu (Peter Kazungu), a so-called beach boy who prostitutes himself to European women. While in Visconti's *Death in Venice* (1971) the beach is the site of Aschenbach's tragic desire for Tadzio, in Seidl's film it is the locus of economic exchange between African men and their European "sugar mamas": the desire for love is costly and results in mutual exploitation. In this film Seidl combined handheld camera work with static shots in the dialogue scenes. Together this creates a documentary effect that is further enhanced by the participation of African lay actors in the cast. *Paradies: Hoffnung* (Paradise: Hope), the third part in the trilogy, relates the experience of Teresa's daughter Melanie (Melanie Lenz), who is forced to spend her holidays in a summer camp for overweight teenagers. The monotonous daily regime of indoor and outdoor exercise and rationed meals is punctuated by the teenagers' nightly chats about love and desire, their night raids on the communal fridge, and the secretive smoking of cigarettes. Melanie falls in love with the director of the camp who eventually enforces professional distance by means of a *Kontaktverbot*, the prohibition to talk to him.[69]

The protagonist of the second part, *Paradies: Glaube*, is Teresa's sister Anna Maria, a middle-aged medical technician and Roman Catholic who spends her holidays spreading the word of God around the impoverished suburbs of Vienna. These excursions to the margins of urban society allow Seidl to depict the dark underside of the neoliberal era: Anna Maria seeks out those who have fallen off the social ladder because they cannot keep up with life in the superfast lane and with the demand for continual innovation

---

69. Florian Mundhenke has shown that Seidl established himself as a controversial filmmaker who traverses the genre boundaries between documentary and fictional filmmaking to new effect. See Florian Mundhenke, "Authenticity versus Artifice: The Hybrid Cinematic Approach of Ulrich Seidl," *Austrian Studies* 19 (2011): 113–25.

in the knowledge economy. Precariousness is thus a prominent theme in a film that places the protagonist's religiosity squarely in the context of the global era. In her domestic environment Anna Maria engages in obsessive cleaning, praying to Jesus, and masochistic acts of self-flagellation and penitential shuffling on her knees through the rooms of her monastic abode. Anna Maria shares her fundamentalist Catholicism with a small group of like-minded zealots who call themselves Legio Cordis Jesu and gather in her house to pray for Austria to become Catholic again: these zealots view themselves as "the spearhead of true faith" (25:46). Even though the protagonist is a Roman Catholic, the institution of the church no longer articulates her faith. Anna Maria is never shown to attend official mass or to go to confession. In her search for the great transcendence she has developed private rituals that take place within the four walls of her home.

The establishing shot shows us a dimly illuminated and Spartan-looking study in the evening: the static camera is positioned in the doorway facing a window covered by slatted blinds. The artificial light coming in through the window barely illuminates a crucifix on the left wall and a religious painting of Christ on the right, which is hanging above a desk with laptop, printer, and desk lamp. While the setting is strikingly Spartan and geometrical, the laptop and printer indicate that the story unfolds in our present age. Seidl predominantly employs a static camera for the scenes that take place inside Anna Maria's home. Diegetic sound is used to indicate movement: we hear how the door is being unlocked and opened before we see Anna Maria entering the room and switching on the desk lamp (0:50). A profile medium long shot shows her praying in front of the crucifix: "Beloved Jesus, please accept my sacrifice today for the grave sin of unchastity. So many people are obsessed with sex. Free them from their hell" (1:06). Unlocking the drawer of the desk, she takes out a whip, strips to the waist, and—falling on her knees—begins to ritually and violently flagellate herself until red abrasions appear on her back (1:37–2.32), the stigmata of her fervent love of Christ. While the static camera alternates medium-long profile shots of Anna Maria with rear views, it never shows a close-up of Anna Maria's face: the viewer has no access to her emotions. The lack of extradiegetic music emphasizes the documentary and voyeuristic effect of Seidl's cinematography.

The topography in the film symbolically foregrounds the sharp separation between Anna Maria's public front and her private belief system. However, the privacy of Anna Maria's religious world is of course destroyed by the voyeuristic and perhaps even pornographic exposure of her sexual and religious practices, which transforms her from professional expert into a precarious subject. The different locations also stand for the different temporal trajectories associated with the various social spheres that Anna Maria traverses. While her house is the guarded location for the enactment of a premodern religion, the film also brings into view the contemporary urban world, as, for example, represented by the hospital, Anna Maria's workplace. In scene 2 she is shown working in the radiology department of her hospital, using high-tech CT scanners and a laptop to screen the patients. In this setting Anna Maria perceives the human body from a scientific and objective view: when carrying out mammograms and magnetic resonance imagining (MRI) on various patients, she instructs them calmly not to move while the image is being taken. In a rare point of view shot we are shown Anna Maria studying the MRI of a human brain on a laptop in the lab (4:09). In her professional role, Anna Maria is a highly skilled medical technician who adopts a rational and scientific perspective. The scene ends with a brief conversation with her boss about her holiday plans. In her professional life, there is no indication that Anna Maria's connection to the contemporary world is so precarious. After work she exits from a subway station, and then walks along a busy road before traversing a park en route to her house. The park is a recurring motif and a heterotopia in Foucault's sense. "Heterotopias are something like counter-sites," comments Foucault, "a kind of effectively enacted utopia in which the real sites . . . that can be found within culture, are simultaneously represented, contested and inverted."[70] The park is both a

---

70. Michel Foucault, "Of Other Spaces: Utopias and Heterotopias," trans. Jay Miskowiec, *Diacritics* 16/1 (1986): 24.

place of reprieve—on her way home, she stops and sits down on a bench, enjoying a moment of idleness (5:58)—and the site where she encounters a grotesque group sex scene at night (38:10) that is reminiscent of Hieronymus Bosch's triptych *The Garden of Earthly Delights* (ca. 1490). Bosch's central panel depicts a garden teeming with an abundance of strange fruits and plants, fantastic animals, and nude male and female figures who are engaged in all kinds of sensual and amorous activities.

The suburbs and apartment blocks that Anna Maria visits to proselytize are a fourth type of location. Knocking on the doors of strangers, many of them immigrants or social dropouts, she announces, "Good morning: the mother of God has come to visit you today" (11:16). That mother is a two-foot clay statue of the Virgin Mary, to which she insists they pray. When Anna Maria interacts with the outside world, Seidl employs the handheld camera and long takes for the scenes unfolding inside the apartments that Anna Maria visits. For example, in one particularly grotesque scene Anna Maria tries to convert an immigrant woman from Russia or the former Soviet Union who is an alcoholic and lives in a run-down apartment. The woman represents the modern precariat: her filthy flat suggests that she has been living alone for quite some time and that Anna Maria is a rare visitor. At the opening of this scene, which is shot in one long take, we see the woman opening a beer bottle at her kitchen sink in which piles of dirty crockery are stacked up. Entering the living room where Anna Maria is sitting on a sofa, she asks whether Anna Maria is from the police or a saleswoman. When Anna Maria replies that she is from the church, the woman comments, "Church—that's harmless" (1:28), and offers Anna Maria a beer. Anna Maria now gets down to her real business by gifting a set of rosary beads to the woman, explaining that praying the rosary can cure her from beer, vodka, and sex with men (1:28). When Anna Maria asks the woman where she is from, she responds: "Selber kommen her. Da bin ich." (1:29; Mind yourself where you from. I am here now.) Anna Maria's questions about the woman's origins are met with heightened emotions—eventually she reveals that her mother did not care for her because she "was fucking 100,000 men" (1:29), a comment that allows Anna Maria to introduce Maria as heavenly mother. As Anna Maria is proselytizing, the woman tries to grab Anna Maria's breasts, tearing at her skirt and underwear. Moments of intimacy alternate with aggressive attacks on Anna Maria, who persists in her attempt to save the woman from the demon of drink. The scene moves to the kitchen, where an extended physical battle ensues, which is rendered in one long take with a handheld camera. As Anna Maria tries to wrest the beer bottles from her, the woman embraces her, declaring: "I love you, my beautiful woman" (1.31). Even though the woman's emotional neediness translates into increasing violence, Anna Maria attempts to calm her down. The scene ends with the woman opening another bottle of beer and Maria praying at the door: "Jesus, help this poor woman. Jesus. She really needs your help" (1.35). The high-angle shots, the long takes, the handheld camera, and the improvised dialogue endow this scene with dramatic intensity and rare intimacy: even though Anna Maria is a zealous proselytizer, she shows genuine humanity and care for the woman. By expressly taking his time, shooting this lengthy scene in long takes, Seidl adopts a documentary format that foregrounds social deprivation and precariousness as motivating factors for Anna Maria's longing for transcendence.

Anna Maria's house is a heterotopic space in which she observes the rituals of her premodern religion. When she returns home after work, she crosses the threshold into another world: hanging up her keys and taking off her shoes, she enters the domain of her private belief system that, even though it draws on Catholic dogma, runs counter to official church teachings. By positioning his static camera in the hallway at a 90° angle to the door, Seidl accentuates the importance of the threshold, which divides the private domain from the public sphere. Anna Maria starts her time off work by feverishly washing and polishing the floors (6:58)—once she enters her house, her modern desire for hygiene transmutes into a premodern act of cleansing from the dirt of this world. The film shows, however, that her obsessive rituals are symptomatic of a pathological obsession that does not engender happiness.

The different spaces and locations in the film evoke different temporal trajectories: the hospital stands for a high-tech society in which well-being can be engineered with the help of diagnostic technologies. The suburbs are depressing places of abandonment and stagnation on the fringes of society: they represent a geography of disempowerment that is the by-product of the disembedding forces of globalization. While the park is an ambivalent site that can engender moments of horror and happiness, Anna Maria's home is the site of obsessive control: within the four walls of her house, Anna Maria attempts to fend off social precariousness by observing a ritualistic and obsessive timetable.

On the first morning of her holiday, we see Anna Maria playing religious hymns on her electronic keyboard under the window of her sitting room before she embarks on her religious mission. Returning home, she reenters the study—her private torture chamber—this time in full daylight (14:35): removing an alarm clock and a belt with metal rings from her desk she fastens the belt tightly around her waist in preparation for yet another sacrifice to her beloved Christ. Having set her alarm clock, she begins shuffling on her knees through the house, praying Holy Marys with the rosary beads in her hands. While Anna Maria moves ever more quickly on her knees from room to room, praying feverishly, the camera remains static. Anna Maria's sadomasochistic punishment takes back the domestification of the "wild transcendental experiences" that, as Luckmann argues, remained part of the medieval church tradition but were later harnessed, controlled, and ultimately rejected by the modern church. This premodern ritual ends when the alarm bell goes off (17:17): we then watch how Anna Maria tends to her wounds with modern disinfectants—her escape into a premodern heterotopia of religious fervor is framed and controlled by clock time and modern technologies.

At one point the filmic narrative points to the etiology of Anna Maria's religious neurosis: when her estranged and paraplegic Muslim husband, Nabil, unexpectedly returns home after a period of two years (27:53), we learn that her quest for religion was probably triggered by the accident that left him wheelchair bound. Before long, they are waging a personal religious war: as Anna Maria keeps refusing to have any physical relationship with him, Nabil begins to view Christ as his rival. Alone in the house, he symbolically resumes his marital role by, for example, replacing the image of Christ on Anna Maria's bedside table with their wedding photograph (42:35). However, even though Anna Maria takes care of his physical needs, it is clear that she has long since left Nabil for her new lover, Jesus. Having moved her bed into her study to safeguard her privacy, she is shown masturbating holding the crucifix in her arms under the duvet (1:08). Nabil's pleading becomes increasingly abusive and violent as he tries to enforce his "marital rights."[71] Their marital warfare culminates in an attempted rape scene: one night Nabil calls for Anna Maria's help as he is lying helplessly on the floor. When she tries to lift him back into his bed, he drags her down on the floor (1:40). A wrestling match ensues in which he attempts to roll on top of her, pushing his hand between her legs, while she is desperately fending him off. Rolling around on the floor, they slap and hit each other. As in the scene with the drunken woman, Seidl employs a handheld camera to capture the shocking eruption of violence in one long take. The viewer is put in the position of the distanced and perhaps Olympian observer of pathological behavior.

These rare dramatic scenes contrast sharply with Seidl's strikingly slow and artificial cinematography that favors symmetry and stillness. The use of a static camera for much of the action that is set inside Anna Maria's house produces a sequence of stylized *tableaux vivants* that create both a hyperreal and antirealist effect.[72] And so a gap opens up between the depiction of religious fanaticism and

---

71. When Anna Maria attempts to exorcise his demons by spraying him with holy water while he is asleep on the sofa bed, Nabil wakes up screaming (1:18). Nabil retaliates the next day by forcefully removing all Christian icons and symbols from the walls. He recovers from his iconoclastic rage by flouting Islamic rule and drinking a beer in the kitchen (1:20). Anna Maria then strikes back by stowing his wheelchair in the garage: Nabil is now forced to drag himself in reptile fashion on his belly on the floors of the house (1:23).

72. Mundhenke's observation about Seidl's earlier films also applies to his Paradise trilogy: "The anti realism or hyperrealism can be said to work similarly to a Brechtian alienation effect, breaking through both the solidity of documentary sobriety and/or the completeness of situational illusions. . . . The images seem offending and insulting in terms of the actions depicted, but quite artificial and conceptualized in terms of aesthetic techniques." Mundhenke, "Authenticity versus Artifice," 124.

marital warfare in a documentary format, on the one hand, and the self-reflexive artificiality of the *tableau vivant*, on the other. This tension does not allow the viewer to settle into a comfortable position of moral judgment. A striking example of Seidl's aesthetics of stillness is the scene in which Anna Maria plays religious hymns on her electronic keyboard under the window (8:40; fig. 8).

Here the visual representation and diegetic sound contradict each other: even though Anna Maria is comically out of tune and even though her keyboard playing is not very accomplished, the mise-en-scène exudes a sense of pictorial stillness. This scene can be read in conjunction with the strikingly similar image in Petzold's *Barbara* where the protagonist is shown at the piano with landscape pictures. In both films piano music and the electronic keyboard are part of a particular soundscape that symbolizes the protagonists' desire for an alternative to the disenchanted here and now. But in both films music cannot fulfill the desire for transcendence because the acoustic space of the film is overlaid by audible threats. In addition, both films employ diegetic sound to foreground their protagonists' experience of time: while in *Barbara* the emphasis is on time as a weight, in Seidl's film diegetic sound (ranging from trees blowing

Figure 8. Film still from Ulrich Seidl, *Paradies: Glaube* (2012), directed and produced by Ulrich Seidl. © Ulrich Seidl Film Produktion.

in the wind to rainfall or thunderstorms) reminds the viewer of a premodern cyclical time that coexists with the modern time of urban Vienna. Ironically, Anna Maria's longing for premodern time is symbolized by an electronic prosthesis, her keyboard. Seidl dignifies her religious quest by tapping into the tradition of Dutch interior painting: the keyboard scene under the window evokes Jan Vermeer's *The Music Lesson* (early 1660s) with its photorealist attention to detail and remarkable sense of geometry (fig. 9).

Figure 9. Jan Vermeer, *Lady at the Virginal with a Gentleman, "The Music Lesson"* (early 1660s). Royal Collection Trust. Public Domain.

The similarity invites contrasting analysis: while the female figure in Vermeer's painting is practicing her music in the presence of a male teacher or cavalier, Anna Maria is alone. In Vermeer's painting, the face of the female figure is reflected in the tilted and framed mirror above the virginal. In European painting, mirrors often represent vanity or the quest for self-awareness and truth. The mirror in Vermeer's painting also reflects a bit of the foreground carpet and some of the floor tiles as well as a leg and the crossbar of the easel, which introduces the artist into the painting. The viewer is thus presented with a scene of a young woman making music with her music teacher or a gentleman cavalier as an unseen artist is painting them. In Seidl's shot of the first keyboard scene the slatted blinds prevent the reflection of Anna Maria's face. Later on, Seidl too employs a mirror effect when Anna Maria is shown playing her keyboard in her study at night (1:38): the reflection of the ceiling lamp in the window sliced through by the seams of the net curtain not only evokes Anna Maria's desire for transcendence but also attracts attention to modern technologies of representation. What Vermeer's *Music Lesson* and Seidl's keyboard scenes share is a great sense of distance from the figures: with their backs turned to the viewer, they remain ultimately impenetrable. The intertextual allusion to Vermeer's work thus accentuates the dignity of Anna Maria's aspiration as well as her extreme loneliness. It is important to note that Anna Maria's and Nabil's longing for a better world is visually represented in analogous terms: Nabil too is shown praying at the window with the blinds slanted and the blue fir tree visible in the middle distance (1:13).

Shortly before the end we see Anna Maria weeping over the body of Nabil, who lies prostrate on the couch in the living room and appears like the dead body of Christ (1:37): regardless of whether one reads this scene as a visual allusion to various pictorial representations of the Lamentation of Christ or as a Pietà in reverse view, Anna Maria's pain is aesthetically ennobled by the strong chiaroscuro effect that is evocative of Renaissance art. The lamp on the wall exudes a warm light that contrasts starkly with a dark framed painting showing an Alpine scene. Seidl combines the hyperrealist depiction of small details with the symbolic use of lighting that shifts from light to dark with some intermediate value. In this way, he constructs a tableau of suffering that places Anna Maria in a long line of martyrdom. What we have here then is a filmic representation of religious fervor that employs two opposing registers: on the one hand, the story pathologizes Anna Maria by suggesting a causal link between her faith in Christ as her savior and Nabil's accident. On the other hand, the cinematography undercuts this causal logic through an aesthetic of stillness that places her quest in the framework of the European history of art.

Seidl's film remains poised between the clinical exploration of the protagonist's religious fervor and the aesthetic rehabilitation of her quest for release from worldly pain. While we follow the plot with titillating horror and a good dosage of voyeuristic pleasure, the film ennobles the protagonist through an intertextually enriched filmic language that places Anna Maria's longing in a long art-historical tradition. The scenes shot in a documentary format in the deprived suburbs of Vienna remind the viewer of the abject deprivation and loneliness suffered by those who have not managed to keep up with global capitalism. The scene with the alcoholic woman brings into view Anna Maria's humanity: even though she is driven by religious fanaticism, she is also shown to be quite tender and caring. By foregrounding what cries out to heaven, Seidl legitimates the protagonist's desperate quest for release from a disenchanted world.

Disruptive Performances: Maren Ade's
Toni Erdmann

German filmmaker Maren Ade (1976–) studied at the Hochschule für Fernsehen und Film in Munich and is loosely associated with the Berlin School of German cinema: she made her debut with the feature film *Der Wald vor lauter Bäumen* (The Forest for the Trees, 2003), which won the Sundance Film Festival Special Jury Prize in 2005. Six years later the romantic drama *Alle Anderen* (Everyone Else, 2009) followed and was awarded the Große Preis der Jury at the Berlin Film Festival. Her third feature film, the internationally acclaimed tragicomedy *Toni Erdmann*, was released in 2016.[73] In an interview Ade explained that it took her almost four and a half years to write the *Toni Erdmann* script, shoot the film, and edit 100 hours of footage down to 156 minutes.[74] As a film director, Ade shares with Christian Petzold the preference for long takes, and in keeping with the realism of the Berlin School, the film employs no extradiegetic music.

Toni Erdmann tracks the fraught relationship between Winfried Conradi (Peter Simonischek), a retired music teacher in his sixties living in the West German city of Aachen, and his daughter Ines (Sandra Hüller), a successful business consultant currently working in Bucharest. Winfried is a member of the left-leaning German post-war generation that, having worked through the National Socialist past, has embraced the idea of a pluralistic, open, and socially responsible society. His daily life revolves around his music, looking after his blind dog, Willie, and caring for his ailing mother.

---

73. It was nominated for the Palme d'Or and won the competition award at the Cannes Film Festival in 2016. It won the European Film Awards for Best Film, Best Director, Best Screenwriter, Best Actor, and Best Actress in 2016. Other awards include the German Film Awards for Best Feature Film, Best Performance, Best Screenplay, and Best Director; the German Film Critics Association Award in 2017; the New York Film Critics Circle Awards for the Best Foreign Language Film in 2016; and the Toronto Film Critics Association Awards in 2016, among many others.

74. See Jonathan Romney, "Maren Ade: Toni Erdmann's Humour Comes out of a Big Desperation," *The Observer*, 21 January 2017, https://www.theguardian.com/film/2017/jan/21/maren-ade-toni-erdmann-humour-comes-out-of-desperation-director; Wenke Husmann, "Tränen gelacht und ein bisschen gegruselt," *Die Zeit*, 14 May 2017, http://www.zeit.de/kultur/film/2016-05/toni-erdmann-cannes-filmfestival-maren-ade; Dietmar Dath, "Jetzt mach mir hier aber mal bitte keine Zähne," *Frankfurter Allgemeine Zeitung*, 13 July 2016, http://www.faz.net/aktuell/feuilleton/kino/video-filmkritiken/maren-ades-toni-erdmann-im-kino-14337456.html; Christina Tillmann, "Der Widerspenstigen Zähmung," *Neue Zürcher Zeitung*, 20 July 2016, https://www.nzz.ch/feuilleton/kino/toni-erdmann-der-widerspenstigen-zaehmung-ld.106521; Richard Brady, "A Stilted Vision of a Declining Europe," *The New Yorker*, 21 December 2016, http://www.newyorker.com/culture/richard-brody/a-stilted-vision-of-a-declining-europe-in-toni-erdmann; A. O. Scott, "Dad's a Prankster Trying to Jolt His Conformist Daughter," *New York Times*, 22 December 2016, https://www.nytimes.com/2016/12/22/movies/toni-erdmann-review.html.

His life is governed by the routine of "long-term, and incremental and above all predictable time" that, according to Richard Sennett, organized citizens' lives from cradle to grave in the era of social capitalism.[75] The establishing scene shows that Winfried has a penchant for practical jokes: when a delivery man arrives with a parcel at his front door, he claims that the package must be for his brother Toni who has just been released from prison. Calling for Toni, he disappears inside the house only to return in the guise of his fictional brother: clothed in a disheveled dressing gown and wearing joke-shop false teeth, which he keeps in his shirt pocket, he plays the part of the sleazy crook before revealing that it was a prank and dispatching the bewildered courier with a generous tip. The scene is shot from the perspective of the courier, who has to wait for Winfried at the door: the company logo *Global Packaging* on his uniform is an early signal that this film unfolds in the context of global turbocapitalism.

While Winfried's life is rooted in his local community, Ines is part of a globally mobile professional elite: she inhabits a stylish apartment in Bucharest and moves with ease through glitzy hotels, bars, restaurants, gyms, and shopping malls. Her social map shares the sterile yet ostentatious idiom of global capitalism that enforces uniformity on how to display and spend lucre. Dislocated from locality and history, these locations are nonplaces in Marc Augé's sense of the word.[76] Ines's life takes place in the fast lane: she has long internalized the neoliberal norms of global capitalism: flexibility, ruthless competition, and short-term gains are prioritized above loyalty, stability, and experience. Her colleagues and friends are potential competitors who maintain shifting friendships while competing against each other in the production of the best deal in the quickest time possible. Outwardly Ines is a successful business consultant, but her life is precarious, lonely, and largely devoid of attachments.

---

75. Sennett, *The Culture of the New Capitalism*, 23.

76. Marc Augé, *Non-Places: Introduction to an Anthropology of Supermodernity*, trans. John Howe (London: Verso, 1995).

We meet Ines for the first time on a brief return to Germany for an early birthday party organized by her mother, Winfried's ex-wife: while her family is talking admiringly about Ines's recent business trip to Shanghai and her future prospects, Ines neglects her scarce family time for business calls on her cell phone in the garden. When Ines finally joins the family gathering, Winfried inserts his false teeth for comic relief, announcing that he will have to visit her in Bucharest to personally deliver her birthday present. Their relationship is clearly awkward and strained: Winfried knows little about his daughter's life, and she is unaware of her father's health issues and resists close communication.[77] When he goes looking for her in the garden to have a chat she pretends to be on her phone to avoid a personal conversation (14:05). Ines informs him that she cannot join him and her grandmother for breakfast the next morning; Winfried quips that he will invite Inge instead, his new hired daughter. After Ines has dashed back to Bucharest to prepare her company's plan to outsource the work of a Romanian oil company by shedding the indigenous workforce, Winfried settles back into his predictable and orderly life. The death of his beloved dog then frees him up for a surprise trip to Bucharest. The scene shifts to a slick lobby of a corporate building in Bucharest, where Winfried is waiting for Ines, who eventually turns up surrounded by suited executives. Inserting his fake teeth, Winfried is planning a jocular appearance only to find that Ines passes through the security gates with her entourage without acknowledging his presence. She has noticed him out of the corner of her eye and sends her personal assistant, Anca (Ingrid Bisu) to inform Winfried about the various hotel options in the city. When Winfried inquires about what his daughter is like as a boss, Anca replies euphemistically that Ines provides her with lots of feedback about her performance (20:51–21:36).

---

77. He is wearing a blood-pressure monitor under his shirt, which inflates from time to time. Ines notices the noise and inquires whether she needs to be worried, but Winfried fobs her off.

Winfried.	Performance—this means the—describes your job?
Anca.	Nein, performance ist also meine Arbeit im Allgemeinen—z.B. im [*sic*] Meetings, im äh—mit dem Team, im Kontakt mit dem Klient.
W.	Und was ist da wichtig, ich meine das Wichtigste, im Kontakt mit dem Klienten?
A.	. . . Die Kunst ist, dem Klient zu erklären, was er eigentlich will.
W.	Na, das kann meine Tochter bestimmt gut.
W.	Performance—this describes your job?
A.	Performance—that's my work in general, in meetings with the team, and in contact with the client.
W.	And what is most important in the contact with the client?
A.	. . . The art of telling the client what he really wants.
W.	I am sure that my daughter can do that very well.

Ines and her colleagues move in a corporate world that is governed by normative behavioral scripts and business targets that can be measured by KPIs (Key Performance Indicators). In this pressurized environment, performance denotes conformity with the neoliberal values of perpetual innovation, profitability, competitiveness, and advancement. Disguised by the jargon of "team building," the corporate idea of performance turns colleagues into competitors without solidarity. Corporate socializing is therefore no less competitive than the workplace. Ines spends her free time working out in the gym, eating in expensive restaurants and drinking in slick bars, making cheerless trips to strip clubs with colleagues, and doing the odd line of coke—all of this is done as part of the team. Even her sex life is governed by competition: meeting her male colleague who is her lover in a hotel room, Ines avoids intercourse with him by spurring him on to ejaculate onto a petit four that she promises to eat, if he manages to hit his target.[78] Because sex is just another form of performance, it is devoid of intimacy. As a female

---

78. Her lover told her that her boss advised him not to "fuck her too frequently" (1:16) because otherwise she might lose her drive. Refusing intercourse, Ines picks this up and observes sarcastically that she does not want to lose her drive (1:17).

consultant in a macho corporate environment, Ines regularly encounters deeply ingrained gender stereotypes: even though she has been assigned a major project, Henneberg (Michael Wittenborn), a powerful client, introduces Ines to his wife, Natalia, as a "specialist for shopping" (25:40). The next day she has to undertake the demeaning role of accompanying Henneberg's wife to a faceless shopping mall: the biggest mall in Europe is, however, largely empty because the locals cannot afford to go shopping there.

The movie also explores opposing generational perspectives about what constitutes fulfilling time and the good life. When father and daughter get to spend some leisure time together by the indoor swimming pool of a stylish fitness center, the membership at which comes with Ines's job, Winfried brings up the topic of happiness (39:05–40.00):

Winfried.   Na, bist du eigentlich auch ein bisschen glücklich hier?

Ines.   Was meinst'n mit Glück? Glück ist ein starkes Wort.

W.   Ich meine, ob du mal ein bisschen zum Leben kommst, auch?

I.   Mal ins Kino gehen, oder so?

W.   Na ja, mal was machen, was Spaß macht.

I.   Da schwirren jetzt ganz schön viele Begriffe hier rum, ne: Spaß—Glück—Leben—musst de mal ein bissschen ausdünnen. Was findest du den lebenswert? Wenn du schon die großen Themen hochbringst? (Pause)

W.   Das kann ich jetzt so spontan gar nicht sagen; ich wollte eigentlich nur wissen, wie's dir geht.

I.   Das ist mir schon klar, aber dann must du auch ne Antwort haben. (Pause)

W.   And, are you a little bit happy?

I.   What do you mean by happiness? Happiness is a loaded term.

W.   I mean whether you have time to live a little.

I.   Going to the movies or that sort of thing?

W.   Well, doing things now and then that are fun.

I.   Your language is peppered with quite a number of different terms: fun, happiness, life—you need to tone it down a bit. What do you find worth living for, since you are bringing up the big issues?

W.   I cannot answer that on the spot. I only wanted to know how you are.

I.   I got that, but you should really have an answer.

Ines's sarcastic response to her father's care rejects his idealism, which she finds misplaced, naive, and out of sync with the hard realities of turbocapitalism. After some hurtful exchanges over the course of the next day, Winfried takes his farewell, pretending to return home to Aachen: we watch him board a taxi from Ines's point of view: standing on the balcony of her designer apartment with a badly injured toe, she waves at him with tears running down her face: it is left open whether she is weeping because of the pain in her toe or because of the difficult relationship with her father.

In reality Winfried's seeming departure gives birth to Toni Erdmann. He pops up in a stylish restaurant at the very moment that Ines is telling her female friends that she has just had the worst weekend of her life. Equipped with a long-haired wig and his false set of joke teeth, and wearing a sharkskin suit and tie, a look that makes him appear like a crooner, he adopts the role of Toni Erdmann, freelance management coach. Even though his appearance is outlandish and characterized by deliberate slippage, he manages to pose as Henneberg's personal life coach, inveigling his way into his daughter's circles in order to disrupt their arrogance, superiority, and sense of entitlement. His role-playing is characterized by an unsettling slippage: while Ines sees through his act straightaway, her colleagues and friends are intrigued and bemused, as they fail to disentangle role play from reality. Even though it should be blatantly evident that he is playing a role, their own entanglement in constant professional role play and a world of simulation has crippled their sense of judgment about the underlying reality. Because the fanciful figure of Toni Erdmann could after all herald a new management style, they collectively buy Toni's story. Winfried's carnivalesque performance in the guise of Toni Erdmann is thus *the* pivotal device in the film that exposes the collectively enacted social conformity of Ines's circle.

But the carnivalesque not only disrupts consensus about the prevailing social order; it also brings into view alternative temporalities that challenge the rational definition of time as an economic resource. The film hints at a cyclical notion of time early on when

Winfried's school choir performs a humorous song on the occasion of a colleague's retirement. Winfried and the kids appear on stage in the guise of Death with their faces painted black and white. The symbolic conjoining of humor and death places Winfried's ensuing roles in the long tradition of the carnivalesque, which, through burlesque and grotesque exaggeration, reminds us that life is cyclical and a prelude to death.[79]

Even though Ines is outraged by her father's fanciful acts, she cannot resist his encroachment on her life. And so, in the course of the film, Winfried's increasingly outlandish role-playing cracks her social veneer, (re)establishing a precarious bond with his daughter: while they are visiting the Romanian woman that he met at a reception, Winfried passes himself off as the German ambassador and Ines as his secretary, Miss Schnuck.[80] The scene involves the painting of Easter eggs and culminates in their joint performance of the iconic Frank Sinatra song "My Way": Winfried plays the keyboard, and Ines hollers the song with increasing emotion in front of the astonished Romanian family. In this scene her vocal performance is a form of self-expression that literally gives voice to her longing for personal empowerment. The handheld camera stays focused on Ines for the duration of the song to capture her vulnerability, underscoring her emotional need beneath the veneer of success.

Over time Winfried's antics do have an infectious effect. The birthday party scene deserves close scrutiny because here Ines engages in an impromptu drama that disrupts her acquiescence with the corporatization of all aspects of life. As she is making final

---

79. Michail M. Bachtin, *Literatur und Karneval: Zur Romantheorie und Lachkultur*, trans. Alexander Kämpfe (Frankfurt a. Main: Fischer, 2000); M. Bachtin, *Rabelais und seine Welt: Volkskultur als Gegenkultur*, ed. Renate Lachmann (Frankfurt a. Main: Suhrkamp, 1995).

80. His Romanian host sees through his act but allows him to carry on because she senses that it has to do with the father-daughter relationship. Later on, after Ines's abrupt departure, Winfried reveals to the woman why he is playing his role.

preparations in her apartment, she is shown struggling with a newly bought designer dress. Ripping off the price tag, she struggles to zip it up with the help of a kitchen fork. We then see her laboring over a pair of high heels in the corridor: crouching on the floor she pauses, before returning to her bedroom, where she tries to take off the tight dress. This comical scene is a fine-tuned observation of the irksomeness of life. When the doorbell rings, she has managed to tear the dress off and, only in her underwear, opens the door to her American female friend who awkwardly inquires as to whether she has come too early. Ines offers her embarrassed friend a drink, rejecting her offer to help her choose a dress from her "bursting" closet (2:05). The doorbell rings again, and her friend volunteers to open the door so that Ines can get dressed. Refusing once more, Ines takes her underwear off and opens the door naked to her boss, Gerald (Thomas Loibl), explaining to the stunned man that her party is a "Nacktempfang," a naked reception in the interest of "team-building" (2:06). Explicitly stating that he does not have to participate, she surreptitiously appeals to his competitiveness and the corporate ethos. Gerald leaves, and Ines returns to her American friend, suggesting that she should also take her clothes off; when the friend explains that this is not her thing Ines asks her to leave the party. In Ade's film the intrusive sound of the doorbell intensifies the dramatic buildup: each time it rings, Ines dons her nakedness as a novel party style.[81] Her lover Tim (Tristan Pytter) is the next guest to arrive: believing that he has been set up, he departs too, and Ines remains alone and naked in her apartment. Lying face down and diagonally on her bed with the designer dress covering her head, she does not answer her cell phone. Ines knows that she has knowingly transgressed the corporate norm of a false discretion that commits its sexual and other violations behind closed doors. When the doorbell rings with increasing insistence, Ines opens the door now

---

81. The recurring motif of the ringing doorbell may also reference Petzold's *Barbara*. While in Petzold's film the doorbell stands for a menacing atmosphere of surveillance and intrusion, in Ade's film it lends the scene the dramatic tension of a play in the tradition of theater of the absurd. Harold Pinter springs to mind as a possible precursor.

wearing a light dressing gown: Anca is the first guest to arrive naked because she has been told that this is a novel challenge.[82]

In this pivotal scene Ines stages a new version of *The Emperor's New Clothes*, Hans Christian Andersen's famous tale about the two rogue weavers who promise their vain emperor a new suit that will be invisible to those who are stupid or incompetent.[83] When the ministers and various court officials are sent in to check on the weaving, they can see no garment at all. Afraid that they may be deemed to be incompetent and therefore unfit for office, they report to the king the elaborate description of the fictional robe that was offered by the rogue weavers. When the king himself is shown the invisible garment, he too faces the dilemma that he may be unfit to govern. He therefore announces that the suit is beautiful and displays himself naked in front of his subjects until a small boy cries out that he has nothing on. With this ending Andersen privileges the romantic figure of the little boy in a scene of revelation that confirms the human ability to establish the truth. With this gendered ending, the story seemingly links the motif of nakedness with transparency: even though the truth should be apparent to the naked eye, it is repressed by all except for the male child.[84]

---

82. The scene subtly exposes the cowardliness of the male colleagues, who know that Anca, the PA, is likely to rise to the challenge because, as a female Romanian employee, she occupies the lowest position in the corporate hierarchy.

83. For Sigmund Freud the story exemplifies the secondary revision that characterizes the work of dreams: the emperor is the dreamer who, ashamed of his public nakedness, clothes his dream. While for Freud the weavers are agents of secondary revision, the boy is the analyst who removes the cloak of repression. See Sigmund Freud, *The Interpretation of Dreams*, trans. James Strachey (London: Basic Books, 2010), 260–66.

84. Hollis Robbins has offered a persuasive reading against the grain by analyzing the roles of the weavers, the emperor, the court officials, the public, and the boy. She argues that "by foregrounding questions of sociability against a backdrop of political and economic turmoil, Andersen's tale clearly suggests that social discretion can engender democratic social solidarity." Looked at from this angle, the boy's voice reflects a socially conservative position according to which emperors should be robed in clothes that reflect their status, wealth, and power. See Hollis Robbins, "The Emperor's New Critique," *New Literary History* 34/4 (2003): 666.

Returning to Ines's birthday party, the scene maintains and transforms the key elements of Andersen's story. In Andersen's tale the king is the butt of the weavers' conceit; in Ade's film Ines herself is the author of the ploy. In Andersen's version the king, his court officials, and the broader public pretend not to notice his nakedness; in Ade's film the participants in the birthday party pretend that their nakedness is a new form of team-building. In both stories anxiety about social incompetency and failure prevails. In the last analysis Ines restages *The Emperor's New Clothes* to expose the self-abasing humiliations that she has to endure in the male-dominated world of corporate conformity. Whereas Andersen's tale ends with the comforting reinstatement of a simply truth, Ade's retelling culminates in another disruptive performance. As the doorbell rings once more, a huge furry monster arrives, handing Ines a small bunch of flowers that has been ripped from a flower bed. This is Winfried, who has borrowed the Bulgarian Kuker costume from the Romanian host to drive out evil spirits. Reanimating pagan beliefs and practices, the Kuker's appearance symbolizes the revival of nature, fertility, a good harvest, and, more generally, happiness.[85] The figure thus stands for a mythopoetic reality that disrupts Ines's entrapment in the corporate world. As Ines tries to establish who is underneath the costume, the doorbell rings again: Gerald has come back naked after mustering up his courage over a beer. Standing close behind Gerald, the hairy monster spooks him by gently touching him on his shoulder. Anca explains to the startled Gerald that the creature is Bulgarian in origin and that it drives out evil spirits—a purpose that the boss refashions as an exercise in team-building. Even naked the man flaunts his corporate identity. As the Kuker leaves the party, Ines walks out too, pretending that she has to pay the actor. She follows the strange creature as it makes its way through a local park, where she observes how the locals

---

85. The Bulgarian Kukeri Festival is celebrated after New Year's Eve and before Lent. It involves men who dress up in animal furs, horns, and sequins, wearing wooden masks, as they drive out evil spirits. See Christo Vakarelski, *Bulgarische Volkskunde* (Berlin: De Gruyter, 1969), 380–89.

smile at the Kuker or touch its fur coat for good luck. Shot in one uninterrupted long take, the scene culminates in a brief moment of reunion between father and daughter when Ines approaches and hugs the hairy monster in the park setting (2:18; fig. 10). This rare moment of tenderness between Beauty and the Beast is the result of a ritualistic performance of otherness that draws on ancient practice: by appearing in the pagan guise of the Kuker, Winfried performs a radical alterity that suspends our embeddedness in a disenchanted present.

This precarious moment of togetherness remains just that: the film ends with Ines briefly stopping off at home for the funeral of her grandmother, who has died in the meantime. After the funeral, father and daughter share a few minutes in the garden before Ines needs to leave in pursuit of a new job in China. Winfried uses the occasion to provide Ines with a belated answer to her earlier question about his notion of happiness: explaining that the daily routine of life has often bogged him down too, he then recounts a few episodes from Ines's childhood. The memory of how she learned to ride a bicycle or when he rescued her from a bus stop exemplifies a rare moment of a precarious togetherness that is only

Figure 10. Film still from *Toni Erdmann*, directed and written by Maren Ade, produced by Maren Ade, Jonas Dornbach, Janine Jackowski, and Michael Merkt 2016. © Komplizen Film.

retrospectively recuperated. At this poignant moment Ines reaches out to him by taking his false set of teeth from his shirt pocket and inserting them in her mouth to try out his guise. As Winfried steps inside the house to fetch his camera to capture this moment, Ines remains alone in the garden setting: wearing his fake teeth, she is her father's daughter, a funny monster that, for a brief moment, breaks out of the cage of conformity.[86] The final shot shows Ines without the fake teeth alone in the garden. Evidently, the garden is a temporary heterotopia: Ines will resume her hectic life as part of the corporate business elite. But there is the suggestion that the memory of the disruptive performances of father and daughter will have a lasting effect.

Ade's film employs a conflict-laden choreography of social performance to foreground a generationally inflected conflict between father and daughter about the good life. Their different lifestyles and incompatible outlooks translate into opposing notions of a good performance: Winfried's jocular and crude acts on- and offstage not only enact carnivalesque freedom from social constraints, but also aim to overcome his estrangement from his daughter. In addition, his performances are meant to disrupt his daughter's unquestioning acceptance of the pernicious rules of a corporate world that, as he observes on numerous occasions, forces her to accept deeply ingrained sexism. In sharp contrast to her father's unsettling antics, Ines's performances are about the alignment of all aspects of her life with her professional interests. In the world of corporate capitalism, performances are measurable and profit-oriented: they aim to engender a uniform mode of behavior that seemingly obliterates differences of class, race, gender, and age while in reality sustaining the dominance of the Western white male. The notion of the team is an essential component in this performance script because it curbs individuality in favor of collective identity. In the birthday party scene, Ines enacts a self-reflexive form of performance that

---

86. The garden and park scene in Ade's film thus works by analogy with Seidl's park scene in *Paradies: Glaube*. In both cases gardens and parks symbolize Foucault's heterotopias. See Foucault, "Of Other Spaces," 24.

seemingly maintains her professional veneer while in reality subverting her overt conformity with the system. Pretending that her
impromptu naked appearance is part of the normal team-building
exercise, she lays bare the pervasiveness of social conformity as well
as the absence of any real intimacy in that world.

Conclusion

In 2016 various British newspapers, including the popular *Evening Standard*, reported that the average daytime speed on London roads had plummeted to 7.8 miles per hour, that is, far below
the speed of 10 to 15 miles per hour of a horse and cart.[87] Congestion, road work, traffic diversions, online shopping deliveries,
and the dramatic rise in the capital's population were blamed for
continuously declining speed on London's roads. A comparison of
average speeds between 2016 and 2017 shows that speed has been
decreasing in all major British cities. And yet, in spite of the common daily experience of gridlock in urban centers, congestion on
highways, and long lines of traffic at stoplights or crossroads, the
fantasy of high speed seems to be just as seductive as it was a century ago when the transportation revolution ushered in modern
speed politics.

The unparalleled success of the BBC television program *Top
Gear* is a case in point: the motoring magazine that started airing
in 2002 was one of the most widely watched factual television pro-
grams globally until the firing of one its key presenters in 2015.[88]

---

87. Ross Lydall, "Revealed: How Average Speed of London Traffic Has Plummeted to Just 7.8mph," *Evening Standard*, 9 December 2016, https://www.
standard.co.uk/news/transport/revealed-average-speed-of-london-traffic-is-just-
78mph-a3416446.html (accessed 8 January 2018).

88. See https://en.wikipedia.org/wiki/Top_Gear_(2002_TV_series). Acclaimed
for its slick format, the show was regularly criticized for ridiculing environmental
issues and advocating irresponsible driving. Complaints by the public to the British
broadcasting regulator Ofcom included the presenters' sexist, homophobic, and
racist remarks. To this day, then, speed politics links the pleasure of speed with
power, gender, privilege, and consumption. See Duffy, *The Speed Handbook*, 7.

Hosted by an all-male cast, the show included car reviews, power laps, long-distance races, and occasional specials with car stunts. *Top Gear* viewers and fans of online racing games get their kicks from a speed fantasy that suspends the daily reality of enforced immobility and inertia.[89] Clearly in our era of traffic congestion, overcrowded transport systems, and long security lines, high speed is mostly a simulation. Our digital devices help us to recycle the waste of empty time that we spend waiting. The news alerts, computer games, and social media apps that we constantly access on our cell phones and tablets transform passive immobility into restless immobility. For the Korean philosopher Byung-Chul Han (see chapter 1) our digital connectivity is merely symptomatic of a pervasive dyschronia that, in his view, destroys the very possibility of temporal anchorage.[90] Han argues that, by browsing social media, gaming online, and surfing the internet, we only intensify the atomization of time, thereby destroying the very condition of time as duration.[91]

Against this background of fragmented time and the simulation of experience through speed, the question is whether slow art can disrupt the speed politics that governs our daily lives. Can it offer more than enclaves of cultured respite or therapeutic moments of

---

89. The simulation of speed favors a particular representation of space. We often race through vast deserts, sublime mountain ranges, or along empty overland roads that seem to be made for competitive racing. As such, these locations are passive recipients of phallic projectiles that conquer passive (feminine) space. The deep imbrication of speed politics in colonialism and capitalism has been widely debated by critics such as Harvey, Virilio, Lefebvre, and Duffy, who have charted the capitalist conquest of space.

90. See chapter 1 on Han's analysis of atomized time.

91. Various slow life movements have responded to the exhausting experience of modern speed politics by advocating a return to a more sustainable lifestyle: for example, the slow food movement, which was founded by a group of activists in the 1980s, originally promoted regional cuisines and a slower pace of life. It has now evolved into a global grassroots organization campaigning for the sustainable production of fair and affordable food for all. Koepnick's assessment that such movements "couple their quest for deceleration and tranquillity to desires for re-enchantment and salvation" misses the politicization of the slow food movement. Koepnick, *On Slowness*, 253.

deceleration in our era of stagnation at top speed? In his book *On Slowness* Lutz Koepnick answers this question in the affirmative. He theorizes slow art "not merely as an attempt to decelerate and invert the speed of modern life but as a mode of movement, perception, and experience that allows us to engage with the present in all its temporality."[92] Rather than inverting speed, "slowness plays out the virtual against the deterministic, dispersal against the trajectorial. As it invites us to hesitate and delay immediate responses, slowness makes a case for the open rather than the timeless, but also for the finite and mortal rather than for stalwart visions of progress, for experience rather than fate."[93] For Koepnick slow art can "uphold what phenomenologies of speed tend to deny, namely to encounter the present as a place of potentiality and contingency."[94] In many ways Koepnick's observations read like a commentary on high modernism, which, as he argues himself, also opened up multiple temporal trajectories that punctured the modern vision of speed as progress. In the last analysis, for Koepnick, the defining feature of slow art is the reinstatement of historical contingency and openness through aesthetic practices that, instead of reducing complexity, explore the temporality of presentness.[95]

This chapter has explored a diverse range of artworks, from performance art to photography and film, that share many of the features of slow art as discussed above. However, while Koepnick emphasizes the potentiality of contingency, the artworks under discussion in this chapter accentuate the precariousness of living in the present. Even though both terms overlap to an extent, they are by no means synonymous: the term "contingency" designates the end of a deterministic universe and the modern shift toward

---

92. Koepnick, *On Slowness*, 251.

93. Koepnick, *On Slowness*, 251–52.

94. Koepnick, *On Slowness*, 251.

95. Koepnick, *On Slowness*, 261. Koepnick draws on Siegfried Kracauer to advance the notion of hesitancy as a nonjudgmental mode of reception and optics that enables the viewer to "measure and assess the complex interactions between subjective and nonsubjective temporalities" (252).

chance combined with free will.[96] Opposed to necessity, contingency is the child of the historicist turn that, in the words of philosopher Richard Rorty, "has helped free us, gradually but steadily, from theology and metaphysics—from the temptation to look for an escape from time and chance."[97] Rorty embraces contingency in the figure of the "liberal ironist" who "faces up to the contingency of his or her own most central beliefs and desires—someone sufficiently historicist and nominalist to have abandoned the idea that those central beliefs and desires refer back to something beyond the reach of time and chance."[98] While contingency is for philosophers from Nietzsche to Rorty the very foundation of freedom, the notion of precariousness as I have used it in this study loosens the link between contingency and freedom. I deliberately us the verb "loosen" rather than "cut" to avoid the alarmist register of the contemporary debates about precarization. Aesthetic precariousness recasts contingency in terms of a radical uncertainty about the past, the present, and the future. While some slow artworks seek, in the words of Koepnick, "to warrant the possibility of . . . experience in the face of today's acceleration," others no longer mediate between individual perception and social meaning. However, the examples discussed in this chapter accentuate once more the fallacy of binary oppositions: the terms "contingency" and "precariousness" are situated on a sliding scale.

Of the examples discussed here Wesely's time photography is closest to Koepnick's version of slow art as a recovery of contingency as potentiality. Wesely's various experiments with extreme exposure time create layered images in which different temporal stages are copresent. His early photographs of European railway stations draw on the notion of the timetable, only to overturn the linearity and synchronicity of modern time. The present is a site of

---

96. See Dirk-Martin Grube, "Contingency and Religion—A Philosophical Tour D-Horizon," in *Religions Challenged by Contingency: Theological and Philosophical Approaches to the Problem of Contingency*, ed. Dirk-Martin Grube and Peter Jonkers (Leiden: Brill, 2008), 1–43.

97. Rorty, *Contingency, Irony, and Solidarity*, xiii.

98. Rorty, *Contingency, Irony, and Solidarity*, xv.

enfolded temporalities that collapse the linearity of past, present, and future. The Potsdamer Platz series of the late 1990s marks a further radicalization of his work: with its extremely long exposure times these photographs offer uncanny images of a rebuilding process that symbolized the birth of ultramodern Germany. While the man-made structures appear as transitory and indeed ghostly, the trees in these pictures point to the permanence of nature. As a constant presence in these images, they evoke the ecological timescale of natural history. It is precisely this shift from human history to natural history that characterizes Wesely's photobook *Ostdeutschland:* the extraterrestrial and abstract landscapes of this series explode the timescales of human history. Here Wesely brings into view an absolute time that evokes both the geophysical timescales of geology and transcendental "other" time.

While Wesely works with long exposure times to recover radical other temporalities that may be seen to recover the contingency of human history, Ulrich Wüst's *Später Sommer/Letzter Herbst* employs yet undercuts the aesthetic conventions of the photobook. Instead of staging 1989 as a series of electrifying turning points, Wüst's strategy of decontextualization raises questions about representational conventions and viewing practices. Analogical comparisons between serialized images replace the recognition of their referent. The photobook does not record a chronological view of history but a series of uneventful and inconclusive journeys that resist conventional narration. The grainy black-and-white photography displaces the idea of historical agency in favor of the precariousness of human experience. Here the mediation between individual perception and social meaning is precarious. In addition, we have seen that Wüst's aesthetic of the unfinished produces a profound sense of inertia and stagnation that seems to eliminate the possibility of change. And so the most representational series in the conventional sense, that is, the beach images, depicts people looking at a horizon that is gray, leaden, and closed-off from an open future. While Wesley enfolds different temporal stages or eliminates human time altogether through long exposure times, Wüst creates a sense of stagnation through serialization.

Turning to cinema, we have seen that Petzold eschews the conventions of mainstream cinema's love affair with speed. The slow unfolding of plot, sparse dialogue, the long take, and symbolically laden diegetic sound work toward an aesthetic that envisages a particular form of attention and care for the Other as a viewing experience. And yet, my analysis of diegetic sound in *Barbara* has also exposed the political dimension of attention: in the context of GDR state surveillance, attention is not just a form of ethical engagement with the Other through collaborative work in the hospital. It is above all a mode of vigilance that aims to protect Barbara from state interference. And so in the acoustic space of the GDR both stillness and sound can exude a threat as well as engender significant moments of *Eigenzeit*. The anticlimactic ending of the film further underlines Petzold's aesthetic of precariousness. Barbara's decision to stay in the GDR is highly ambivalent: her relationship with André remains precarious and open to state interference.

Ulrich Seidl's *Paradies: Glaube* explores an extreme case of religiosity in the age of turbocapitalism. The protagonist's quest for transcendence involves premodern practices of penance as well as feverish proselytizing in the depraved suburbs of Vienna. Anna Maria (and with her the viewer) encounters extreme forms of social precariousness: the figures of the middle-aged hoarder who presents himself in his underwear and of the alcoholic Russian immigrant who is simultaneously aggressive and emotionally needy bring into view more than the erosion of the social security systems of the postwar order. Seidl shoots these scenes in a documentary style: these characters allow Anna Maria to enter their homes because, in all likelihood, she is a rare visitor in their disembedded and lonely existences.

However, what makes this film a further example of an aesthetic of precariousness is the cinematographic tension between two opposing perspectives. The documentary format promotes a clinical and perhaps Olympian view of Anna Maria's religious practice. Looked at through the documentary lens, her extreme acts of self-flagellation appear as symptoms of an obsessive disorder, the etiology of which lies in her relationship to her paraplegic Muslim husband, Nabil. Their estrangement is depicted in the naturalist style of an Ibsen drama in which the battle between the sexes assumes grotesquely violent proportions. But the documentary format is held in check by Seidl's stylized cinematography, which creates a strikingly antirealist effect. Intertextual allusions to artworks place Anna Maria's religious quest in the long tradition of Western art history and its quest for transcendence. The irresolvable tension between the documentary format and Seidl's cinematography of stillness suspends the viewer's moral judgment. And so Anna Maria's religiosity is both highly pathological and deeply humane: it cries out to heaven in response to a disenchanted world.

Maren Ade's *Toni Erdmann* also explores the precariousness of social relations in the context of globalization. The conflict between father and daughter allows Ade to foreground generationally inflected perspectives on what constitutes fulfilled time and the good life. While Winfried Conradi is the beneficiary of the social agenda of the postwar era—his comfortable retirement in the West German town of Aachen revolves around his local community—his daughter Ines represents the globally mobile management class that enjoys the spoils of neoliberal entrepreneurship without any apparent social hang-ups. Their different lifestyles and incompatible outlooks translate into opposing notions of a good performance: Winfried's jocular and crude acts on- and offstage not only enact carnivalesque freedom from social constraints; they also aim to overcome his estrangement from his daughter. In addition, his performances are meant to disrupt his daughter's unquestioning acceptance of the pernicious rules of a corporate world that, as he observes on numerous occasions, forces her to accept deeply ingrained sexism. In sharp contrast to her father's unsettling antics, Ines's performances seek to align all aspects of her life with her professional interests. In the world of corporate capitalism, performances are measurable and profit-oriented: they aim to engender a uniform mode of behavior that seemingly obliterates differences of class, race, gender, and age, while in reality sustaining the dominance of the Western white male. The notion of the team, an essential component in this performance script, serves to curb individuality in favor of collective identity. In the pivotal birthday party scene, Ines then enacts a self-reflexive mode of performance that seemingly maintains her professional veneer, while in reality subverting her overt conformity with the system. Pretending that her impromptu naked appearance is part of the normal team-building exercise, she lays bare at once the pervasiveness of social conformity as well as the absence of any real intimacy in this world. Winfried's appearance in the guise of the ancient Kuker engenders a genuine reaction in Ines precisely because the Kuker symbolizes the revival of life and happiness. And so, by the end of the film, father and daughter have rebuilt a precarious relationship through their disruptive performances.

The examples discussed here differ in terms of genre, thematic concerns, and artistic sensibilities: Wesely shifts from an aesthetic of copresence to an aesthetic of abstraction. Both modes are concerned with the recovery of temporal potentiality in Koepnick's sense. By contrast, Wüst's aesthetic of the unfinished works within the human timescale to expose the precariousness of historical experience: his representation of the summer and autumn of 1989 raises the issue of the readability of history. Petzold's s aesthetic of attention explores the precariousness of *Eigenzeit* under conditions of extreme surveillance, a theme that resurfaces in his later film *Etwas Besseres als den Tod*.[99] Seidl's aesthetic of intertextual tension explores the longing for transcendence in our disenchanted age. The documentary representation of social precarization and of Anna Maria's pathological religiosity contrasts sharply with the aesthetic of stillness and intertexuality that dignifies Anna Maria's search for meaning. Finally, Maren Ade's aesthetic of performance explores the corporatization of social relations in the world of global capitalism alongside intergenerational conflict over the meaning of the good life.

I classify the photography and films under discussion here as "slow art" not because they advocate retreat into havens of respite and calm in response to the experience of a high-speed culture.

---

99. See Andrew J. Webber, "The Seen and Un-Seen: Digital Life-Time in Christian Petzold's *Etwas Besseres als den Tod*," in "*Ästhetische Eigenzeit* in Contemporary Literature and Culture, Part II," ed. Anne Fuchs and Ines Detmers, special issue, *Oxford German Studies* 46/4 (2017): 345–59.

Rather than merely designating decelerated tempo, slow art involves complex aesthetic practices that probe the often inconclusive experience of both subjective and social time. Time in these works is a performative category that brings forth *Eigenzeit* as a precarious and unstable experience. Slow art requires the work of "close looking" from an attentive recipient who is prepared to engage in self-reflexive, contemplative modes of reception.

4

Narrating Precariousness

Dis/connectedness in Contemporary German Literature

The great modernist novelists of the early twentieth century, including Joyce, Proust, Woolf, Musil, Kafka, Schnitzler, and Mann,
explored untimely modes of slowness through new experimental literary forms that, by calling on the reader's sustained attention, queried the relentless valorization of speed and rapid change.
Mann's and Musil's essayistic excursions in their novels interrupt
narration; Joyce, Woolf, and Schnitzler experiment with interior
monologue and stream of consciousness to open up an interior
world. Robert Walser's meandering narrative voice and strategy
of deviation defy the social order of time; and in Kafka's world
metaphysical time unpredictably punctures modern time. Modernism produced a wide spectrum of avant-garde literary forms that
displaced linear narrative and with it the chronological imagination. What Mann calls the "großzügige Zeitwirtschaft" (DZ, 202;

generous time management) of the magic mountain is indeed the signature of literary modernism. Modernist texts employ tropes of both extreme slowness and extreme speed to capture the unevenness of the modern experience, while also engendering *Eigenzeit*. The question then is to what extent contemporary literature still operates within these parameters or whether its particularity derives from engagement with the temporal anxieties of our age. Or to put it differently, how does the precarious experience of our own time affect the narratological strategies of these texts?

It may be useful to return briefly to the by-now established distinction between modernist and postmodernist literature before addressing these issues in texts that cover divergent historical experiences from German unification to the present day. Brian McHale argued in his classic study of the postmodern novel that the narratological experiments of modernist novels pose epistemological questions, such as "What is there to be known?; Who knows it?; How do they know it, and with what degree of certainty?; . . . How does the object of knowledge change as it passes from knower to knower?"[1] By contrast, the postmodern text asks ontological questions: "What is a world?; What kinds of world are there, how are they constituted, and how do they differ? . . . What is the mode of existence of a text?"[2] Ursula Heise too contrasts the psychologically motivated disruption of linear plotting in modernist novels through repetition, metalepsis, and the nesting or spatialization of time with the altogether more radical purposes these techniques serve in the postmodern novel:[3]

> The postmodernist novel confronts the more radically contingent future of Western societies in the late twentieth century by projecting the temporal mode of the future into the narrative present and past. Narrative, in other words, takes on the temporal structure of a future that can no longer be envisioned without great difficulty, so that the experience of the future is displaced into the reading experience.[4]

---

1. Brian McHale, *Postmodernist Fiction* (New York: Methuen, 1987), 9.

2. McHale, *Postmodernist Fiction*, 10.

3. Ursula Heise, *Chronoschisms: Time, Narrative, and Postmodernity* (Cambridge: Cambridge University Press, 1997), 53.

4. Heise, *Chronoschisms*, 67.

Heise's observation that postmodern literature can no longer envision the gap between the present and a radically better future accentuates the crisis of historicity (i.e., the relationship between the stable past, the present, and the future that has defined modern consciousness). Johannes Pause too notes that contemporary fiction stages the experience of a present in crisis and entrapment in a permanent now without any perspective.[5]

I would argue, however, that the opposition between modernism and postmodernism is too binary: while the prevailing mode in the modernist novel may be epistemological, it can also raise the type of ontological questions that McHale attributes to the postmodern mode. Heise rightly emphasizes the nondirectionality of time in much of contemporary fiction by observing that in the postmodern novel "the present is trapped in its own mutations, without any possibility of linkage to past and future."[6] And yet, similar experiences can already be found in nuce in modernist texts where the experience of time is often slow, achronic, nonteleological, and disorientating. Seen from this perspective, modernism and postmodernism are terms on a continuum that "straddles the great divide of twentieth-century aesthetic culture." Contemporary culture, argues Lutz Koepnick, "urges us to reconsider monolithic definitions of both the modern and the postmodern."[7]

Compared to Heise's corpus of rarefied postmodern novels, which includes works by Pynchon, Robbe-Grillet, and Beckett, the literary texts discussed in this chapter may appear more conventional: they do not always dispense with established modes of narration, such as plot, characterization, and a unified narrative voice. Nevertheless, they all explore temporal itineraries that collide with the contemporary scripts of instant delivery and the cult

---

5. Johannes Pause, *Texturen der Zeit: Zum Wandel ästhetischer Zeitkonzepte in der deutschsprachigen Gegenwartsliteratur* (Cologne: Böhlau, 2012), 120. Following Hartmut Rosa, Pause paints a grim picture of our social enslavement in a present that, on the one hand, is characterized by a pluralization of *Eigenzeit* and, on the other, requires social actors to chase the perpetual innovations of the digital era.

6. Heise, *Chronoschisms*, 58.

7. Koepnick, *On Slowness*, 11.

of immediacy. Exploring the relevance of history after 1989, they experiment narratologically with modes of dis/connectedness and achronicity. In many of the texts discussed here considerable performative effort is required for the temporary and precarious recuperation of *Eigenzeit*.

Acceleration and Point Time: Clemens Meyer's *Als wir träumten*

When published in 2006, Clemens Meyer's celebrated first novel, *Als wir träumten* (As We Were Dreaming), was compared to Danny Boyle's iconic *Trainspotting* (1996).[8] Boyle's film follows a group of young male heroin addicts growing up in a deprived area of Edinburgh in the late 1980s who fill their days with gang violence, theft, and drug taking.[9] Directed by Andreas Dresen, the film version of *Als wir träumten* was first screened in the main competition of the Berlin Film Festival in 2015.[10] Like *Trainspotting*, Meyer's novel and Dresen's film also revolve around a gang of young male dropouts in Reudnitz, a run-down suburb in eastern Leipzig, where, after the *Wende*, they kill time street-fighting other gangs (especially the neo-Nazis who also live in Reudnitz and the so-called Zecken [ticks], i.e., punks from Connewitz), committing all sorts of crime, destroying property, boozing, drug-taking or discussing the ill fortune of their local football club Chemie Leipzig.[11] Born in 1976, the first-person narrator Danie (Daniel Lenz) reviews his own life and the lives of his gang friends, Rico

---

8. Clemens Meyer, *Als wir träumten* (Frankfurt a. Main: Fischer, 2011); cited as Awt in the text.

9. See Kolja Mensing, "Mit den Dämonen sprechen," *tageszeitung*, 1 March 2008.

10. *Als wir träumten*, director: Andreas Dresen; script: Wolfgang Kohlhaase; producer: Peter Rommel (Germany, France, 2015).

11. For an analysis of the representation of masculinity in the novel, see Frauke Matthes, "Clemens Meyer, *Als wir träumten*: Fighting 'Like a Man' in Leipzig's East," in *Emerging German-Language Novelists in the Twenty-First Century*, ed. Lyn Marven and Stuart Taberner (Rochester, NY: Camden House, 2011), 89–104.

Grundmann, Stefan Schulte (Pitbull), Walter Richter, Mark Bormann, Paul Jendroschek, and Alfred Heller (Fred), from within the four walls of an institution, in all likelihood a prison. His narrative is delivered in the epic preterite and covers the period from the mid-1980s, when the boys were in fifth grade, right up to the mid-1990s, when they watch the live transmission of a boxing match between Henry Maske and Rocky Rocchigiani, which took place in 1995. Other datable events include the Monday demonstrations in Leipzig in the autumn of 1989 and the infamous football match between the FC Sachsen Leipzig (formerly the BSG Chemie Leipzig) and the BFC Dynamo on 3 November 1990, when Mike Polley, a supporter of BFC Dynamo, was shot dead by a policeman during outbursts of hooligan violence. These scarce historical reference points are embedded in an anachronic and, as one critic observed,[12] cinematographic narrative structure that combines descriptions of repetitive events, behavioral patterns, and group habits with frequent flashbacks that home in on the boys' lives in the GDR. The retrospective chapters offer insight into the GDR education system: for example, chapter 2 recalls the exercises of the *Wehrkundeunterricht* (military training classes), which involved trainee rescue operations for the war injured or a collective search for fake mines in a forest (grotesquely represented by colorful balloons). Chapter 8, "Immer bereit" (Always Prepared), then exposes the coercion of the Junge Pioniere (Young Pioneers), the mass organization for children in the GDR, which, by the late 1980s, was joined by most children. Danie recalls here an investigation by the authorities after his friend Rico burnt his Pioneer necktie in response to feeling abandoned by his father, an officer of the Nationale Volksarmee (NVA), who had left his wife and family for another woman. In the course of the official inquiry Danie tells on Rico after being severely pressured by the school authorities. The chapter finishes with a further school episode: as Danie is asked to read a passage

---

12. Martin Jörg Schäfer, "Die Intensität der Träume: Clemens Meyers Poetik des Kinos," in "Inszenierungen von 'Intensität' und 'Lebendigkeit' in der Gegenwartsliteratur," ed. Martin Jörg Schäfer and Niels Werber, special issue, *Zeitschrift für Literaturwissenschaft und Linguistik* 170 (2013): 57–58.

from the history book he is overwhelmed by the memory of how Rico had refused to read aloud a passage about the Red Army's fight against Hitler and Fascism, a further offense that leads to Rico's admission to an institution for young offenders. The blurring of the two schoolbook episodes conveys the traumatic nature of Danie's memories.

While these flashback chapters capture the massive biographical rupture that separates the GDR past from the boys' present lives, there are other retrospective episodes that emphasize the continuity of dysfunctional family relations before and after the *Wende*. "Nachspielzeit" (Extra Time) concerns memories of Danie's father, who used to spend his Sundays boozing and bragging with his drinking mates in a run-down football bar. The homosocial and yet deeply homophobic undercurrent of their conversations heralds the swagger of the boy gangs who will later also bolster their weak egos through male bonding rituals. The chapter ends with Danie imagining his mother waiting for them with the Sunday dinner gone cold, an image that recurs when Danie himself returns home to his mother after various escapades that leave him battered. Family life before and after the *Wende* is thus shown to be dysfunctional and out of sync with the historical master narratives of the GDR and of unified Germany.

Throughout the narrative Danie's account captures the age and experiential horizon of his protagonists linguistically through youth- and gender-inflected idioms, paratactic sentence structure, and filmic dialogue, all of which is reminiscent of Salinger's *The Catcher in the Rye*. Danie's narration largely abstains from a psychologizing perspective that, by accessing their inner selves, would explain the motivation for and causes of their bouts of extreme violence and destruction. In line with a predominantly external narrative perspective that tracks routinized behavior, there is practically no reflection on the psychological effects of the fall of the Berlin Wall. And so the Leipzig Monday demonstrations of 1989 feature in the novel not as a historical event of seismic proportions but merely as a theatrical spectacle filtered through the uncomprehending eyes of male adolescents who are excited by crowd power. Stripped of political significance, the events of 1989 represent the thrill of disobedience that, after the fall of the Wall, Danie and his friends endlessly reenact in their post-*Wende* lives. Even though 1989 is a dramatic caesura that separates the protagonists' GDR biographies from their post-*Wende* existence, the experience of history in this narrative is fundamentally dyschronic, atomized, and empty of significance. In line with this the narrative employs circular loops that foreground the repetitiveness of drug abuse and gang violence, which are interrupted only by the protagonists' deaths or imprisonment.

The title *Als wir träumten* evokes neither merely the loss of the former hope that the end of the GDR would bring happiness, freedom, and material wealth (Helmut Kohl's "blühende Landschaften," blooming landscapes), nor simply the memories of the boys' GDR childhood and their early adolescence immediately after the *Wende*.[13] As a central leitmotif dreaming connotes rather a fundamentally transgressive and dyschronic temporality brought forth by intense states of intoxication and frenzy at night that collapse the protagonists' ability to distinguish between past, present, and future. At the beginning of chapter 1 Danie explains that, immediately after the *Wende*, the boys sought contact with a radically new reality by drinking themselves senseless and engaging in endless orgies of destruction (Awt, 7). He vividly describes fast-paced chases in stolen cars through Leipzig at night that gave rise to the short-lived feeling of unbounded freedom and independence (Awt, 9). But these "traumartige Flugnächte" (dreamlike night flights) crashed "mit der Landung in einer Ausnüchterungszelle oder auf dem Flur des Polizeireviers Südost, mit Handschellen an die Heizung gekettet" (Awt, 7; with a landing in a cell for drunkards or in the corridor of the police station south-east, chained with handcuffs to a radiator). *Als wir träumten* transforms Shakespeare's *A Midsummer Night's Dream* into a contemporary midsummer nightmare, or in Danie's words, "ein Albtraum in einer Sommernacht bei dreißig Grad" (Awt, 14; a nightmare on a summer's night at 30°).

---

13. Matthes, "Clemens Meyer, *Als wir träumten*," 92.

Simultaneously intense and boring, the violent episodes produce an experience of time that is repetitive. From a temporal angle, *Als wir träumten* can thus be seen to stage Byung-Chul Han's point time: deprived of any direction or aim, the various accounts of gang violence remain fundamentally atomized and discontinuous.[14] In its repetitive structure gang violence is shown to propagate empty intervals, which produce the insatiable need to overcome the threat of empty time with even more intense violence. Point time therefore manifests itself symptomatically as the hysterical acceleration of episodic events that, even though they are sensational, are without proper narrative tension or meaning. For Han atomized time produces a mode of attention that demands the continual production of new and ever more drastic sensations rather than duration.[15] Social structures and practices that used to enact duration through the social promise of loyalty or faithfulness have been swept away by the radical experience of discontinuity that only engenders social precariousness, fear, and violence. This would also explain why Danie and his friends do not even manage to uphold their own masculine code of everlasting loyalty: Stefan (alias Pitbull) deals heroin to Mark, who then dies of an overdose—in Danie's eyes an unforgivable act of betrayal that ends their friendship. But Danie too fails to live up to the gang ethos when he passively observes from a window how Mark and Rico are being beaten up by the neo-Nazis. The atomization of time manifests itself in the experience of a disconnectedness that is barely masked by the performance of masculinity in the group.

The following analysis focuses on three central episodes that chronotopically enact the atomization of lived time in the protagonists' lives through the ruination or fragmentation of space: the chapters "Palast-Theater" (Palace Theater), "Schüsse" (Shots), and "Versammlungen" (Meetings) foreground the contestation over three heterotopic spaces that, in Foucauldian fashion, represent counter-sites, "a kind of effectively enacted utopia in which the real

---

14. Han, *Duft der Zeit*, 13.
15. Han, *Duft der Zeit*, 13.

sites, all the other real sites that can be found within the culture, are simultaneously represented, contested and inverted."[16]

In chapter 3 Danie returns to the Palast-Theater, their former cinema, in search of his drug-addicted friend Mark who has abandoned a drug rehabilitation program and, as Danie learns from Trinker Thilo, now hangs out in the burnt-down ruin of the former cinema. During GDR times Mark and Danie used to visit the Palace cinema regularly to escape the hated Pionier meetings and watch various *Winnetou* screenings that, even though they were produced in the West and loosely based on Karl May, whose works were frowned upon in the GDR, could be seen in the cinema (Awt, 22). Located on the fringes of Leipzig, only a few hundred meters from the sign demarcating the city boundaries (Awt, 47), the Palace Theater (in spite of its aspirational name) was a small and liminal place that, even during "Zonenzeiten" (GDR times; literally "the time of the Zone"), was mostly ill attended. The Palace Theater was a site where the boys could practice their male virility by masturbating in the darkness of the cinema. A heterotopic space par excellence, the cinema is the locus where heterochronic time unfolds through homosocial time: as Mark, Danie, and the tramps watch how Winnetou dies in the arms of Old Shatterhand, they are transported into an alternative time-space of enduring male friendship and love (Awt, 51). But the image of eternal brotherhood remains a filmic projection of freedom in a fictional Wild West that, in its unbounded vastness, represents a seemingly unlimited and yet-untamed space where interracial male friendship can flourish. In the context of the enclosed GDR it is precisely this vision of limitless freedom and friendship that makes the film a heterotopic site for adolescent longing.

The ruination of the Palace Theater in the immediate post-*Wende* era then designates the crisis of a shared heterotopic social fantasy alongside a broader crisis of time. Under the dyschronic

---

16. Foucault, "Of Other Spaces," 24. See also Mikhail M. Bakhtin, *The Dialogic Imagination: Four Essays*, ed. Michael Holquist, trans. Caryl Emerson and Michael Holquist (Austin: University of Texas Press, 1981).

conditions of accelerated change, the heterotopic space of the cinema is destroyed: it goes up in flames; according to local rumor it was an act of arson by the owner, who wanted to draw down the insurance money. What is left of the former Palace is a blackened, windowless ruin with broken seating, ripped posters, piles of rubbish, and the empty beer bottles left by the local dropouts (Awt, 48). Not surprisingly, then, the reenactment of friendship in this setting is bound to fail: Danie attempts in vain to persuade Mark to return to the rehab clinic because Mark has relapsed and is shooting up heroin. The bond of trust between them was already broken when Danie body-searched Mark on the suspicion that his friend had stolen 50 DM from him to feed his drug habit (Awt, 52). The chapter ends with Danie's frantic attempt to repair the friendship through a biographical narration that summarizes their lives and the content of the ensuing chapters:

> "Weißt du noch", sagte ich, "damals, in der Lagerhalle, wie wir's den Bullen gezeigt haben . . ." Aber er wollte davon nichts wissen, "ich bin so scheiße, Danie, ich bin so scheiße", aber ich erzählte einfach weiter, erzählte von den alten Zeiten, vom kleinen Walter, von Fred, von der Eastside, von Goldies Kneipe, in der wir so oft zusammengesessen und getrunken hatten, erzählte von der 'Grünen Aue' und wie Goldie sie gehasst hat . . . , erzählte von der Alten und dem Apfelkorn der Alten, "wie der geleuchtet hat, golden, weißt du noch", erzählte von Pitbulls Hund, als Pitbull noch Stefan hieß, aber er antwortete nicht, und ich erzählte und erzählte. (Awt, 55)

> "Do you remember," said I, "back then in the depot, when we really had a go at the cops . . ." But he did not want to hear about this, "I'm such shit, Danie, I'm such shit," but I kept yakking on, about the old times, about little Walter, about Fred, the Eastside, Goldie's pub, in which we often sat together drinking, I blathered on about the "Grüne Aue" and how much Goldie hated it . . . , about the old woman and her apple schnapps, "how it was glowing golden, do you remember," about Pitbull's dog, when Pitbull was still Stefan, but he did not answer me, and I talked and blubbered on.

Danie's frenzied narration of the old times evokes the unfulfilled hopes of the immediate post-*Wende* times when Rico still aspired to pursue a professional boxing career, when the boys envisaged the promotion of their football club Chemie Leipzig, and when they expected to encounter true romantic love. Instead of reaching out to an attainable future, Danie's narration assigns their dream to a past that has been superseded by a disenchanted present. Emphatically appealing to their shared vision, Danie ends up addressing the empty and dark auditorium of the burnt-out cinema, which only accentuates his acute sense of desperation and loneliness. The frantic and fragmented nature of his narrative is indicative of precisely the lack of narrative integration that defines the experience of atomized time. Later on Mark will die alone in the stairwell of a ruin, the so-called Nazi House, without the comfort of his best mate. Pitbull, who has established himself as the main drug dealer in the district, will deal the lethal dosage to Mark.

The chapter "Schüsse" relates the destruction of the second heterotopia, the BSG Leipzig soccer club, which, during GDR times, represented for its local fans both a real and a mythical site of countercultural hope or in Foucault's terms a "heterotopia of deviation," a site where, to a degree, some deviant behavior could be enacted. The fortune of the club is a constant topic of conversation between Danie, his father, and his father's drinking mates, who regularly invoke the club's mythical championship victory in the GDR League in 1951. In 1988 when Danie was twelve he visited the Silberhöhle, the football pub where his father was a regular before being imprisoned for the assault on "a Lok-Schwein" (Awt, 273; a Lok pig), that is, a supporter of FC Lokomotive Leipzig. The publican relays the father's "big fight" against the Lok supporter, his friends, and the police (Awt, 275) before gifting Danie the championship pennant from 1951, a symbolic act that obliges Danie to continue the role of macho Chemie Leipzig fan (Awt, 276). The fortune of Chemie Leipzig is a leitmotif in a narrative in which nearly all versions of happiness revolve around a community of men.

In 1990 Rico and Danie want to attend the match between Chemie Leipzig (which has now been renamed FC Grün-Weiß Leipzig) and the hated BFC Dynamo (now FC Berlin), the Berlin club that, during GDR times, was headed by Erich Mielke and known as the Stasi club.[17] It is a time of many transitions: the match takes place in the final year of the GDR, which is also the final year of the GDR Oberliga (upper football league) and on the very day that Danie's parents get divorced. Danie and Rico arrive late at the S-Bahn station in Leutzsch and end up among a large mob of BFC hooligans. Frightened, they stuff their Chemie Leipzig scarves down the toilet in the S-Bahn carriage and pretend to be BSG fans in the agitated mob (Awt, 334). As the doors of the S-Bahn open, the dream of a male heterotopia turns into the nightmare of uncontrolled hooligan violence and a threatening bodily proximity that unveils Danie's and Rico's utter vulnerability: "Ich sah keinen Bahnhof mehr, keine Häuser, keine Straße, nur Männer, nur BFC, neben mir waren Springerstiefel, und ich sah, wie klein meine Füße waren" (Awt, 335; I no longer saw the railway station, no houses, no street, just men, only BFC fans, next to me army boots, and I noticed how small my feet were). The contrast between the hooligan's large and clunky combat boots and Danie's small feet is striking. In the ensuing vivid and cinematographic description of the unfolding violence, Meyer then foregrounds the boys' total lack of spatial and temporal orientation as they are swept along by the hooligan mob, which is being tackled by the police. Blinded by tear gas they try to run back to the station but bump into hooligans who smash up cars (Awt, 338). Eventually Danie and Rico crouch down by a wall, disorientated and frightened, as the angry mob now hurls cobblestones at the police (Awt, 339). Here the close proximity between the boys designates a state of absolute fear. As shots are fired, the crowd disperses, and the injured are dragged along like rag dolls. Danie observes the unfolding events in filmic fashion without comprehending them. The chapter ends with the relegation of Chemie Leipzig to amateur status after unification. The relegation also marks the end of the football club as a

---

17. In 2012 the office of the Bundesbeauftragte für Stasiunterlagen organized the exhibition Fußball für die Stasi: Der Berliner Fußball-Club Dynamo, which documented the Stasi's influence over the club and its ideological function. See http://www.ddr-fussball.net/heute/ausstellung-fussball-fuer-die-stasi-der-berliner-fussball-club-dynamo/ (accessed 6 August 2014).

heterotopia. Even though the boys invest in new club scarves, the tenor of Danie's commentary is disenchanted.

"Versammlungen" stages the famous Monday demonstrations in Leipzig not as a historical turning point of global consequence but as a thrilling opportunity for adolescent misdemeanor and as a farce in Marx's sense.[18] The chapter begins with a humorous description of how the boys hold their own private assembly every Monday in order to plan their weekly schedule, which includes activities such as attending the next match of Chemie Leipzig or sneaking into the Leipzig Trade Fair in order to collect plastic bags, stickers, and ballpoint pens with Western brand names. On this occasion Walter is not present because, as he explained to them, together with his mother he regularly takes part in the Monday demonstrations (Awt, 418). Intrigued by the long convoy of police cars and police trucks that makes its way to the city center, they decide to attend the next Monday demonstration because it promises thrilling excitement (Awt, 423). Meyer highlights the boys' naivete through subtle narrative details that foreground their detachment from and incomprehension of any political aspiration: as Danie enters the term "marschieren" (marching) into their agenda for the following week, Mark announces that he will bring along his Pioneer flag, which he kept after the state celebrations of International Workers' Day on 1 May (Awt, 424). Stefan, a member of the school's photography club, plans to win the annual photography competition by taking photographs of the demonstrations. The ensuing description of the Monday demonstration adopts the naive perspective of the boys, who see it merely as an exhilarating disruption of their regimented everyday lives. As the crowd chants, "Wir sind

---

18. Quoting Hegel, Marx famously begins his *The Eighteenth Brumaire of Louis Bonaparte*: "Hegel remarks somewhere that all great world-historic facts and personages appear, so to speak, twice. He forgot to add: the first time as tragedy, the second time as farce. Caussidière for Danton, Louis Blanc for Robespierre, the Montagne of 1848 to 1851 for the Montagne of 1793 to 1795, the nephew for the uncle. And the same caricature occurs in the circumstances of the second edition of the Eighteenth Brumaire." Karl Marx, *The Eighteenth Brumaire of Louis Bonaparte*, https://www.marxists.org/archive/marx/works/download/pdf/18th-Brumaire.pdf (accessed 17 August 2014).

das Volk!" (We are the people!), Mark joins in, excitedly waving his Pioneer flag, while Stefan takes pictures of the demonstrators and the police (Awt, 433). Chanting the demonstrators' slogan, the boys jump up and down in the crowd, adding their well-rehearsed football rallying cry to the protest: "Wir sind das Volk"! Wir sind das Volk! Wer nicht wippt ist ein Club-Schwein." (Awt, 432; We are the people! We are the people! If you don't jump up and down, you are a club-pig.) The boys' participation in the demonstration only accentuates how divorced they are from any political perspective. While the politically motivated demonstrators articulate their dissatisfaction with a stagnating and repressive political reality, demanding the democratization of the GDR, the boys see in the events merely a carnivalesque happening that comes with the type of extroverted animation that they associate with the matches of their beloved football club. The cinematographic descriptions of the demonstrations offer a dissociated series of diverse visual and aural impressions that are not interpreted from the perspective of a comprehending narrator. By representing the events in terms of a series of atomized happenings, Meyer overturns the logic of the prevailing historical master narrative according to which the events leading up to the end of the GDR were ultimately inevitable in a Hegelian sense.

The farcical effect of the depiction derives from a narrative perspective that never deviates from the limited experiential horizon of the boys, who are being pulled along by the crowd without understanding the political agenda of the democracy movement. Even though Danie and his friends register the Monday demonstration in terms of a titillating event, in their biographies it remains a mere episode that is detached from narrative integration and developmental potential. By representing the Monday demonstration in terms of an atomized incident, Meyer divorces the event precisely from the type of retrospective interpretation that, in the aftermath of the fall of the Wall, served to either corroborate or challenge prevailing master narratives.[19] Stripped of all ideological messages,

---

19. Fritzsche, "1989 and the Chronological Imagination," 18.

1989 signals here merely a sensational and short-lived moment of utter heterochronia that for Meyer's protagonists leads nowhere.

Empty Time and the Extended Present: Julia Schoch's *Mit der Geschwindigkeit des Sommers* and Karen Duve's *Taxi*

In *Mit der Geschwindigkeit des Sommers* (With the Speed of the Summer, 2009), Julia Schoch explores the fractured and precarious experience of the end of the GDR from the perspective of a female protagonist for whom the fall of the Berlin Wall signifies not so much a decisive moment of liberation as a frightening contingency that leaves her stranded in the past.[20] Set in a small and remote East German community close to the Polish border where time appears to stagnate, the narrative captures the evacuation of historical time from provincial places in the wake of the fall of the Berlin Wall. Concerned with the exterritorialization of the Eastern province from history, it foregrounds a poetics of localization that probes the disabling effects of the acute polarization of place and time in the global age. However, in sharp contrast to recent ostalgic literary representations of life in the former GDR, *Mit der Geschwindigkeit des Sommers* does not idealize a lost *Heimat*.[21]

---

20. Julia Schoch, *Mit der Geschwindigkeit des Sommers* (Munich: Piper, 2009); cited as MdG in the text.

21. On *Ostalgie*, see the contributions in "From Stasiland to Ostalgie: The GDR Twenty Years After," ed. Karen Leeder, special issue, *Oxford German Studies* 38 (2009). Peter Thompson argues that *Ostalgie* is not just a sentimental hankering after the security of daily life in the GDR but a retrospective longing for the unrealized potential of the socialist dream. Peter Thompson, "Die unheimliche Heimat: The GDR and the Dialectics of Home," *Oxford German Studies* 38/3 (2009): 278–87. See also Susanne Ledanff, "Neue Formen der 'Ostalgie'—Abschied von der 'Ostalgie'? Erinnerungen an Kindheit und Jugend in der DDR und an die Geschichtsjahre 1989/90," *Seminar: A Journal of Germanic Studies* 43/2 (2007): 176–93; Andrew Plowman, "Westalgie? Nostalgia for the 'Old' Federal Republic in Recent German Prose," *Seminar* 40/3 (2004): 249–61; Paul Cooke, "Performing 'Ostalgie': Leander Haußmann's *Sonnenallee* (1999)," *German Life & Letters* 56 (2003): 156–67; Anthony Enns, "The Politics of Ostalgie: Post-Socialist Nostalgia in Recent German Film," *Screen* 48/4 (2007): 475–91; Linda Shortt, "Reimagining the West: West Germany, Westalgia, and the Generation of 1978," in *Debating German Cultural Identity since 1989*, 156–70.

Although it investigates multiple local reverberations of globalization, it does not suggest that the province was endowed with local agency and symbolic value in the GDR. Schoch's text is reminiscent of the French *nouveau roman* in that it offers a detailed and extremely objectified symptomatology of the protagonist's temporal disorder without, however, providing a psychological explanation of the causes of her state of unhappiness. Instead the text spatializes temporal stagnation: set in the most godforsaken Eastern province, namely, an East German military outpost close to the Polish border, it enacts the passage of empty time through a topography of lifelessness that is devoid of all energy and vitality.

The garrison town in Schoch's story is stripped of all conventional markers of identity that could designate it a lost *Heimat*. Its sole function during the Cold War derives from its camouflaged setting on the eastern border of the GDR. Here 1989 was a rupture that served only to widen the existing gulf between a faraway center and the forgotten province. Schoch employs what one might call a vocabulary of disembedding that divorces the Eastern province from its meaning-generating capacity. The military garrison town is "ein aus dem Nichts gestampfter Ort, nahe der polnischen Grenze" (MdG, 16; a place knocked together from nothing, close to the Polish border) whose remoteness and woodland setting provided convenient camouflage for the military buildings and training maneuvers during the Cold War. Designed around the barracks, which are plunked down in the middle of woodlands, the town exemplifies the dislocation of modern planning from preexisting contexts and cultural memory: the prefabricated apartment blocks appear like stacked-up boxes without any relation to the natural environment or the old village, which predates the military settlement (MdG, 19). In their sterile execution these islands of modernity defy the idea "daß sich in dieser Art Beton etwas einnisten, dass hier irgend etwas würde zurückbleiben können von uns" (MdG, 20; that something could begin to nest in this type of concrete, that something would be left behind from us). The collective memories that might have the capacity to turn sterile space into lived place are bound to bounce off the impenetrable concrete walls of these prefab buildings. But the natural environment too seems to conspire against the inhabitants: the nearby lagoon that

separates the place from the Polish town Szczecin is a false sea
without any movement or horizon. In summer it degenerates into a
large algae-covered pond whose stench penetrates the whole region
(MdG, 26–27). Inertia triumphs over all human hope that a different existence might be had elsewhere (MdG, 65).

The narrative is set in train by the narrator's attempt to understand her sister's suicide in a hotel room in New York. The motive
and the metropolitan location of the suicide propel the narrator to
piece together the sister's provincial life before and after the *Wende*.
While both the narrator and her sister grew up in this miserable
place as daughters of a NVA officer, the narrator left this "Ödnis"
(MdG, 24; wasteland) soon after the fall of the Berlin Wall to pursue a mobile career that epitomizes the global age. Continually
engaged in "Abfliegen oder Ankommen" (MdG, 12; taking off or
landing), she remembers that during the last phone conversation
with her sister she was packing her suitcase for an extended trip
to Asia. In sharp contrast to the narrator's busy global schedule,
the sister remains marooned in the province, weighed down by the
abundance of empty time. And yet, despite this oppressive sense of
stagnation, the sister harbored no secret dream to travel to exotic places
or to seek out adventures through foreign encounters (MdG, 12). The
narrator recalls that her sister hardly ever ventured farther than the
nearest bigger town (which was still very small) for her shopping
trips (MdG, 13). But her stubborn disengagement with the global
world is not a reflection of her embeddedness in local life but
rather a fundamental disbelief that place has the capacity to bring
forth any meaningful attachment. Arguably, the story of the sister
concerns much more than the lifting out of social relations from
local contexts, which, according to Anthony Giddens, is one of
the hallmarks of globalization. While the narrator's mobile global
lifestyle does indeed exemplify such disembedding from local context, the sister's stationary existence in the remote province foregrounds something even more worrying: the disembedding of the
locality from any meaning-generating contexts and as such from
the possibility of generating attachment to space and time. *Mit der
Geschwindigkeit des Sommers* thus offers a radical exploration of
the failure of conventional "techniques for the spatial production

of locality," which, as Arjun Appadurai suggests, serve to social-
ize and localize space and time "through complex and deliberate
practices of performance, representation, and action."²² Although
the sister goes through the motions of some of these rituals of
localization—for example, she gets married, has children, and,
after the *Wende*, moves from the prefab apartment block into a
newly built house with a garden on the periphery of the town—
her existence remains "ein stetiges Schlingern durch einen dunklen
Raum" (MdG, 53; a constant swaying movement through a dark
room). Even the post-*Wende* renewal of her affair with a former
soldier with whom she had a relationship before the fall of the Wall
does not induce a sense of connectedness with the place.

At first, however, their relationship reenacts a post-*Wende* version of an ostalgic alternative life that was prematurely ended by
the events of 1989. As the sister and the soldier revisit the decaying
ruins of the former garrison town, they suddenly discover meaning
in "wegbröckelnde Ladenaufschriften, überwucherte Denkmäler
oder rostige Springbrunnen" (MdG, 62; crumbling shop signs,
overgrown monuments, or rusty fountains). Even the photographs
of queues of people outside the barren GDR shops become cher-
ished souvenirs, projecting a lost attachment into the future ante-
rior of the GDR. But such romance with the bygone GDR remains
short-lived; it is soon superseded by the bitter realization that people's dreams in the GDR had been so small that their fulfillment
after the *Wende* was swift and totally unspectacular (MdG, 109).
The revolution of 1989 thus stands for the end of all utopian aspirations: now that one's material wish list has been exhausted, people no longer know "welcher Art von Träumen in dieser anderen
Gesellschaft nachzuhängen war" (MdG, 110; what type of dream
to hanker after in this different society).

And yet Schoch's text abstains from the type of ostalgia that per-
meates much of post-Wall literature. As Mary Cosgrove notes, "The
sense of non-place . . . enshrouds pre- and post-Wende existence,"

---

22. Arjun Appadurai, *Modernity at Large: Cultural Dimensions of Globalisation*, 2nd ed. (1996; Minneapolis: University of Minnesota Press, 2000), 180.

and "the lack of future orientation is also part of both world orders."[23] There is, however, one significant difference between the sister's pre- and post-*Wende* existence: as a teenager she could still dream of leaving a place that, at this point in her life, merely stood for a transitional phase in a fulfilling future. Hence her hope that this "unpassender Beginn" (MdG, 22; improper beginning) in the remote province was nothing but a glitch that would be corrected when she assumed her prescribed role "an einem Platz, den es doch zu geben schien, für jeden" (MdG, 22; in a spot, which appeared to exist for everybody). But the promise that social and ideological conformity with the system produces placed identity rings hollow in a garrison town populated by stranded expellees, a few local farmers, disappointed army families, and drafted soldiers who embark on heavy weekend drinking sessions out of sheer boredom and despair (MdG, 24). Together they make up a motley bunch of untied ends. When the Berlin Wall comes down, the officers' wives watch this event on TV in disbelief before grasping the opportunity it offered them to leave their bewildered husbands for a new and autonomous life elsewhere: "Es war, als hätte ihnen der Lauf der Geschichte plötzlich ein Argument für ein eignes Leben gegeben." (MdG, 50; It seemed as if, all of a sudden, the course of history had given an argument for a self-determined life.) It is precisely the utterly unpredictable and contingent nature of the events of 1989 that imbues, at least temporarily, their lives with liberating emancipatory agency. Occurrences are experienced as events when they "can be separated ex post from the infinity of circumstances."[24] The rupture of 1989 introduces the officers' wives to a momentous reconnection of their individual biographies with world history. According to Reinhart Koselleck historical experience requires a

---

23. Mary Cosgrove, "Heimat as Non-Place and Terrain Vague in Jenny Erpenbeck's *Heimsuchung* and Julia Schoch's *Mit der Geschwindigkeit des Sommers*," in "Transformations of German Cultural Identity, 1989–2009," ed. Anne Fuchs and Kathleen James-Chakraborty, special issue, *New German Critique* 116 (2012): 83.

24. Reinhart Koselleck, "Representation, Event, and Structure," in *Futures Past: On the Semantics of Historical Time*, trans. Keith Tribe (New York: Columbia University Press, 2004), 105.

"significant unity that makes an event out of incidents."[25] Prior to 1989, the absence of meaningful temporal sequencing in the province produced a deadening inertia, sucking all hope from the lives of its inhabitants. In the garrison town nothing ever happened that could overcome the "threshold of fragmentation below which an event dissolves into unrelated incidents."[26] As Peter Fritzsche comments, "The watersheds of 1789 and 1989 indicated the historical and basically impermanent, even unstable nature of all social and political constructions. The events of 1989 restored the role of surprise to history and underscored the role of contingency."[27] Accordingly, for Schoch's protagonists 1989 reintroduces an awareness of history in the guise of historical surprise. The narrator's sister is no exception: she too acknowledges that 1989 was an event that sliced her life into a before and an after, producing a radically new and "andere Geschwindigkeit der Zeit" (MdG, 118; different speed of the times). And yet, in her case the experience of historical acceleration results only in a "Galopp auf der Stelle . . . , bei dem man sich eingrub" (MdG 118; canter in the same spot . . . that buried you).

The sister's historical consciousness then begs the question of why she remained behind when so many others packed up and left. Rather than resolving this conundrum by way of psychological explanations that, for example, would diagnose her as suffering from depression, the narrator reflects on the sister's negative attachment to a hollowed-out place for which she becomes a sort of disenfranchised ambassador: "Mein Eindruck, der Ort schiebe sich vor, und meine Schwester wäre nur ihre Botschafterin. Als seien ihre beiden Geschichten vermengt, und ihre hätte in gar keiner Weise woanders stattfinden können." (MdG, 91; My impression was that the place pushed itself forward, and my sister was its ambassador.

---

25. Koselleck, "Representation, Event, and Structure," 106.

26. Koselleck, "Representation, Event, and Structure," 106.

27. Debating Samuel Huntington's *The Clash of Civilizations*, Fritzsche shows that this manifesto signaled the reinstatement of national histories: "The 'hardness of culture' rested on endurance, not change, so that the dominant metaphors of historical interpretation after 1989 were spatial: *bounded* identities, *deep* essences, in contrast to *surface* ideology." Fritzsche, "1989 and the Chronological Imagination," 20.

As if their stories were entangled and as if her story could not have happened elsewhere.) For the sister the empty time of provincial existence continues to dominate, evaporating all hope for a meaningful chronology beyond one's biological clock. When the sister and her ex-soldier lover revisit the nearly demolished town she notes that even its disappearance is completely unspectacular and banal. The ex-soldier observes that the evacuation of the province from historical time is part of a

> gewaltigen Prozesses . . . , der in der ganzen Welt vor sich ging. Woanders versiegt ein Meer, Häfen wurden geschlossen, Bodenschätze gingen zur Neige, man legte Zechen still, Werke, Industrien verschwanden, aus Fischerdörfen wurden Urlaubsanlagen, ganze Städte versteppten (MdG, 85).

> phenomenal process . . . , which was happening all over the world. Somewhere else the sea was drying up, harbors were being closed, natural resources came to an end, mines were being closed, factories and whole industries disappeared, fishing villages turned themselves into holiday resorts, whole cities turned into deserts.

In this dystopian perspective, globalization has effected a fundamental dislocation of place: the termination of production in former heartlands of the Industrial Revolution, the closure of harbors and mines, and the decline of natural resources usher in a universal deterritorialization that may render the globe a barren wasteland. In this view, the erosion of locality in the East German province is not just the effect of German unification but also the corollary of an anxiety-inducing global "disjuncture between territory, subjectivity and collective social movement."[28] Under these new conditions conventional techniques for the production of locality are precarious if not ineffective. In Schoch's narrative 1989 only momentarily connects the province with world affairs; it does not, however, root it in a multidimensional cultural geography where temporal and geographical axes could create dynamic lines of exchange between the periphery and the center. The polarization of space and time in the global age has robbed the province of all contexts and thus of the very possibility of generating attachment to places.

---

28. Appadurai, *Modernity at Large*, 189.

While Schoch stages the disjuncture between her protagonist's personal history and the chronological imagination in the Eastern province, Karen Duve's female protagonist, Alex, in her novel *Taxi* experiences an abysmal sense of stagnation in urban Hamburg before and immediately after the fall of the Wall.[29] The narrated time in this first-person narrative comprises six years: the 140 pages of part 1 cover the period from 1984 to 1986, and part 2, which comprises 170 pages, deals with the short but historically eventful time span from September 1989 to June 1990, with the intervening years omitted. However, rather than giving prominence to the fall of the Berlin Wall, the extension of narrative time in the second part only accentuates the protagonist's profound sense of disconnectedness from life. Accordingly, she barely registers the fall of the Berlin Wall when she notices in passing how a Trabi (the iconic East German Trabant car for which people had to wait for ten years or more) is being repaired at a local garage.

At the beginning of the narrative we learn that Alex takes up the job of taxi driver in Hamburg on a temporary basis in order to avoid making any binding decision about her future. In contrast to her former schoolmates, who have entered university, Alex has been hanging around at home reading books about chimpanzees. A prominent leitmotif, her interest in primates already points to her inability to plan the future and fulfill conventional social expectations. Instead of subscribing to the temporal discipline of the bourgeois subject, which accrues social capital by pursuing professional success within a normative setting, Duve's protagonist precariously drifts through life without a sense of biographical direction.

The male-dominated world of taxi drivers in the West Germany of the 1980s is, as Alex finds out quickly, characterized by a deep-seated misogyny that entraps her in a repetitive series of dissatisfying relationships with deeply sexist men. Alex sustains a relationship with her taxi colleague Dietrich because she cannot muster the energy to end an affair that she began only out of

---

29. Karen Duve, *Taxi* (Frankfurt a. Main: Eichborn, 2008); cited as T in the text.

sheer boredom. Rüdiger, another taxi driver and a close friend of Dietrich, embarks on frequent misogynist rants that are peppered with quotes from Weininger and Nietzsche and, in their predictability, lose the edge of contrariness. When Alex meets Marco, a former schoolmate, she enters into a clandestine affair with him without, however, committing to a relationship. While Marco is the only male character who takes her seriously, he too denigrates her by slapping her during rough sex. In part 2, Alex is briefly attracted to the journalist Majewski, who takes her on a fast car ride: as he races through the countryside at a speed of 150 kilometers per hour, engaging in risky passing, Alex is overcome by the unknown thrill of being alive, an experience that remains episodic, however, because Majewski too turns out to be abusive.

Ironically, Duve communicates her protagonist's sense of stasis through the motif of driving: driving through the cityscape in this narrative no longer signifies the thrill of urban life or speed but entrapment in a repetitive routine that grinds down the difference between past, present, and future. At first in her new job as a taxi driver Alex feels a welcome sense of adventure as she speeds through Hamburg at night without a seat belt and picks up passengers from sleazy bars or brothels (T, 35). But such excitement is short-lived: the initial titillation of discovering the unknown underworld of Hamburg soon turns into permanent disgust at the predictability of human behavior. The stench of drunk and filthy passengers who are rude, abusive, and unwilling to pay their fare makes Alex reflect on the "Ausmaß der Schlechtigkeit meiner Mitmenschen im Umgang mit Dienstleistenden" (T, 29; extent of my fellow human being's abusiveness when dealing with service providers). Instead of reenacting the modern fantasy of liberation, the narrative employs the chronotope of driving through the cityscape to map out a topography of repetitions and recursions that mirrors Alex's sense of disenchanted stagnation. As Mary Cosgrove argues, "Subverting the road narrative as the special domain of the white (American) male on a voyage of self-discovery, success, and fast movement, Duve conveys gender stasis as well as social stasis in the spatio-temporal motif of driving around and around the same routes, year in, year out." [30] The absence of any significant temporal markers in Alex's life is matched by her deep sense of spatial disorientation: in spite of her best efforts to remember street names, she forgets even those place-names that she had already learned by heart (T, 56). Alex's notorious sense of disorientation thus points to a profound crisis of the biographical imagination: because of the deadening repetitiveness and routine she can no longer relate her life in terms of a coherent biography that draws on the past as a resource for shaping an open and dynamic future. And so at the beginning of part 2 five years have passed and Alex is still driving her taxi:

> Und dann waren fünf Jahr um und ich fuhr immer noch Taxi. Zur Reeperbahn. Zum Flughafen. Zum Mittelweg. . . . Am Ende einer Nacht konnte ich mich nicht einmal mehr erinnern, in welchen Stadtteilen ich gewesen war. Die Touren verschmolzen zu einem Brei aus Lichtern, Straßen, Zigarettenrauch und immer gleichem Gerede. (T, 145)

> And then five years had passed and I was still driving a taxi. To the Reeperbahn. To the Airport. To Mittelweg. . . . At the end of a night I could not even remember in which districts I had been. My taxi tours morphed into a pulp of lighting, streets, cigarette smoke, and repetitive chitchat.

The novel ends with a dramatic climax when Alex drives off at top speed with a chimpanzee that she wants to rescue from the shackles of its oppressed circus existence. As Alex is racing away in her taxi, the chimp takes control of the steering wheel, causing an accident that will end Alex's time as taxi driver:

> Und so schoss das Taxi am Ende über eine Böschung. Ich schrie, der Affe schrie, die Bremse quietschte, Zweige prasselten von allen Seiten auf die Fenster, dünne Zweige, dicke Äste, Holz krachte, Metall knirschte. Dann hob sich das Vorderteil des Taxis in die Luft, das Scheinwerferlicht erfasste den Rand einer Baumkrone, und dann sah ich über mir nur noch den schwarzblauen, sternenübersäten Himmel. (T, 309)

---

30. Mary Cosgrove, "The Temporality of Boredom in the Age of Acceleration: The Car Crash in Contemporary German Literature," in *Time in German Literature and Culture*, 211. See also Heike Bartel, "Of Alpha Males, Apes, Altenberg, and Driving in the City," in *Emerging German-Language Novelists*, 179–94.

And so the taxi was shooting over the embankment at the end. I was screaming, the ape was screaming, the brakes were screeching, twigs were hitting the car window from all sides, thin twigs, and big branches, wood was splintering, and metal was grinding. And then the front part of the car was being lifted into the air, the headlights illuminating the edge of a tree top, and then I saw only the black and blue sky above me, covered by stars.

Filippo Marinetti's *Futurist Manifesto* imagined a car crashing into a ditch as a supreme moment of rupture, freeing his cyborg subject from the shackles of a decrepit social order. But as Enda Duffy argues, the thrill of speed as promised by the modern car culture was intimately bound up with consumerism and "bracketed as a leisure experience: it offered no real new power to the driving subject."[31] While driving at high speed could simulate freedom, the crash marks "the intrusive revenge of the real on a culture whose pleasures are built on the dream of escaping the illusionary world of consumerist simulation."[32] Both moments already featured in chapter 1 of Robert Musil's *Der Mann ohne Eigenschaften* (*The Man without Qualities*, 1930–43), where motorcars are depicted shooting from deep, narrow streets into the bright squares of Vienna before an accident involving a truck and a pedestrian brings the traffic to an abrupt halt.[33] In Musil's novel the protagonist Ulrich, an engineer by training, rationalizes the traumatic moment of the accident by means of the technical explanation that the breaking distance of these heavy trucks is far too long. As a mere engineering problem, the accident loses its core meaning, namely, that accidental violence can occur unpredictably at any time and with full catastrophic force. Ulrich's final observation that car accidents kill 190,000 people every year in the United States further normalizes the traffic accident.

When read in dialogue with modernist texts, Duve's crash scene appears as a parodic reenactment of the Futurist speed fantasy.

31. Duffy, *The Speed Hand-Book*, 202.
32. Duffy, *The Speed Hand-Book*, 203.
33. Robert Musil, *Der Mann ohne Eigenschaften*, in *Gesammelte Werke in neun Bänden*, ed. Adolf Frisé (Reinbek: Rowohlt, 1978), 1:9–11.

Instead of Marinetti's vision of the new cyborg subject we are faced here with a hominoid primate whose primitive physical power brings into play the vitalistic nature.

The Cult of Immediacy and the Search for Resonance: Wilhelm Genazino's *Das Glück in glücksfernen Zeiten*

Wilhelm Genazino's poetics lectures *Die Belebung der toten Winkel* (The Reanimation of the Dead Corners, 2006) address the transformation of human experience in the contemporary arena.[34] Genazino approaches his topic by elaborating the fundamental difference between the modern figure of the flâneur, who emerged in the nineteenth century, and his contemporary successor, the stray city walker. Referring to Walter Benjamin's Baudelaire essays, he argues that the flâneur's enjoyment of modernity's electrifying visual spectacles depended on an urban environment that, in spite of the increased pace of life, could still be assimilated by the receptive individual (BtW, 95).[35] Joyce's work in particular stages for Genazino a subjectivity that manages to derive pleasure from the urban environment by transforming fleeting impressions into moments of quasi-metaphysical vision. The Joycean epiphany thus accentuates the sovereignty of the modern self that is at liberty to mobilize a heightened attention in the service of the subject's own creative imagination (BtW, 93). But this modern aesthetic of *Plötzlichkeit* (instantaneity), to use Karlheinz Bohrer's term, depended on the ability of individuals to select whether, when, and for how long to direct their gaze at specific phenomena.[36] As a sovereign

---

34. Wilhelm Genazino, *Die Belebung der toten Winkel: Frankfurter Poetikvorlesungen* (Munich: Carl Hanser, 2006); cited as BtW in the text.

35. In line with this Benjamin writes that the leisurely mode of the flâneur is made possible by the arcades, which turn the boulevard into an *intérieur* and as such into a sphere of domesticity. See Walter Benjamin, "Das Paris des Second Empire bei Baudelaire," in *Abhandlungen—Gesammelte Schriften*, ed. Rolf Tiedemann and Hermann Schweppenhäuser (Frankfurt a. Main: Suhrkamp, 1991), I.2:539.

36. Karlheinz Bohrer, *Plötzlichkeit: Zum Augenblick des ästhetischen Scheins* (Frankfurt a. Main: Suhrkamp, 1981).

subject the flâneur commanded modernity's culture of speed by means of two codependent cultural techniques that helped to filter modernity's dazzling sensations through two modes of perception: attention and distraction. Fin de siècle discourse discovered attention as a vital cultural strategy that could ward off the danger of too much distraction and ultimately of psychic disintegration. Attention as the ability to focus for a defined period of time on selected external phenomena contained and disciplined the perpetual production of the new as one of modernity's striking features.[37] Distraction as the flip side of attention indicated a temporality of leisure brought about by this wealth of intoxicating external stimuli. The modern subject thus entertained fleeting interests in a rapid succession of visual attractions that, at the point of their appearance, were already destined to be superseded by new excitements and thrills. Georg Simmel's essay "Die Großstädte und das Geistesleben," Siegfried Kracauer's "Der Kult der Zerstreuung" ("The Cult of Distraction"), and, of course, Benjamin's elaborations on the flâneur articulate and explore specifically modern strategies of coping with such radically new conditions of perception. In chapter 2 we saw how the new tempo of life unleashed new aesthetic possibilities that found articulation in modern poetry, short prose, fiction, film, and fine art. In his Frankfurt lectures Genazino argues that the conditions of early modernity were still sufficiently stable to fuse the observing self and the observed object through a temporality of meaningful observation. He agrees with Hartmut Rosa's diagnosis that late modernity has destroyed the momentary stability of this fourfold constellation of subject, object, time, and mode of seeing (BtW, 92). The contemporary metropolis is an illegible jungle that has lost the "strukturiertes, eingängiges Stadtbild"

---

37. On the discourse on attention around 1900, see Crary, *Suspensions of Perceptions*; Anne Fuchs, "Why Smallness Matters: Smallness, Attention, and Distraction in Franz Kafka's and Robert Walser's Short Short Prose," in *Kafka und die kleine Prosa der Moderne/Kafka and Short Modernist Prose*, ed. Ritchie Robertson and Manfred Engel (Würzburg: Königshausen & Neumann, 2010), 167–79; Carolin Duttlinger, "Kafkas Poetik der Aufmerksamkeit von *Betrachtung* bis *Der Bau*," in *Kafka und die kleine Prosa der Moderne*, 79–97.

(BtW, 104; structured and coherent cityscape) that, according to Genazino, was a central condition of the flâneur's epiphanic connectivity with the urban environment (BtW, 104). The flâneur's contemporary successor is a stray self who roams the city, exposed to the "Durcheinander der verwischten Bilder" (BtW, 104; mess of blurred images):

> Die Figur des Flaneurs hat in der zerstückelten Stadt abgedankt und ist ersetzt worden durch einen moderneren Typus, den des Streuners. Der Streuner ist jemand, der selbst der Ungemütlichkeit noch einen Reiz abgewinnen möchte und dabei oft erfolgreich ist. . . . Der Streuner fühlt sich als displaced person, aber er weiß auch, daß es andere Plätze für ihn nicht mehr gibt. Die Identität des Streuners ist genauso beschädigt wie die Gestalt der Metropole selbst. (BtW, 103)

> The figure of the flâneur has had it in the dismembered city; he has been replaced by a more modern type, the stray. The stray is someone who tries to extract pleasure even from the discomforting coldness and he is often successful in this. . . . The stray sees himself as a displaced person but he knows that there are no longer any alternative places for him. The identity of the stray is as damaged as that of the metropolitan cityscape.

With its glitzy surfaces and flat projection screens, the contemporary city has, in the eyes of Genazino, morphed into a fake stage set that engenders nothing but "fake Tagesgefühle, die genauso prekär sind wie die Kulissen der Stadt, denen sie mühsam abgefühlt worden sind" (BtW, 105; fake temporary feelings that are as precarious as the stage set of the city from which they have been painfully derived). Because the quick succession of rapid images has destroyed the conditions of intimacy, the only options left to the stray self of late modernity is to retreat momentarily into "die Ordnung seiner Innerlichkeit" (BtW, 106; the order of his inner self) or to adopt various tactics of temporal resistance, which I will discuss below. Genazino summarizes the difference between early capitalism and its late version as follows:

> Früher, sagen wir in der prähysterischen Phase des Kapitalismus, richtete sich der Blick der Menschen auf die Dinge. Heute richtet sich der Blick der Dinge auf den Menschen. Niemand entgeht den Übergriffen ihrer Kaufappelle. Die Zudringlichkeit kassiert die betrachtende Distanz, auf die der Flaneur einmal Wert gelegt hatte. Die Penetranz der

Waren macht den Flaneur zum Streuner und ist der Grund für die
Fluchtförmigkeit seines Umherstreifens. In Umgebungen ohne Diskre-
tion kann es Flaneure deshalb nicht mehr geben. (BtW, 107)

In earlier times, say the prehysterical phase of capitalism, human beings
directed their gaze at things. In today's world it is the things that are di-
recting their gaze at humans. No one escapes the attack of their urgent
appeal to be bought. Pushy impropriety has replaced the contemplative
distance that was once valued by the flâneur. The omnipresence of merchandise turns the flâneur into a stray, and it is the reason for the hastiness of his flânerie. The flâneur cannot survive in environments without
discretion.

Philosopher Byung-Chul Han celebrates the emergence of a deterritorialized and disembedded global culture that he envisions as
populated by "hypercultural tourists" who neither long for nor
fear the encounter with a "there."[38] He claims that the figure of the
hypercultural tourist knows no difference between here and there
as he "windows" the world—a term coined on the analogy of the
ubiquitous computer operating system.[39] For Han this new state
of hyperculturality has the potential to realize freedom if it abandons prevailing notions of fulfilled time and narration in favor of
what he calls "point time" or "event time."[40] Without past and future horizon, this "point time" carries no meaning and is thus not
burdened by "gravitation," the term by which Han captures conventional ideas of narration and history. "Das Sein," according to
Han, "zerstreut sich zu einem Hyperraum aus Möglichkeiten und
Ereignissen, die, statt zu gravitieren, darin gleichsam nur schwirren" (Being disaggregates into a hyperspace of opportunities and
events which, instead of gravitating, buzz around).[41] Han's eulogy

---

38. Zygmunt Bauman's critique of globalization, Byung-Chul Han argues, lacks
appreciation of the hypercultural tourist: "Für Bauman ist der Tourist noch ein Pilger,
der zerrissen ist zwischen der Sehnsucht nach dem Dort und der Furcht vor diesem.
Der hyperkulturelle Tourist dagegen hat weder Sehnsucht noch Furcht." (For Bauman the tourist is still a pilgrim torn between the longing for and the fear of a There.
By contrast the hypercultural tourist knows neither fear nor longing.) Byung-Chul
Han, *Hyperkulturalität: Kultur und Globalisierung* (Berlin: Merve, 2005), 45 and 47.
39. Han, *Hyperkulturalität*, 49.
40. Han, *Hyperkulturalität*, 54.
41. Han, *Hyperkulturalität*, 54.

for hyperculturality clearly contradicts his critique of point time as discussed in chapter 2. It also completely ignores the negative effects of global capitalism, as manifest in the sharp disjuncture between a mobile extraterritorial elite and "the ever more 'localized' rest" that, as Zygmunt Bauman argues, are left behind as human debris in largely disenfranchised localities.[42] In contrast to Han's rather euphoric view, Genazino emphasizes the pathologies of late capitalism: its hysterical phase is characterized by the "Penetranz der Waren" (BtW, 107; the omnipresence of merchandise), which has destroyed the contemplative distance between subject and object. While the nineteenth-century flâneur still managed to exploit this distance in the pursuit of an epiphanic connectivity, his Genazinean successor inhabits an environment without contemplative distance and discretion. Surrounded by the impoverished trappings of hysterical capitalism, as Genazino's figures wander through the city they suffer from the enduring consciousness that they are ridiculously out of place and time. But as Ernst Bloch's famous formulation suggests, history is marked by the contemporaneity of the noncontemporaneous.[43] The seeming defect turns out to be a strategic position: Genazino's figures discover their noncontemporaneity with the contemporary to be a creative resource that allows them to exercise a degree of temporal sovereignty in an era that is otherwise ruled by the hectic just-in-time ideology. In the following I will illustrate such resistance to the prevalent

---

42. Zygmunt Bauman, *Globalization: The Human Consequences* (Cambridge: Polity, 1998), 3.

43. See Ernst Bloch, *Erbschaft dieser Zeit* (Frankfurt a. Main: Suhrkamp, 1962), 1. Bloch coined the phrase "Gleichzeitigkeit des Ungleichzeitigen," but the concept goes back to the late eighteenth century, when European civilization was set as a benchmark for overseas cultures seen as having been left behind. See Reinhart Koselleck, "'Neuzeit': Remarks on the Semantics of Modern Concepts of Movement," in *Futures Past: On the Semantics of Historical Time* (New York: Columbia University Press, 2004), 236–38. See also Hanns-Georg Brose, "Das Gleichzeitige ist ungleichzeitig: Über den Umgang mit einer Paradoxie und die Transformation der Zeit," in *Unsichere Zeiten: Herausforderungen gesellschaftlicher Transformationen; Verhandlungen des 34. Kongresses der Deutschen Gesellschaft für Soziologie in Jena 2008*, ed. Hans-Georg Soeffner, Kathy Kursawe, Margrit Elsner, and Manja Aldt (Wiesbaden: Springer, 2010), 547–62.

zeitgeist with reference to Genazino's novel *Das Glück in glücks-fernen Zeiten.*

Nearly all of Genazino's heroes abhor the drudgery of the world of work whose alienating effects are amplified in the contemporary open-plan office environment where employees become agents of mutual surveillance. The *Abschaffel* trilogy of the late 1970s, which consists of *Abschaffel* (1977), *Die Vernichtung der Sorgen* (The Abolition of Worries, 1978), and *Falsche Jahre* (False Years, 1979), relates the story of a male employee who is the embodiment of the unhappy white-collar worker in the latter part of the twentieth century and as such a successor of Kafka's Josef K.[44] Aged thirty-one and single, he feels trapped by his job in the open-plan office of a transport company. The boring routine of his working life is punctuated only by office gossip, long and empty Sundays, dissatisfying leisure activities, including casual relationships with women, the occasional visit to a brothel, and far too many cigarettes.

Thirty years later we encounter Gerhard Warlich, the protagonist of *Das Glück in glücksfernen Zeiten*, who is manager of a big laundry company that services hotels in the Frankfurt region.[45] In the opening scene we encounter Warlich after work in a street café in Frankfurt where he observes "die endlich zur Betrachtung freigegebenen feierabendlichen Goldränder unserer Leistungsgesellschaft" (GigfZ, 7; the golden rims of our society of achievers which have finally been released at the end of their working day). This setting bears all the tacky signs of global capitalism: the café's menu of drinks has been printed on the back of the employees' T-shirts, half a dozen Russian immigrants are playing a slot machine, and a young couple next to Warlich are slurping their green drinks so loudly that Warlich feels tempted to pay them a fiver to stop their noisy sucking. Warlich himself is self-consciously aware of the consumer slogans on his plastic bags, which he shoves in embarrassment under the table. Reflecting on his desire for change in his life,

---

44. Wilhelm Genazino, *Abschaffel* (Munich: dtv, 2002).

45. Wilhelm Genazino, *Das Glück in glücksfernen Zeiten* (Munich: Hanser, 2009); cited as GigfZ in the text.

he then observes a begging trumpeter who, in spite of his poor performance, manages to collect some money (GigfZ, 9). Overcome by this "allgemeine Ödnis des Wirklichen" (GigfZ, 9; general dreariness of reality), Warlich is desperately in need of a small-scale occurrence that could appease his injured soul.

Although Warlich is a version of Genazino's earlier protagonist, his situation has become much more precarious in the age of neoliberalism and the erosion of the social securities of the postwar era. In many ways Warlich is the embodiment of the new, educated precariat facing social and economic decline.[46] He wrote a doctoral dissertation on Heidegger, in all likelihood on the phenomenology of time, but landed his permanent job because he introduced just-in-time deliveries at the laundry company. Warlich has long abandoned the naive belief that the conventional pathway through the education system can influence one's prospects in life: the alienating reality of the world of work has exposed his academic qualifications as "Bildungslametta" (educational tinsel) without use or value (GigfZ, 45). In his professional life Warlich is not only responsible for further rationalizations, such as the introduction of the one-day laundry service, but also for spying on the deliverymen whom his boss suspects of wasting time. As he follows the company drivers Wrede and Ehrlicher through the outskirts of Frankfurt he is struck by the drab appearance of these urban edgelands, which bear all the signs of long-term neglect. Disused shopping malls line the streets, sheltering the homeless, the drunk, and other misfits, along with Asian discount stalls that flog tacky wares:

> Die Leute leben zwar, aber sie haben vergessen, wo sie einmal zu Hause waren, so ähnlich wie traurige Tiere im Zoo. Der Blick fällt auf verstopfte Abfallkörbe, nicht weggeräumte, vermoderte Blätter vom Vorjahresherbst, leerstehende Geschäfte, in den Kaufhauseingängen herumliegende Obdachlose und Gestrandete, dazu immer mehr

---

46. On this topic, see chapter 1 in this study. Heinz Bude and Andreas Willisch, eds., *Exklusion: Die Debatte über die "Überflüssigen"* (Frankfurt a. Main: Suhrkamp, 2007); Robert Castel and Klaus Dörre, eds., *Prekariat, Abstieg, Ausgrenzung: Die soziale Frage am Beginn des 21. Jahrhunderts* (Frankfurt a. Main: Campus, 2009).

Asiatenbasare, wo es Plastiksandalen, Gummirosen und Strohperücken
zu kaufen gibt. (GigfZ, 41)

People may still be alive but they have forgotten where they are from,
just like the sad animals in the zoo. He is scanning overflowing rubbish bins, the leaves from last year that have not been swept up; derelict
shops; the homeless and dropouts who are hanging around the entrance
of a store; and in the midst of all this Asian discount stalls where you
can buy plastic sandals, plastic roses, and straw wigs.

The visual and emotional deprivation in this scene accentuates the
sharp disjuncture between, on the one hand, Frankfurt's financial
center and global investment hub that proudly showcases its signature buildings and, on the other, its down-at-the-heels urban
fringes, which have swept up the trash of globalization, losing all
connection with place as a "field of care" (Yi-Fu Tuan). And yet,
this shabby *non-lieu* houses a small oasis, a Volksgarten or people's garden that offers a retreat for mothers, children, and the elderly. As a communal space, the Volksgarten represents a social
locality that reanimates the damaged bond between the environment and its inhabitants. However, for Warlich it is a tainted paradise because of his hateful "Observierungsauftrag" (GigfZ, 41;
surveillance task): in the park's beer garden he then spots the two
company drivers, who are enjoying a drink during their working
hours. As he considers his unenviable role as a company snoop,
he realizes his systemic enmeshment in existing power structures
(GigfZ, 41).

In his encounter with a reality that is simultaneously drab and
demanding, Genazino's hero pursues five tactics of resistance:[47]
melancholy self-absorption, the performance of private rituals, the
fabrication of stories, the prolonged gaze, and, finally, a tactical
slowness. This ensemble of tactics creates a multilayered temporal

---

47. Michel de Certeau distinguishes between strategy as an operation of institutionalized power and tactics "which cannot count on a proper (a spatial or institutional) location, nor thus on a borderline distinguishing the other as a visible
totality. The place of the tactic belongs to the other. A tactic insinuates itself into
the other's place, fragmentarily, without taking it over in its entirety, without being
able to keep it at a distance." Michel de Certeau, *The Practice of Everyday Life*,
trans. Steven Rendall (Berkeley: University of California Press, 1984), xix.

ecology that allows the protagonist either to cultivate a melancholy subjectivity at a remove from the world or to periodically experience "topophilia," that is, attachment to local places.[48]

All of Genazino's heroes foster a highly self-conscious mode of melancholy. Their regular retreat into melancholy self-absorption creates a form of Bergsonian *durée* that suspends the "Zwangsabonnement der Wirklichkeit" (GigfZ, 10; the enforced subscription to reality) and as such the obligation to be "always connectable, available and public."[49] By indulging in bouts of "melancholische Verwilderung" (GigfZ, 23; melancholic wilderness)—a term that possibly alludes to Benjamin's short essay on Robert Walser[50]— Warlich gains access to his innermost self, where all disturbing interaction with the outside world is temporarily suspended. In his depiction of Warlich's melancholy, Genazino clearly plays with the ancient tradition of melancholy as a physiological condition (caused by too much black bile and the influence of the planet Saturn) and as a sign of the genius.[51] However, in Genazino's novel the reactivation of this tradition, which, from antiquity to the present day, provides a rich cultural narrative, is always lined with humor. Warlich is therefore not a creative genius but merely "ein Beinahe-Künstler . . . ; ich mache Collagen. Ich zeichne und male. Ich filme, ich schreibe Nonsens-Gedichte, aber nichts davon so richtig." (GigfZ, 17; Nearly an artist . . . , I produce collages. I draw and paint. I make films and I write nonsense poetry, but all of this

---

48. See Gaston Bachelard, *The Poetics of Space*, trans. Maria Jolas (Boston: Beacon Press, 1969); and Tuan, *Topophilia*.

49. Nowotny, *Time*, 34.

50. Benjamin's comments on Walser's style resonate with Genazino's poetics of melancholy opposition: for Benjamin, Walser confronts the reader with a "scheinbar, völlig absichtslosen und dennoch anziehenden und bannenden Sprachverwilderung. Vor einem sich Gehenlassen, das alle Formen von Grazie bis zur Bitternis aufweist" (seemingly unintentional and at the same time fascinating and gripping form of linguistic unruliness. It is abandonment which comes with all forms of grace and bitterness). Walter Benjamin, "Robert Walser," in *Über Robert Walser*, ed. Katharina Kerr (Frankfurt a. Main: Suhrkamp, 1978), 1:126.

51. See Raymond Klibansky, Erwin Panofsky, and Fritz Saxl, *Saturn and Melancholy: Studies in the History of Natural Philosophy, Religion, and Art* (London: Thomas Nelson & Sons, 1964).

without real effort.) And while his periodic spells of "Verrücktheit" (GigfZ, 86; madness) are a further indication of his melancholy inclination, they are divorced from the grand cosmological context of the mad genius. Once he reaches the recesses of his melancholy "Innenraum" (inner space), he can wallow in a form of self-pity that is framed by a good dosage of self-knowledge:

> Dort bedauert mich niemand so kenntnisreich wie ich selber. Die Leisigkeit, mit der ich neben Traudel sitzen bleibe und gleichzeitig verschwinde, wirkt auch auf mich unangenehm. Ich bin in einer Stimmung, in der ich kaum ertrage, daß es abends immer Abend wird und daß die Dunkelheit draußen auch in unsere Wohnung eindringt. (GigfZ, 23).

> In there nobody commiserates with me as professionally as I do. I find the quiet manner in which I remain seated next to Traudl while simultaneously disappearing disagreeable. I am in a mood in which I can barely tolerate the fact that every evening it is evening time and that the darkness outside will make its way into our flat too.

The whimsical expression of selfhood presented here revitalizes a sentimental subjectivity that, by analogy with the age of *Empfindsamkeit* (Sentimentality), links the physiological and emotional spheres through an all-encompassing mood.[52] It comes as no surprise that Warlich understands his hyperconscious melancholy as a mode of refinement that recuperates the purity of a subjectivity that otherwise feels assaulted by the demands of a runaway world: "Etwas von der Feinheit, die ich zum Leben brauche," reflects Warlich, "finde ich nur in meiner Melancholie." (GigfZ, 63; I only find some of the refinement that I need for life in my melancholy.) By tapping into his melancholy disposition, Genazino's hero restores interiority as a basic condition of intimacy. As shown before, in his poetics lectures Genazino describes the contemporary city environment as dominated by reflective surfaces, projection

---

52. On *Empfindsamkeit*, see Catherine J. Minter, "Literary *Empfindsamkeit* and Nervous Sensibility in Eighteenth-Century Germany," *Modern Language Review* 96/4 (2001): 1016–28. On the return of "Stimmung" as a literary category, see Hans Ulrich Gumbrecht, *Stimmungen lesen: Über eine verdeckte Wirklichkeit der Literatur* (Munich: Carl Hanser, 2011); See also Anna Katherina Gisbertz, ed., *Stimmung: Zur Wiederkehr einer ästhetischen Kategorie* (Munich: Fink, 2011).

screens, and the rapid sequence of indiscreet images (BtW, 105). This new surface reality has eliminated intimacy because as a spatiotemporal relationship between social actors intimacy presupposes interiority as well as access to private time or *Eigenzeit*. As Helga Nowotny argues, *Eigenzeit* designates the modern subject's ability to cultivate "temporal sovereignty" over local time in the face of the commodification and acceleration of time in the public sphere.[53] The digital era has complicated the modern quest for *Eigenzeit* by eroding the clear-cut division between the self's public time and private time along with spaces of intimacy.

The melancholy disposition of the Genazinean protagonist fuels a mode of empty longing following from loss of any vision for a better life. For example, as Warlich happens upon an anarchist demonstration in the financial center of Frankfurt, he observes wryly that he has lost belief in the possibility of change: "Dafür dauert das, was hätte verändert werden müssen, schon zu lange an. Trotzdem haben meine Wünsche ihre Nichterfüllung überlebt." (GigfZ, 98; That which should have been changed has endured for too long. And yet my hopes have still survived their nonfulfillment.) Ironically, the next day he is fired without notice because a colleague mistakenly reported him for participating in the demonstration during regular working hours.

The fabrication of stories is the second tactic employed by Warlich in the search for meaning and attachment. In the course of the novel he fantasizes about founding a "Schule der Besänftigung" (School of Appeasement), which, as he explains to his old friend Gerd Angermann, will teach what people really want to know (GigfZ, 57). Later on we learn that this alternative knowledge should focus on the composition of happiness in environments at a remove from happiness: "Das ist mein Spezialgebiet. Wir müssen uns das Außerordentliche selber machen, sonst tritt es nicht in die Welt." (GigfZ, 80; That's my specialization. We have to create the extraordinary ourselves, otherwise it won't appear in this world.) Although this is initially an entirely fabricated story, the

---

53. Nowotny, *Time*, 13.

project gains momentum when Warlich applies to the city council for funding, a request that is granted on the condition that the School of Appeasement will be a Pop Academy for young celebrity wannabes.

Such cock-and-bull stories are a regular occurrence: they give metaphoric expression to Warlich's deepening sense of alienation and a crisis of connectedness that he tries to contain with "borrowed" forms of emotional identification. For example, when Warlich concocts a story about his mother's childhood (he tells his colleague Frau Weiss that his mother nearly died as a young child in the bombing raids) his fabricated story produces half a false tear in his eye, then a sense of shame, and, finally, a genuine tear in recognition of his own neediness (GigfZ, 100). Warlich's stories unleash emotional responses in the recipient, including in Warlich himself, who adopts the dual perspective of author and listener when inventing stories about an alternative life. But these fictions also point to an imminent crisis that finally erupts when, after many years, he accidentally meets his old friend Annette with her teenage son in the street. Warlich passes her a slice of stale bread that he had earlier slipped inside the inner pocket of his jacket (GigfZ, 127–28). With its biblical connotations, this abject gesture symbolizes a moment of utter exposure and vulnerability. The episode ends with him breaking down in sobs and his admission to a psychiatric hospital.

Warlich's third tactic involves symbolic performances and private rituals that suspend the perceived impoverishment of life. A prime example in this regard is his clothing: he reveals early on that he enjoys wearing an old rag of a vest under an impeccable shirt. This small act of resistance allows him to fantasize about his future as a "Kleiderkünstler" (artist of clothing) or "Verwesungskünstler" (artist of decomposition), who, as he explains, enacts the slow dissolution of life through his sense of dress (GigfZ, 18). When his girlfriend, Traudel, asks him to buy new clothes, he acquiesces but quietly hatches the plan to leave his old and worn trousers hanging out on the balcony so that he can observe their slow decay (GigfZ, 25). He also plans to keep a diary about the dissolution of his trousers and their gradual return to a state of nature. Later

on, the memory of his rotting trousers releases a sense of content-
ment in Warlich because they are weathering away in his place,
thus banning the threat of death (GigfZ, 44). The trousers are a
sort of humorous totem pitched against the commodity fetishism
that, according to Marx, regulates social relations in capitalism.[54]
Warlich idolizes the loss of exchange value in objects and thus their
ability to escape the capitalist circuit of exchange. As curator of his
old trousers he symbolically salvages the contemporaneity of the
noncontemporaneous by dispensing with capitalist prestige indicators such as price, novelty, and up-to-date design. Every evening he
feels comforted by his weathered trousers on the balcony because
they represent the passage of time: "Es ist das Gefühl, das Vergehen
der Zeit sei anschaulich geworden. Manchmal denke ich sogar, es
handle sich um das Vergehen meiner Zeit." (GigfZ, 83; It gives
me the feeling that the passage of time has become visible. Sometimes I even think that it is the passage of my time.) For Warlich
his Beuys-like project equips a mass-produced consumer product
with symbolic resistance to the zeitgeist; for Traudel it is a sign that
he is clearly going over the edge. While the comic nature of this
episode may be seen to underline the futility of such acts of resistance, which arguably shrink into pathetic gestures with cast-off
clothing, it nevertheless communicates the protagonist's desperate
search for connectedness with an environment that fetishizes innovation and change. Even though Genazino's protagonists appear
as comical heroes of futility, their seemingly absurd ideas bring
to the fore a fundamental emotional need. As Genazino argued in
his poetics lectures, in the contemporary city environment the continual onslaught of shrill images leaves nothing to the imagination.
Global capitalism and its flashy simulacra in the cityscape have
disrupted intimacy and deterritorialized the public sphere and its
inhabitants so that enormous effort is required to retrieve moments
of intimacy.

---

54. See Karl Marx, *Das Kapital: Kritik der politischen Ökonomie*, vol. 1, *Der
Produktionsprozess des Kapitals*, ed. Rosa-Luxemburg-Stiftung (Berlin: Dietz,
1962).

The fourth and perhaps most strategic technique of connecting the fragile self with the city is, however, the practice of the "prolonged gaze," which recuperates the possibility of experience in face of the continual production of obsolescence. In an essay devoted to this subject, Genazino explains this notion as follows: "Der gedehnte Blick sieht auch dann noch, wenn es nach allgemeiner Übereinkunft, die schon längst beim nächsten und übernächsten Bild angekommen ist, nichts mehr zu sehen gibt." (The extended gaze continues to look when, according to the general viewpoint, which has already moved on to the next few images, there is nothing else to see.)[55] Its work consists of a constant transformation of the image that, by breaking through habitual patterns of perception, rediscovers the enigmatic quality of the perceived object. For Genazino this transformative effect of the prolonged gaze is most evident when social actors are perplexed by the realization that they can no longer make sense of an image. He writes: "Die Perplexion ist das allmähliche Vertrautwerden mit der uns melancholisch stimmenden Zumutung, daß wir immer nur Splitter und Bruchstücke von etwas verstehen." (Perplexity is the process of becoming used to the unreasonable and melancholy-inducing state of affairs that we can only ever understand splinters and fragments of reality.)[56] While such puzzled perplexity disrupts the ordinariness of everyday life, it also draws attention to the semiotic nature of the relationship between self and object. In this way, the prolonged gaze enables Genazino's protagonists to anchor themselves temporarily in a phenomenological reality. Their perplexing observations are an antidote to the absence of sustained attention in the city environment. Scanning the environment for quirky encounters, Genazino's hero is always on the lookout for unexpected situations that challenge the rationalization of attention, that hallmark of turbocapitalism. As Georg Franck has argued in two books on the subject, the new digital era is marked by a fundamental shift from the modern economy of exchange toward a new economy of

---

55. Wilhelm Genazino, *Der gedehnte Blick* (Frankfurt a. Main: dtv, 2007), 42.
56. Genazino, *Der gedehnte Blick*, 51.

attention where attention itself is a prized good.[57] Of course this does not mean that the ever more accelerating circuit of production and consumption is no longer the driver of capitalism. Rather, attention has become a scarce capitalist resource, requiring constant investment and management.

Das Glück in glücksfernen Zeiten adds a new component to the prolonged gaze: here Genazino introduces the notion of the "Blickkette" (chain of glances), which involves more than one social actor. An example occurs at the beginning of the novel when Warlich discovers a half-eaten piece of cake on the roof of a parked car. As he preoccupies himself with construing various stories about how the owner and his cake might have been separated, a young man arrives on the scene and starts eating the cake. Engaging in further speculation as to whether or not the young man is the rightful cake owner or a possible cake thief, Warlich then realizes that he too is being observed by a fruit vendor who might view him as a potential fruit thief:

> Ich beobachte den Kuchendieb und werde selbst des geplanten Obstdiebstahls beargwöhnt, das heißt ich kann mich in diesen Sekunden als Erfinder einer Blickkette fühlen, die unbekannte Ereignisse miteinander verbindet und mich selber auf unaussprechliche Weise auszeichnet beziehungsweise erhöht beziehungsweise in eine andere Wirklichkeit hineinhebt. (GigfZ, 13)

> As I am observing the cake thief I am being observed as a potential fruit thief; this means I can see myself for a few seconds as the inventor of a chain of glances that interconnects unrelated events, while distinguishing me in an inexpressible way or elevating me or lifting me into a different reality.

The "Blickkette" between himself, the fruit vendor, and the young man establishes a network of speculative relations and as such a space for imaginary stories that make both space and time open to alternative practice. The "Blickkette" is a fleeting spatiotemporal constellation that reinstates an extremely fragile cultural connectedness between Warlich and the city environment. As a performance

---

57. See Franck, *Ökonomie der Aufmerksamkeit*; Franck, *Mentaler Kapitalismus*.

that creates imaginary relations between social actors who do not know each other, it exemplifies Doreen Massey's notion of space as "a sphere of possibility of the existence of multiplicity."[58] Furthermore, by equipping a banal observation with such imaginary potential, Warlich reenacts the flâneur's modern epiphany.

Warlich invests great hope in such imaginary relations, as he takes them as evidence "daß es hinter der ersten Wirklichkeit eine zweite und eine dritte gibt, an denen ich teilhabe und die ich, so ich Glück habe, irgendwann zu meinem Beruf machen möchte" (GigfZ, 17; that behind the first reality there is second or third one, which, if I am lucky, I will turn into my new calling). This is of course misleading because it mistakes a particular moment of connectedness for the idea of transcendence. While his ensuing plan to start up his School of Appeasement founders, this humorous episode is exemplary of the subject's longing for happiness in unhappy times. Genazino's humor never belittles his protagonist's various endeavors; rather, it accentuates the potential of an eccentric otherness to disrupt habitual modes of perception and patterns of behavior.

Slowness is the fifth tactic employed by Warlich to protect himself from the culture of speed. As a stigmatized temporality, slowness disrupts an economic performance ideology that aims to close the gap between here and there and now and then in favor of instant delivery. Even though the very idea of slowness is in itself a by-product of a modernity that prioritized an ever-faster speed, it can be used tactically to open up a self-conscious space of reflection. And while his strategy of slowing down may look pathetic and defensive, it nevertheless allows Warlich to defy the temporal serfdom of the culture of immediacy: "In der Langsamkeit verarbeite ich, daß ich wenig verstehe und nicht viel Neues kennenlernen möchte. Das Nichtverstehen wird in der Langsamkeit aufbewahrt und die Langsamkeit im Nichtverstehen." (GigfZ, 73; Through my slowness I come to terms with the fact that I understand very little and that I don't wish to encounter too many novelties. My

---

58. Massey, *For Space*, 8.

noncomprehension is kept alive in my slowness and my slowness in my sense of noncomprehension). By extending the present into a prolonged duration that is divorced from fast-paced activities, slowness strategically disrupts the idea of the right moment, which is an essential part of modern chrono-politics. And so slowness reinstates temporality as a mode of experiencing real presence without any gain or purpose.

The ensemble of Warlich's various tactics aims to rehabilitate the self's *Eigenzeit* by way of a temporal ecology that recovers place as a sphere of possibility. But this recovery requires tremendous performative effort that comes at a price. In the course of the novel Warlich loses not only his job but also his mental health. As a patient of the psychiatric hospital he finally finds an attentive listener in his therapist, Dr. Treukirch, who invites Warlich to explore his melancholy disposition. In the protective and slow environment of the clinic Warlich develops a new sense of tranquility that is, however, also induced by a cocktail of medication. As Warlich considers the topics of his next therapy session with Dr. Treukirch, he awaits the appearance of a chicken in a courtyard: "Eine Art Glück durchzittert mich. Offenbar kann ich, trotz allem, immer noch wählen, wie ich in Zukunft leben will." (GigfZ, 158; Some kind of happiness is vibrating through my body. Apparently, I am still able to choose how I wish to live in the future.)

The Search for Transcendence: Arnold Stadler's *Sehnsucht: Versuch über das erste Mal* and *Salvatore*

From the Enlightenment period onward, modern literature underwent a process of aesthetic secularization that absorbed, recoded, and replaced the notion of religious transcendence with the idea of aesthetic transcendence. By transmuting a formerly religious semantics into the aesthetic domain, modern literature could claim autonomy: it became a quasi-religious but nevertheless inner-worldly vehicle for the expression of transcendental longing, political beliefs, and ethical questions as well as for modern aesthetic concerns in defiance of religious transcendence. As Silvio Vietta and Herbert Uerlings comment, the modern period is thus defined by "the radical recasting of Christian beliefs on a new stage: the stage of aesthetics."[59] However, Vietta and Uerlings also emphasize that this process of aesthetic conversion remains deeply ambivalent because it involves both a break with and continuity of tradition.[60] Novalis's famous designation of Friedrich Schlegel as an "Apostel in unserer Zeit" (apostle in our time) captures this ambivalence well:[61] even though Novalis accentuates modern literature's link to messianic hope, he celebrates not the Christian apostles but Schlegel, the modern artist, as the harbinger of truth. The question then is whether and how literature in the contemporary arena can recover the idea of religious belief without being religiously dogmatic and aesthetically naive. Or is it perhaps the case that religion has been rediscovered as a convenient register that lends itself to the poetic articulation of the limits of the purely rational morality that governs postmetaphysical thinking? Does the return of religion in contemporary fiction underscore the failure of Enlightened reason "to awaken, and to keep awake, in the minds of secular subjects, an awareness of the violations of solidarity throughout the world, an awareness of what is missing, of what cries out to heaven," as suggested by Jürgen Habermas?[62] The following section discusses the awareness of what is missing and the longing for transcendence with reference to the motif of voyeurism in Arnold Stadler's novel *Sehnsucht: Versuch über das erste Mal*. I will then examine Stadler's sophisticated remediation of desire in his hybrid text, *Salvatore* (2009), which combines elements of the novel with essayistic explorations of Pasolini's

---

59. Silvio Vietta and Herbert Uerlings, "Einleitung: Ästhetik, Religion, Säkularisierung," in *Ästhetik, Religion, Säkularisierung I: Von der Renaissance zur Romantik*, ed. Silvio Vietta and Herbert Uerlings (Munich: Wilhelm Fink, 2008), 22; *Ästhetik, Religion, Säkularisierung II: Die klassische Moderne*, ed. Vietta and Uerlings (Munich: Wilhelm Fink, 2009).

60. Vietta and Uerlings, "Einleitung," 13.

61. Quoted in Vietta and Uerlings, "Einleitung," 22.

62. Jürgen Habermas, "An Awareness of What Is Missing," in *An Awareness of What Is Missing: Faith and Reason in a Post-Secular Age*, trans. Ciaran Cronin (Cambridge: Polity, 2010), 19.

film *The Gospel According to Matthew* (1964) and Caravaggio's painting *The Calling of St. Matthew* (1599–1600).

Arnold Stadler, a former Catholic seminarist and philologist with a PhD about the poetry of Bertolt Brecht and Paul Celan, is no longer a marginal figure in contemporary German literature.[63] A recipient of several major book prizes, including the Marie-Luise-Kaschnitz Preis in 1998 and the Büchner-Preis in 1999, author of travelogues and several collections of poetry, and translator of the Psalms from ancient Hebrew (*"Die Menschen lügen. Alle" und andere Psalmen*, "All Human Beings Are Liars" and Other Psalms, 2005), Stadler made his name with the semiautobiographical trilogy *Ich war einmal* (I Was Once Upon a Time, 1989), *Feuerland* (Tierra del Fuego, 1992), and *Mein Hund, meine Sau, mein Leben* (My Dog, My Sow, My Life, 1994). Republished in revised and enlarged form under the title *Einmal auf der Welt. Und dann so* (Once Alive and Then Like This) in 2009, this quixotic first-person narrative tracks the narrator's life story from his origins in a provincial landscape and family, both marked by telling names: Himmelreich, a village in southern Germany near Meßkirch, where he was born into the Schwanz clan, a powerful pig dynasty that claims the Austrian seventeenth-century divine Abraham a Santa Clara and the philosopher Martin Heidegger as relatives.[64] *Feuerland* relates the protagonist's first departure from Himmelreich, the Swabian kingdom of heaven, through a journey to Patagonia at the end of the world (EadW, 223). The final part, *Mein Hund, meine Sau, mein Leben* then chronicles his failed attempt to become a priest in Rome. "Mit dem Ehrgeiz eines Kindes ausstaffiert, das in den Himmel kommen wollte"

63. For an introductory essay on Stadler, see Stuart Taberner, "'Nichts läßt man uns, nicht einmal den Schmerz, und eines Tages wird alles vergessen sein': The Novels of Arnold Stadler from *Ich war einmal* to *Ein hinreissender Schrotthändler*," *Neophilologus* 87 (2003): 119–32. On the trilogy, see Pia Reinacher, "Verzweiflung und Glücksgier," in *"Als wäre er ein anderer gewesen": Zum Werk Arnold Stadlers*, ed. Pia Reinacher (Frankfurt a. Main: Fischer, 2009), 29–36.

64. Arnold Stadler, *Einmal auf der Welt. Und dann so* (Frankfurt a. Main: Fischer, 2009); cited as EadW in the text.

(EadW, 315; equipped with the ambition of a child who wanted to go to heaven), he is taken under the wing of Franz Sales Obernosterer, a titular bishop in Rome full of carnal desire for the young Schwanz—the names speak ever more loudly! In the end he leaves Rome as he arrived: "trostlos, im Grunde unbelehrt, ins Ungewisse" (EadW, 353; wretched, fundamentally ignorant into uncertainty). The specific timbre of Stadler's storytelling comes from a mode of humor reminiscent of Robert Walser that yokes the sublime and the ridiculous to articulate what Stadler calls "Stellvertretersätze. . . . Für diese Welt, die ihren Schmerz noch nicht formuliert hat" (deputy sentences. . . . For this world which has not yet realized its pain).[65] The very term Stadler uses here exemplifies the program: Christ was God's "Stellvertreter" (deputy), his vicar on earth. But the term "Stellvertretersätze," used to convey to the world its as-yet unformulated suffering, mixes the biblical gospel with the current mundane sense of a deputy or second-best stand-in. As Martin Walser wittily observed, Stadler is a "Selbstbezichtigungsvirtuose," a virtuoso in self-accusation who balances the desire to save the world—and, one might add, to be saved himself—with a linguistic "Zerreibungszwang" (compulsion to dissect) in the manner of Robert Walser.[66] While the quixotic ironies of Stadler's style frustrate dogmatic religious belief, he nevertheless articulates a sense of longing that encompasses both the carnal and the transcendental. Instead of posing a Manichaean opposition, Stadler makes sexual desire an inner-worldly variant of transcendental longing. In this he touches obliquely

---

65. Arnold Stadler, "Im Grunde war alles nach Hause geschrieben: Dankrede zur Verleihung des Marie-Luise-Kaschnitz-Preises 1998," in *"Als wäre er ein anderer gewesen,"* 124.

66. Martin Walser, "Über das Verbergen der Verzweiflung: Laudatio zur Verleihung des Marie-Luise-Kaschnitz Preises 1998," in *"Als wäre er ein anderer gewesen,"* 115–16. On Stadler's literary humor as a signature of transcendence, see Anton Philipp Knittel, "'Glaube, Hoffnung, Erinnerung': Anmerkungen zu Komik und Transzendenz im Werk Arnold Stadlers," in *"Als wäre er ein anderer gewesen,"* 69–80. See also Karl Wagner, "'Eine gewaltige Scham': Arnold Stadlers Schreiben zwischen Mündlichkeit und Schriftlichkeit; Hebel—Stifter—Handke," in *"Als wäre er ein anderer gewesen,"* 95–104.

on a resonant mystic tradition stretching back to Hildegard of Bingen in the early Middle Ages or Saint Teresa of Avila in the Counter-Reformation.[67]

This interrelationship is precisely the territory of *Sehnsucht: Versuch über das erste Mal*, which tells the story of a first-person manic-depressive narrator who describes himself as "ein Unding aus Gläubigem und Voyeur, ein katholisches Ferkel" (an impossible combination of believer and voyeur, a catholic piglet).[68] Middle-aged and long married to Hilde, with whom he entertains irregular and tired intercourse enabled by Viagra, he ekes out his living with "Verbrauchervorträge" (consumer advice presentations), an idea that he developed after dropping out of his university program in forestry during a period when he earned a meager income with slideshows about the Tessin and other popular holiday destinations to an ever-diminishing public (Se, 47). The narrative is set around the Feast of the Ascension, which coincides with Father's Day: on the eve of Ascension Day he delivers his consumer talk at the Rotary Club in Bleckede in northern Germany, ironically "der Ort, wo das Kapital von Marx verlegt wurde" (Se, 34; the place where Marx's *The Capital* was published) and close to the very spot where Eckermann studied the dykes for Goethe's *Faust II*. Equipped with a sex guide, he intends to reward himself for his effort by visiting the Blue Moon, a swinger club near Fallingbostel with a three-star excellence rating. On the morning of Father's Day, he spots two anglers on the banks of the Elbe who appear "als Mittelpunkt einer impressionistischen Skizze, als ob es für immer wäre, als Seelen der Landschaft mit dem Wasser, das schon auf halbem Wege in die Abstraktion war (Se, 54; as the center of an impressionistic sketch, as if it was meant to last forever, like the souls of the watery landscape that was turning into abstraction).

---

67. Stadler's self-feminization can also be read as a nod toward the presence of women in the mystic tradition. On Hildegard von Bingen's mysticism, see Barbara Newman, ed., *Voice of the Living Light: Hildegard of Bingen and Her World* (Berkeley: University of California Press, 1998).

68. Arnold Stadler, *Sehnsucht: Versuch über das erste Mal* (Cologne: DuMont, 2002), 61; cited as Se in the text.

Throughout the narrative the river represents a transience overlaid with multiple art-historical associations: there are earlier comparisons of the landscape with Joos de Momper's paintings and with Emil Nolde's expressionist art.[69] With its art-historical and biblical overtones, the image of the two anglers unleashes a longing for transcendence in the protagonist for whom this moment of visual pleasure then transforms into an icon of faith in the unseen:

> Ich glaubte immer noch an Dinge, die nicht sichtbar waren in dieser Welt. Ich glaubte immer noch. Die Hoffnung und die Liebe waren ja auch nicht sichtbar, oder nur ganz selten wie ein Wunder. Ich hoffe, daß das Unsichtbare mehr war als das Sichtbare. So wie die beiden da standen. Das, was ich sehen konnte, war wenig; und doch so viel. (Se, 54)

> I still believed in things that were invisible in this world. I still believed. Hope and love were not visible either or only very rarely like a miracle. I am hoping that the invisible was more than the visible. Like the two fellows standing there. What I could see was very little and yet so much.

The metaphysical conversion of the painterly landscape stands, of course, in the Romantic tradition. The disenchanting experience of modernity as manifest in today's overexposure to televised images of daily horrors further fuels the narrator's longing for the unseen (Se, 54). Disillusioned by a world in which, as he puts it, hope has been replaced by fun, desire by the wellness sector, and the human being by the consumer (Se, 97), the protagonist regularly succumbs to longing for transcendence. The expression "wenn ich meine Tage hatte" (Se, 58; when I was having my period), which deliberately evokes the female menstrual cycle, is a recurring leitmotif employed in nearly all of Stadler's narratives to give expression to the protagonist's disaffection with the state of affairs. Accordingly, when he

---

69. "Die Kühe standen wie bei den holländischen Landschaftsmalern des 17. Jahrhunderts, wie bei Joos de Momper halb im Wasser, halb an Land." (Se, 29; The cows were standing half in the water, half on the shore, just as in Dutch landscapes of the seventeenth century, as in a painting by Joos de Momper.) "Aber der Expressionismus lebte noch in den Elbtalauen, dieser Morgen war der reinste Emil Nolde." (Se, 37; But Expressionism lived on in the meadows of the Elbe valley; this morning was like a pure Emil Nolde painting.)

has "his period," he is overcome by a longing for God, which then motivates his attendance at the Ascension mass in a local Catholic church that was built after the war in a "post–Mies van der Rohe" style for the fugitives from Silesia (Se, 57). The fear that this sterile building cannot be expressive of hope is corroborated when during Mass the priest nervously admonishes the small congregation not to sing too loudly so as not to disturb the neighbors (Se, 59). His indignation at the priest's apparent shame for holding Mass motivates a verbose polemic against rationalism and the functionaries of the church, who, the narrator claims, cared more about the contradictions of the Bible than the "Ungereimtheiten dieser Welt" (Se, 60; contradictions of this world). The protagonist's disappointment with the impoverished mass unleashes the most impure thoughts about the swinger club: "Was soll's, dachte ich, bald werde ich wieder unter Frauen mit Fußkettchen sein, die sich an behaarten Toupeträgern hocharbeiten." (Se, 58; Never mind, I thought, soon I will lie below women with bracelets around their feet who work their way up the bodies of hairy men with toupees.) The enactment of such fantasies later on in the narrative constitutes a mortal sin, which, according to Catholic moral theology, would require repentance through confession and a firm resolution to sin no more to restore the link to God's saving grace.[70] This is precisely where Stadler's poetics of longing challenges and overturns church dogma: as the longing for the "big transcendence" cannot find fulfillment beyond the aesthetic realm, sex promises at least the temporary attainment of "little transcendences" or, as the narrator puts it when he finally enters the playground of the Blue Moon, "überschaubare Sehnsucht" (Se, 246; manageable longing).[71]

---

70. See *Catechism of the Catholic Church*, Vatican.va (accessed 13 March 2012).

71. On this issue, see Thomas Luckmann's theory of the invisible religion, which provides a functional, nondoctrinal, and anthropological definition of religion. For Luckmann religion defines man's ability to transcend his biological life by constructing interpretive frames that produce "Weltansichten" (worldviews). While the "Weltansicht" designates a universal social form, "Kirchlichkeit" refers to the internalization of doctrinal practices and beliefs. Luckmann distinguishes between our little transcendences, that is, man's ability to transcend the immediacy

And so the rising gaze of the protagonist's transcendental longing turns downward in an act of voyeurism: the day before his
consumer talk, he observes a couple who are having sex near the
Elbe in the former *Todesstreifen* (death strip) of the inner German
border. Speculating that the pair really wanted to be observed in
the act of copulation, the narrator describes how he watched them
with his binoculars "ganz unverhohlen . . . , entschuldigen Sie, wie
ein Voyeur, der Vögeln beim Vögeln zuschaut" (Se, 32; openly . . . ,
excuse my words, like a voyeur who enjoys watching birds screw-
ing each other) before being discovered by the man, who attempts
to capture the voyeur on his digital camera. While the binoculars
aid voyeurism by offering ocular proximity from a safe physical
distance, the secretive visual control over the scene, so essential
in the economy of voyeurism, is reversed when the protagonist is
himself threatened with being filmed by a digital camera that has
the capacity to zoom in on the offender and on the license plate
of his car. The protagonist's ensuing panic communicates not only
the voyeur's fear of exposure but, more importantly, his concern
that his voyeurism will be misunderstood as merely a perverse sexual act: "Als ob aus mir ein Voyeur geworden wäre. Keiner der
Zeugen, die ich hätte aufrufen können, daß ich kein Schwein war,
daß ich nur so schaute, war noch am Leben." (Se, 33; As if I had
become a voyeur. None of the witnesses who could have vouched
that I was not a pig, that I only stared like one, was still alive.) The
expression "so schauen" (to stare) connects this passage with the
opening section, in which the narrator remembers how as a child
he was either admonished not to look at things too long or praised
for his own sweet looks: "Warum schaust du so? Schau nicht so!
Oder auch: Jetzt schaut er aber! Ist es nicht süß, wie er schaut?"
(Se, 9; Why do you have that look? Don't look like that! Or: Look
how he is watching! Isn't it sweet how he is looking?) A Freudian

---

of the here and now by means of protention and retention, and the big transcen-
dences, which require mediation in ritual acts, language, and icons of "letzte
Bedeutungen." See Thomas Luckmann, *Die unsichtbare Religion* (Frankfurt a.
Main: Suhrkamp, 1991); Hubert Knoblauch, "Die Verflüchtigung der Religion ins
Religiöse," in Luckmann, *Die unsichtbare Religion*, 7–41.

scene of "aktive and passive Schaulust" (active and passive voyeurism),[72] the opening narrative moment sets up the economy of scopophilia by interweaving the prohibition and the incitement to look and to be looked at.[73]

Voyeurism in this narrative thus has two meanings: while it denotes classical Freudian *Schaulust* and as such the protagonist's sexually charged scopophilic curiosity, it always points to an awareness of what is missing and the attendant desire for transcendence. And this is precisely the context in which the narrator's later declaration "Schauen war meine erste Sehnsucht" (Se, 256: Looking was my first form of longing) makes sense: even though the voyeur's prime impulse can be temporarily satisfied in the Blue Moon or with the help of a pair of binoculars out on the dyke, the act of "Schauen" is a mode of longing for the unseen that keeps open the possibility of a nondoctrinal faith in transcendence.

Stadler's *Salvatore* (2009) develops the poetics of longing for transcendence in new directions. Comprising a fictional narrative and two essays on Pasolini's film *The Gospel According to Matthew* and on Caravaggio's painting *The Calling of St. Matthew*, the three texts in *Salvatore* deploy a process of remediation as a path toward the recovery of transcendence. In the fictional narrative the sexually charged voyeurism of *Sehnsucht* undergoes a process of sublimation that channels erotic desire into faith without, however, erasing its sexual vector. *Salvatore* is the companion piece to *Sehnsucht* in that the narrative relates a parallel story in a similar setting: after the delivery of his talk at the Rotary Club, Salvatore, the eponymous protagonist whose name associates him

---

72. See Sigmund Freud, *Über Psychoanalyse: Fünf Vorlesungen*, in *Gesammelte Werke*, 8:46.

73. Laura Mulvey's seminal 1975 article, "Visual Pleasure and Narrative Cinema," unleashed countless responses that explore and challenge the validity of the psychoanalytic approach and its normative emphasis on the phallus, the patriarchal nature of the gaze, the status of the female viewer, the issue of hetero- and homosexuality, pleasure versus masochism, and so on. See Laura Mulvey, "Visual Pleasure and Narrative Cinema," *Screen* 16/3 (1975): 6–18; Clifford T. Manlove, "Visual 'Drive' and Cinematic Narrative: Reading Gaze Theory in Lacan, Hitchcock, and Mulvey," *Cinema Journal* 46/3 (2007): 83–108.

with Christ, like his predecessor, also observes two anglers on the banks of the Elbe on the morning of Ascension Day. Inspired by the image, which he explicitly associates with Christ's recruitment of the apostles at the Sea of Galilee,[74] Salvatore too decides to attend the Ascension mass. However, after the uninspiring mass the two protagonists' pathways biforcate: whereas in *Sehnsucht* he spends the rest of the day dedicated to carnal delights at the Blue Moon, Salvatore follows his loftier "Sehnsucht, danach, ergriffen zu sein" (S, 17; longing to be moved) by watching a poorly attended screening of Pasolini's *The Gospel According to Matthew*. Stadler foregrounds the interrelationship of the two texts through narrative metalepsis or *mise en abyme*:[75] halfway through the novel Salvatore remembers having attempted to read Stadler's *Sehnsucht: Versuch über das erste Mal*. Even though he identified with the protagonist of Stadler's novel, he explains, he was ultimately bored and ended up putting it aside (S, 82). By employing metalepsis as a device that transgresses the "shifting but sacred frontier between two worlds, the world in which one tells, the world of which one tells," Stadler creates that narrative vertigo that induces epistemological doubt about the status of reality.[76]

Like his author, Salvatore lost his attachment to Catholic Church teachings when he studied theology (S, 22). We learn that his "Abbruch des Glaubens" (loss of faith) was caused by modern theologians who, according to Salvatore, were steeped in historical-critical Bible exegesis, behaving like car mechanics and dismantling the Gospel "wie ein altes Auto" (S, 46; like an old car), a point to which I return later. Even though in this novel too the Ascension mass is an impoverished affair, in the end the priest's reading of

---

74. Arnold Stadler, *Salvatore* (Frankfurt a. M: Fischer, 2009), 23; cited as S in the text.

75. Genette defines narrative metalepsis as "any intrusion by the extradiegetic narrator or narratee into the diegetic universe (or by diegetic characters into a metadiegetic universe, etc.) or the inverse." Gerard Genette, *Narrative Discourse: An Essay in Method*, trans. Jane Lewin (Ithaca, NY: Cornell University Press, 1980), 234–35. Also Doritt Cohn, "Metalepsis and Mise en Abyme," *Narrative* 20/1 (2012): 105–14.

76. Genette, *Narrative Discourse*, 236.

Christ's final lines from the Gospel of Matthew affects Salvatore to his very core: "'Seid gewiss: Ich bin bei euch alle Tage bis zum Ende der Welt.' Das hätte eigentlich jeden Menschen umhauen müssen. Aber an diesem blauen Tag war es wahrscheinlich nur Salvatore, den es umhaute." (S, 62; "Be assured: I will stay with you until the end of the world." This should have knocked every human being over. But on this blue day it was probably only Salvatore who was knocked over.) His "Sehnsucht nach dem ganz Anderen" (S, 46; longing for something completely different) is then played out as he watches Pasolini's rendition of the biblical narrative. This triggers a participatory mode of reception that Stadler sets in opposition to the aberrations of modern Bible criticism, as he sees it. Salvatore praises Pasolini not only for his Marxist partisanship with the poor and disenfranchised (S, 85) but above all for a film that remains true to the biblical narrative. When Salvatore leaves the film screening, he is transformed (S, 84).

And yet, this transformation is not just the effect of the original true message of the Gospel, but rather of a complex process of remediation on several levels: after watching the film, Salvatore retells the biblical narrative through the lens of the film, which, on a third level, is filtered through the narrative medium of the novel. The conversion of biblical text into film and its reconversion into fictional text create a circuit of intermedial exchange that requires the reader's imaginative participation. Faith is not a matter of doctrinal teaching here but an intermedial experience that unlocks longing for transcendence in the film viewer and in the reader. Stadler also emphasizes how Pasolini's film aesthetic combines neorealist effects with a highly stylized visual register that subtly draws on Renaissance representational art practice. Accordingly, the Christ figure in Pasolini's film appeals to Salvatore on both erotic and aesthetic grounds: he was "einer nach dem sich alle umdrehten" (S, 93; one who turned everybody's heads) and "schön anzusehen, wie auf dem Bild des Caravaggio in der Kirche San Luigi degli Francesi" in Rome (S, 97; lovely to look at, like in the painting by Caravaggio in San Luigi degli Francesi). By intertwining the erotic appeal of the actor with Renaissance representations of Christ, the novel links erotic desire with an aesthetically charged longing for transcendence. For Stadler and his hero the filmic medium in particular has the capacity to create faith by means of an aesthetics of presence:

> Die Bilder waren so, dass Salvatore und auch den anderen, die dies nicht gesehen haben, wenn sie es gesehen hätten, auf der Stelle "Ja!" gesagt hätten und es geglaubt: dass dies der Messias war, der Sohn des lebendigen Gottes, wenn sie auch nach wie vor kein Wort davon verstanden hätten. Das war die Macht der Bilder. Die Augen besaßen Definitionshoheit über den Menschen. Und die Wörter waren oftmals nicht mehr als Bildlegenden. (S, 129)

> The images were so powerful that Salvatore and the others, who did not see this but if they had seen it would have immediately said, "Yes!" and they would have believed that this was the Messiah, the son of the living God—even if they would not have understood a single word. Such was the power of images. The eyes ruled with sovereignty over human beings, and the words were often nothing but captions of images.

Salvatore's emphatic belief in Christ's presence is triggered here by the rendering visible of the biblical narrative in film, such filmic remediation of presence in turn enclosed within Stadler's narrative. By remediating the aesthetic immediacy of Pasolini's film through Salvatore's retelling of his filmic experience, Stadler engenders a circuit of exchange designed to instill awareness of what is missing through continual remediation. While Pasolini's neorealism anchors the narrative in the phenomenological world, the intertextual allusions to Renaissance and Baroque art turn faith into a mode of mediatized memory.[77] Each level of remediation carries the imprints of previous experiences: Pasolini's reception of the Gospel as represented in the film becomes a source of reception for Salvatore whose own filmic experience is then passed on to the reader. Such hypermediation at once rehabilitates faith in the unseen and aspires to create a participatory discipleship based on the persuasiveness of aesthetic images.

---

77. When in Pasolini's film Christ arrives in Jerusalem on the back of a donkey, Salvatore compares the jubilant crowd to paintings by Piero della Francesca, Fra Angelico, Botticelli, and van Eyck (S, 133).

A further level of remediation is introduced through Salvatore's memories of an earlier film viewing when, as a child, he watched the film with his family after its release in 1965. We learn that many of Salvatore's southern Italian relatives were lay actors in Pasolini's film. However, regardless of whether they played the devil or the apostles, they all ended up on the island of Procida, in the biggest prison in Italy (S, 79), because of involvement with the Mafia. As repeat offenders, his southern Italian relatives thus represent the majority of the people who, according to Salvatore, don't succeed in life: "Sie hatten es alle nicht geschafft. Das Glücken war eine Episode geblieben, ein Filmauftritt." (S, 70; They didn't manage it. Their luck had been an episode, a short appearance in a film.) By opening up the gap between the prosaic reality of Mafia-ridden southern Italy and the filmic representation of the Gospel in terms of a sublime message of hope, Stadler reinstates the epistemological difference between a primary social reality in the here and now and the various remediated and aestheticized worlds that are sources of transcendental longing. On the other hand, the superimposition of Salvatore's memory of his first film viewing onto the second greatly enhances his personal investment in the biblical message: the apostles are not just distant mythical figures but his own relatives. Instead of creating metatextual distance, the multiple remediations of the Gospel as an original source text that is filtered through Pasolini's film, which is then watched, remembered, and retold by Salvatore within the fictional universe of the novel, aim to emphatically recover faith in the unseen. But is this experience of transcendence in the present really only the aesthetic effect of the perception of images, as Silke Horstkotte suggests,[78] or does it communicate genuinely religious experiences?

To address the status of aesthetics as a medium or an end in itself, one needs to consider Stadler's essays on Pasolini and Caravaggio, which complement the fictional narrative. For Stadler

---

78. Silke Horstkotte, "Poetische Parusie: Zur Rückkehr der Religion in der Gegenwart," in "Deutschsprachige Literatur(en) seit 1989," ed. Norbert Otto Eke and Stefan Elit, special issue, *Zeitschrift für deutsche Philologie* 131 (2012): 281.

Pasolini's film is a "Joint Venture aus Bild, Wort und Klang" (S, 157; joint venture of images, words, and sound) that renders visible the eschatological promise of the last sentence of the Gospel of Saint Matthew: "Ich bin bei euch alle Tage bis zum Ende der Welt." (S, 154; I am with you always, even to the end of the world.) With its episodic structure the film remained true to the original biblical text and, for Stadler, has the capacity to arouse faith in the viewer. According to Stadler, Pasolini was inspired by the totality of the biblical narrative, which, as Stadler sees it, demands a participatory mode of reading that could not be more removed from the principles of modern Bible criticism, which appeals to a modern audience steeped in a scientific worldview.[79] For Stadler it is precisely such methodical demythologization that reduced theology to a "gigantisches Schrottgewerbe" (S, 159; gigantic scrapyard business), depriving the biblical text of its poetic totality (S, 158). Because Pasolini did not read the Bible in the disenchanted spirit of modernity (S, 188), he was inspired to render a filmic representation of his own engaged reading. Like the biblical text, Pasolini was able to furnish his audience with "Partituren der Hoffnung . . ., dass es nicht aus ist mit ihnen" (S, 188; scores of hope . . . that they are not yet finished). According to Stadler, by lending Christ filmic presence Pasolini managed to turn faith in the unseen into self-evidential reality: "Ich muss ja nicht mehr glauben, ich sehe es ja, alles ist einleuchtend und evident." (S, 186; I don't need to merely believe because I see it, it's all clearly visible and evident.) For Stadler Pasolini's film is thus neither merely about the aesthetic power of images nor is it a simple assertion of faith.

Stadler's essay on Caravaggio's *The Calling of St. Matthew* concludes his deliberations on transcendence. His detailed interpretation of the painting challenges the conventional art-historical view, according to which the elderly bearded man on the left-hand side of

---

79. Stadler specifically targets Bultmann's principle of formal criticism, which essentially aimed at demythologizing the message of the New Testament by distinguishing secondary additions in the biblical text. See Rudolf Bultmann, *New Testament and Mythology and Other Basic Writings*, ed. Schubert M. Ogden (Philadelphia: Fortress Press, 1984).

the picture is summoned by Christ. It was Giovanni Bellori who in 1672 provided a canonical description: "Several heads are drawn from life, among them the saint, who interrupts his counting of the money and, with one hand on his breast, turns toward the Lord."[80] Following Bellori, art historian Walter Friedländer reaffirmed the view that the elderly man with his well-kempt beard, fine attire, and pointed index finger represents Matthew. In contrast, Stadler argues that for both pictorial and theological reasons Matthew must be the seemingly indifferent or uninterested young man who is focusing on the money on the table in front of him. For Stadler two pictorial moments in particular identify this young fellow as Matthew: firstly, the physical distance between him and Christ, which symbolizes their separation at the moment when Christ enters his life; secondly, the diagonal shaft of light that connects the two figures. In this way Caravaggio's pictorial symbolism high-lights the young man's great need of salvation. The raised index finger of the bearded old man is thus not a "Who me?" gesture but merely an extension of Christ's raised arm, which points at the young man, who is desperately trying to ignore the imperative of this gesture. Having established the identity of Matthew, Stadler then foregrounds the representation of sexual desire in Caravaggio's painting: he sees in the tax collector's illuminated leg under the table a gigantic phallus that represents the daily involvement of the depicted men in the common sinfulness of life (S, 202). By shedding light on what goes on above and below the table Caravaggio conjoins transcendental longing and carnal desire: "Bei Caravaggio kommen so das Himmlische und Irdische auf engstem Raum zusammen und werden von einem Licht ausgeleuchtet." (S, 203; In Caravaggio the most heavenly and worldly moments are conjoined and illuminated by light.) Instead of excluding sexual desire from pictorial representation, Caravaggio—according to Stadler—thus brings to the fore the physical and sensual undercurrent of

---

80. Giovanni Bellori, "Le vite de' pittori, scultori e architetti moderni" (Rome, 1672); cited in Walter Friedländer, *Caravaggio Studies* (Princeton, NJ: Princeton University Press, 1955), 248.

all desire, including the desire for transcendence. Stadler's later comment that the painting is so beautiful "dass ich es abschlecken möchte" (S, 213; that I want to lick it) further underlines the voyeuristic and erotic impulse of the longing for transcendence, which was already the central theme of *Sehnsucht*.

To conclude, the awareness of what is missing and the attendant longing for transcendence emerge as key themes in Stadler's narrative universe. Stadler's world is peopled by melancholy characters who, even though their experience tells them that "Sehnsucht ist Hoffnung minus Erfahrung" (Se, 308; longing is hope minus experience), invest in the utopian longing for an alternative world. The imaginative scarcity of modernity prompts them to search for moments of transcendence that, although aesthetically imbued, carry the imprint of religious faith in the unseen. While the semantics of faith in Stadler's work eschews theological dogma, it emphatically recovers the notion of the possibility of salvation as an act of partisanship with the majority of people, who, like Salvatore's relatives, do not make it in life (S, 82). His insistence that the last line of the Gospel contains a promise that is worth preserving in a disenchanted world lends Stadler's narratives a religious orientation beyond the aesthetic domain. On the other hand, the emphatic reinstatement of the validity of this promise relies on an aesthetic of remediation that involves various sources, including the Gospel, Renaissance art, Pasolini's film, and the fictional universe of Stadler's own texts. By engendering a complex circuit of exchange between diverse genres and media, Stadler aims to create a participatory discipleship that unleashes the experience of aesthetic presence in the recipient through visual pleasure. A central element of this aesthetics of presence is thus a semantics of voyeurism that negates the Manichaean division between sexual desire and transcendental longing. Even though the sexually charged voyeurism of *Sehnsucht* undergoes a process of sublimation in *Salvatore*, erotic desire and visual pleasure fuel the desire for transcendence. His protagonists' sexual desire and their loftier aspirations are thus two variants of a poetics of longing that gives expression to the modern self's existential dislocation. From this perspective transcendence is not an attainable goal but the vector for human desire.

Precarious Times, Precarious Lives: Jenny Erpenbeck's *Gehen, ging, gegangen*

It is appropriate to conclude a study of the precariousness of the times of and lives in the twenty-first century with Jenny Erpenbeck's award-winning *Gehen, ging, gegangen* (2015; *Go, Went, Gone*, 2017),[81] as this novel addresses "the central moral question of our time," the unresolved global crisis of the enforced displacement of millions of people.[82] Before analyzing the novel against the backdrop of the 2015 European refugee crisis, it may be useful to briefly touch upon Erpenbeck's handling of history and time in her previous two novels, which explore the vagaries of twentieth-century German history.

Heimsuchung (2008; *Visitation*, 2010) traces the stories of the inhabitants of a house from the late nineteenth century through the Second World War, Soviet occupation, and GDR times right up to the fall of the Berlin Wall. Set in a grand house on the shores of the Scharmützelsee in provincial Brandenburg, the narrative adopts a cyclical mode of narration that undermines the idea of historical progression. The sequential owners of the house and garden—a farmer in Imperial Germany, German Jews, Nazis, expellees, and Communist functionaries—are eventually expelled from a domestic paradise that allegorizes German history from the Kaiserreich to postunification Germany in the 1990s.[83] In the end, a Western

---

81. Jenny Erpenbeck, *Gehen, ging, gegangen* (Munich: Knaus, 2015); cited as GGG in the text; Jenny Erpenbeck, *Go, Went, Gone*, trans. Susan Bernofsky (London: Portobello Books, 2017); cited as GWG in the text.

82. James Wood, "A Novelist's Powerful Response to the Refugee Crisis," *The New Yorker*, 25 September 2017, https://www.newyorker.com/magazine/2017/09/25/a-novelists-powerful-response-to-the-refugee-crisis (accessed 26 September 2017). The English-language reviews were on the whole far more enthusiastic than the German reviewers. See Eileen Battersby, "*Go, Went, Gone* by Jenny Erpenbeck—Humanising Migration," *The Guardian*, 23 September 2017; Catherine Taylor, "*Go, Went, Gone* by Jenny Erpenbeck—No Place Like Home," *Financial Times*, 1 September 2017; Neel Mukherjee, "*Go, Went, Gone*: A Profound, Beautiful, and Deeply Affecting Novel of Migration," *The New Statesman*, 17 October 2017.

83. Jenny Erpenbeck, *Heimsuchung* (Berlin: Eichborn, 2008); Jenny Erpenbeck, *Visitation*, trans. Susan Bernofsky (New York: New Directions, 2010). On

investor purchases the house with the intention of demolishing it along with all those historical traces that have imbued the place with rich meaning. *Heimsuchung* engenders historical nostalgia for the unrealized utopian potential of the socialist dream; it also suggests that globalization obliterates history through accelerated innovation. The chronological narration along generational lines is disrupted by the mythological figure of the gardener who recurs throughout regardless of who owns the house. His timeless presence represents an uncanny alterity that remains unaffected by historical change. Erpenbeck's narrative is fueled by the acute anxiety that the fall of the Berlin Wall signaled not only the triumphant victory of global capitalism over socialism but also the arrival of an indiscriminate obliviousness to history that assigns junk status to the very idea of alternative historical itineraries. The real specter in *Heimsuchung* is thus not the historical uncanny that the narrative evokes through its richly layered and highly poeticized topography but the vision of a world devoid of all historical shadows.

Erpenbeck's later novel *Aller Tage Abend* (2012; *The End of Days*, 2014) approaches history by means of a poetics of reversals that overturns the chronology of birth and death.[84] The female protagonist of mixed Jewish and gentile origins is born at the beginning of the twentieth century at a time of eastern European pogroms: she dies a natural death in early infanthood in book 1. She is then resurrected in four further books that explore alternative biographies that take the reader from the early twentieth

---

Erpenbeck's spectral descriptions, see Cosgrove, "Heimat as Non-Place," 63–86; Gillian Pye, "Jenny Erpenbeck and the Life of Things," in *Transitions: Emerging German Women Writing in German-Language Literature*, ed. Gillian Pye and Valerie Heffernan (Amsterdam: Rodopi, 2013), 111–30; Monika Shafi, *Housebound: Selfhood and Domestic Space in Contemporary German Fiction* (Rochester, NY: Camden House, 2012).

84. Jenny Erpenbeck, *Aller Tage Abend* (Munich: Knaus, 2012); Jenny Erpenbeck, *The End of Days*, trans. Susan Bernofsky (London: Portobello, 2014). See Iris Hermann, "Heimsuchung in Jenny Erpenbecks Roman *Aller Tage Abend*," in *Wahrheit und Täuschung: Beiträge zum Werk Jenny Erpenbecks*, ed. Friedhelm Marx and Julia Schöll (Göttingen: Wallstein, 2014), 145–56.

century through to the 1990s. While the first book focuses on the aftermath of the pogrom that killed her Galician Jewish grandfather to the infant's early death, book 2 features her as an eighteen-year-old who has moved with her family to Vienna before she dies falling down a staircase. Book 3 then resurrects her by showing her as a thirty-seven-year-old communist in Moscow in exile with her husband. At the end of book 3 she dies once more, this time as a victim of Stalin's purges. In book 4 we encounter her as an honored GDR artist in East Berlin, where she dies a natural death in 1962. Finally, book 5 depicts her in a care home as a ninety-one-year-old patient who is suffering from dementia after German unification. Rather than offering a revisionist reading of twentieth history, the five biographical trajectories accentuate the uncontrollable contingency of survival and death. Ultimately the exploration of alternative biographies through a strategy of narrative reversals reinforces the kind of cyclical and melancholy structure that was already a central device in *Heimsuchung*: insofar as the experience of history always results in death, the historicity of history is erased here in favor of a far grander, anthropological temporality.

By contrast, *Gehen, ging, gegangen* eschews the mythologizing tendencies that characterize these earlier works. Here the time frame is much shorter, and the focus shifts from German history in the twentieth century to transnational displacement in the twenty-first century. While both *Heimsuchung* und *Aller Tage Abend* reactivated the idea of cyclical time to disrupt both linear historical time and chronological narrative time, here Erpenbeck explores entrapment in circular movement and the weight of empty or traumatic time, which the narrative then transforms dialogically into relational time. This is a semidocumentary novel, so before analyzing the novel in more detail, it will be useful to summarize the European refugee crisis of 2015.[85]

---

85. In a postscript, Erpenbeck expressed her gratitude to thirteen individually named refugees for the many good conversations she enjoyed with them, while also thanking other helpers for their assistance (GGG, 350; GWG, 285).

The European Refugee Crisis of 2015

According to the United Nations Human Rights Council (UNHRC) 2015 Report migration reached new heights in 2015 when 65.3 million people were forcibly displaced worldwide, "as a result of persecution, conflict, generalized violence, or human rights violations." In 2015 the main route for refugees who wanted to reach Europe shifted from the dangerous Mediterranean crossing from Libya to Italy to a new route from Turkey across the Aegean to Lesbos in Greece. An estimated 3,770 people drowned when attempting the haphazard crossing on overloaded and unsuitable boats (including dinghies); more than 1 million people arrived in Europe by boat during that momentous year.[86] Twenty-five percent were children (many unaccompanied), 17 percent women, and 58 percent men. Half of the Mediterranean arrivals came from Syria, 21 percent from Afghanistan, 9 percent from Iraq, and 4 percent from Eritrea, followed by Pakistan, Iran, Nigeria, Somalia, Morocco, and Sudan.[87] Monthly arrivals in Italy, Greece, Spain, and Malta rose steadily from April onward, peaking in October with a figure of more than 200,000 in that month alone. Those who arrived in Greece made their way along the Balkan route into Hungary where they hoped to travel on to other European destinations, above all to Germany and Sweden. Even though the refugee crisis underlined the need for a coordinated European response, based on solidarity, responsibility, and shared humanitarian values, European leaders were unable or unwilling to agree on a common solution. Instead they relied on the Dublin II agreement of 2003, which established the problematic principle that "only one Member State is responsible for examining an asylum application."[88] According to the UNHRC, Germany was "the largest single recipient of new asylum applications, with 441,900 registered during 2015. This is more

---

86. See UNHRC, *Global Trends: Forced Displacement in 2015*, 32. See http://www.unhcr.org/576408cd7.pdf.

87. UNHRC, *Global Trends: Forced Displacement in 2015*, 34.

88. Seehttp://eur-lex.europa.eu/legal-content/EN/TXT/?uri=LEGISSUM:l33153.

than double those registered a year earlier (171,100) and the eighth consecutive increase."[89]

At the height of the 2015 crisis thousands of refugees were stranded in Hungary. Early in September 2015 the German chancellor, Angela Merkel, opened the German borders to allow the refugees to travel from Budapest via Vienna to Germany. It was a momentous decision that changed the image of Germany worldwide. Many international commentators who had previously criticized Merkel for her hard-line stance toward Greece after its financial crash now applauded the German chancellor for her humanitarian response and moral leadership at a time when most European leaders showed little or no solidarity with the refugees.

In June 2015 Viktor Orbán, the right-wing prime minister of Hungary, announced that his country would build a fence along the Serbian-Hungarian border to block the Balkan route for refugees.[90] Building began in July 2015 and continued to the end of the year. On 21 August 2015, a senior government official at the German Federal Office for Migration and Refugees sent an internal memo that was leaked to the media; the memo suspended the Dublin II agreement, according to which refugees had to be registered and provided for in the country where they entered Europe. A few days later the Office for Migration and Refugees released the following tweet without Merkel's prior knowledge and consent: "We are at present no longer enforcing Dublin procedures for Syrian refugees." Unsurprisingly, it spread like a wildfire among

---

89. The US was second with 172,700 new asylum claims, followed by Sweden, which received 156,400 new applications. Russia, Turkey, and Austria were ranked fourth, fifth, and sixth, respectively. Other EU countries include Hungary, the eighth-largest recipient with approximately 74,200 applications, closely followed by France, which received a similar number. UNHRC, *Global Trends: Forced Displacement in 2015*, 38. For further details on German figures, see Bundesamt für Migration und Flüchtlinge, *Das Bundesamt in Zahlen 2015: Asyl, Migration und Integration*, http://www.bamf.de/SharedDocs/Anlagen/DE/Publikationen/Broschueren/bundesamt-in-zahlen-2015.pdf?__blob=publicationFile.

90. The German weekly newspaper *Die Zeit* published a meticulously researched account of the dramatic events. See "The Night Germany Lost Control," *Die Zeit Online*, 30 August 2016, http://www.zeit.de/gesellschaft/2016-08/refugees-open-border-policy-september-2015-angela-merkel.

refugees along the Balkan route who now refused to register in Hungary in order to be eligible for registration in Germany.[91] The humanitarian crisis reached a new climax when, on 28 August 2015, seventy-one bodies of refugees and migrants were found in an abandoned truck on a highway in Austria: they had paid traffickers to take them to Germany but suffocated in the back of the refrigeration truck. This horrific story touched many people globally, drawing further attention to the unresolved urgency of the crisis. On 31 August Merkel gave a historic press conference in which she announced that, in all likelihood, more than 800,000 refugees would enter Germany in that year alone. Quoting the German constitution, which enshrines the right to asylum, she compared the challenges of accommodating and integrating the refugees with the difficult process of German unification, declaring: "Wir haben so Vieles geschafft—wir schaffen das! Wir schaffen das, und dort, wo uns etwas im Wege steht, muss es überwunden werden, muss daran gearbeitet werden." (We have managed so many things—we will manage that too. We will manage it, and wherever we encounter obstacles, we will work to overcome them.)[92] On 4 September the body of the three-year-old Syrian boy Aylan Kurdi washed up on a Turkish beach: the image of this small boy wearing a red T-shirt with his face pressed into the sand sent shock waves round the world. In Hungary things came to a head on 5 September when some 2,000 refugees began to march out of Budapest in protest of the Hungarian government's refusal to provide trains for their onward journey: the refugees wanted to become visible and used social media effectively to produce global pictures of their plight. As they marched along the main highway toward Austria, the

---

91. However, in its official pronouncements the German government continued to insist that Hungary had a legal duty to register all refugees in accordance with Dublin II, even though it knew perfectly well that if Dublin II still applied, the refugees should have been registered and provided for in Greece rather than in Hungary. In the context of the Greek financial crisis and given the sheer number of refugees arriving in Greece from Turkey this was an unrealistic demand.

92. Die Bundesregierung, "Im Wortlaut Sommerpressekonferenz von Bundeskanzlerin Merkel," https://www.bundesregierung.de/Content/DE/Mitschrift/Pressekonferenzen/2015/08/2015-08-31-pk-merkel.html.

group was led by a man waving a European flag; other marchers had pinned photos of Merkel onto their T-shirts, and a woman was shown being pushed along in a wheelchair. These emotive images were rapidly shared around the globe on social media with the hashtag "marchofhope." On the same day, the Hungarian ambassador in Berlin informed the German government that the country would no longer register the refugees and would bus them to the Austrian border instead. In that way, the country gave the migrants what they wanted—a free passage to Germany—while also getting rid of its refugee problem. The Austrian chancellor informed Merkel that he could not wait any longer because the situation at the Hungarian-Austrian border was becoming far too explosive. After sporadic consultation Merkel agreed to open the German border. Within one week 20,000 refugees arrived at Munich's railway station. From then on approximately 13,000 people crossed into Germany every single day. Faced with seemingly insurmountable logistical problems of how to process, shelter, and provide for the refugees, the German federal government briefly considered the option of closing the border but abandoned this plan. By the end of 2015, 890,000 refugees had arrived in Germany.

Die Zeit sums up its forensic analysis of the political drama with the following assessment:

> The reporting conducted by ZEIT and ZEIT ONLINE shows that the historic decision made by Merkel was not based on some spontaneous humanitarian impulse, emotional affect or sense of moral self-exaltation. Merkel had to make the decision under considerable pressure, within barely three hours, after Viktor Orbán succeeded in creating a situation for which there was practically no alternative.
>
> It's possible that historians will establish one day that this dramatic situation only became possible because communication had broken down in the European Union, because Brussels, Berlin and Budapest were all blaming each other rather than showing solidarity, because everyone was insisting they were right even as public order was collapsing. One thing, however, can be said with a reasonable degree of certainty: If the refugees had not decided on the morning of September 4 to start marching on foot from Budapest's Keleti station to Vienna, European history that weekend would have turned out differently.[93]

---

93. "The Night Germany Lost Control," *Die Zeit Online*, 30 August 2016.

Narrative Style and Perspective

Erpenbeck's novel deals with a group of male refugees from African countries who have arrived in Germany and made it to Berlin after highly perilous journeys across the Mediterranean to Italy. The events of the story are told from the perspective of Richard, a widower and recently retired professor of classics who becomes increasingly involved with these asylum seekers.

The title of the narrative—the conjugation of the irregular verb *gehen*—refers firstly to the language classes that the refugees attend while waiting for their asylum claims to be processed. But it also evokes the refugees' shared experience of displacement and dislocation from home: most of them have been on the move for years without any sense of stability. Their lives are precarious in the most immediate way: separated from their families and homes, they inhabit an insecure space defined by temporary accommodation and enforced mobility as they cannot settle down or work before their cases have been adjudicated. Their lack of attachments and inability to work leaves them stranded in an extended present that, as I will argue below, is haunted by a traumatic past and cut off from an open future. But displacement also applies to Richard, who, as we will see, is also experiencing a sense of biographical rupture in his life.

Erpenbeck's style can best be described as wry and restrained. In the main, her third-person narrative tracks Richard's thoughts, perceptions, and experiences in the narrative present. As in much contemporary fiction, the employment of the present tense services a "reflector-mode narrative" that "concentrates on the psychology of the protagonist,"[94] thereby emphasizing the experiential nature of reality while maintaining a sense of ironic distance. In this way, the present-tense narration creates proximity to and distance from Richard. The chronological narration in the present tense is regularly ruptured by analeptic flashbacks in the epic preterite that feature aspects of Richard's and his wife's past, including his

---

94. Monika Fludernik, "Chronology, Time, Tense, and Experientiality in Narrative," *Language and Literature* 12/2 (2003): 125.

nonmarital affair, his wife's alcoholism, and her death as well as early traumatic childhood memories from the end of the Second World War. While Richard is the main focalizer throughout, Erpenbeck briefly reverses the narrative perspective in chapter 27 where we view Richard through the eyes of Awad, one of the refugees with whom Richard strikes up a friendship. This temporary reversal reminds the reader that the narrative perspective is deliberately subjective: the story is not about what happens but rather about how Richard and the refugees relate to one another over time.

The chronological story has a clear timeline and setting: it starts in the summer of 2013 shortly after Richard's retirement, and it ends in spring 2014 when the cases of the refugees have been processed, and most are being returned to Italy, their first country of entry and registration in Europe. Erpenbeck regularly employs temporal markers that alternate between precise dates and more general temporal indicators that signal the objective passage of time. While the narrative perspective emphasizes the subjective experience of time, the narration is framed by a historical consciousness that objectifies the events. In the end, historical time cuts through subjective time when the men receive their deportation letters.

The Weight of Empty Time

The opening chapter introduces Richard reflecting on his new status as a recently retired professor of classics with a lot of time on his hands. The schedules and timetables that, up until now, have structured his working life no longer govern his days, and, in principle, he is free to do what he pleases without too many temporal imperatives:

> Vielleicht liegen noch viele Jahre vor ihm, vielleicht nur ein paar. Es ist jedenfalls so, dass Richard von jetzt an nicht mehr pünktlich aufstehen muss, um morgens im Institut zu erscheinen. Er hat jetzt einfach nur Zeit. Zeit, um zu reisen, sagt man. Zeit, um Bücher zu lesen. Proust. Dostojewski. Zeit, um Musik zu hören. Er weiss nicht, wie lange es dauern wird, bis er sich daran gewöhnt hat, Zeit zu haben. (GGG, 9)

> Perhaps many more years lie before him, or perhaps only a few. In any case, from now on Richard will no longer have to get up early to appear at the Institute. As of today, he has time plain and simple. Time to

travel, people say. To read books. Proust. Dostoevsky. Time to listen to music. He doesn't know how long it will take him to get used to having time. (GWG, 3)

The irony inherent in the narrative voice is effected by the distancing "sagt man" (people say) and the implied dialogism of the entire passage:[95] in all likelihood, Richard remembered here the voices of his colleagues during his retirement party, which features later in the chapter. Narrative irony already signals that Richard is struggling with the unsettling effect of unstructured time: unlike previous leisure breaks and vacations, Richard's time is now open-ended and, after his retirement, a symbol of his mortality. Having the time to read the mighty tomes of Dostoevsky or Proust is not so much a promising opportunity as the anxiety-inducing premonition of death. Rather than a mode of liberating idleness,[96] such unfilled time is a weight that causes the type of brooding melancholy that, according to Robert Burton, often afflicts the scholar.[97] Erpenbeck further enhances the association of unscheduled time and the passage toward death by the setting: from his desk Richard is looking out at the lake where a man drowned earlier this summer—his body has not yet surfaced, the significance of which I will explore later.

Recalling the time when he discovered that his lover was cheating on him, Richard remembers how he got over the ensuing separation by following Ovid's advice that the best cure for love is work. However, this strategy no longer works because "nun . . . quält ihn nicht die Zeit, die mit einer unnützen Liebe ausgefüllt ist, sondern die Zeit an sich. Vergehen soll sie, aber auch nicht vergehen" (GGG, 11; "now . . . he is being tormented, not by time filled with pointless love but by time itself. Time is supposed to pass but not just that"; GWG, 4). Without work and love Richard's experience of time is devoid of purpose, orientation, and social context,

---

95. See Bakhtin, *The Dialogic Imagination*, 275–300.
96. On idleness, see Leonhard Fuest, *Poetik des Nicht(s)Tuns: Verweigerungsstrategien in der Literatur seit 1800* (Munich: Wilhelm Fink, 2008).
97. Richard Burton, *The Anatomy of Melancholy*, ed. with an introduction by Holbrook Jackson (New York: New York Review of Books, 2002), 301.

and as such is strangely atemporal: it consists of discrete Newtonian moments that are atomized and without the temporal horizon that, according to Edmund Husserl, shapes human experience.[98] Of course, this momentary impression of an atomistic now is just that: a fleeting realization of dread that is embedded in the flow of Richard's temporal consciousness in chapter 1. Richard's self-reflexive engagement with the experience of time is aided by the free indirect speech, which creates a present-time effect, regardless of whether or not the preterite or present tense is used.

Remembering his retirement party at the beginning of August, Richard retrospectively attempts to normalize the event by emphasizing the ordinariness of a transition that, in spite of his best efforts, is a major biographical break: "Jeder wurde ja irgendwann alt. War irgendwann alt." (GGG, 13; "After all, everyone got old sooner or later. Was old sooner or later"; GWG, 6.) The transition phase from work into retirement was still busy, with Richard packing up his books and moving out of his office. Reflecting on the curious convention that it is the retiree who must arrange his own retirement party, Richard realizes that he cannot comprehend that, for his colleagues, his retirement is part of ongoing life, whereas for him it signifies an absolute ending (GGG, 14). In his eyes his scholarly learning and knowledge accumulated over a lifetime have been reduced to "Privateigentum" (GGG, 15; private property; GWG, 8), that, in the form of his books and scripts, is stored away in the basement of his house. Since Richard has no family, he wonders whether there is any point in unpacking what his late wife used to call his "Krempel," his stuff, which now exists for his pleasure alone (GGG, 15; GWG, 8). Erpenbeck's ironic employment of the label "private property" for Richard's classical scholarship draws attention here to the commodification of knowledge in contemporary capitalism: outside the rarefied academic context, Richard's learning is accumulated junk without much exchange value. And so

---

98. See Michael R. Kelly, "Phenomenology and Time-Consciousness," *Internet Encyclopedia of Philosophy: A Peer-Reviewed Academic Resource*, http://www.iep.utm.edu/phe-time/ (accessed 10 January 2018).

the first chapter stages a crisis of time and temporality in Richard's life, which then motivates his interest in the fate of the refugees.

Erpenbeck delays this new beginning in Richard's life by recounting in chapter 2 how he passes by the refugees' protest camp at the Rote Rathaus—the Red Town Hall, residence of the mayor of Berlin and the Senate—lost in his own thoughts. He is on his way to an archaeologist friend, who wants to show him a dig with medieval tunnels, and fails to pay attention to the protest. In chapter 3 their demonstration features in the evening news, and he briefly wonders why he did not notice the men (GGG, 29; GWG, 19). But it is only in chapter 4 after a news report that the hunger strike has been ended and the men have been removed that Richard's attention is aroused: he compares the men's strategy of hiding their identity while making themselves visible in the public domain to Odysseus's ruse of calling himself Nobody to escape from the Cyclops's cave (GGG, 32; GWG, 22). The episode thus shows that his learning is not useless junk at all: the poetic analogy to Homer's *Odyssey* mobilizes a new energy in Richard, whose interest in the refugees is ignited. During a visit to the refugee camp on Oranienplatz in Kreuzberg he overhears a German helper explaining to a journalist that the men end up doing nothing all day because they are not allowed to work: "Wenn das Nichtstun zu schlimm wird, organisieren wir eine Demo." (GGG, 48; "When doing nothing gets too much for them we organize a demonstration"; GWG, 35.) It is precisely the realization of the weight of empty time that motivates Richard's ensuing dedication to the cause of the refugees. Later on he recalls these words and suddenly realizes why he visited Oranienplatz in the first place: "Über das sprechen, was Zeit eigentlich ist, kann er wahrscheinlich am besten mit denen, die aus ihr hinausgefallen sind. Oder in sie hineingesperrt, wenn man so will." (GGG, 51; "Speaking about the actual nature of time is something he can probably do best with those who have fallen out of it. Or been locked up in it, if you prefer"; GWG, 38.) The chapter finishes with the description of his wife's empty bed, which is covered with the clothes he has worn over the last few days—a poignant detail that externalizes a significant absence in Richard's life.

Richard finally visits the asylum home in chapter 11 and gains permission to carry out interviews. In chapter 12, he meets some of the refugees for the first time: when the director of the temporary asylum home knocks on one of the doors and opens it, Richard is reminded of a hospital ward because some of the men lie asleep on their cots, while other beds are empty (GGG, 59; GWG, 45–46). Faced with this depressing image of inertia and stagnation, Richard's first impulse is to retreat but instead he begins to interview Rashid, a refugee from Nigeria, and the other room occupants, who explain that they are not allowed to work: "Es ist schwer, sagt Zair, sehr schwer. Ein Tag ist genauso wie der andere, sagt der lange Ithemba." (GGG, 63; "It is hard, Zair says, very hard. One day is just the same as another, says tall Ithemba"; GWG, 48.) Without work and recognition as asylum seekers, these young men are stranded in an empty but restless present.

Chronotopes

The previous section has already mentioned a range of Erpenbeck's carefully crafted chronotopes that map the protagonists' temporal and spatial dislocation. The camps in front of the Rote Rathaus in the city center and later at Oranienplatz in Kreuzberg are public locations that make visible the refugees' existential uprootedness from home. Their nomadic tents in the middle of Germany's capital contrast with Berlin's imposing signature buildings, above all the tall TV tower in Alexanderplatz, which features early on: it was constructed in the mid- to late 1960s at a time when the GDR had made considerable economic progress and gained new confidence. With a total height of 365 meters, a rotating Telecafé at the top, modeled on Sputnik, it symbolized the GDR's competition with the West. When inaugurated in 1969, it was the third-tallest freestanding building in the world after Ostrankino in Moscow and the Empire State Building in New York. Richard remembers a story for children about a construction worker who fell from the top as the tower was being built: because it was so high, people had enough time to pile up mattresses at the bottom so that he landed softly and unharmed like the "Erbsenprinzessin im Märchen"

(GGG, 21), the princess and the pea in the fairy tale. As he passes the fountain at Alexanderplatz—another GDR landmark—he wryly reflects on the communist promise of happiness in a future "die irgendwann für alle Menschen erreicht sein würde, nach treppenförmig angeordnetem Fortschritt bis in schwungvolle, kaum zu glaubenden Höhen hinein, so in ein-, zwei oder spätestens dreihundert Jahren" (GGG, 22; "that mankind would eventually make its way to via a sort of staircase of progress leading into dazzling, astonishing heights, a state to be achieved in the next hundred, two hundred, or at the very most three hundred years"; GWG, 14). The TV tower, the fountain, and the world clock at Alexanderplatz (which features later in the narrative) represent the communist investment in the future as the place of collective happiness. After the fall of Communism these socialist landmarks are *lieux de mémoire* of a utopia that has been catapulted from the distant future into the world of fairy tales.

The camps, tents, and temporary homes inhabited by the refugees also contrast with the domestic setting of Richard's house, which is located on the shores of a lake on the outskirts of East Berlin. Even though Richard and his wife lived in the house for decades, it too evokes a sense of temporal and spatial dislocation: since his wife's death, Richard has lived there on his own, surrounded by stranded objects from their shared past, including an Advent wreath that he has not stored away for years. The lake adds an uncanny element to this setting: a man drowned there earlier that summer, but his body has not yet surfaced. The drowned man serves as a leitmotif, evoking the tension between surface and depth that runs through the narrative as a whole. A third significant type of location are the asylum homes of the refugees: neither a camp nor a proper home, the disused old people's home near Richard's house and the asylum home in Spandau represent the temporary nature of the refugees' accommodation in Germany and thus their precarious status as their cases are processed according to the Dublin II regulations. Other recurring locations include the supermarket—during GDR times it was the *Kaufhalle*—where Richard does his shopping with the help of a list that he writes in the order of the products on the shelves that he passes (GGG, 72). He also visits the house of his friends Detlef and Sylvia for birthday parties and other celebrations. Erpenbeck embeds Richard in a topography of ordinariness that highlights his slightly obsessive need for structure in everyday life. The narrator describes with ironic detachment Richard's pleasure when he finally masters the best way of cutting an onion (GGG, 24; GWG, 16).

But this sense of an ordered ordinariness is an extremely fragile construct. In West Berlin, Richard feels disoriented and out of place, even though the fall of the Berlin Wall happened more than twenty years previously. When his wife Christel was still alive, she used to guide him through the rapidly changing city with a map on her knees. After her death, he bought a satellite navigation system: "Jetzt sagt eine Frauenstimme, mit der er nicht verheiratet ist, zu ihm: Biegen Sie rechts ab, biegen Sie links ab." (GGG, 192; "Now, when he drives, the voice of a woman to whom he isn't married says to him: Turn right, turn left"; GWG, 155.)

Richard's lack of direction contrasts sharply with the Tuareg's astonishing sense of orientation, which derives from transgenerational knowledge. Richard learned from the refugee he thinks of as Apollo in the previous chapter that the Tuareg manage their way across the Sahara without any signposts or maps; they find their route because they know what happened to their forefathers on their established tracks. They cross the desert as Apollo crosses the heavens. These stories are retold and passed down the generational chain; they form a memory map that interweaves space and time into a meaningful whole (GGG, 187, GWG, 150). Richard, the professor of classics and reader of Homer, recognizes that proper emplacement depends precisely on such performative acts of narration that create a poetic time-space:

Natürlich hat er immer gewusst, dass zum Beispiel die *Odyssee* und die *Ilias*, bevor Homer oder wer auch immersie zum ersten Mal aufgeschrieben hat, mündlich weitergegebene Erzählungen waren. Aber noch nie ist ihm der Zusammenhang zwischen Raum, Zeit und Dichtung so klar gewesen wie in diesem Moment. Vor dem Hintergrund einer Wüste sah man es nur besonders deutlich, aber im Prinzip war es doch an

keinem Ort auf der Welt je anders: Ohne Erinnerung war der Mensch
nur ein Stück Fleisch auf einem Planeten. (GGG, 187)

Of course he's always known that the *Odyssey* and the *Iliad* are stories
that were passed on orally long before Homer or whoever it was wrote
them down. But never before has the connection between space, time,
and words [poetry, AF] revealed itself so clearly as at this moment. The
backdrop of the desert shows it off in sharp relief: without memory man
is nothing more than a bit of flesh on the planet's surface. (GWG, 151)

In the context of urban Berlin, which is visibly marked by the upheavals of recent world history, such anchorage in a stable poetic
time-space appears as a retrospective utopia. As they drive across
Berlin, Richard attempts to explain to Rufu that a wall sliced
through the city, dividing it into East and West for nearly thirty
years, and that it was not possible to cross over from the East into
the West.

Bei dem Versuch, über die Grenze zu kommen, wurden manchmal sogar
    welche erschossen
Ah, capisco, man wollte sie im Westen nicht haben.
Nein, man wollte sie aus dem Osten nicht rauslassen.
Okay. (GGG, 156)

Some people were even shot trying to cross the border.
Ah, capisco, they didn't want them in the West.
No, they did not want to let them leave the East.
Okay. (GWG, 156)

This rather humorous exchange exposes the strangeness of Cold
War history from the perspective of a refugee who understands
perfectly well why the West would not allow people *in* but who
cannot make sense of why the East would not have allowed them
out. Their ensuing conversation about walls and fences that inhibit
free movement is constantly punctured by the voice of the satellite
navigation system that steers Richard safely across the former border (GGG, 195). As they are passing the Soviet War Memorial in
Treptow Park, Richard abandons the idea of explaining the meaning of the monument, which depicts a Soviet soldier carrying a
German child "zum Zeichen eines Neubeginns nach dieser letzten

Schlacht des Weltkriegs" (GGG, 95; "to symbolize the rebirth of Berlin after this final battle of the World War"; GWG, 157). In her description of Richard's and Rufu's journey across Berlin, Erpenbeck thus articulates the incommensurable nature of historical experience: from the perspectives of the African refugees, the German experience of the war is not particularly special or different. Their own experiences of extreme violence, mass deaths, displacement, and loss relativize the Western historical consciousness. Richard's failure to adequately translate German history into a meaningful time-space narrative that can be shared communally perhaps also reflects his position as a former GDR citizen who has learned to distrust any kind of shared historical narrative. However, it may also have to do with his deep-seated and, ultimately, traumatic sense of dislocation. Richard loves the surface order of his life because it conceals disturbing memories. Richard and his wife hung onto a shared sense of order because their early childhoods were marked by war trauma: at the age of three his wife had been shot in the legs by German strafing planes as she and her family were fleeing the advancing Russian army. Christel drew the following lesson from history: "Alles, was man nicht überblickt, ist tödlich, hatte seine Frau so schon mit drei Jahren gelernt." (GGG, 25; "So his wife had learned at the age of three that everything you can't size up properly is potentially lethal"; GWG, 17.) In the "Kriegswirren," the mayhem of war, Richard was nearly separated from his mother at the overcrowded train station, had it not been for a Russian soldier who handed the small infant back to his mother through the train's window.[99] His early experience of chance survival feeds into his view of history as an accidental and ultimately haphazard force that, in sharp contrast to the Marxist view of a teleological history, cannot be controlled, engineered, or steered toward a better future.

---

99. Erpenbeck employs here typical features of the recent German family novel, which filters twentieth-century German history through the lens of family history. See Anne Fuchs, *Phantoms of War in Contemporary German Literature, Films, and Discourse: The Politics of Memory*, 2nd ed. (2008; Houndmills: Palgrave Macmillan, 2010); Friederike Eigler, *Gedächtnis und Geschichte in Generationenromanen seit der Wende* (Berlin: Erich Schmidt, 2005).

Richard responds to the radical contingency of history by seeking meaning in everyday order and practice.

Fragile Relationships

At the heart of the narrative is the changing relationship between Richard and the refugees. At first, their encounter is asymmetrical and governed by unconscious cultural bias. The director of the asylum home gives Richard permission to interview the refugees because of his academic title. And so, in their initial meetings, he behaves like a Eurocentric anthropologist who records the stories of exotic Others. Because he struggles to recall their African names, he assigns aliases from Greek or German mythology (Apollo, Tristan, the Olympian) to some of the young men. Over time, however, Richard's relationship with the young men changes as he listens to their individual stories about the traumatic loss of their families, friends, and homes. By interspersing their dialogues in German with Italian and English phrases, Erpenbeck captures the trans- and multilingual reality of the refugees, who often command more than three or four languages. For example, Apollo, the young Tuareg from the Sahara who worked as a slave from an early age, speaks Tamasheq, Hausa, Arabic, and French, and he is now learning German (GGG, 68; GWG, 52–53). As he listens to Apollo's description of his former nomadic life, Richard feels like a child again because he is hearing so many things for the first time (GGG, 70; GWG, 54). Rashid, the so-called Olympian, is a refugee from Nigeria: he explains the five pillars of Islam to Richard and also reveals how thirteen years ago on the eve of Eid Mubarak, the religious holiday marking the end of Ramadan, a radical Islamist group modeled on Boko Haram carried out a horrific massacre in his community, burning down his village and killing his father among many others. One of Rashid's most poignant memory icons is the image of the tidy and scrubbed family home, which had been prepared by the women for the festivities of Eid Mubarak before it was burned to the ground. In the course of the novel we also find out that Rashid was married with two children in Libya: when he crossed the Mediterranean on an overcrowded boat with his two children, it capsized, and 550 people, including his children, drowned. His wife who had stayed behind in Tripoli divorced him and remarried. Awad (Tristan) was born in Ghana and grew up in Libya with his father. Life was good until his father was murdered by the army during the war against Gaddafi, and Awad, together with many other African immigrants and Arabs, was rounded up by militia and taken to barracks where he and the others were beaten and dispossessed of their few belongings, including the SIM cards in their mobile phones—"sagt Awad. Das Gedächtnis zerbrochen" (GGG, 79; "Broke the memory, says Awad"; GWG, 61)— before they were put on boats to Europe. Awad does not know whether it was the pro- or anti-Gaddafi factions that drove them from Libya, his only homeland (GGG, 79, GWG; 62):

> Der Krieg zerstört alles, sagt Awd: die Familie, die Freunde, den Ort, an dem man gelebt hat, die Arbeit, den Alltag. Wenn man ein Fremder wird, hat man keine Wahl mehr. Man weiß nicht wohin. (GGG, 80)

> War destroys everything, Awad says: your family, your friends, the place where you lived, your work, your life. When you become foreign, Awad says, you don't have a chance. You don't know where to go. (GWG, 63)

From a temporal perspective, then, the traumatic stories of Awad, Rashid, and the others disturb the sense of chronological order that governs the narrative discourse. Trauma time is anachronic and deeply disruptive as it turns the past into a never-ending nightmare that slices into the present. Trauma time is always retroactive: it involves what Freud calls "Nachträglichkeit," the belated recalling of a prior event that was overwhelming and could not be processed by the traumatized self when it occurred.[100] The retroactivity of

---

100. For an excellent account of Freud's theory of trauma and a compelling critique of poststructuralist readings of Freud, see Ruth Leys, *Trauma: A Genealogy* (Chicago: University of Chicago Press, 2000); Sigrid Weigel, "Téléscopage im Unbewußten: Zum Verhältnis von Trauma, Geschichtsbegriff und Literatur," in *Trauma: Zwischen Psychoanalyse und kulturellen Deutungsmustern*, ed. Elisabeth Bronfen, Birgit Erdle, and Sigrid Weigel (Cologne: Böhlau, 1999), 51–76; John Fletcher, *Freud and the Scene of Trauma* (New York: Fordham University Press, 2013). See also Anne Fuchs, "'Der Zauberrhytmus des Lebens': Freuds *Jenseits des Lustprinzips* und der Zeitdiskurs der Gegenwart," *Westend: Neue Zeitschrift für Sozialforschung* 1 (2015): 27–44.

trauma also explains its "presentist" nature: precisely because it involves the confrontation with an event that has not yet been processed and symbolized, it can erupt at any moment in the present in the form of intrusive flashbacks. The nightmarish nature of the troubling "presentism" of trauma is particularly evident in chapter 27 where we perceive Richard through Awad's eyes: suffering from post-traumatic stress disorder (PTSD) and a range of psychosomatic symptoms such as migraines, nausea, and restless pacing, Awad perceives Richard as an older gentleman "der sehr höflich ist, aber vielleicht auch verrückt ist" (GGG, 165; who is very polite but perhaps also crazy"; GWG, 132). The fastidious care with which Richard writes everything down in his notebook contrasts sharply with the chaotic disorder in Awad's own head where the memories of his traumatic past are lodged like painful shards. And so when Awad is asked to take a medical blood test, he is overcome by panic and escapes back to his room. Free indirect speech allows us to witness how Awad's perception of the here and now is overlaid by the traumatic presentism of his memories.

Erpenbeck gives each character a personal voice that she then filters through Richard's perspective. Indirect speech alternates with direct speech to accentuate the testimonial nature of these dialogues. Instead of an undifferentiated collective of refugees, Richard and the reader thus get to know individuals from different backgrounds with different stories and expectations. What unites them is their shared experience of suffering, traumatic displacement, and loss. And so this polyphony of voices strives for "narrative equality" and coevality between the different refugees and Richard as witness.[101]

There are, however, two characters who have a more pronounced role in the course of the narrative: Karon Anubo, the thin man from Ghana, for whom Richard purchases a piece of land; and Osarobo from Niger, to whom Richard teaches the piano for

---

101. On witnessing, see Dori Laub, "Bearing Witness, or the Vicissitudes of Listening," in *Testimony: Crises of Witnessing in Literature, Psychoanalysis, and History*, ed. Shoshana Felman and Dori Laub (New York: Routledge, 1992), 57–74.

some time. Both stories explore the possibility of friendship across the sociocultural, linguistic, and generational divide that separates Richard from the African young men. According to Jochen Dreher, friendship is an imagined construct "which transcends the world of everyday life of individuals and, as a special form of 'encounter with fellow human beings', creates a specific bond between people."[102] Even though friendship can overcome major sociocultural, generational, and experiential differences, it tends to occur more easily between people who share symbolic worlds. Richard's circle of friends exemplifies the type of we-relationship based on reciprocity and collectively shared experiences and values: he has known most of his close friends half his life, and some almost his entire life (GGG, 88; GWG, 69). In contrast, the African men forge homosocial ties of comradeship with one another, based on the need to cooperate in order to cope with the hardship of migration.[103] In dealing with them, Richard starts out as academic anthropologist in pursuit of a project, and then adopts the role of mentor and helper who finally sees himself as their friend. The question as to how far Richard's friendship with them remains unequal and one-sided can be illuminated with reference to book 8 of Aristotle's *Nicomachean Ethics*, which Richard, a professor of classics, would of course know well. Aristotle distinguishes between three types of friendship: friendship of pleasure, friendship of utility, and friendship of virtue.[104] For Aristotle, the first two forms are accidental because they are grounded in the gratification or benefit that arises from the friendship. Friendships of pleasure and utility are therefore tainted: while the first is motivated by the enjoyment or

---

102. Jochen Dreher, "Phenomenology of Friendship: Construction of an Existential Social Friendship," *Human Studies* 32/4 (2009): 407.

103. See Thomas Kühne, *The Rise and Fall of Comradeship: Hitler's Soldiers, Male Bonding, and Mass Violence in the Twentieth Century* (Cambridge: Cambridge University Press, 2017). Kühne writes: "While friendship caters to the individual self, it is rooted in mutual sympathy of individuals, and may be abandoned at any time, comradeship denotes the relationship of people who cooperate, work, live together not by choice but by coercion, by accident, or by fate" (291).

104. Aristotle, *Nikomachische Ethik*, trans. Frank Dirlmeier (Stuttgart: Reclam, 1969), 212–42.

comfort one gains from the other, the second type feeds on the expectation of some kind of advantage. Aristotle exemplifies this with reference to a gift: when A makes a gift to B, the gift is made with the expectation of some kind of return—in other words, it is not a genuine gift but a loan.[105] For Aristotle, genuine friendship must be based on equality, reciprocal affection, goodwill, and mutual choice.[106]

The issue of the gift is raised in relation to Osarobo. In their first conversation the eighteen-year-old tells Richard that he has lost all his friends, and that he witnessed how many of them died while crossing over from Libya to Italy (GGG, 125). He has already spent three years in Europe without any sense of a future (GGG, 126).

> Ich will wieder zu meinen Freunden zurück.
> Richard weiß nicht, ob Osarobo seine Freunde im Altersheim meint oder die Toten. Richard scheitert an diesem Jungen. Aber es geht nicht darum, dass er scheitert. Es geht überhaupt nicht um ihn.
> (GGG, 126)

> I want to go back to my friends, he says.
> Richard doesn't know if Osarobo means his friends in the nursing home or the ones who are dead. With this boy, Richard has run aground. But his failure isn't what matters here. He's not what matters.
> (GWG, 100)

Attempting to draw the boy back into life, Richard asks him whether there is anything at all he would like to do, if he had the opportunity (GGG, 127; GWG, 101). When Osarabo reveals that he would love to play the piano, Richard offers his instrument and begins to teach him after realizing that the boy has never touched a keyboard before. In chapter 32 Richard plays a video recording of his favorite pianists, and he and Osarobo listen to the music for a few hours (GGG, 201). This sense of a shared bond is in all likelihood a misconception because Richard is the sole focalizer of the episode. In chapter 37 we learn that Richard has bought Osarobo

---

105. Aristotle, *Nikomachische Ethik*, 239.
106. Aristotle, *Nikomachische Ethik*, 217.

a Christmas present, a keyboard that can be rolled up and fits into a small backpack so that he could earn a little money playing it on the street (GGG, 216). Ashamed by his admission that Osarobo's future is unlikely to be bright, he wonders at what point he transmuted from a man with great hopes into an almsgiver. In Aristotelian terms then, Richard entertains a friendship of pleasure, and for Osarobo it is a friendship of utility. Having moved in with a friend from Ivory Coast who lives in a different part of the city, Osarobo eventually abandons the piano lessons altogether. When Richard returns home from a conference and finds that his house has been burgled, he is troubled by the thought that perhaps Osarobo broke into his house because he knew that Richard would be away. His ensuing attempts to meet Osarobo to talk things over are unsuccessful: the latter keeps sending evasive text messages and fails to turn up for their meetings. Richard's final attempt to meet Osarobo at the World Clock in Alexanderplatz ends with Richard returning home and sitting at his desk weeping as he wept only when his wife died (GGG, 323; GWG, 262). Faced with the feeling of having been betrayed, Richard finally recognizes that his relationship with Osarobo had remained asymmetrical. The kind of commitment, reciprocity, and trust that Richard, the professor of classics and reader of Aristotle, would expect from his friends is the prerogative of someone who inhabits a stable social world.

And yet, Erpenbeck is careful not to rule out the possibility of friendship between social actors whose realities are very divergent. The story of Karon Anubo from Ghana acts as a counterpart to the Osarobo story. Karon is introduced as the thin man who keeps sweeping the stairs in the nursing home; in chapter 23 Richard replays his lengthy conversation with him when he is back home: the thin man's account revolves around entrapment in absolute poverty and his inability to provide for his mother and siblings in Ghana. Caught up in a vicious circle of precarious and exploitative employment, he finally made his way to Libya, where he worked on a building site; when the war broke out, he escaped to Europe aided by traffickers. What makes Karon's story so remarkable is the way in which Erpenbeck interlaces his first-person account with the description of Richard as he recalls their conversation: turning on the lights in the sitting room, library, and kitchen, as he always does when he comes home at night, Richard is unable to resume his routine. As he replays the thin man's first-person narration in his mind, the latter turns into a specter sweeping Richard's house. The first sentence uttered by the man—"Ich schaue nach vorn und nach hinten und sehe nichts" (GGG, 136; "I look in front of me and behind and I see nothing"; GWG, 108)—becomes a spectral leitmotif that adds a repetitive and cyclical rhythm to a narration that centers on entrapment in the vicious cycle of poverty. The external symbol of this is his careful but pointless sweeping: the thin man sweeps the stairs from bottom to top, moving up one step at a time with the dust from each step falling down on the one he has just swept (GGG, 144; GWG, 115).[107]

Karon sends most of the social benefits he receives as remittances to his family because, as the oldest son, he must provide for them (GWG, 202). When he is summoned to the police in Berlin to produce his identity papers he is worried that, after the interview, he will be sent back to Italy and be unable to feed his family: "Ich habe keine Frau und keine Kinder, sagt er, ich bin klein. Aber das Problem ist sehr groß, es hat eine Frau und viele, viele Kinder." (GGG, 251; "The problem is very big, Karon says. I have no wife and children, he says—I am small. But the problem is very big, it has a wife and many, many children"; GWG, 203.) Karon explains to Richard that a piece of land that could feed his family would be one-third the size of Oranienplatz and would cost between 2,000 and 3,000 euros. When Richard offers to buy a piece of land for Karon's family in Ghana, Karon's reaction remains muted: Richard realizes that his worries have ground him down to such an extent that he is afraid to invest in hope (GGG, 255; GWG, 206).

---

107. In *Spectres of Marx* Derrida interweaves a reading of Shakespeare's *Hamlet* with an interpretation of the pervasive ghost imagery in Marx. "Haunting," writes Derrida, "is historical, to be sure, but it is not dated, it is never docilely given a date in the chain of the presents, day after day, according to the instituted order of the calendar." Jacques Derrida, *Specters of Marx*, trans. Peggy Knauf (New York: Routledge, 1994), 3. The figure of the ghost thus displaces presence through a movement of return and inauguration that Derrida captures in the term "hauntology."

The successful transaction and purchase of the land on behalf of "his friend Karon" (GGG, 282) concludes with Karon sending a text message to Richard:

> Hi Richard. I just want to see how are you doing, Richard. I don't know how to thank you. Only God no my heart but anyway wat I can say is may God protect you. always Good morning. karon Immer Guten Morgen, denkt Richard, mehr kann man nicht wünschen. (GGG, 282 *sic*)

> Hi Richard. I just want to see how are you doing, Richard. I don't know how to thank you. Only God no my heart but anyway wat I can say is may God protect you. always Good morning. karon. Always good morning, Richard thinks, indeed, one can't ask for more.[108]

The grammatical and punctuation errors in Karon's message enhance this expression of gratitude: they are unedited and therefore genuine. While Richard's generosity may have been initially motivated by the expectation of a return, it is Karon's response that overcomes the economy of exchange in favor of a fragile reciprocity. And so the recipient of the gift, Karon, becomes the giver by transforming the gift-loan into a proper gift.

Erpenbeck's story ends with Richard and his friends taking in as many refugees as they can when they lose their asylum cases and are about to be deported to their first country of entry into the EU. This last-minute rescue, however, does not sugarcoat the reality of deportation for the majority. As the objectifying third-person narrative voice observes, "Von 476 haben auf diese Weise, 147 einen Schlafplatz bekommen" (GGG, 334; "In this way, 147 of the 476 men now have a place to sleep"; GWG, 272), but the remaining 329 are unaccounted for.

The novel concludes with a social vision of sharing: together with his old and new friends, Richard has organized a barbecue in his garden. When a group photo is taken, he notices that Sylvia is missing. Detlef's revelation that her cancer is now reaching the

---

108. Bernofsky translates this sentence as follows: "Always good morning, Richard thinks, indeed what better thing to wish a friend?" (GWG, 228). The reference to the friend is absent in the German original, which makes Richard's conclusion a little more muted.

terminal stage causes the participants to reflect on the losses or absences of intimate relationships in their lives. It is in this context that Richard finally reveals the real reason for his wife's drinking: as a young woman she had an illegal abortion because Richard did not want to have a child at that point. He remembers how, after the botched abortion, the blood was dripping down Christel's legs as they were traveling home on the local train. Richard's embarrassment at his wife's bleeding is a form of displaced guilt. His sense of shame masked the fear that she might die:

> Damals glaube ich, sagt Richard, ist mir klargeworden, dass das, was ich aushalte, nur die Oberfläche von all dem ist, was ich nicht aushalte.
> So wie auf dem Meer?, fragt Khalil.
> Ja, im Prinzip genauso wie auf dem Meer. (GGG, 348)

> I think that's when I realized, says Richard, that the things I can endure are only just the surface of what I can't possibly endure.
> Like the surface of the sea? Asks Khalil.
> Actually, yes, exactly like the surface of the sea. (GWG, 283)

The novel thus ends with the articulation of a grief that could not surface because it could not be endured alone. "If my fate is not originally or finally separated from yours," comments Judith Butler, "then the 'we' is traversed by a relationality that we cannot easily argue against; or, rather, we can argue against it, but we would be denying something fundamental about the social conditions of our very formation."[109] Indeed, Richard's belated recognition of the depth of his grief takes place among friends who entertain fragile relations based on the mutual recognition of loss. It is for this reason that Richard's act of sharing his buried grief does not follow Freud's economy of mourning, according to which mourning is merely a transitory stage on the pathway to a form of healing that manifests itself in the redirection of one's libidinal energy toward a new love object.[110] Instead,

---

109. Butler, *Precarious Life*, 222.

110. See Sigmund Freud, "Remembering, Repeating, Working-Through," in *The Standard Edition*, 12:147–56. See Gisela Ecker, "Trauer zeigen: Inszenierung und die Sorge um den Anderen," in *Trauer Tragen—Trauer Zeigen: Inszenierungen der Geschlechter*, ed. G. Ecker (Munich: Fink, 1999), 8–25.

the final pages of Erpenbeck's great novel imagine a transitory community founded on respect for the vulnerability of life and care for the Other. Rather than romanticizing the precarious conditions of the refugees who are still facing a very uncertain future, the novel merely gestures toward a precarious politics of relationality that acknowledges our codependency through everyday practice.

Conclusion

It is not surprising that many of the temporal tropes that dominate current theories of time resurface in contemporary literary guise. Point time, atomization, the empty and extended present, acceleration, and the culture of immediacy are terms that capture the social, historical, and existential experience of precariousness at the beginning of the twenty-first century. The texts under discussion confront precariousness through narrative techniques that collapse the chronological imagination, which has underpinned much of modern historical consciousness. The experience of time in these texts is in crisis: they abandon the temporal itineraries that could synthesize past, present, and future into a historical master narrative. Contemporary German fiction queries the chronological imagination and with it the dramatic turning points of history by staging 1989 as a chance happening that shatters its protagonists' lives. The radical contingency of the events of 1989 is further aggravated by the rise of global capitalism and its economic and social insecurities, which feature prominently in much of contemporary literature. In the lives of the protagonists biographical time is no longer incremental and predictable but extremely precarious: the expectation of what ought to happen is displaced by temporal anxiety and the experience of exclusion and of biographical irrelevance.

In Meyer's *Als wir träumten* the loss of the chronological imagination manifests itself in the dreamlike rendition of the frenzied and atomized experience of time. His perspectival narration never deviates from the experiential horizon of his adolescent protagonists who can no longer envision a future beyond the thrill of the intensely lived moment in the here and now. Having abandoned the idea of social advancement through education and work, they opt instead for a homosocial gang identity founded on puerile fantasies of masculine omnipotence. Meyer often employs the present tense for the frequent flashbacks in Danie's first-person narration, which is delivered in the epic preterite. This analeptic structure accentuates the traumatic nature of the successive loss of all his friends, who die as a result of extreme gang violence. And so the atomization of lived time in *Als wir träumten* destroys the very condition of lasting social relations: the boys' vision of friendship was modeled on the filmic projection of eternal brotherhood in *Winnetou*. Such fictional casting of male friendship is an insufficient basis for trust and long-term relations. Because their group identity was extremely phobic, it falls apart from within. Here the atomization of time results in the atomization of social relations: without some kind of future horizon, life is without orientation.

While Meyer focuses on the short-lived thrill of the atomized moment, Julia Schoch's *Mit der Geschwindigkeit des Sommers* explores the sheer weight of empty time. Situated in a garrison town near the Polish border before and after the fall of the Berlin Wall, Schoch's narrative "highlights unsettling continuities between life in the GDR and life in the Berlin Republic."[111] As in Meyer's *Als wir träumten*, the first-person narrator tries to understand the loss of life: her sister spent all her life in the godforsaken East German province but traveled to New York only to commit suicide in some anonymous guesthouse. The incongruity sparks the narrative investigation of the meaning of place and time. The fall of the Berlin Wall liberated the narrator from the shackles of provincial life: her mobility exemplifies the global lifestyle of the educated elite that has embraced the millennial values of individualism, flexibility, and continual innovation. By contrast, her sister remained moored in a province that is as disembedded from the past as it is divorced from the future. Adopting the cool tone and perspective of the *nouveau roman*, Schoch's narrative employs a

---

111. Cosgrove, "Heimat as Non-Place," 70.

forensic descriptiveness to map out a *nature morte* of extended dead time. With its crumbling infrastructure, this East German garrison town could be a rust belt town in the US or a locality in the postindustrial wastelands of northern England or Wales. And yet, the descriptive poetry of stagnation in the marginalized province in *Mit der Geschwindigkeit des Sommers* resists both the socioeconomic analysis of deprivation and the psychological explanation of the sister's suicide. Instead the narrative offers topographical symptoms of a profound unhappiness that, in the last analysis, remains impenetrable. Like the boys in Meyer's novel, the sister lacks both attachment to the past and belief in a better future.

Meyer's and Schoch's texts feature East German protagonists before and after the *Wende*. Duve's *Taxi* covers a similar historical time frame but concerns a Western female protagonist who cannot envision her future either. Set in affluent Hamburg, the narrative explores how Alex's temporary job as a taxi driver transmorphs into long-term entrapment in the repetitive and male-dominated world of taxi driving. Told in the first-person epic preterite, the novel is a postmodern road narrative that also challenges the gender politics of this genre. Instead of the thrill of speed and masculine agency, we are faced here with a female driver whose endless touring through the city symbolizes a debilitating circularity of time. Her sexual affairs with her overwhelmingly misogynist colleagues only reinforce the sense of isolation that dominates Alex's life. And so the car crash does not so much bring about a moment of stylized glamor and self-liberation as a parodic reenactment of the modernist speed fantasy. Neither the chimpanzee nor Alex is a suitable descendant of James Dean, whose death in his Porsche at the age of twenty-four has become one of the most iconic emblems of the nonconformist American hero.

In Meyer's, Schoch's, and Duve's textual universe, the recuperation of meaningful *Eigenzeit* remains hopeless because the protagonists inhabit an atomized or empty present without past attachments and a future horizon. The incapacitating effect of the experience of such timeless time is particularly noticeable in the failure of the biographical imagination across all three works: none of the protagonists can imagine what ought to happen in their lives. They no longer envisage the type of biography that made life in both Germanys in the second half of the twentieth century relatively predictable. After the experience of two world wars the majority of postwar Germans in the GDR and FRG embraced social stability combined with an incremental prosperity that promised to reach all. The acute anxiety caused by the Cold War, especially by the Berlin Crisis (1958–61) and the Cuban Missile Crisis (1962), only underlines the shared value of economic, social, and political stability. Ludwig Erhard, the second chancellor of the Federal Republic of Germany, famously coined the term *Wirtschaftswunder* (economic miracle) for the transformation of postwar West Germany into a prosperous society that was underpinned by a social market economy. Of course avant-garde postwar West German writers criticized a cozy social consensus that simply bypassed responsibility for the Nazi past: their long engagement with *Vergangenheitsbewältigung* aimed to purge society of National Socialism with a view to creating a democratic civic society based on tolerance and diversity. Thus in spite of considerable aesthetic differences and political disagreements, postwar German literature was, on the whole, committed to shaping a better future. By contrast, many of the texts discussed in this chapter entertain a precarious if not dystopian relationship to the future: we have seen that the protagonists have given up on a career plan and upward social mobility. These narratives diagnose an underlying lack of orientation as a signature of our age. They reinstate nihilism in response to disenchantment with history. Nietzsche's famous definition of nihilism—"Was bedeutet Nihilismus? Daß die obersten Werte sich entwerten. Es fehlt das Ziel. Es fehlt die Antwort auf das 'Wozu?'"[112] (What does nihilism stand for? That the highest values have been devalued. A central goal is lacking. The answer to the question "What for?" is lacking)—captures the devaluation of all idealistic belief systems that, for Nietzsche, infected the decadent culture of the late nineteenth century.

---

112. Friedrich Nietzsche, *Werke in drei Bänden*, ed. Karl Schlechta (Munich: Hanser, 1969), 3:557.

The experience of time and space in these texts can articulate both the quest for cultural connectedness and disconnectedness from society. As a precarious positioning within contemporary society, cultural connectedness, as I define it, has little in common with conventional identity politics. In fact, it shifts the emphasis away from the notion of a stable identity toward the idea of a fragile self that continually needs to invest energy in the project of insecure self-assurance. The endeavor required in the maintenance of cultural connectedness always points up the threatening possibility of social redundancy and entry into a state of permanent cultural disconnectedness and exclusion. Instead of the effortless delivery of gratification promised by the culture of immediacy, cultural connectedness in these texts is a precarious project, requiring considerable performative effort on the part of unstable selves, which can only ever achieve temporary attachment to a fickle environment. However, disconnectedness from mainstream society appears not only as a pathological reaction to the overwhelming demands of a world of rapid and indigestible simultaneities but also as a radical affirmation of other temporalities that strategically catapult the protagonists outside the contemporary time regime of enhanced liveness and synchronicity.

And so the heroes of these texts often resort to "principled unsociability" through the performance of melancholy.[113] The long and dazzling European tradition of melancholy discourse[114] provided those postwar German writers who were concerned with the ethical memory of the Holocaust with a rich repertoire of motifs,

---

113. On melancholy traditions in postwar German literature, see Mary Cosgrove, *Born under Auschwitz: Melancholy Traditions in Postwar German Literature* (Rochester, NY: Camden House, 2014).

114. On this issue, see Jennifer Radden, ed., *The Nature of Melancholy: From Aristotle to Kristeva* (Oxford: Oxford University Press, 2000). The scholarship on literary melancholy is too vast to be captured here. For a first insight, see Hans-Jürgen Schings, *Melancholie und Aufklärung: Melancholie und ihre Kritiker in der Erfahrungsseelenkunde des 18. Jahrhunderts* (Stuttgart: Metzler, 1977); Ludger Heidbrink, *Melancholie und Moderne: Zur Kritik der historischen Verzweiflung* (Munich: Fink, 1994); Martina Wagner-Egelhaaf, *Die Melancholie der Literatur: Diskursgeschichte und Textfiguration* (Stuttgart: Metzler, 1997).

images, and figures for a self-reflexive language of remembrance that always articulates its own limitations. Wilhelm Genazino and Arnold Stadler represent the first generation of melancholy postwar writers who no longer engage (directly) with the problem of Holocaust representation. The breaking of this link may symbolize cultural exhaustion with a discourse that, since the 1960s, invoked the nonrepresentability of the Holocaust while producing ever more images of the unimaginable. And yet, even though melancholy in contemporary German literature is no longer tied to *Vergangenheitsbewältigung*, it too taps into a sense of historical crisis. Genazino in particular stages his protagonists' profound disaffection with the here and now through the performance of melancholy. In nearly all of his novels melancholy appears both as a narrative mode and as a subjective tactic that enables his heroes to retreat into an inner world at a remove from the exterior world of the fleeting surface thrills and flashy simulacra of turbocapitalism. Besides cultivating melancholy, Genazino's heroes reclaim *Eigenzeit* through highly eccentric artistic performances. What may seem like pathetic gestures of opposition to the zeitgeist gains poetological significance through the practice of the prolonged gaze, which, as Genazino explains in his poetics lecture, continues to look at an object beyond the habitualized time. By causing perplexity in the viewer, the prolonged gaze creates a Brechtian alienation effect that makes possible different relations between selves and their environment. The attainment of happiness in unhappy times remains, however, a precarious performance that is constantly challenged by what Genazino calls the hysterical phase of capitalism, with its unrelenting onslaught of indiscreet images.

Stadler's novel illuminates the return of a religious imaginary in contemporary German literature. Prominent examples include Sibylle Lewitscharoff's *Consummatus* (2006) and *Blumenberg* (2011), Peter Henisch's *Der verirrte Messias* (The Lost Messiah, 2009), and Martin Walser's *Mein Jenseits: Novelle* (My Hereafter: A Novella, 2010) and *Muttersohn* (Mother-Son, 2011), to name but a few. While this renewed engagement with religion responds to the perceived imaginative poverty of contemporary reality, it rarely signals a return to dogmatic religion. In Stadler's

Salvatore the search for transcendence mobilizes complex cycles of remediation across genre boundaries. Faith is not a matter of doctrinal teaching here but an intermedial experience that is intended to unlock in the reader the longing for the great transcendence. This interplay of visual and narrative media might be held to resist what Hans Ulrich Gumbrecht has described as the erosion of presence in the contemporary world. We could see in chapter 1 that for Gumbrecht global media and information technologies have accelerated the elimination of corporeal presence, which has been underway since the Cartesian split between body and mind. In his view modernity caused a seismic shift from the dominant "Präsenzkultur" (culture of presence), in which knowledge depended on acts of divine revelation, toward a "Bedeutungskultur" (culture of meaning), in which the self-conscious and autonomous subject assumes the position of a disembodied observer of things.[115] In the information age, the conditions of real presence have been replaced, Gumbrecht argues, by the type of special effects that enable Batman to fly.[116] Even though Stadler shares Gumbrecht's anxiety about the creation of a monstrously disembodied and disembedded self in the digital era that is divorced from attachment to place, he aesthetically reinstates the possibility of what he calls the "große Gleichzeitigkeit, in der die Vergangenheit und die Zukunft mit der Gegenwart eins waren" (the great simultaneity in which past and future were fused with the present).[117] Remediation and intertextuality also embed the quest for transcendence historically through a circuit of exchange that takes the reader back to older narratives. From a temporal perspective, then, the quest for transcendence in contemporary German literature is fundamentally anachronic: while it gestures toward a radically different future, this future can be envisaged only through a move backward in time and the performance of cultural memory.

---

115. Gumbrecht, *Präsenz*, 291–308.
116. Gumbrecht, *Präsenz*, 291.
117. Stadler, *Salvatore*, 148.

Finally, Jenny Erpenbeck's semidocumentary novel *Gehen, ging, gegangen* turns away from the self-absorbed protagonists of Genazino's and Stadler's texts by addressing one of the most pressing issues of the twenty-first century: the enforced displacement of millions of people and the so-called refugee crisis, which is in fact a crisis of inequality. Narratologically, the text eschews the problem of speaking on behalf of the disempowered Other by filtering the stories of the African refugees through Richard's eyes, a retired professor of classics who acts as focalizer, witness, and helper. Divided by race, class, education, language, and socioeconomic factors, Richard and the young African men engage in a cautious dialogue about the men's journey to Europe, the losses they endured, their families, and homelands. Over time the asymmetrical relationship turns into a more a equitable affiliation based on the mutual recognition of grief. The exploration of individual experiences of loss and displacement prioritizes discourse over story: dialogue often alternates with free indirect speech that foregrounds Richard's own hidden and troubled past. A further facet is the careful description of a topography of displacement that encompasses Richard's house, the lake, and the temporary dwellings of the refugees as well as the totality of their remembered *lieux de mémoire*. Spatial disorientation translates into anachronic time, disrupting chronological narration: even though the narrative has a clear temporal arc, it is often suspended by the retroactive intrusion of trauma time into the present. The documentary edge of the novel derives from Erpenbeck's critical engagement with the Dublin II regulations that limit the refugees' ability to move from the country of entry to their country of choice. And so in this narrative Hartog's historiographic notion of presentism gains concrete sociohistorical meaning: it designates, firstly, the condition of those who are haunted by trauma; secondly, it refers to the experience of a European bureaucratic machine that keeps the refugees entrapped in circular movement without progress. Thirdly, the presentist reality of the refugees draws attention to their fundamental inability to plan their future. Erpenbeck's text ends with the vision of relational *Eigenzeit* that enables Richard to finally acknowledge his buried grief in the company of his old and new friends. This vision of fellowship turns the recuperation of *Eigenzeit* into a social project that requires mutual effort and time.

The texts discussed here foster asynchronous and nonchronological times. Literary precariousness thus designates the oscillating movement between social diagnosis, on the one hand, and the narration of *Eigenzeit*, on the other. Even though Meyer, Schoch, Duve, Genazino, Stadler, and Erpenbeck explore the temporal malaise of life in the twenty-first century, they depart from the dystopian conclusions that, as we saw in chapter 1, dominate many contemporary theories of social time. Commentators ranging from Rosa and Gumbrecht to Byung-Chul Han diagnose a Spenglerian ending to the modern time regime. In contrast, the writers discussed here experiment with an aesthetics of precariousness that probes the very conditions of interiority and intimacy. Such an aesthetics of precariousness is premised on realization through the act of reading, which enables the reader to experience temporal particularity or *Eigenzeit*. Literary texts are particularly apt at transmuting temporal anxiety precisely because they can suspend our habitual perceptions and expectations in favor of make-believe. They have the power to defamiliarize us from our worlds through acts of fictionalization that, in the words of Wolfgang Iser, involve "a constant crossing of boundaries between the real and the imaginary."[118]

---

118. Wolfgang Iser, "Fictionalizing Acts," *Amerikastudien/American Studies* 31 (1985): 5.

5

Epilogue

Presentist Dystopias or the Case for Environmental Humanities

In 2017 the renowned German writer Juli Zeh published *Leere Herzen* (Empty Hearts), a dystopian novel that imagines life in postdemocratic Germany and Europe.[1] Regula Freyer, the leader of the Besorgte Bürger Bewegung (Concerned Citizens Movement), has taken over from Angela Merkel, who was forced to leave the political stage eight years previously, suddenly looking like a sad old woman. Modeled on various current right-wing movements, the BBB is a democratically elected party that, on its journey to power, successfully exploited the electorate's widespread political apathy. Besides introducing a basic income for all to keep protest at bay, the ruling party has launched various "Effizienzpakete" (efficiency packages), which, in the name of economic efficiency, have

---

1. Juli Zeh, *Leere Herzen* (Munich: Luchterhand, 2017).

already massively curtailed civil rights and undermined central democratic institutions. For example, the German supreme court is now made up of only three judges (instead of sixteen), and the newly established Bundeszentrale für Leitkultur (Federal Agency for the Lead Culture) oversees the government's identitarian politics. Arabic tearooms have been closed down, and the Qu'ran has been banned from bookshops. On the European stage Frexit (the departure of France from the EU) and Spexit (the departure of Spain from the EU) sound the imminent death knell for the EU; in the international arena Trump and Putin have forged an autocratic transatlantic alliance, ending the war in Syria.

Pervasive postdemocratic attitudes and political indifference have enabled Britta Söldner and her business partner Babak Hamwi to develop a new business model. Their company Brücke (Bridge), ostensibly a therapeutic practice for patients with suicidal thoughts, is in reality just a front for an employment agency for suicide bombers. With the help of data mining they identify potential suicide candidates, who, after a careful algorithmic selection process, sign up for a tough psychological and physical "evaluation program" that establishes suicidal intention on a scale of 1 to 10. Nine candidates leave the program in the early stages and resume their ordinary lives, but every tenth candidate reaches level 10 and is thus deemed to be suitable for a suicide attack. The Brücke's clients include radicalized eco and animal rights groups as well as splinter Islamic factions who pay high fees to contract suicide bombers. As a company director, Britta lives in complete harmony with the zeitgeist: the reintegration of nine out of ten potential suicide candidates has produced declining suicide figures, and the careful management of the rare suicide attacks is preventing collateral damage. In a nutshell, Britta embodies a form of "pragmatic nihilism" that has long abandoned the common good in favor of her narrowly defined interests, which revolve around her business, her family, and a few friends.

Zeh's novel does not rank among her highest literary achievements. Many reviewers have criticized the schematic and wooden characterization, her handling of dialogue and clichéd plot elements that too easily reveal their anchorage in current affairs.[2] And yet, from a temporal perspective, *Leere Herzen* is an intriguing novel: it places what one might call a "plausible dystopia" within close reach of our disillusioned age. Dystopia no longer designates the final apocalyptic catastrophe that dramatically unfolds in the distant future but rather the gradual erosion of democracy in the here and now. Some critics have read Zeh's book as a riposte to Michel Houellebecq's controversial *La soumission* (2015; *Submission*, 2015), which imagines the step-by-step islamification of France by democratic means.[3] There is, however, a second allusion that illuminates the profound foreclosure of the future that has featured so prominently in my book. Overtly, the title of Zeh's novel refers to a pop song that, in the novel, is at the top of the charts and sung by Julietta, a young woman from a middle-class background who commits a spectacular suicide attack at the end: "When the future has passed, the past will return. One day you'll be asked what you did, baby. Full hands, empty hearts, it's a suicide world" (LH, 232). But the recurring leitmotif "full hands, empty hearts" also alludes to Fritz Lang's iconic film *Metropolis*, which, as I have shown in chapter 2, projected the revolutionary potential of modern technology onto the figure of the female robot. *Metropolis* reins in its dazzling depiction of a sci-fi future through its conservative handling of class conflict. Intertitles translate the clash between the master of the metropolis and the exploited workers into the fairly conventional dichotomy of "Hirn und Hände" (head and hands) that requires the female heart as mediator. The death of the female robot at the end safeguards conventional gender roles as embodied by Maria, the real woman with a real heart. And so the final intertitle reinstates a traditional vision of social harmony: "Mittler zwischen Hirn und Hand muss das Herz sein" (The mediator

---

2. See Jacqueline Thör, "Gibt es noch Hoffnung in Dunkeldeutschland?," *Die Zeit Online*, 14 November 2017; Julia Encke, "Wo geht's zum Abgrund?," *Frankfurter Allgemeine Zeitung*, 16 November 2017; Gustav Seibt, "Jede Gesellschaft braucht eine Dosis Amok," *Die Süddeutsche Zeitung*, 14 November 2017; Björn Hayer, "Im Inneren der Wohlstandsblase," *Der Spiegel*, 13 November 2017.

3. Michel Houellebecq, *Submission*, trans. Lorin Stein (London: Vintage, 2016).

between head and hand must be the heart). Evidently, Zeh's novel overturns this version of social harmony. Britta is an entrepreneur with a cool and calculating head who skillfully exploits the business opportunities of postdemocracy—her heart only beats for her most private affairs. By contrast, Julietta, the suicide bomber, is a disillusioned moralist who becomes the willing hand in Britta's brainy scheme that will see off a rival suicide agency. There is no place for mediation by the heart: "It's a suicide world, baby."

Fritz Lang's futurist vision was separated from the world of 1927 by 100 years; Zeh's political dystopia is set in 2025 and thus less than ten years from 2019. It shares its shrunken timescale with other recent apocalyptic narratives that also place the catastrophe within our sight.[4] These "presentist" versions radically reduce the temporal horizon and narrative arc of the secular apocalypse that, as Eva Horn has so brilliantly shown, stages a dramatic tipping point as the point of no return.[5] The embodiment of the missed tipping point is the last human being on earth. A genuinely modern figure of thought, he/she is the only survivor on the planet, who inspects the totality of destruction, while realizing the belatedness of this insight.[6] As Horn argues, postapocalyptic narratives look back at life in the future perfect in order to mobilize prevention. Prevention, explains Horn, relies on the fictional emplotment of events that must be stopped from unfolding.[7] The double structure of prevention recasts the present as a point of bifurcation, thereby envisaging two futures, one in which the catastrophic has been prevented and one in which the tipping point has been surpassed.

---

4. See also Karen Duve, *Macht* (Cologne: Kiepenheuer & Witsch, 2016), which is set in Germany in 2031. Vladimir Sorokin's *Day of the Oprichnik*, trans. Jamey Gambrell (New York: Farrar, Straus and Giroux, 2011), is set in Russia in 2028.

5. See Eva Horn, *Zukunft als Katastrophe* (Frankfurt a. Main: Fischer, 2014). See also Silke Horstkotte, "Die Zeit endet und das Ende der Zeit: Apokalyptisches Erzählen in Thomas Lehrs 42 und Thomas Glavinics *Die Arbeit der Nacht*," *Oxford German Studies* 46/4 (2017): 403–15.

6. "Der Letzte Mensch ist die Antizipation einer späten, endgültigen Einsicht, deren ganze Trostlosigkeit darin liegt, dass diese Einsicht nichts mehr nützt." (The last man anticipates a late and definitive insight which is so despondent precisely because it is useless.) Horn, *Zukunft als Katastrophe*, 29.

7. Horn, *Zukunft als Katastrophe*, 304.

The question then is to what extent this preventative logic still applies to the presentist dystopias that I have sketched above. By radically shrinking the temporal gap between now and the future, Zeh's dystopia suspends the future perfect as an enabling perspective that can mobilize preventative action. By contrast to the apocalyptic staging of the tipping point that terminates life on this planet, presentist dystopias envisage the future as unfolding incrementally and cumulatively in our extended present. "The future is now" no longer designates the emancipatory desire of political activists but blocked bifurcation in the present.

Adopting a broader perspective, then, these plausible dystopias could be read to amplify the collapse of the modern time regime that, as this study has argued, preoccupies historians, philosophers, social scientists, cultural theorists, artists, filmmakers, and writers alike. We have seen that the modern experience of historical time required sufficient distance between the experience of the real world and the horizon of expectation. The idea of historical progress thus presupposed the systemic asymmetry between experience and expectation, which, in turn, produced various modern speed fantasies. However, in the Anthropocene this model has spectacularly crashed, leaving us stranded in an omnivorous present with no vision of a stretching horizon. In a manner of speaking we are all gazing at the ominous gray and laden horizon that, in Ulrich Wüst's iconic photograph from 1989, seemed to foreclose the future of the East Germans with their baggage on the beach. For François Hartog and Hans Ulrich Gumbrecht, we are moored in a presentist experience of history that is "shadowed by entropy, consigned to the immediate, the instantaneous, and the ephemeral."[8] While these critics mourn the loss of historicity, others welcome the end of the Western time regime precisely because it brutally promoted linear development at the expense of alternate temporal models in other parts of the world. Christophe Bonneuil and Jean-Baptiste Fressoz remind us that the modern

---

8. Hartog, *Regimes*, 203.

time regime and vision of history were inextricably based on the Cartesian split between nature and culture and the ensuing objectification of and abstraction from nature.[9] The outsourcing of human history from the history of the earth and the epistemological partitioning of the human species from the animal and plant worlds gave rise to and legitimated the anthropocentric worldview that seemingly emancipated human time from the time of nature. The original Cartesian sin also manifests itself in a system of knowledge that completely separated the natural sciences from the social and human sciences, thereby further obfuscating the precarious interdependence of all life on the planet. It is one of the great ironies that the so-called Anthropocene finally unmasks the unsustainability of anthropocentrism. Bruno Latour, Bonneuil, and Fressoz are among those who propose a different ecology of knowledge:

> The new geohistorical epoch signals the irruption of the Earth (its temporality, its limits, its systemic dynamics) into what sought to be a history, an economy and a society emancipating themselves from natural constraints. It signals the return of the Earth into a world that Western industrial modernity on the whole represented to itself as above earthly foundations. If our future involves the geological swing of the Earth into a new state, we can no longer believe in a humanity making its own history by itself. . . . The Anthropocene thus requires the substitution of the "ungrounded" humanities of industrial modernity by new environmental humanities that adventure beyond the great separation between environment and society.[10]

Indeed, environmental humanities steeped in the planetary consciousness of the precariousness of all life systems would be a project worth pursuing. Part of this new project should be a way of

---

9. Christophe Bonneuil and Jean-Baptiste Fressoz, *The Shock of the Anthropocene: The Earth, History, and Us,* trans. David Fernbach (London: Verso, 2017).

10. Bonneuil and Fressoz, *The Shock of the Anthropocene,* 32–33. See also Bruno Latour, *Das terrestrische Manifest,* trans. Bernd Schwibs (Frankfurt a. Main: Suhrkamp, 2018).

thinking about time and temporality that, instead of denigrating alternative trajectories and timescapes, views them as potential sites of Other time(s). The analysis of diverse aesthetics of *Eigenzeit* in works of art and literature, in films and performances, illuminates alternative ecologies of time that, precisely because they are precarious and inconclusive, can attune us to an ethical planetary consciousness.

BIBLIOGRAPHY

Primary Sources

Als wir träumten. Director: Andreas Dresen. Script: Wolfgang Kohlhaase. Producer: Peter Rommel. Germany, France 2015. DVD: Pandora Filme 2015.

Altenberg, Peter. *Auswahl aus seinen Büchern.* Edited by Karl Kraus. Frankfurt a. Main: Insel, 1997.

Barbara. Director: Christian Petzold. Script: Christian Petzold and Harun Farocki. Production: Schramm Film Koerner & Weber 2012. DVD: Indigo 2012.

Berlin: Sinfonie der Großstadt. Director: Walter Ruttmann. Production: Karl Freund. Deutsche Vereins-Film AG/Fox Europa 1927.

Duve, Karen. *Macht.* Cologne: Kiepenheuer & Witsch, 2016.

———. *Taxi.* Frankfurt a. Main: Eichborn, 2008.

Erpenbeck, Jenny. *Aller Tage Abend.* Munich: Knaus, 2012.

———. *The End of Days.* Translated by Susan Bernofsky. London: Portobello, 2014.

———. *Gehen, ging, gegangen.* Munich: Knaus, 2015.

———. *Go, Went, Gone.* Translated by Susan Bernofsky. London: Portobello Books, 2017.

———. *Heimsuchung.* Berlin: Eichborn, 2008.

———. *Visitation*. Translated by Susan Bernofsky. New York: New Directions, 2010.

Genazino, Wilhelm. *Abschaffel*. Munich: dtv, 2002.

———. *Die Belebung der toten Winkel: Frankfurter Poetikvorlesungen.* Munich: Carl Hanser, 2006.

———. *Der gedehnte Blick*. Frankfurt a. Main: dtv, 2007.

———. *Das Glück in glücksfernen Zeiten*. Munich: Hanser, 2009.

Henisch, Peter. *Der verirrte Messias*. Munich: dtv, 2012.

Homer. *The Odyssey*. Translated by A. S. Kline. *Poetry in Translation 2004*, http://www.poetryintranslation.com/PITBR/Greek/Odyssey12.htm#anchor_Toc90268047.

Houellebecq, Michel. *Submission*. Translated by Lorin Stein. London: Vintage, 2016.

Kafka, Franz. *Amerika (The Man Who Disappeared)*. Translated by Michael Hofmann. London: Penguin, 1996.

———. *Josefine, die Sängerin oder Das Volk der Mäuse*. In *Ein Landarzt und andere Drucke zu Lebzeiten*, 274–94. Frankfurt a. Main: Fischer, 1994.

———. *Josefine, the Singer, or The Mouse People*. Translated with an introduction by Michael Hofmann, 228–44. London: Penguin Books, 2007.

———. *Der Proceß: Roman in der Fassung der Handschrift*. Frankfurt a. Main: Fischer, 1995.

———. "Das Schweigen der Sirenen." In *Beim Bau der chinesischen Mauer und andere Schriften aus dem Nachlaß*, 68–70. Frankfurt a. Main: Fischer, 1994.

———. *The Trial*. Translated by Breon Mitchell. New York: Schocken, 1998.

———. *Der Verschollene: Roman in der Fassung der Handschrift*. Frankfurt a. Main: Fischer, 1994.

Kracauer, Siegfried. "Der Kult der Zerstreuung" (1926). In *Das Ornament der Masse: Essays*, 311–17. Frankfurt a. Main: Suhrkamp, 1977.

Lewitscharoff, Sibylle. *Blumenberg*. Frankfurt a. M.: Suhrkamp, 2011.

———. *Consummatus*. Frankfurt a. Main: Suhrkamp, 2010.

Mann, Thomas. *Buddenbrooks: Verfall einer Familie*. Frankfurt a. Main: Fischer, 1997.

———. *The Magic Mountain*. Translated by John E. Woods. New York: Everyman's Library, 2005.

———. *Der Tod in Venedig und andere Erzählungen*. Frankfurt a. Main: Fischer, 1987.

———. *Der Zauberberg*. Frankfurt a. Main: Fischer, 1979.

Marina Abramovic, The Artist Is Present. Directors: Matthew Akers, Jeffrey Dupre. Dogwoof Studio. DVD release 2012.

Metropolis. Director: Fritz Lang. Production: Erich Pommer. UFA 1927.

Meyer, Clemens. *Als wir träumten*. Frankfurt a. M: Fischer, 2011.

Musil, Robert. *Der Mann ohne Eigenschaften*. In *Gesammelte Werke in neun Bänden*, edited by Adolf Frisé, vol. 1. Reinbek: Rowohlt, 1978.

———. *Die Verwirrungen des Zöglings Törless*. In *Gesammelte Werke in neun Bänden*, edited by Adolf Frisé, 6:7–140. Reinbek: Rowohlt, 1981.

Nietzsche, Friedrich. *On the Uses and Disadvantages of History for Life.* Translated by R. J. Hollingdale. Cambridge: Cambridge University Press, 1997.

———. *Vom Nutzen und Nachteil der Historie für das Leben.* Stuttgart: Reclam, 1999.

Paradies: Glaube. Director: Ulrich Seidl. Production: Ulrich Seidl Film Koproduktion 2013. DVD: Good Movies 2013.

Paradies: Hoffnung. Director: Ulrich Seidl. Script: Ulrich Seidl. Production: Ulrich Seidl Film Koproduktion 2013. DVD: Good Movies 2013.

Paradies: Liebe. Director: Ulrich Seidl. Production: Ulrich Seidl Film Koproduktion 2012. DVD: Good Movies 2013.

Schoch, Julia. *Mit der Geschwindigkeit des Sommers.* Munich: Piper, 2009.

Seiler, Lutz. *Kruso.* Berlin: Suhrkamp 2014.

Simmel, Georg, "Die Großstädte und das Geistesleben." In *Gesamtausgabe,* edited by Rüdiger Kramme, 7:227–42. Frankfurt a. Main: Suhrkamp, 1995.

———. "The Metropolis and Mental Life." In *Simmel on Culture,* edited by David Frisby and Mike Featherstone, 174–85. London: Sage, 1997.

Sorokin, Vladimir. *Day of the Oprichnik.* Translated by Jamey Gambrell. New York: Farrar, Straus and Giroux, 2011.

Stadler, Arnold. *Einmal auf der Welt. Und dann so.* Frankfurt a. Main: Fischer, 2009.

———. *Ein hinreissender Schrotthändler.* Cologne: DuMont, 2010.

———. "Im Grunde war alles nach Hause geschrieben: Dankrede zur Verleihung des Marie-Luise-Kaschnitz-Preises 1998." In *"Als wäre er ein anderer gewesen": Zum Werk Arnold Stadlers,* edited by Pia Reinacher, 119–25. Frankfurt a. Main: Fischer, 2009.

———. *Salvatore.* Frankfurt a. Main: Suhrkamp, 2008.

———. *Sehnsucht: Versuch über das erste Mal.* Cologne: DuMont, 2002.

Toni Erdmann. Director: Maren Ade. Script: Maren Ade. Production: Komplizen-Film 2016. DVD: Eurovideo Medien 2016.

Walser, Martin. *Mein Jenseits.* Berlin: Berlin University Press, 2010.

———. *Muttersohn.* Reinbek: Rowohlt, 2011.

Walser, Robert. *Kritische Ausgabe sämtlicher Drucke und Manuskripte.* Edited by Wolfram Groddeck and Barbara von Reibnitz. Vol. III.1, *Drucke im Berliner Tagblatt,* ed. Hans-Joachim Heerde. Frankfurt a. Main: Stroemfeld, 2013.

———. *Sämtliche Werke in Einzelausgaben.* Edited by Jochen Greven. 20 vols. Frankfurt a. Main: Suhrkamp, 1986.

———. *The Walk and Other Stories.* Translated by Christopher Middleton. London: Serpent's Tail, 1992.

Wesely, Michael. *Ostdeutschland.* Edited by Galerie Fahnemann. Cologne: Walter König, 2004.

Wüst, Ulrich. *Später Sommer/Letzter Herbst.* Heidelberg: Kehrer, 2016.

Zeh, Juli. *Leere Herzen.* Munich: Luchterhand, 2017.

Literature on Time and Space

Adam, Barbara. *Time*. Cambridge: Polity, 2004.

———. *Timewatch: The Social Analysis of Time*. Cambridge: Polity, 1995.

Appadurai, Arjun. *The Future as Cultural Fact: Essays on the Global Condition*. London: Verso, 2013.

Assmann, Aleida. *Ist die Zeit aus den Fugen? Aufstieg und Fall des Zeitregimes der Moderne*. Munich: Hanser, 2013.

Bauman, Zygmunt. *Liquid Times: Living in an Age of Uncertainty*. Cambridge: Polity, 2007.

Beck, Ulrich. *Weltrisikogesellschaft: Auf der Suche nach der verlorenen Sicherheit*. Frankfurt a. Main: Suhrkamp, 2008.

Bergson, Henri. *Matter and Memory*. Translated by Nancy Margaret Paul and W. Scott Palmer. London: George Allen and Unwin, 1911.

Berman, Marshall. *All That Is Solid Melts into Air: The Experience of Modernity*. 1982. London: Verso, 2010.

Bloch, Ernst. *Erbschaft dieser Zeit*. Frankfurt a. Main: Suhrkamp, 1962.

Bohrer, Karlheinz. *Plötzlichkeit: Zum Augenblick des ästhetischen Scheins*. Frankfurt a. Main: Suhrkamp, 1981.

Bonneuil, Christophe, and Jean-Baptiste Fressoz. *The Shock of the Anthropocene: The Earth, History, and Us*. Translated by David Fernbach. London: Verso, 2017.

Borscheid, Peter. *Das Tempo-Virus: Eine Kulturgeschichte der Beschleunigung*. Frankfurt a. Main: Campus, 2004.

Bragaglia, Anton Giulio. "Excerpts from Futurist Photodynamism." In *Photography in the Modern Era: European Documents and Critical Writings, 1913–1940*, edited by C. Phillips, 287–95. New York: Metropolitan Museum of Modern Art, 1989.

Brose, Hanns-Georg, "Das Gleichzeitige ist ungleichzeitig: Über den Umgang mit einer Paradoxie und die Transformation der Zeit." In *Unsichere Zeiten: Herausforderungen gesellschaftlicher Transformationen; Verhandlungen des 34. Kongresses der Deutschen Gesellschaft für Soziologie in Jena 2008*, edited by Hans-Georg Soeffner, Kathy Kursawe, Margrit Elsner, and Manja Aldt, 547–62. Wiesbaden: Springer, 2010.

Castells, Manuel. "Grassrooting the Space of Flows." *Urban Geography* 20/4 (1999): 294–302.

———. *The Rise of the Network Society*. 2nd ed. Oxford: Blackwell, 2000.

Crary, Jonathan. *24/7: Late Capitalism and the Ends of Sleep*. London: Verso, 2013.

———. *Suspensions of Perceptions: Attention, Spectacle, and Modern Culture*. Cambridge, MA: MIT Press, 1999.

Dohrn-van Rossum, Gerhard. *Die Geschichte der Stunde: Uhren und moderne Zeitordnungen*. Cologne: Anaconda, 2007.

Duffy, Enda. *The Speed Handbook: Velocity, Pleasure, Modernism*. Durham, NC: Duke University Press, 2009.

Elias, Norbert. *Über die Zeit.* Edited by Michael Schröter. Frankfurt a. Main: Suhrkamp, 1988.

Eriksen, Thomas Hylland. *Tyranny of the Moment: Fast and Slow Time in the Information Age.* London: Pluto Press, 2001.

Fritzsche, Peter. "1989 and the Chronological Imagination." In *Debating German Cultural Identity since 1989,* edited by Anne Fuchs, Kathleen James-Chakraborty, and Linda Shortt, 7–29. Rochester, NY: Camden House, 2011.

Fuchs, Anne. "Defending Lateness: Deliberations on Acceleration, Attention, and Lateness, 1900–2000." In "Figuring Lateness," edited by Karen Leeder, special issue, *New German Critique* 125/42 (2015): 31–48.

———. "'Der Zauderrhythmus des Lebens': Freuds *Jenseits des Lustprinzips* und der Zeitdiskurs der Gegenwart." *Westend: Neue Zeitschrift für Sozialforschung* 1 (2015): 27–45.

Fuchs, Anne, and J. J. Long, eds. *Time in German Literature and Culture, 1900–2015: Between Acceleration and Slowness.* Houndmills: Palgrave Macmillan, 2016.

Glennie, Paul, and Nigel Thrift. *Shaping the Day: A History of Timekeeping in England and Wales, 1300–1800.* Oxford: Oxford University Press, 2011.

Göttsche, Dirk, ed. *Critical Time in Modern German Literature and Culture.* Oxford: Peter Lang, 2016.

Gumbrecht, Hans Ulrich. *Präsenz.* Edited with an afterword by Jürgen Klein. Frankfurt a. Main: Suhrkamp, 2012.

———. *Unsere breite Gegenwart.* Frankfurt a. Main: Suhrkamp, 2010.

Hammer, Espen. *Philosophy and Temporality from Kant to Critical Theory.* Cambridge: Cambridge University Press, 2011.

Han, Byung-Chul. *Digitale Rationalität und das Ende des kommunikativen Handelns.* Berlin: Matthes & Seitz, 2013.

———. *Duft der Zeit: Ein philosophischer Essay zur Kunst des Verweilens.* Berlin: Transcript, 2009.

———. *Hyperkulturalität: Kultur und Globalisierung.* Berlin: Merve, 2005.

Hartog, François. *Regimes of Historicity: Presentism and the Experiences of Time.* Translated by Saskia Brown. New York: Columbia University Press, 2015.

Harvey, David. *The Condition of Postmodernity: An Enquiry into the Origins of Cultural Change.* Cambridge: Blackwell, 1989.

———. *Spaces of Global Capitalism: Towards a Theory of Uneven Geographical Development.* London: Verso, 2006.

Hassan, Robert. "Network Time." In *24/7: Time and Temporality in Network Society,* edited by Robert Hassan and E. Purser, 37–61. Stanford, CA: Stanford Business Books, 2007.

Hengsbach, Friedhelm. *Die Zeit gehört uns: Widerstand gegen das Regime der Beschleunigung.* Frankfurt a. Main: Westend, 2012.

Holford-Strevens, Leofranc. *The History of Time: A Very Short Introduction.* Oxford: Oxford University Press, 2005.

Hölscher, Lucian. *Die Entdeckung der Zukunft*. Frankfurt a. Main: Suhrkamp, 1999.

Horn, Eva. *Zukunft als Katastrophe*. Frankfurt a. Main: Fischer, 2014.

Horstkotte, Silke. "Die Zeit endet und das Ende der Zeit: Apokalyptisches Erzählen in Thomas Lehrs *42* und Thomas Glavinics *Die Arbeit der Nacht*." *Oxford German Studies* 46/4 (2017): 403–15.

Keightley, Emily, ed. *Time, Media, and Modernity*. Basingstoke: Palgrave Macmillan, 2012.

Kelly, Michael R. "Phenomenology and Time-Consciousness." *Internet Encyclopedia of Philosophy. A Peer-Reviewed Academic Resource.* http://www.iep.utm.edu/phe-time/ (accessed 10 January 2018).

Kern, Stephen. *The Culture of Time and Space, 1880–1918*. Cambridge, MA: Harvard University Press, 2003.

Koepnick, Lutz. *On Slowness: Toward an Aesthetic of the Contemporary*. New York: Columbia University Press, 2014.

Koselleck, Reinhart. *Futures Past: On the Semantics of Historical Time*. Translated by Keith Tribe. New York: Columbia University Press, 2004.

———. *The Practice of Conceptual History—Timing History—Spacing Concepts*. Translated by Todd Samuel Presner. Foreword by Hayden White. Stanford, CA: Stanford University Press, 2002.

Leccardi, Carmen. "New Temporal Perspectives in the High-Speed Society." In *24/7: Time and Temporality in the Network Society*, edited by Robert Hassan and Ronald E. Purser, 25–36. Stanford, CA: Stanford Business Books, 2007.

Marx, Karl, and Friedrich Engels. *Das Manifest der kommunistischen Partei*. Kommentierte Studienausgabe, edited by Theo Stammen and Alexander Classen. Munich: Fink/UTB, 2009.

———. *Manifesto of the Communist Party: A Modern Edition*. With an introduction by Tariq Ali. London: Verso, 2016.

Massey, Doreen. *For Space*. London: Sage, 2010.

May, Jon, and Nigel Thrift, eds. *TimeSpace: Geographies of Temporality*. London: Routledge, 2001.

McQuire, Scott. "City Times: Negotiating Public Space in the Twenty-First-Century City." In *Time, Media, and Modernity*, edited by Emily Keightley, 123–42. Basingstoke: Palgrave Macmillan, 2012.

Nowotny, Helga. *Eigenzeit: Entstehung und Strukturierung eines Zeitgefühls*. Frankfurt a. Main: Suhrkamp, 1993.

———. *Time: The Modern and Postmodern Experience*. Cambridge: Polity, 1996.

Osborne, Peter. *The Politics of Time: Modernity and Avant-Garde*. London: Verso, 1995.

Rosa, Hartmut. *Beschleunigung: Die Veränderung der Zeitstrukturen in der Moderne*. Frankfurt a. Main: Suhrkamp, 2005.

———. *Resonance: A Sociology of Our Relationship to the World*. Translated by James C. Wagner. Cambridge: Polity, 2019.

————. *Resonanz: Eine Soziologie der Weltbeziehung*. Frankfurt a. Main: Suhrkamp, 2016.

————. *Social Acceleration: A New Theory of Modernity*. Translated by Jonathan Trejo-Mathys. New York: Columbia University Press, 2015.

————. *Weltbeziehungen im Zeitalter der Beschleunigung: Umrisse einer neuen Gesellschaftskritik*. Frankfurt a. Main: Suhrkamp, 2012.

Schlögl, Karl. *Im Raume lesen wir die Zeit: Über Zivilisationsgeschichte und Geopolitik*. Frankfurt a. Main: Fischer, 2006.

Tomlinson, John. *The Culture of Speed: The Coming of Immediacy*. London: Sage, 2007.

Tuan, Yi-Fu. *Topophilia: A Study of Environmental Perception, Attitudes, and Values*. New York: Columbia University Press, 1990.

van Dijck, José. *The Culture of Connectivity: A Critical History of Social Media*. Oxford: Oxford University Press, 2013.

van Dijk, Jan. "The One-Dimensional Network Society of Manuel Castells." *New Media & Society* 1 (1999): 127–38.

Virilio, Paul. *Negative Horizon: An Essay in Dromoscopy*. Translated by Michael Degener. London: Continuum, 2005.

Wajcman, Judy. *Pressed for Time: The Acceleration of Life in Digital Capitalism*. Chicago: University of Chicago Press, 2015.

White, Hayden. *Metahistory: The Historical Imagination in Nineteenth-Century Europe*. 1975. Baltimore: Johns Hopkins University Press, 2014.

Other Secondary Sources

Adorno, Theodor, and Max Horkheimer. *Dialektik der Aufklärung*. In *Gesammelte Schriften*, vol. 3. Frankfurt a. Main: Suhrkamp, 1981.

Allemann, Beda. "Noch einmal Kafkas *Process*." In *Zeit und Geschichte im Werk Kafkas*, 101–14. Göttingen: Wallstein, 1998.

Althaus, Thomas, Wolfgang Bunzel, and Dirk Göttsche. "Ränder, Schwellen, Zwischenräume: Zum Standort Kleiner Prosa im Literatursystem der Moderne." In *Kleine Prosa: Theorie und Geschichte eines Textfeldes im Literatursystem der Moderne*, edited by Thomas Althaus, Wolfgang Bunzel, and Dirk Göttsche, ix–xxvii. Tübingen: Niemeyer, 2007.

Appadurai, Arjun. *Modernity at Large: Cultural Dimensions of Globalisation*. 2nd ed. 1996. Minneapolis: University of Minnesota Press, 2000.

Aristotle. *Nikomachische Ethik*. Translated by Frank Dirlmeier. Stuttgart: Reclam, 1969.

Assmann, Jan. *Die mosaische Unterscheidung oder der Preis des Monotheismus*. Munich: Hanser, 2003.

————. *Religion and Cultural Memory: Ten Studies*. Translated by Rodney Livingstone. Stanford, CA: Stanford University Press, 2006.

Auerochs, Bernd. "Innehalten vor der Schwelle: Kafkas 'Vor dem Gesetz' im Kontext der traditionellen Parabel." In *Grenzsituationen: Wahrnehmung, Bedeutung und Gestaltung in der neueren Literatur*, edited by Dorothea

Lauterbach, Uwe Spörl, and Ulrich Wunderlich, 131–50. Göttingen: Vandenhoeck & Ruprecht, 2002.

Augé, Marc. *Non-Places: Introduction to an Anthropology of Supermodernity.* Translated by John Howe. London: Verso, 1995.

Bachelard, Gaston. *The Poetics of Space.* Translated by Maria Jolas. Boston: Beacon Press, 1969.

Bachtin, Michail M. *Literatur und Karneval: Zur Romantheorie und Lachkultur.* Translated by Alexander Kämpfe. Frankfurt a. Main: Fischer, 2000.

———. *Rabelais und seine Welt: Volkskultur als Gegenkultur.* Edited by Renate Lachmann. Frankfurt a. Main: Suhrkamp, 1995.

Bakhtin, Mikhail M. *The Dialogic Imagination: Four Essays.* Edited by Michael Holquist. Translated by Caryl Emerson and Michael Holquist. Austin: University of Texas Press, 1981.

Barthes, Roland. *Camera Lucida: Reflections on Photography.* Translated by R. Howard. New York: Vintage Classics, 1993.

Bauman, Zygmunt. *Globalization: The Human Consequences.* Cambridge: Polity, 1998.

Bazin, André. "The Ontology of the Photographic Image." In *Classic Essays on Photography*, edited by A. Trachtenberg, translated by H. Gray, 237–44. New Haven, CT: Leete's Island Books, 1980.

Benjamin, Walter. "Das Paris des Second Empire bei Baudelaire." In *Abhandlungen—Gesammelte Schriften*, edited by Rolf Tiedemann and Hermann Schweppenhäuser, I.2:513–604. Frankfurt a. Main: Suhrkamp, 1991.

———. "Robert Walser." In *Über Robert Walser.* Edited by Katharina Kerr, 1:126–29. Frankfurt a. Main: Suhrkamp, 1978.

Binder, Hartmut. *Vor dem Gesetz: Einführung in Kafkas Welt.* Stuttgart: Metzler, 1993.

Blees, Thomas. *Glienicker Brücke: Schauplatz der Geschichte.* Berlin: Berlin Edition, 2010.

Boa, Elizabeth. "Global Intimations: Cultural Geography in *Buddenbrooks*, *Tonio Kröger*, and *Der Tod in Venedig.*" *Oxford German Studies* 35 (2006): 21–33.

———. *Kafka: Gender, Class, and Race in the Letters and Fictions.* Oxford: Clarendon, 1996.

———. "Karl Rossmann and, or the Boy Who Wouldn't Grow Up: The Flight from Manhood in Franz Kafka's *Der Verschollene.*" In *From Goethe to Gide: Feminism, Aesthetics, and the French and German Literary Canon, 1770–1936*, edited by Mary Orr and Lesley Sharpe, 168–83. Exeter: University of Exeter Press, 2005.

Boa, Elizabeth, and Rachel Palfreyman. *Heimat—A German Dream: Regional Loyalties and National Identity in German Culture, 1890–1990.* Oxford: Oxford University Press, 2000.

Bourdieu, Pierre. "First Lecture: Social Space and Symbolic Space; Introduction to a Japanese Distinction." *Poetics Today* 12 (1991): 627–38.

Boym, Svetlana. *The Future of Nostalgia.* New York: Basic Books, 2001.

Bragaglia, Anton Giulio. "Excerpts from Futurist Photodynamism." In *Photography in the Modern Era: European Documents and Critical Writings, 1913–1940*, edited by C. Phillips, 287–95. New York: Metropolitan Museum of Modern Art, 1989.

Bronfen, Elisabeth. *Der literarische Raum: Eine Untersuchung am Beispiel von Dorothy M. Richardson's "Pilgrimage."* Tübingen: Niemeyer, 1986.

Bude, Heinz, and Andreas Willisch, eds. *Exklusion: Die Debatte über die "Überflüssigen."* Frankfurt a. Main: Suhrkamp, 2008.

Bultmann, Rudolf. *New Testament and Mythology and Other Basic Writings.* Edited by Schubert M. Ogden. Philadelphia: Fortress Press, 1984.

Burton, Richard. *The Anatomy of Melancholy.* Edited with an introduction by Holbrook Jackson. New York: New York Review of Books, 2002.

Butler, Judith. *Precarious Life: The Powers of Mourning and Violence.* London: Verso, 2004.

Castel, Robert, and Klaus Dörre, eds. *Prekariat, Abstieg, Ausgrenzung: Die soziale Frage am Beginn des 21. Jahrhunderts.* Frankfurt am Main: Campus, 2009.

Cohn, Doritt. "Metalepsis and Mise en Abyme." *Narrative* 20/1 (2012): 105–14.

Comay, Rebecca. "Adorno's Siren Song." *New German Critique* 81 (2000): 21–48.

Cooke, Paul. "Performing 'Ostalgie': Leander Haußmann's *Sonnenallee* (1999)." *German Life & Letters* 56 (2003): 156–67.

Corrigan, Timothy. "Still Speed: Cinematic Acceleration, Value, and Execution." *Cinema Journal* 55/2 (2016): 119–25.

Cosgrove, Mary. *Born under Auschwitz: Melancholy Traditions in Postwar German Literature.* Rochester, NY: Camden House, 2014.

———. "Heimat as Non-Place and Terrain Vague in Jenny Erpenbeck's *Heimsuchung* and Julia Schoch's *Mit der Geschwindigkeit des Sommers.*" In "Transformations of German Cultural Identity, 1989–2009," edited by Anne Fuchs and Kathleen James-Chakraborty, special issue, *New German Critique* 116 (2012): 63–86.

———. "The Temporality of Boredom in the Age of Acceleration: The Car Crash in Contemporary German Literature." In *Time in German Literature and Culture, 1900–2015: Between Acceleration and Slowness*, edited by Anne Fuchs and J. J. Long, 204–17. Houndmills: Palgrave Macmillan, 2016.

———. "The Time of Sloth in Terézia Mora's *Der einzige Mann auf dem Kontinent.*" In "*Ästhetische Eigenzeit* in Contemporary German Literature and Culture, Part II," edited by Anne Fuchs and Ines Detmers, special issue, *Oxford German Studies* 46/4 (2017): 374–88.

De Luca, Tiago. "Slow Time, Visible Cinema: Duration, Experience, and Spectatorship." *Cinema Journal* 56/1 (2016): 23–42.

Derrida, Jacques. *Specters of Marx.* Translated by Peggy Knauf. New York: Routledge, 1994.

Di Bello, Patrizia, and Shamoon Zamir, eds. *The Photobook: From Talbot to Ruscha and Beyond.* London: I.B. Tauris, 2012.

Dreher, Jochen. "Phenomenology of Friendship: Construction of an Existential Social Friendship." *Human Studies* 32/4 (2009): 401–17.

Duttlinger, Carolin. "Kafkas Poetik der Aufmerksamkeit von *Betrachtung* bis *Der Bau*." In *Kafka und die kleine Prosa der Moderne/Kafka and Short Modernist Prose,* edited by Manfred Engel and Ritchie Robertson, 79–97. Würzburg: Königshausen & Neumann, 2010.

Echte, Bernhard, and Andreas Meier, eds. *Die Brüder Karl und Robert Walser: Maler und Dichter.* Zurich: Rothenhäusler Verlag Stäfa, 1990.

Ecker, Gisela. "Trauer zeigen: Inszenierung und die Sorge um den Anderen." In *Trauer Tragen—Trauer Zeigen: Inszenierungen der Geschlechter,* edited by G. Ecker, 8–25. Munich: Fink, 1999.

Eigler, Friederike. *Gedächtnis und Geschichte in Generationenromanen seit der Wende.* Berlin: Erich Schmidt, 2005.

Enns, Anthony. "The Politics of Ostalgie: Post-Socialist Nostalgia in Recent German Film." *Screen* 48/4 (2007): 475–91.

Enzensberger, Hans Magnus. *Eine Theorie des Tourismus* (1958). In *Einzelheiten I & II,* 177–203. Hamburg: Spiegel Verlag, 2006.

Faulstich, Werner. *Medienwandel im Industrie- und Massenzeitalter 1830–1900.* Göttingen: Vandenhoeck & Ruprecht, 2004.

Firebrace, William. "Slow Spaces." In *Camera Constructs: Photography, Architecture, and the Modern City,* edited by Andrew Higgott and Timothy Wray, 247–54. Farnham: Ashgate, 2014.

Fleig, Anne. "Lesen im Akkord? Uwe Tellkamp's *Der Turm* als Bildungsroman zwischen Realismus und Fantastik." In *Poetiken der Gegenwart: Deutschsprachige Romane nach 2000,* edited by Silke Horstkotte and Leonhard Herrmann, 83–98. Berlin: De Gruyter, 2013.

Fletcher, John. *Freud and the Scene of Trauma.* New York: Fordham University Press, 2013.

Fludernik, Monika. "Chronology, Time, Tense, and Experientiality in Narrative." *Language and Literature* 12/2 (2003): 117–34.

Foucault, Michel. "Of Other Spaces: Utopias and Heterotopias." Translated by Jay Miskowiec. *Diacritics* 16/1 (1986): 22–27.

Franck, Georg. *Mentaler Kapitalismus: Eine politische Ökonomie des Geistes.* Munich: Hanser, 2005.

———. *Ökonomie der Aufmerksamkeit: Ein Entwurf.* Munich: Hanser, 1998.

Freud, Sigmund. *Drei Abhandlungen zur Sexualtheorie.* In *Gesammelte Werke,* edited by Anna Freud et al., 5:27–145. Frankfurt a. Main: Fischer, 1999.

———. "Fetishism." In *The Standard Edition of the Complete Psychological Works of Sigmund Freud,* translated by James Strachey, 21:149–57. London: Hogarth Press, 1953–74.

————. *The Interpretation of Dreams*. Translated by James Strachey. London: Basic Books, 2010.

————. *Der Mann Moses und die monotheistische Religion*. In *Gesammelte Werke*, edited by Anna Freud et al., 16:101–246. Frankfurt a. Main: Fischer, 1999.

————. "Remembering, Repeating, Working-Through." In *The Standard Edition of the Complete Psychological Works of Sigmund Freud*, translated by James Strachey, 12:147–56. London: Hogarth Press, 1953–74.

————. *Studien über Hysterie*. In *Gesammelte Werke*. Edited by Anna Freud et al., 1:75–312. Frankfurt a. Main: Fischer, 1999.

————. *Über Psychoanalyse: Fünf Vorlesungen*. In *Gesammelte Werke*, edited by Anna Freud et al., vol. 8. Frankfurt a. Main: Fischer, 1999.

Frisby, David. *Fragments of Modernity: Theories of Modernity in the Work of Simmel, Krakauer, and Benjamin*. Cambridge, MA: MIT Press, 1986.

Fritzsche, Peter. *Reading Berlin 1900*. Cambridge, MA: Harvard University Press, 1996.

Fuchs, Anne. *After the Dresden Bombing: Pathways of Memory, 1945 to the Present*. Houndmills: Palgrave Macmillan, 2012.

————. "After the Flâneur: Temporality and Connectivity in Wilhelm Genazino's *Belebung der toten Winkel* and *Das Glück in glücksfernen Zeiten*." *Modern Language Review* 109/2 (2014): 435–50.

————. "An Awareness of What Is Missing: Voyeurism and the Remediation of Transcendence in Arnold Stadler's *Sehnsucht* and *Salvatore*." *German Life & Letters* 67/3 (2014): 435–49.

————. *Phantoms of War in Contemporary German Literature, Films, and Discourse: The Politics of Memory*. 2nd ed. 2008. Houndmills: Palgrave Macmillan, 2010.

————. "A Psychoanalytic Reading of *The Man Who Disappeared*." In *The Cambridge Companion to Kafka*, edited by Julian Preece, 25–41. Cambridge: Cambridge University Press, 2002.

————. "The Trouble with Time: Kafka's *Der Proceß*." In *Franz Kafka's The Trial*, edited by Espen Hammer, 173–200. Oxford: Oxford University Press, 2018.

————. "W. G. Sebald's Painters: Some Reflections on Fine Art in W. G. Sebald's Prose Works." *Modern Language Review* 101/1 (2006): 167–83.

————. "Why Smallness Matters: Smallness, Attention, and Distraction in Franz Kafka's and Robert Walser's Short Short Prose." In *Kafka und die kleine Prosa der Moderne/Kafka and Short Modernist Prose*, edited by Ritchie Robertson and Manfred Engel, 167–79. Würzburg: Königshausen & Neumann, 2010.

Fuchs, Anne, and Kathleen James-Chakraborty, eds. "Transformations of German Cultural Identity, 1989–2009." Special issue, *New German Critique* 116 (2012).

Fuchs, Anne, Kathleen James-Chakraborty, and Linda Shortt, eds. *Debating German Cultural Identity since 1989*. Rochester, NY: Camden House, 2011.

Fuest, Leonhard. *Poetik des Nicht(s)Tuns: Verweigerungsstrategien in der Literatur seit 1800.* Munich: Wilhelm Fink, 2008.

Geertz, Clifford, *The Interpretation of Cultures.* New York: Basic Books, 1973.

Genette, Gerard. *Narrative Discourse: An Essay in Method.* Translated by Jane Lewin. Ithaca, NY: Cornell University Press, 1980.

Geschichte der Frankfurter Zeitung von 1856 bis 1906. Edited by Verlag der Frankfurter Zeitung. Frankfurt a. Main: August Osterrieth, 1911.

Giddens, Anthony. *Runaway World: How Globalisation Is Reshaping Our Lives.* 2nd ed. London: Profile Books, 2002.

Gisbertz, Anna Katherina, ed. *Stimmung: Zur Wiederkehr einer ästhetischen Kategorie.* Munich: Wilhelm Fink, 2011.

Gómez-Montero, Karina. *Sinnverlust und Sinnsuche: Literarischer Nihilismus im deutschsprachigen Roman nach 1945.* Cologne: Böhlau, 1998.

Göttsche, Dirk. "Epistemology, Poetics, and Time in Modernist Short Prose around 1900." In *Time in German Literature and Culture, 1900–2015: Between Acceleration and Slowness,* edited by Anne Fuchs and J. J. Long, 71–92. Houndmills: Palgrave Macmillan, 2016.

———. *Kleine Prosa in Moderne und Gegenwart.* Münster: Aschendorff, 2006.

———. *Zeit im Roman: Literarische Zeitreflexion und die Geschichte des Zeitromans im späten 18. und im 19. Jahrhundert.* Munich: Wilhelm Fink, 2001.

Gross, Ruth V. "Of Mice and Women: Reflections on a Discourse in Kafka's *Josefine, die Sängerin oder Das Volk der Mäuse.*" *Germanic Review* 60 (1985): 59–68.

Grube, Dirk-Martin. "Contingency and Religion—A Philosophical Tour D-Horizon." In *Religions Challenged by Contingency: Theological and Philosophical Approaches to the Problem of Contingency,* edited by Dirk-Martin Grube and Peter Jonkers, 1–43. Leiden: Brill, 2008.

Gumbrecht, Hans Ulrich. *Stimmungen lesen: Über eine verdeckte Wirklichkeit der Literatur.* Munich: Carl Hanser, 2011.

Habermas, Jürgen. "An Awareness of What Is Missing." In *An Awareness of What Is Missing: Faith and Reason in a Post-Secular Age,* translated by Ciaran Cronin, 15–23. Cambridge: Polity, 2010.

Hake, Sabine. "Urban Spectacle in Walter Ruttmann's *Berlin, Symphony of the Big City.*" In *Dancing on the Volcano: Essays on the Culture of the Weimar Republic,* edited by Stephen Brockmann and Thomas W. Kniesche, 127–37. Rochester, NY: Camden House, 1994.

Hansen-Löve, Aage. "Vor dem Gesetz." In *Interpretationen—Franz Kafka: Romane und Erzählungen,* edited by Michael Müller, 146–58. Stuttgart: Reclam, 1994.

Harman, Mark. "Wie Kafka sich Amerika vorstellte." *Sinn und Form* 60 (2008): 794–804.

Hegel, Georg Wilhelm Friedrich. *Vorlesungen zur Ästhetik.* Edited by Friedrich Bassenge. Vol. 1. Berlin: Aufbau, 1965.

Heidbrink, Ludger. *Melancholie und Moderne: Zur Kritik der historischen Verzweiflung.* Munich: Wilhelm Fink, 1994.

Heimböckel, Dieter. "'Amerika im Kopf': Franz Kafkas Roman *Der Verschollene* und der Amerika-Diskurs seiner Zeit." *DVjs* 77 (2003): 130–47.

Heise, Ursula. *Chronoschisms: Time, Narrative, and Postmodernity.* Cambridge: Cambridge University Press, 1997.

Hermann, Iris. "Heimsuchung in Jenny Erpenbecks Roman *Aller Tage Abend.*" In *Wahrheit und Täuschung: Beiträge zum Werk Jenny Erpenbecks,* edited by Friedhelm Marx and Julia Schöll, 145–56. Göttingen: Wallstein, 2014.

Hickel, Jason. *The Divide: A Brief Guide to Global Inequality and Its Solutions.* London: William Heinemann, 2017.

Hiebel, Hans H. "Schuld oder Scheinbarkeit der Schuld? Zu Kafkas Roman *Der Proceß.*" In *Das Schuld-Problem bei Franz Kafka,* edited by Wolfgang Kraus and Norbert Winkler, 95–117. Klosterneuburg: Böhlau, 1993.

Hillard, Derek. "Walter Ruttmann's Janus-Faced View of Modernity: The Ambivalence of Description in *Berlin: Die Sinfonie der Großstadt.*" *Monatshefte* 96/1 (2004): 78–92.

Hillebrand, Bruno. *Ästhetik des Nihilismus: Von der Romantik zum Modernismus.* Stuttgart: Metzler, 1991.

Hodgin, Nick. "East Germany Revisited, Reimagined, Repositioned: Representing the GDR in Dominik Graf's *Der rote Kakadu* (2005) and Christian Petzold's *Barbara.*" In *East, West, and Centre: Reframing Post-1989 European Cinema,* edited by Michael Gott and Todd Herzog, 237–51. Edinburgh: Edinburgh University Press, 2015.

Hoffmann, Felix. "Leporello/Time/Memory: On Ulrich Wüst and His Leporello *Später Sommer/Letzter Herbst.*" In Ulrich Wüst, *Später Sommer/Letzter Herbst,* 85–88. Heidelberg: Kehrer, 2016.

Horstkotte, Silke. "Poetische Parusie: Zur Rückkehr der Religion in der Gegenwart." In "Deutschsprachige Literatur(en) seit 1989," edited by Norbert Otto Eke and Stefan Elit, special issue, *Zeitschrift für deutsche Philologie* 131 (2012): 265–82.

Hoskins, Andrew. "Anachronisms of Media, Anachronisms of Memory: From Collective Memory to a New Memory Culture." In *On Media Memory: Collective Memory in a New Media Age,* edited by Motti Neiger, Oren Meyers, and Eyal Zandberg, 278–88. Basingstoke: Palgrave Macmillan, 2011.

Huyssen, Andreas. "Modernist Miniatures: Literary Snapshots of Urban Spaces." *PMLA* 122/1 (2007): 27–42.

———. "The Vamp and the Machine: Technology and Sexuality in Fritz Lang's *Metropolis.*" *New German Critique* 24/25 (1981/82): 221–37.

Immelmann, Thomas. *Der unheimlichste aller Gäste: Nihilismus und Sinndebatte in der Literatur von der Aufklärung zur Moderne.* Bielefeld: Aisthesis, 1992.

Iser, Wolfgang. "Fictionalizing Acts." *Amerikastudien/American Studies* 31 (1985): 5–15.

———. *The Fictive and the Imaginary: Charting Literary Anthropology.* Baltimore: Johns Hopkins University Press, 1993.

Jäger, Christian, and Erhard Schütz, eds. *Glänzender Asphalt: Berlin im Feuilleton der Weimarer Republik.* Berlin: Fannei & Waltz, 1994.

———. *Städtebilder zwischen Literatur und Journalismus: Wien, Berlin und das Feuilleton der Weimarer Republik.* Wiesbaden: Deutscher Universitätsverlag, 1999.

Jameson, Fredric. *The Cultural Turn: Selected Writings on the Postmodern.* London: Verso, 1983.

Joas, Hans. "Morality in the Age of Contingency." *Acta Sociologica* 47/4 (2004): 392–99.

Judd, Tony. *Postwar: A History of Europe since 1945.* London: Random House, 2007.

Kaes, Anton. "Leaving Home: Film, Migration, and the Urban Experience." *New German Critique* 74 (1998): 179–92.

Karthaus, Ulrich. "*Der Zauberberg*—ein Zeitroman (Zeit, Geschichte, Mythos)." *Deutsche Vierteljahresschrift für Literaturwissenschaft und Geistesgeschichte* 44 (1970): 269–305.

Kavaloski, Joshua. "Performativity and the Dialectics of Time in Thomas Mann's *Der Zauberberg*." *German Studies Review* 32/2 (2009): 319–42.

Kelly, Michael R. "Phenomenology and Time-Consciousness." *Internet Encyclopedia of Philosophy: A Peer-Reviewed Academic Resource.* http://www.iep.utm.edu/phe-time/ (accessed 10 January 2018).

Kendall, Tinda. "Staying on, or Getting off (the Bus): Approaching Speed in Cinema and Media Studies." *Cinema Journal* 55/2 (2017): 112–18.

Kittler, Wolf. "Burial without Resurrection: On Kafka's Legend 'Before the Law.'" *Modern Language Notes* 121/3 (2006): 647–78.

Klibansky, Raymond, Erwin Panofsky, and Fritz Saxl. *Saturn and Melancholy: Studies in the History of Natural Philosophy, Religion, and Art.* London: Thomas Nelson & Sons, 1964.

Knittel, Anton Philipp. "'Glaube, Hoffnung, Erinnerung': Anmerkungen zu Komik und Transzendenz im Werk Arnold Stadlers." In *"Als wäre er ein anderer gewesen": Zum Werk Arnold Stadlers,* edited by Pia Reinacher, 69–80. Frankfurt a. M.: Fischer, 2009.

Knoblauch, Hubert. "Die Verflüchtigung der Religion ins Religiöse." In Thomas Luckmann, *Die unsichtbare Religion,* 7–41. Frankfurt a. Main: Suhrkamp 1991.

Kohl, Katrin. "Conceptualizing the GDR—20 Years After." *Oxford German Studies* 38 (2009): 265–77.

Kracauer, Siegfried. "Der Kult der Zerstreuung" (1926). In *Das Ornament der Masse: Essays,* 311–17. Frankfurt a. Main: Suhrkamp, 1977.

Kristianson, Borge. "Thomas Mann und die Philosophie." In *Thomas Mann Handbuch,* edited by Helmut Koopmann, 259–83. 3rd ed. Stuttgart: Kröner, 2001.

Kühne, Thomas. *The Rise and Fall of Comradeship: Hitler's Soldiers, Male Bonding, and Mass Violence in the Twentieth Century*. Cambridge: Cambridge University Press, 2017.

Latour, Bruno. *Das terrestrische Manifest*. Translated by Bernd Schwibs. Frankfurt a. Main: Suhrkamp, 2018.

Laub, Dori. "Bearing Witness, or the Vicissitudes of Listening." In *Testimony: Crises of Witnessing in Literature, Psychoanalysis, and History*, edited by Shoshana Felman and Dori Laub, 57–74. New York: Routledge, 1992.

Ledanff, Susanne. "Neue Formen der 'Ostalgie'—Abschied von der 'Ostalgie'? Erinnerungen an Kindheit und Jugend in der DDR und an die Geschichtsjahre 1989/90." *Seminar: A Journal of Germanic Studies* 43/2 (1007): 176–93.

Leys, Ruth. *Trauma: A Genealogy*. Chicago: University of Chicago Press, 2000.

Liska, Vivian. "Was weiß die Literatur? Das Wissen der Sirenen: Adorno, Banchot, Sloterdijk." *KulturPoetik: Zeitschrift für kulturgeschichtliche Literaturwissenschaft* 4 (2004): 1–18.

Lister, Martin. "The Times of Photography." In *Time, Media, and Modernity*. Edited by Emily Keightley, 45–65. Houndmills: Palgrave Macmillan, 2012.

Long, Jonathan J. "Photography/Topography: Viewing Berlin, 1880/2000." *New German Critique* 116 (Summer 2012): 25–45.

Lotman, Jurij M. *Die Struktur literarischer Texte*. Translated by Rold-Dietrich Keil. Munich: Wilhelm Fink, 1972.

Löw, Martina. *Raumsoziologie*. Frankfurt a. Main: Suhrkamp, 2001.

Luckmann, Thomas. *The Invisible Religion: The Problem of Religion in Modern Society*. New York: Collier-Macmillan, 1967.

———. *Die unsichtbare Religion*. Frankfurt a. Main: Suhrkamp, 1991.

Lützeler, Paul Michael. "Schlafwandler am Zauberberg: Die Europa-Diskussion in Hermann Brochs und Thomas Manns Zeitromanen." *Thomas-Mann-Jahrbuch* 14 (2001): 49–62.

Luyken, Gunda. *Hannah Höch Album*. Ostfildern-Ruit: Cantz, 2004.

Mach, Ernst. *Die Analyse der Empfindungen und das Verhältnis des Physischen zum Psychischen*. 9th ed. Jena: Fischer, 1922. Reprint, Darmstadt: Wissenschaftliche Buchgesellschaft, 1991.

Makreel, Rudolf. "Imagination and Temporality in Kant's Theory of the Sublime." *Journal of Aesthetics and Art Criticism* 42/3 (1984): 303–15.

Manlove, Clifford T. "Visual 'Drive' and Cinematic Narrative: Reading Gaze Theory in Lacan, Hitchcock, and Mulvey." *Cinema Journal* 46/3 (2007): 83–108.

Marinetti, Filippo Tommasso. "The Founding and Manifesto of Futurism." In *Futurist Manifestos*, edited by Umbo Apollonio, 19–24. London: Thames and Hudson, 1973.

Marx, Karl. *The Eighteenth Brumaire of Louis Bonaparte*. https://www.marxists.org/archive/marx/works/download/pdf/18th-Brumaire.pdf (accessed 17 August 2014).

————. *Das Kapital: Kritik der politischen Ökonomie.* Vol. 1, *Der Produktionsprozess des Kapitals*, edited by Rosa-Luxemburg Stiftung. Berlin: Dietz, 1962.

Matthes, Frauke. "Clemens Meyer, *Als wir träumten*: Fighting 'Like a Man' in Leipzig's East." In *Emerging German-Language Novelists in the Twenty-First Century*, edited by Lyn Marven and Stuart Taberner, 89–104. Rochester, NY: Camden House, 2011.

McBride, Patrizia. "Narrative Resemblance: The Production of Truth in the Modernist Photobook of Weimar Germany." *New German Critique* 115/39 (2012): 169–97.

McHale, Brian. *Postmodernist Fiction.* New York: Methuen, 1987.

Metz, Christian. "Photography and Fetish." *October* 34 (1985): 83–84.

Middeke, Martin. *Die Kunst der gelebten Zeit: Zur Phänomenologie literarischer Subjektivität im englischen Roman des ausgehenden 19. Jahrhunderts.* Würzburg: Königshausen & Neumann, 2004.

Minden, Michael. "Kafka's *Josefine die Sängerin oder Das Volk der Mäuse.*" *German Life & Letters* 62 (2009): 297–310.

Minter, Catherine J. "Literary *Empfindsamkeit* and Nervous Sensibility in Eighteenth-Century Germany." *Modern Language Review* 96/4 (2001): 1016–28.

Mores, Zofia. *Nihilistische Gedankenexperimente in der deutschen Literatur von Jean Paul bis Georg Büchner.* Frankfurt a. Main: Peter Lang, 2007.

Motakef, Mona. *Prekarisierung.* Bielefeld: Transcript, 2015.

Mulvey, Laura. "Visual Pleasure and Narrative Cinema." *Screen* 16/3 (1975): 6–18.

Mundhenke, Florian. "Authenticity versus Artifice: The Hybrid Cinematic Approach of Ulrich Seidl." *Austrian Studies* 19 (2011): 113–25.

Neumann, Gerhard. "'Blinde Parabel' oder Bildungsroman? Zur Struktur von Franz Kafkas *Proceß*-Fragment." In *Franz Kafka: Experte der Macht*, 101–36. Munich: Hanser, 2012.

————. "Der Zauber des Anfangs und das 'Zögern vor der Geburt'—Kafkas Poetologie des 'riskantesten Augenblicks.'" In *Nach erneuter Lektüre: Franz Kafkas "Der Proceß,"* edited by Hans Dieter Zimmermann, 121–42. Würzburg: Königshausen & Neumann, 1992.

Newman, Barbara, ed. *Voice of the Living Light: Hildegard of Bingen and Her World.* Berkeley: University of California Press, 1998.

Nietzsche, Friedrich. *Werke in drei Bänden.* Edited by Karl Schlechta. Munich: Hanser, 1969.

Nünning, Ansgar, and Roy Sommer. "Die Vertextung der Zeit: Zur narratologischen und phänomenologischen Rekonstruktion erzählerisch inszenierter Zeiterfahrungen und Zeitkonzeptionen." In *Zeit und Roman: Zeiterfahrung im historischen Wandel und ästhetischer Paradigmenwechsel vom sechzehnten Jahrhundert bis zur Postmoderne*, edited by Martin Middeke, 33–56. Würzburg: Königshausen & Neumann, 2002.

Oesterle, Günter. "'Unter dem Strich': Skizze einer Kulturpoetik des Feuilletons." In *Das schwierige neunzehnte Jahrhundert: Germanistische Tagung zum 65. Geburtstag von Eda Sagarra im August 1998*, edited by Jürgen Barkhoff et al., 230–50. Tübingen: Niemeyer, 2000.

Parr, Martin, and Gerry Badger. *The Photobook: A History*. 2 vols. London: Phaidon, 2004, 2006.

Pause, Johannes. *Texturen der Zeit: Zum Wandel ästhetischer Zeitkonzepte in der deutschsprachigen Gegenwartsliteratur*. Cologne: Böhlau, 2012.

Petzold, Christian. *Barbara: Ein Drehbuch*. Edited by Fred Breinersdorfer and Dorothee Schön. Berlin: Deutsche Filmakademie, 2012.

Philippi, Klaus-Peter. "'K. lebte doch in einem Rechtsstaat': Franz Kafkas *Der Proceß*—ein Prozeß des Mißverstehens." In *Aufklärungen: Zur Literaturgeschichte der Moderne*, edited by Werner Frick, 259–82. Tübingen: Niemeyer, 2003.

Pinfold, Debbie. "The End of the Fairy Tale? Christian Petzold's *Barbara* and the Difficulties of Interpretation." *German Life & Letters* 67/2 (2014): 280–300.

Pinkerneil, Beate. "Ewigkeitssuppe kontra schöpferisches Werden: Zum Thema Thomas Mann—Bergson." In *Thomas Mann und die Tradition*, edited by Peter Pütz, 250–83. Frankfurt a. Main: Athenäum, 1970.

Plowman, Andrew. "Westalgie? Nostalgia for the 'Old' Federal Republic in Recent German Prose." *Seminar* 40/3 (2004): 249–61.

Preisendanz, Wolfgang. "Voraussetzungen des poetischen Realismus in der deutschen Erzählkunst des 19. Jahrhunderts." In *Wege des Realismus: Zur Poetik und Erzählkunst im 19. Jahrhundert*, 68–91. Munich: Wilhelm Fink, 1984.

Pütz, Peter. "Thomas Mann und Nietzsche." In *Thomas Mann und die Tradition*. Edited by Peter Pütz, 225–49. Frankfurt a. Main: Athenäum, 1970.

Pye, Gillian. "Jenny Erpenbeck and the Life of Things." In *Transitions: Emerging German Women Writing in German-Language Literature*, edited by Gillian Pye and Valerie Heffernan, 111–30. Amsterdam: Rodopi, 2013.

Radden, Jennifer, ed. *The Nature of Melancholy: From Aristotle to Kristeva*. Oxford: Oxford University Press, 2002.

Reed, T. J. *Thomas Mann: The Uses of Tradition*. 2nd ed. 1973. Oxford: Clarendon, 1996.

Reinacher, Pia, ed. *"Als wäre er ein anderer gewesen": Zum Werk Arnold Stadlers*. Frankfurt a. Main: Fischer, 2009.

Robbins, Hollis. "The Emperor's New Critique." *New Literary History* 34/4 (2003): 659–75.

Robertson, Ritchie. "Reading the Clues: Franz Kafka, *Der Proceß*." In *The German Novel in the 20th Century: Beyond Realism*, edited by David Midgley, 59–79. Edinburgh: Edinburgh University Press, 1993.

Rorty, Richard. *Contingency, Irony, and Solidarity*. Cambridge: Cambridge University Press, 2009.

Rüsing, Hans Peter. "Quellenforschung als Interpretation: Holitschers und Soukups Reiseberichte über Amerika und Kafka's Roman *Der Verschollene*." *MAL* 20 (1987): 1–38.

Rutsky, R. L. "The Mediation of Technology and Gender: Metropolis, Nazism, Modernism." *New German Critique* 60 (1993): 3–32.

Schäfer, Martin Jörg. "Die Intensität der Träume: Clemens Meyers Poetik des Kinos." In "Inszenierungen von 'Intensität' und 'Lebendigkeit' in der Gegenwartsliteratur," edited by Martin Jörg Schäfer and Niels Werber, special issue, *Zeitschrift für Literaturwissenschaft und Linguistik* 170 (2013): 53–66.

Schings, Hans-Jürgen. *Melancholie und Aufklärung: Melancholie und ihre Kritiker in der Erfahrungsseelenkunde des 18. Jahrhunderts.* Stuttgart: Metzler, 1977.

Schivelbusch, Wolfgang. *Geschichte der Eisenbahnreise: Zur Industrialisierung von Raum und Zeit im 19. Jahrhundert.* 5th ed. Frankfurt a. Main: Fischer, 2011.

Schoonover, Karl. "Wastrels of Time: Slow Cinema's Labouring Body, the Political Spectator, and the Queer." *Framework: The Journal of Cinema and Media* 51/1 (2012): 65–78.

Sennett, Richard. *The Culture of the New Capitalism.* New Haven, CT: Yale University Press, 2006.

Shafi, Monika. *Housebound: Selfhood and Domestic Space in Contemporary German Fiction.* Rochester, NY: Camden House, 2012.

Shortt, Linda. "Reimagining the West: West Germany, Westalgia, and the Generation of 1978." In *Debating German Cultural Identity since 1989*, edited by Anne Fuchs, Kathleen James-Chakraborty and Linda Shortt, 156–69. Rochester, NY: Camden House, 2011

Smith, Graham. "H. Fox Talbot's 'Scotch Views' for *Sun Pictures in Scotland* (1845)." In *The Photobook: From Talbot to Ruscha and Beyond*, edited by Patrizia Di Bello, Colette Wilson, and Shamoon Zamir, 17–34. New York: I.B. Tauris, 2012.

Sontag, Susan, *On Photography.* New York: Doubleday, 1973.

Stäheli, Urs. "Entnetzt euch! Praktiken und Ästhetiken der Anschlusslosigkeit." *Mittelweg* 36/22 (August/September 2013): 3–28.

Standing, Guy. *The Precariat: The New Dangerous Class.* London: Bloomsbury, 2014.

Taberner, Stuart. "'Nichts läßt man uns, nicht einmal den Schmerz, und eines Tages wird alles vergessen sein': The Novels of Arnold Stadler from *Ich war einmal* to *Ein hinreissender Schrotthändler.*" *Neophilologus* 87 (2003): 119–32.

Thompson, Peter. "Die unheimliche Heimat: The GDR and the Dialectics of Home." *Oxford German Studies* 38/3 (2009): 278–87.

Utz, Peter. *Tanz auf den Rändern: Robert Walsers "Jetztzeitstil."* Frankfurt a. Main: Suhrkamp, 1998.

Vakarelski, Christo. *Bulgarische Volkskunde.* Berlin: De Gruyter, 1969.

van Gelder, Hilde, and Helen Westgeest. *Photography Theory in Historical Perspective: Case Studies from Contemporary Art.* Oxford: Wiley-Blackwell, 2011.

Vietta, Silvio, and Stephan Porombka, eds. *Ästhetik, Religion, Säkularisierung II: Die klassische Moderne*. Munich: Wilhelm Fink, 2009.

Vietta, Silvio, and Herbert Uerlings, eds. *Ästhetik, Religion, Säkularisierung I: Von der Renaissance zur Romantik*. Munich: Wilhelm Fink, 2008.

Wagner, Karl. "'Eine gewaltige Scham': Arnold Stadlers Schreiben zwischen Mündlichkeit und Schriftlichkeit; Hebel—Stifter—Handke." In *"Als wäre er ein anderer gewesen": Zum Werk Arnold Stadlers*, edited by Pia Reinacher, 95–104. Frankfurt a. Main: Fischer, 2009.

Wagner-Egelhaaf, Martina. *Die Melancholie der Literatur: Diskursgeschichte und Textfiguration*. Stuttgart: Metzler, 1997.

Walser, Martin, "Über das Verbergen der Verzweiflung: Laudatio zur Verleihung des Marie-Luise-Kaschnitz Preises 1998." In *"Als wäre er ein anderer gewesen": Zum Werk Arnold Stadlers*, edited by Pia Reinacher, 115–18. Frankfurt a. Main: Fischer, 2009.

Webber, Andrew J. "'Good Work': Speed, Slowness, and Taking Care in Christian Petzold's *Barbara*." In *Time in German Literature and Culture, 1900–2015: Between Acceleration and Slowness*, edited by Anne Fuchs and J. J. Long, 173–88. Houndmills: Palgrave Macmillan, 2016.

———. "Topographical Turns: Recasting Berlin in Christian Petzold's *Gespenster*." In *Debating German Cultural Identity since 1989*, edited by Anne Fuchs, Kathleen James-Chakraborty, and Linda Shortt, 67–81. Rochester, NY: Camden House, 2011.

Weigel, Sigrid. "The Symptomatology of a Universalized Concept of Trauma: On the Failing of Freud's Reading of *Tasso* in the Trauma of History." *New German Critique* 90 (2003): 85–94.

———. "Téléscopage im Unbewußten: Zum Verhältnis von Trauma, Geschichtsbegriff und Literatur." In *Trauma: Zwischen Psychoanalyse und kulturellen Deutungsmustern*, edited by Elisabeth Bronfen, Birgit Erdle, and Sigrid Weigel, 51–76. Cologne: Böhlau, 1999.

Weissberg, Liliane. "Myth, History, Enlightenment: The Silence of the Sirens." *Journal of the Kafka Society of America* 9 (1985): 131–48.

Whittell, Giles. *Bridge of Spies—A True Story of the Cold War*. London: Simon and Schuster, 2011.

Wickerson, Erica. *The Architecture of Narrative Time: Thomas Mann and the Problems of Modern Narrative*. Oxford: Oxford University Press, 2017.

Wimmer, Ruprecht. "Zur Philosophie der Zeit im *Zauberberg*." In *Auf dem Weg zum Zauberberg: Die Davoser Literaturtage 1996*, edited by Thomas Sprecher, 251–72. Frankfurt a. Main: Klostermann, 1997.

Yerushalmi, Yosef Hayim. *Freud's Moses: Judaism Terminable and Interminable*. New Haven, CT: Yale University Press, 1991.

INDEX

Page numbers followed by letters *f* and *n* refer to figures and notes, respectively.